STRANGE ANTICS

STRANGE ANTICS

A History of Seduction

Clement Knox

WILLIAM
COLLINS

William Collins
An imprint of HarperCollins*Publishers*
1 London Bridge Street
London SE1 9GF

WilliamCollinsBooks.com

First published in Great Britain in 2020 by William Collins

1

A catalogue record for this book is available from the British Library

ISBN 978-0-00-828567-8 (hardback)
ISBN 978-0-00-828568-5 (trade paperback)

Typeset in Minion Pro by Palimpsest Book Production Ltd, Falkirk, Stirlingshire
Printed and bound in UK by CPI Group (UK) Ltd, Croydon CR0 4YY

To My Parents

When we behold two males fighting for the possession of the female, or several male birds displaying their gorgeous plumage, and performing strange antics before an assembled body of females, we cannot doubt that, though led by instinct, they know what they are about, and consciously exert their mental and bodily powers.

Charles Darwin, The Descent of Man, *Chapter VIII*

CONTENTS

Introduction   1

1 Rake Culture   13
2 The Transit of Venus   79
3 An Unsentimental Education   141
4 Circling Mary Shelley   195
5 Of Mann and Men   249
6 Blood Out   318
7 Seduction Remains   372

Afterword   416
Endnotes   431
List of Illustrations   491
Acknowledgements   493
Index   495

INTRODUCTION

In 1873, a Georgia court heard the appeal of Myron Wood against his conviction in a seduction case involving Emma Chivers. Wood was a reverend, schoolmaster and Civil War veteran, a pillar of the community in Decatur, the seat of DeKalb County, north-east Georgia. Chivers was fifteen when she first met Wood, who was her teacher at school and her pastor at church. She was the daughter of a destitute widow, so poor that Wood took the family into his own home to help relieve their poverty. But Wood had other motives. His own wife was terminally ill and he seduced Chivers, promising her that he would marry her once his sick spouse died. Chivers trusted him, respected him, and probably somewhat feared him, and she submitted to his advances, the first time she had ever done so. A child was born, whereupon Wood went back on his word and denied all responsibility.

This was the background to Chivers' initial, successful lawsuit. On appeal Wood adopted a new strategy. He did not deny that the affair had taken place, simply that Chivers was ineligible for protection under the seduction statute as she was a lascivious girl, sluttish, and primed for sin. Wood's lawyers marshalled an array of witnesses willing to testify to Chivers' low morals and lustful nature. The sins of the mother were visited upon the daughter. A spinster was found who claimed that Chivers' mother was rumoured to have consorted with black men and may even have run a brothel in Atlanta. Classmates took to the stand. They revealed that Chivers was not in the habit of concealing her legs as a good Christian girl was expected to do. Some had seen her hug and kiss young men. Others noted her penchant for unfruitful fruit-picking expeditions with local boys. Was it not true, the counsel for the defence asked her, that she was known to go 'blackberry hunting with young men and [bring] no blackberries back'?

The state supreme court sided with Wood. Emma Chivers, the justices ruled, was not a seducible woman.[1]

What happened in that Georgia courtroom 150 years ago was a waypoint in a social transformation whose consequences we all live with today. Before the Enlightenment, the sexual existences of Europeans and North Americans were closely monitored. Sexuality was a public matter, subject to observation and discipline. Sexual freedoms were few and sexual protections were scarce. Today, almost the exact opposite is the case. We are striving towards a juncture where broad sexual freedoms for consenting adults will co-exist with substantive controls on the predatory protections for the vulnerable. How we got from then to now is in a large part the history of seduction. Almost all the reluctant concerns of that history were present in the case of Emma Chivers. To investigate seduction is to think about power, desire, race, class, agency and the law. Less visible but omnipresent – including in the Chivers' case – is a question of storytelling. The history of seduction is about the sum of stories – in other words, of narrative.

Every aspect of human experience has its history; the problem is identifying how best to measure it. The unit of measurement for the history of seduction is that strange and powerful thing, the seduction narrative. The basic claim of this book is that the seduction narrative is a product of the modern world and serves as a vehicle for the exploration of modern values, modern experiences and modern concerns.

This is not to say that seduction *never* existed in fact or fiction before the onset of modernity. The moons of Jupiter are named for four of Zeus's most celebrated seductions. The nymph Io he enshrouded in darkness and turned into a snow-white heifer to conceal her from his jealous wife. Callisto, the 'Arcadian virgin [who] suddenly caught his fancy and fired his heart with a deep-felt passion', he approached in the guise of her mistress, the goddess Diana, before taking her in his arms and revealing his true identity. To win the Phoenician princess Europa, he 'discarded his mighty sceptre and clothed himself in the form of a bull'. Once he had lured her to sit on his back, he swam out to sea, taking her all the way to Crete where they eventually had three children together. To secure the Trojan youth Ganymede, he took the form of an enormous eagle, swooping down from the skies and carrying him away to Mount Olympus. All these stories are recorded in the *Metamorphoses*, written by the Roman poet Ovid, who is also famous for authoring the first-ever seduction manual, the *Ars Amatoria*, in the second century BC.

Ovid's frank treatment of seduction scandalised the emperor Augustus and he was sent into exile on the Black Sea. Whatever tribulations he experienced in his own lifetime, however, Ovid's legacy endured. In the pre-modern world he was the paradigmatic writer on seduction, name-checked by Chaucer and Shakespeare and avidly read by every educated young man. Indeed, Ovid's influence was so great that it became an inspiration for perhaps the first proto-feminist analysis of seduction. Writing in the early fifteenth century, Christine de Pizan mocked the clerks who lived by Ovid's sexual commandments while lamenting that the sexual culture his writings had helped forge made life impossible for women. For a beautiful woman to keep herself chaste, de Pizan wrote, is 'like being in the midst of flames without getting burnt' on account of her having 'to fend off the attentions of young men and courtiers who are eager to have affairs'.[2]

Classical writers aside, the other major influence on how pre-moderns thought about seduction was Christianity. In the Christian tradition, the problem of seduction had begun not with Ovid but with Eve in the Garden of Eden. From the earliest days of the Christian faith, theologians had identified the first woman, Eve, and consequently *all* women, with lust. St Augustine had claimed that mankind's original sin was the lustfulness uncovered in Eve after she ate the apple at the serpent's urging. Augustine believed that the 'legacy of Eve' was the 'sorrow she brought into the world' through her discovery of her sexuality. As a result of this mythology, early Christian culture was astonishingly misogynistic. St Jerome was so aghast at the carnality he associated with women that he counselled chastity for men wherever possible. Indeed, he identified men with sexual restraint (with 'the virtue of continence'), whereas women were marked with the 'command to increase and multiply' associated with the expulsion from Eden and with 'the nakedness and the fig-leaves which speak of sexual passion'. The writer and apologist Tertullian described women as 'each an Eve . . . You are the devil's gateway: you are the unsealer of that forbidden tree: you are the first deserter of divine law.' For the eleventh-century Benedictine monk St Peter Damian, women were 'bitches, sows, screech-owls, night owls, she-wolves, blood suckers . . . harlots, prostitutes, with your lascivious kisses, you wallowing places for fat pigs, couches for unclean spirits, demi-goddesses, sirens, witches'.[3]

The consequence of theological misogyny was a literary tradition in which the dominant seduction narrative was that of a woman seducing a man. In 'The Wife of Bath's Tale' in Chaucer's *The Canterbury Tales*, this trope was mocked by the female narrator who describes how men, drunk on Ovid, Jerome, Tertullian and all the rest, have come to believe that women are intrinsically licentious and that they 'cannot keep the vow of marriage'. When at the end of fourteenth-century romance *Sir Gawain and the*

Green Knight, Gawain discovers that the witch Morgan Le Fay has been toying with him throughout the tale, he gives vent to his frustrations concerning male powerlessness in the face of female manipulation:

> But it's no wonder a fool should lose his senses and be brought to his downfall through the wiles of women. For Adam in this world was misled by one, and Solomon by several, and Samson after him – Delilah was his ruin – and David afterwards, was blinded by Bathsheba and suffered much misery. Since all of these were deluded, it would be a fine thing to love them well without trusting, if a man could do it.[4]

Many of these concerns spilled over into the popular fear about witches. 'All witchcraft comes from carnal lust,' intoned the *Malleus Maleficarum*, the classic treatise on the subject, 'which in women is insatiable.'[5]

In the sixteenth and seventeenth centuries these attitudes began to soften. The continental tradition of courtliness popularised by writers like Baldassare Castiglione and Philip Sidney encouraged socialising among the sexes – at least at an elite level – and emphasised that courtship could be an aesthetic pleasure and not a moral hazard. This attitude is certainly in evidence in Shakespeare's comedies, where the game of love is played out in an endless carnival of disguise, gender confusion and enchantment. In figures like Richard III, who seeks to seduce the widow Lady Anne, gloating that he will triumph though he has 'nothing to back my suit at all, But the plain devil and dissembling looks', Shakespeare also looks forward to more modern conceptions of the seduction narrative where men are predators and women are prey.

These precursors are interesting but they feel intellectually distant. The cause of that distance – and the reason that this book begins at the start of the eighteenth century and not before – is the Enlightenment. The seduction narrative was born out of a series of intellectual developments and value shifts that took place in this period.

In short, the seduction narrative was a byproduct of the rise of liberalism. The growing belief – that by 1800 had solidified into a consensus across much of Europe and North America – that individuals had the basic right to chose their husband or wife was one consequence of the widespread acceptance of liberal attitudes.

It was also the decisive development in the history of seduction because it raised a raft of issues. If marriage was now a private choice then individuals, especially women, had to be trusted to make their own decisions. But could they be trusted to make the right ones? What if they were deceived? If they were misled, were they owed any special sympathies or even particular legal protections? Conversely, if men were judged to have behaved in a deceptive or exploitative manner, how were they to be dealt with? Should they be punished? Should they be reformed? Or, as the hackneyed saying goes, is all fair in love and war? As we shall see, these questions occupied the attention of some of the most celebrated minds of the past. They still concern us now.

Underpinning all these debates is a more fundamental question. Are we rational decision-makers or flighty, manipulable creatures, subject to our passions? Whether reason or passion exerts greater sway on human decision-making was one of the foundational debates of the Enlightenment. And – in numerous variants – it is with us to this day.[6] The argument of this book is that this debate finds expression in the seduction narrative. Key to its expression is the fact that seduction narratives come in two forms. Each takes a different side of this debate. Each tells a complementary story about the modern world. In the classic seduction narrative – what me might call the 'Villainous' kind – the seducer uses guile, deception and mental games to overcome their target's resistance. It implies a psychological vulnerability on the part of seduced – a fact reflected in etymology of the word: *se + ducere*, to lead away. Seduction assumes one person is manipulating another, leading them away from their true preferences. This was the basis for the crucial legal distinction between rape and seduction. Whereas rape was coercive, seduction admitted consent while assuming that consent had somehow been degraded by the techniques of the seducer. As one New York court put it in 1896: 'to constitute seduction, the defendant must use insinuating arts to overcome the opposition of the seduced and must by wiles, without force, debauch her.'[7] In common law the classic example of seduction was a woman who agreed to sex after accepting a disingenuous marriage proposal. This, in the eyes of society and the law, was a species of fraud as consent had been obtained by a lie. Early nineteenth-century feminists campaigning for increased legal protections for women and girls understood the threat of seduction as being pervasive. In a pamphlet from 1910, one wrote that seduction – the 'ultimate inferno' – was brought about by the assault on the rational mind 'by the toils of unreasoning and prejudiced ignorance.'[8] Nowadays the language used to describe such scenarios tends to focus on structures of power and patterns of grooming and assault.

The common feature is that the seduction narrative dramatises powerlessness. This is why, from *Clarissa* (1748) to *Cruel Intentions* (1999), the victims of seducers are portrayed as naive, unworldly women. This is not to say that there have been no seduction narratives that feature women seducing men – as we shall see, this has been a recurring counter-current from the eighteenth century to the twenty-first – simply that they rely on the premise that men are the powerless playthings of predatory, powerful women, a contention that has lacked credibility for almost all recorded history. This speaks to the political, feminist dimension of these seduction narratives. They tell a story about women's place in society. They allegorise their oppression.

If the villainous seduction narrative dwells on psychological vulnerability, the other kind of seduction narrative focuses on the power of reason. Enlightenment philosophers believed that individuals were endowed with reason and could use it to make decisions in their own best interests. In one of the foundational manifestos of the Enlightenment, the Declaration of Independence, the founding fathers of the United States declared that among the 'unalienable Rights' of free men were 'Life, Liberty, and the Pursuit of Happiness'. The other kind of seduction narrative – the one which portrays the seducer as a hero, not a villain – is intensely interested in that pursuit.

Throughout this book we shall meet writers and intellectuals who believed that the rational pursuit of sexual pleasure was an endeavour characteristic to the enlightened individual. In England, one of the earliest champions of this position was the writer and dramatist Henry Fielding who considered men's and women's desires natural 'and productive not only of corporeal delight, but of the most rational felicity'. In continental Europe, philosophers like Voltaire and Casanova argued much the same. Nor was it just men who trumpeted the virtues of sexual freedom. The pursuit of what she called 'rational desires' was central to the intellectual project of Mary Wollstonecraft. Among the Romantics, 'free love' was embraced in theory and practice by women such as Mary Shelley and Claire Clairmont as much as it was by men like Percy Shelley and Lord Byron. In the latter half of the twentieth century, this view of human sexuality became basically unchallenged. From James Bond to Brigitte Bardot, seducers were celebrated in the culture as symbols of sexual freedom, free agents who had unburdened themselves of the irrational prejudices of custom, religion and taboo. In the twenty-first century the rise of algorithmic online dating represents the triumph of seduction as a logical exercise.

These rival traditions in the seduction narrative – reason versus passion; the seducer as hero versus the seducer as villain – coexist. They are, in fact, deeply intertwined. In the period of three centuries covered by this book, both kinds of narrative exist in every time and in every place that is studied. Indeed, the foundational conflict between reason and passion that is at the heart of this history is often found within seduction narratives themselves. For example, in the eighteenth-century novel *The Man of Feeling*, the seduced and betrayed Emily Atkins contrasts her passionate abandon with her seducer's cold, calculating nature:

> It was gratitude, it was pride, it was love! Love which had made too fatal a progress in my heart, before any declaration on his part should have warranted a return: but I interpreted every look of attention, every expression of compliment, to the passion I imagined him inspired with, and imputed to his sensibility that silence which was the effect of art and design.

This dynamic tension between reason and passion also accounts for another recurrent theme in this book: the use of hypnosis as a metaphor for seduction. As we shall see in the chapters on Mary Shelley and Bram Stoker, hypnotism was a potent symbol of seduction, as it was a transitional psychological state that bridged the worlds of reason and passion. Seduction is bewildering, exciting and dangerous because it occupies this grey zone of agency.

It is for precisely the same reason that seduction has repeatedly been the subject of legal interest. As we shall see in the later chapters of this book, the legal principles that brought Emma Chivers to the courtroom in the 1870s were born of passionate public debates about the limits of rational sexual decision-making and consequently with the limits of consent.

Such tension creates paradoxes – contradictions that will surface again and again in this narrative. Those who believe that individuals are prone to violent passions and vulnerable to manipulation tend to argue for the creation of laws and rules that will try to rationally regulate sexual desire. As we shall see, the successful campaigns on both sides of the Atlantic in the nineteenth and early twentieth centuries to bring about a body of law to regulate seduction mobilised these 'villainous' seduction narratives in order to achieve their goals. Out of the chaos of the passionate mind was born the need for a set of logical legal codes. Yet these supposedly rational laws were quickly revealed to be capricious themselves. As the example of Emma Chivers showed, far from being impartial, seduction laws were used to police arbitrary boundaries of class, race and gender.

Conversely, the 'Heroic' seduction narrative uses the claim of rationality to advance a culture of sensual revelry. From the hedonism of Enlightenment London, Paris and Venice, to the free love doctrines of the Romantics, to the 'sexual revolution' of the 1960s and 1970s, sexual rationalism has been used to justify a culture of pleasure, permissiveness and emotional authenticity. Yet time and again, the promise of sexual freedom in theory has run up against the problem of sexual freedom in practice. The dream of emotional authenticity underpinned by a model of rational decision-making has all too often led to a reality of sexual exploitation motivated by an unfeeling transactionalism that conceals itself within a masque of sexual liberation. At the height of the sexual revolution, Germaine Greer observed as much when she wrote in *The Female Eunuch* that 'sex for many has become a sorry business, a mechanical release involving neither discovery nor triumph, stressing human isolation more dishearteningly than ever before'.[9]

These paradoxes, these brawling contradictions, are the engine of this book. But what follows is not an attempt to endlessly restate the arguments made above. These are intended to function only as the poles, pegs and guy ropes that give structure to the marquee of the book. Crowded under the canopy are a dozen or so major figures, and a selection of minor figures, through whose lives and relationships and writings the history of seduction will be explored.

1

RAKE CULTURE

He could not fidget – as a man well might, standing in the dock of the Old Bailey charged with a capital offence – because his thumbs were bound together with twine. This seemed to be the end of the road for Colonel Francis Charteris. After a long and infamous career as Britain's most notorious rake, Charteris, now in his late sixties, stood accused of the rape of his former maid-servant Anne Bond. Standing before a judge and jury in February 1730 he had little hope of obtaining an acquittal. He was one of London's most renowned sexual predators, so detested for his lechery and his abusive methods that his house in Hanover Square had been attacked on more than one occasion by angry mobs. He had only managed to have annulled a previous conviction for rape through generous bribery (what was then known as a 'Golden Nol. Pros.'). His trial took place amid a blizzard of Grub Street pamphlets that chronicled his misdeeds, real and fictional, and denounced him as 'the Rape-Master-General of Great Britain'. In taverns, coffee-houses and salons throughout the capital the most scandalous rumours were spread about him, including allegations that he had raped his own grandmother.[1]

When Charteris was duly found guilty the courtroom erupted in cheers. A few days later he was summoned to the same place for sentencing. Dressed in a cavalry officer's uniform, attended to by a brace of footmen, he was sentenced to hang at Tyburn along with nine other common criminals brought before the magistrate in the same session. His carriage back to Newgate Prison was followed by a large crowd of happy Londoners, eager to advertise and celebrate the imminent demise of the nation's most prolific and unprincipled sexual adventurer. 'The most popular Whore-master in the three Kingdoms', as one contemporary account had it, 'said to have lured as many Women into his toils as would set up a *Sultan*'.[2]

***

Charteris had been born in Edinburgh at some point in the 1660s. His father was a wealthy landowner in Dumfriesshire and the Charterises were a family with ancient ties to the Scottish aristocratic elite. His youth was almost exactly coterminous with the reign of the restored Charles II, the Merry Monarch, whose priapic rule signalled a dramatic end to Cromwell's Puritan Protectorate. The libidinism of Charles's court was without parallel in English history. The king very much led by example. 'His scepter and his prick are of a length,' the Earl of Rochester reported, 'And she may sway the one who plays with th' other.' St James's was a long way from the Charteris family seat in Amisfield. Nevertheless, the cyprian spirit of the age made itself felt on the young man and would find morbid expression in him in his later years.

Charteris's devilish ways first became a matter of public record in the 1690s, when he joined the army of the Duke of Marlborough in Flanders. It is unclear how much, if any, combat Charteris saw. What is known is that he soon became a figure of general loathing for his ill-treatment of his brother officers. Charteris had become an inveterate card cheat as well as a ruthless loan shark. It seems as though he used his skills in one arena to create customers for the other. These demoralising activities, combined with various unspecified abuses of the local population, secured his expulsion from the army twice, the second occasion shortly before the Battle of Blenheim in 1704. Thereupon Charteris returned to Scotland where he paid his way back into the army, came into his inheritance following his father's death, and, to general amazement, managed to marry. The details of this union, like so much about his earlier life, are unknown, but it yielded a daughter, Janet Charteris, who would later do no service to the cause of British women through her loyalty to her villainous father.

Rich and married, Charteris now embarked on a phenomenal spree. He invested his income at the card table, where he systematically bilked the Scottish elite of their wealth. The master of the marked card and the loaded die, he had soon multiplied his net worth. On one particularly scandalous occasion he managed to inveigle his way into the Edinburgh salon of the Duchess of Queensberry and, with the aid of a strategically situated mirror, rob his hostess blind during a card game in her own drawing room. (This enraged her husband the Duke so much that he lobbied Parliament to change the law concerning the amount of money one could wager while gaming.)

This incident and many others like it served to make Charteris *persona non grata* in Scottish society. But ostracism could little restrain a man with Charteris's capacity for roguery, nor did it hinder the indulgence of his other appetites: women and property. Acquiring the latter was fairly straightforward. As for the former, Charteris used money, force and fraud to obtain sex, travelling far and wide to do so. His preference was for working-class women, 'strong, lusty, fresh Country Wenches', one account records, 'of the first Size, their B–tt–cks as hard as Cheshire Cheeses, that should make a Dint in a Wooden Chair and work like a Parish Engine at a Conflagration'. The accumulation of a substantial property portfolio created the need for large permanent staffs upon whom Charteris could prey. In 1713 he purchased Hornby Lodge in Lancashire, a place which became host to any number of proto-Sadean scenes as Charteris remodelled the house for his own debauched purposes – including the installation of secret passages that led to trapdoors in the servants' bedrooms – and then sent his agents out into the neighbouring countryside to find victims for his orgies. Soon the residents of the surrounding villages knew better than to send their wives and daughters to work for Charteris, and his panders had to search further afield for suitable targets.

On one famous occasion, Charteris's valet John Gourley found a girl looking for work as a maidservant, but willing only to enter the service of either an unmarried woman or a widow. Gourley lured her to Hornby Hall on the promise of work with his benign and virtuous mistress. Upon arrival she was told her potential new employer would interview her from her bed. Halfway through the conversation, her would-be mistress sprang from beneath the covers and disrobed to reveal the degenerate form of Francis Charteris, struggling to free himself from his disguise. He presently tried to seduce the shocked girl and, when that failed, drew a pistol and demanded sex. She pretended to comply, but when Charteris laid down the gun in readiness for his ministrations, she seized it, turned it upon her attacker and 'swore by all that was sacred, she would discharge it into his Body, if he did not return instantly to his Bed'. Charteris obliged and the girl was able to make her way safely out of the building, gun in hand.[3]

The great number of properties Charteris owned necessitated a considerable amount of travel between them, and it was during these sojourns that much of his most despicable business was carried on. On one such occasion Charteris was travelling between Musselburgh and Edinburgh when he came across a solitary woman carrying a sack of corn. Charteris solicited her, and when she refused both his advances and his money, he raped her at pistol point. Afterwards, having escaped, she told her husband, who sought personal revenge, and when that was not forthcoming, legal redress. Charteris's customary attempts to bribe his way out of trouble failed, and an Edinburgh court summoned him to appear before it charged with rape. Fearing that justice would be done, Charteris fled south to England and made his way to London.

***

London in the early eighteenth century, according to one jaundiced contemporary, was

> like the Ocean, that receives the muddy and dirty Brooks, as well as the clear and rapid Rivers, swallows up all the *Scum* and *Filth*, not only of our own, but of other Countries: *Wagons, Coaches,* and *Carrivans; Pack-Horses, Ships,* and *Wooden-Shoes; French, Dutch, German,* and *Italian* tattered Garments, being constantly emptying and discharging themselves into this *Reservoir,* or *Common-Sewer* of the World.[4]

With a population of over half a million it was the largest city in Europe and the largest conurbation by far in the United Kingdom, accounting for a tenth of the total population and dwarfing the next largest city, Bristol, which was home to a mere 30,000 people.

London was dirty, crowded and dangerous. There were innumerable ways to die. Highwaymen worked the roads between the built-up centre and the nearby villages and market towns of Kensington, Camberwell, Hampstead and Islington. Swords were worn in public and used in street fights, tavern brawls, and confrontations in the theatre. Smallpox was the terror of every citizen; the sexually indulgent, or even just the unlucky, faced an agonising death from the venereal diseases that claimed several thousand lives each year. The poor died of gin-drinking and starvation and upon the ravenous scaffolds at Tyburn. The old wooden houses in Covent Garden and Drury Lane came cheap – as little as twopence a night – but collapsed with regularity and were at perpetual risk of fire. 'Here malice, rapine, accident, conspire,' Samuel Johnson wrote in *London, a poem*:

> *And now a rabble rages, now a fire;*
> *Their ambush here relentless ruffians lay,*
> *And here the fell attorney prowls for prey;*
> *Here falling houses thunder on your head,*
> *And here a female atheist talks you dead.*

The city's capacity to kill was offset by the enormous quantity of sexual activity going on among its populace. To read the London press of the day is to enter a world that seems exclusively populated by coquettes, coxcombs, cuckolds and prudes engaged in a permanent carnival of amorous intrigue. 'I confess,' wrote one despairing Londoner to a country friend, 'if you have a Design to make your self a good Proficient in the Arts of *Whoring,* and *Drunkenness,* or to understand exactly the Methods of *Debauchery* and *Profaneness,* this is indeed the Place of the World.'[5] Sexual profligacy was then the fashion and the men of London competed with one another to prove their seductive powers. The mania for sexual adventure and amorous expertise found innumerable means of expression. A whole new vocabulary sprang to life to describe the mores of the day. Seemingly every man aspired 'to keep cully', the more prodigious being known as 'Whore-mongers'; for those with limited resources a couple of shillings could afford a visit to a 'Vaulting School' kept by an 'Abbess' or 'Mother', though doing so brought with it the risk of contracting the 'Drury-Lane Ague' or the 'Covent Garden Gout'. Among the Quality, 'Whoring, Drinking and Gaming, are reckon'd among the Qualifications of a fine Gentleman'. These well-born, moneyed syba-rites were the rakes who, either as individuals or gathered together in clubs – the Mohocks, the Hell-Fire Club, and many more – roved the city searching for trouble and pleasure. One ballad recorded in print in 1719 records the sexual escapades of these leisured men:

But the Town's his Seraglio, and still he lives free;
Sometimes she's a Lady, but as he must range,
Black Betty, or Oyster Moll serve for a Change:
As he varies his Sports his whole Life is a Feast,
He thinks him that is soberest is most like a Beast:
All Houses of Pleasure, breaks Windows and Doors,
Kicks Bullies and Cullies, then lies with their Whores:
Rare work for the Surgeon and Midwife he makes,
What Life can Compare with the jolly Town-Rakes.

Such behaviour was by no means limited to the wealthy elite. Scandalised observers recorded the democratic nature of the phenomenon. One complained of the '*Suburbs gallant Fop that takes delight in Roaring, / He spends his time in Huffing, Swearing, Drinking, and in Whoring*'. A Portuguese visitor singled out for criticism the legal clerks who 'are under no manner of government; before their times are half out, they set up for gentlemen; they dress, they drink, they game, frequent the playhouses, and intrigue with the women'. In London, even the humblest apprentice could don his finest clothes and go to the theatre or to the Vauxhall Leisure Gardens for a shilling and mingle, unobserved, with other young men and women looking for adventure. For this was not a man's world. Women were active and perceptive participants in the London frolics. There were, in the first instance, the thousands – perhaps tens of thousands – of active sex workers: '*The* Sisterhood *of* Nightingale-lane, Ratcliff-high-way, Tower-Ditch, Rose-mary-lane, Hatton-Wall, Saffron-hill, Wetstone's-Park, Lutener's-lane', the women of Bankside, known as the Stewes Bank for its great quantities of prostitution, and, of course, the wealth of formal, informal and opportunistic sex work going on in amid the storied 'Hundreds of Drury Lane' – the vast and murky warren of back alleys, dim courtyards and precarious tenements that ran between Drury Lane and the Piazza of Covent Garden. These women were understood to be tempters as much as temptations, and it became almost a matter of form to warn young men to steer well clear of their siren call:

> *Of Drury's mazy courts, and dark abodes,*
> *The harlot's guileful paths, who nightly stand,*
> *Where Katherine-street descends into the Strand.*
> *Say, vagrant Muse, their wiles and subtil arts,*
> *To lure the strangers unsuspecting hearts;*
> *So shall our youth on healthful sinews tread,*
> *And city cheeks grow warm with rural red.*

Prostitution was not then understood in the same clear terms as it is now. Language was used loosely, and who or what was a 'whore' and what their motives were at any one moment was always in flux. James Boswell recorded that he picked up two girls in Covent Garden with nothing more than the promise of 'a glass of wine and my company'. Even the hardened regulars of the trade understood their position as being essentially a gamble on social mobility, preferable to a lifetime as a domestic servant. Jacob Ilive, confined in Clerkenwell Prison, vividly recalled the imprisoned prostitutes trading stories of jaunts down to Bath, nights out at the theatre, and days out at the races with their 'Gallants', as they beat hemp together.

To be sure, the opportunities for social mobility on offer for those who chose a life as a courtesan operated at the vertiginous extremes – but there were those who made it. Lavinia Fenton, the first woman to play the female lead in *The Beggar's Opera*, wound up as the Duchess of Bolton. Fanny Murray came to London after being seduced by the Duke of Marlborough's grandson and worked her way up from Covent Garden to be the mistress of the Earl of Sandwich before ending up happily married to the actor David Ross. In the next generation, Soho native Kitty Fisher became one of the most famous women in the country, charming her way to the top through a deft manipulation of men, the media, and her own potent sexual allure. These are just some of the most famous examples. That the average female Londoner could be just as sexually adventurous as any man was attested to by the immense literature in which worries were expressed about the morality of modern women. One pamphleteer complained in the 1730s that women were running riot 'on account of the promiscuous liberty allowed both Sexes' and that consequently even 'the best Husbands are often hornified, as well as bad ones'. The spectre of the seductress loomed large in the consciences of god-fearing Englishmen:

> 'tis a deplorable Truth, that our young ladies . . . are wise, and more, knowing in the Arts of Coquetry, Galantry [sic], and others Matters relating to the Differences of Sexes, &c. before they come to be Twenty, than our Great-Grandmothers were all their lives.[6]

More equanimous observers of the London scene agreed with the famous and oft-repeated lines from Alexander Pope's *Moral Essays*: 'Men, some to Bus'ness, some to Pleasure take; / But ev'ry Woman is at heart a Rake.'

It was into this world that Francis Charteris entered at some time around 1720, living at first in Poland Street, Soho, before moving to Great George Street, near Hanover Square, by 1729. He was soon immersed in the sexual demi-monde of Georgian London. With the help of his faithful deputy, John Gourley, and the assistance of the West End's many bawds and procuresses – Mother Needham of Park Place, St James's, emerged as his preferred intermediary – Charteris was soon well supplied with women. His methods remained much the same as they had in the provinces. In 1724 Isabella Cranston applied for poor relief in St Margaret's Parish, Westminster, following her seduction by Charteris. She reported that she had been ruined by him after she was lured to the house of one Mrs Jolly in Suffolk Street under the promise of domestic service. Many more girls would share Cranston's fate.

One victim who departed from the typical profile was a young widow in Marylebone whom Charteris wooed while in disguise as a foreign nobleman. Thus compromised, she found herself extorted out of her jewels, causing her such torment in the process that she went mad and had to be committed to an asylum. On another occasion Charteris was drawn to an actress at Lincoln's Inn Theatre. After the performance ended he found her backstage and, when his advances failed, raped her at pistol point in the green room, while four of his lackeys guarded the door with their swords drawn. Some of his more egregious transgressions – such as this assault at the theatre – did not go unanswered and Charteris was regularly obliged to bribe victims, judges and husbands to forget about his crimes. But for the most part justice was not forthcoming.[7]

Then came Anne Bond. Tricked into working for 'Colonel Harvey' of Hanover Square, Bond was raped by Charteris, then beaten by his servants and thrown out onto the street. She found a friend, one Mrs Parsons, and together they went to court to file a suit against Charteris. A Middlesex jury agreed to indict the Colonel – a fact made retrospectively inevitable when it emerged that Charteris had once attempted to seduce the sister of one of the jurors – and in a matter of months he had been sentenced to hang.

Charteris's life was saved through the intervention of his daughter Janet. In 1720 she had married the eldest son of the Earl of Wemyss, a prominent Scottish peer. George II relied upon such men to keep the peace in Scotland, where the prospect of Jacobite rebellion still lurked just beneath the surface of daily life. When Janet, operating through influential Scottish intermediaries in London, sought her scoundrel father's pardon, the king had little choice but to comply. In April 1730, a pardon was issued through the Privy Council and Charteris was released from Newgate. He was obliged to pay damages to Anne Bond and, all told, the price of his freedom was £15,000 – an immense amount for the time. But freedom did not buy security. London was no longer safe for him. In a reversal of his previous fortunes, he now fled up north – doubtless encouraged in his decision when he was pulled from his carriage and beaten by an angry mob as he swept through Chelsea.[8] He was now an old and ravaged man, and he died two years later in Edinburgh. His estate was valued at a plum[9] (or two, depending on whether one believed his lawyers or his Grub Street obituarists), the awesome gains of a lifetime of fraud, larceny and extortion. He left the bulk of his estate to his grandson, the future 7th Earl of Wemyss, whose grateful descendants have borne the name of Charteris ever since.[10]

His burial in Edinburgh was as turbulent as his life. Enraged crowds repeatedly attacked the constables present to keep the peace in an attempt to seize and destroy the body. They failed to do so, but succeeded in pelting the service from afar, and so Colonel Francis Charteris's coffin was lowered into the ground accompanied by a hail of dead dogs, dead cats, living cats and offal.

Charteris's was a uniquely eighteenth-century life. His was the era of the rake, and he was the rake nonpareil. His ignominious achievements in the field secured him lasting recognition as the great sexual villain of his time. He passed directly from life into art. Alexander Pope paired him with the Devil in the third of his *Moral Essays* (1733); Jonathan Swift did likewise on more than one occasion. Charteris, his henchman Gourley, and his bawd of choice, Mother Needham, all appear together in the first plate of William Hogarth's *The Harlot's Progress*, the phenomenally popular 1732 series of etchings that made the young artist's name. Most significantly, Charteris, the class of rakes he exemplified, and the problem he posed to women, morals and society found their clearest and most enduring expression in a trilogy of books by a man who, more than any other individual, codified and popularised the modern concern with seduction: Samuel Richardson.

***

William Hogarth's *The Harlot's Progress* (1732). Colonel Francis Charteris and his henchman, John Gourley, lurk in the background on the right.

Samuel Richardson was born in 1689, on the marches of two worlds. The year before his birth the Dutch king, William of Orange and his English wife, Mary Stuart, had been invited to take the throne from Mary's father, James II, in the so-called Glorious Revolution. This bloodless handover of power was accompanied by a new constitutional settlement embodied by two Acts of Parliament instituted in the year of Richardson's birth. The Bill of Rights codified the rights and liberties of English subjects and confirmed Parliament's sovereignty; the Act of Toleration granted religious freedom to dissenting Protestants (though to no Catholics), so ending the attempt to impose religious uniformity on the nation from above. In the spirit of the new, liberty-infused age, the Printing Act was allowed to lapse in 1695, bringing an end to pre-publication censorship; marking England's arrival as a pragmatic, mercantile power, the Bank of England was established in

1694. These bureaucratic landmarks were not intended to transform the moral worlds of regular English men and women, but the second-order effect of the upheavals of the late seventeenth century was to inaugurate a revolution in social conduct and sexual attitudes. The celebration of individual political liberty opened the door to libertinism. The toleration of religious minorities implied a willingness to turn a blind eye to private peccadilloes. A Swiss visitor in the early eighteenth century was in awe, like so many continental visitors, of English freedoms, but appalled at the permissiveness unleashed thereby in society at large. 'They cherish their liberty to such an extent,' he wrote, 'that they often let both their religious opinions and their morals degenerate into licentiousness. . . . Debauch runs riot with an unblushing countenance.'[11]

In one of the few extant autobiographical accounts of his early life, Richardson made a conscious effort to link his own family to the events of 1688. His father was a humble London joiner who, he claimed, enjoyed the patronage of the Duke of Monmouth. In 1685 Monmouth staged an ill-fated uprising against the rule of James II. When it failed, Richardson's father, in his son's telling, 'thought proper, on the Decollation of the first-named unhappy Nobleman, to quit his London Business & to retire to Derbyshire; tho' to his great Detriment; & there I, & three other Children out of Nine, were born'. Richardson Sr, however, was on the right side of history. After the Glorious Revolution he and his family returned to London and had his remaining sons baptised in his native parish of St Botolph's, Aldgate. At first the family lived in Tower Hill, a poor neighbourhood just outside the eastern limit of the City of London, on a street called Mouse Alley that sat in the shadow of the Tower of London, connecting the city's commercial centre to the docks. Later the family would move a short distance north, to Rosemary Lane just inside the City. In neither location were the family considered rich, or even prosperous, but in both the young Richardson would have been exposed to the hectic realities of daily life in the capital.

Given his silence about his youth it is hard to accurately reconstruct what Richardson absorbed from the city in these years. One likes to think that as a child he would have been privileged to live so close to the Tower of London, known then not just for its prison but for the menagerie of exotic animals – including a famous pride of lions – that were kept on public display in its precincts. More prosaically, it seems likely that Richardson's lifelong fascination with clothing and the details of fashionable dress must have begun in the thronged streets of the City where the parvenu 'Cits' (the merchants and tradesmen made good) mixed with apprentices, journeymen, foreign businessmen, off-duty servants, clerks, molls, vendors and pedlars eager to display themselves and their finery. The City was still a distinct entity from Westminster and had its own fashions, typically more democratic (some would say garish) than those prevailing in the haughtier neighbourhoods that surrounded St James's. The 'mix'd Crouds of saucy Fops and *City* Gentry' that thrived in the streets of Richardson's childhood were ripe targets for social satire.

The vibrancy of London life attracted the concern of moralists as well as the condescension of snobs. The neighbourhoods around the Tower, the aptly named Tower Hamlets, were the epicentre of the movement to transform English manners. The freedoms enshrined in the post-1688 settlement were extended only grudgingly to the common people. The recognition that the state could no longer prescribe moral and religious conformity from the top down was balanced by a countervailing belief that individuals were amenable to suasion, instruction and shame from the bottom up. Encouraged by Queen Mary, citizens in Tower Hamlets set up a Society for the Reformation of Manners in 1690 to suppress brothels and to stymie immoral behaviour in their community. Over a dozen companion societies were active elsewhere in the city by the mid-1690s, and they would remain features of London life until the 1730s, when they finally abandoned their Sisyphean task. Even if their mission was ultimately in vain, the attempt at moral reformation made a great impression on Richardson. The animating ideal of the societies – the notion that individuals were moral agents susceptible to reason, whose better impulses could be cultivated by instruction and example – was to shape his entire worldview.

One of the first glimpses we get of the young Richardson is his admission that as a teenager he sent anonymous letters to dissipated members of his community urging them to reform their ways. This was an early manifestation of his lifelong love of letter writing. A shy boy, Richardson immersed himself in books and was known in his neighbourhood for his literary abilities. His bashfulness and his way with words made him a favourite of the local women, who had him read to them while they sat at their needlework and, later, recruited him to help manage their correspondence with their suitors:

I was not more than thirteen when three of these young women, unknown to each other, having an high opinion of my taciturnity, revealed to me their love secrets, in order to induce me to give them copies to write after, or correct, for answers to their lovers letters: Nor did any of them ever know, that I was the secretary to the others. I have been directed to chide, and even repulse, when an offence was either taken or given, at the very time that the heart of the chider or repulser was open before me, overflowing with esteem and affection; and the fair Repulser dreading to be taken at her Word; directing this word, or that expression, to be softened or changed. One, highly gratified with her lover's fervor, and vows of everlasting love, has said, when I have asked her direction: 'I cannot tell what to write; But (her heart on her lips) you cannot write too kindly.' All her fear only, that she should incur slight for her kindness.

Better training for an epistolary novelist can scarcely be imagined.

Richardson's obvious intelligence and eagerness to learn put him on the path to train as a clergyman, and one can glimpse an alternative reality where he joined the ranks of the great Georgian scribbler-divines: Jonathan Swift, Lawrence Sterne and Charles Churchill. But this would have required a university education, and his family's poverty precluded that eventuality. Unable to afford an education, in July 1706 Richardson was bound as an apprentice to John Wilde, a London printer. At any one time London had a floating population of around ten thousand apprentices, paying their dues in trades as diverse as tweezer-making, bridle-cutting and calico-printing. Bound to their respective masters for seven years and taken into their homes and families to live, work and learn, apprentices – aside from actual criminals – constituted the most suspect of London's demographics. 'The Blood runs warm in their young veins,' a commentator observed in one of the innumerable tracts decrying the moral threat posed by these rampant young men, 'against this Evil the young Apprentice must exert all the Force of Reason, Interest, and Religion.' Morality and the urges of young manhood aside, apprentices were trapped in an economic bind: they vastly outnumbered their masters. In the printing industry there were only a hundred or so master printers, each employing at any one time between four and ten apprentices on top of a regular staff of journeymen printers. With only faint prospects of ever matching their employers' prosperity, the loyalty of apprentices to their masters and their commitment to society as a whole was always contingent. The vast cultural effort that went into preaching to apprentices on matters of morals, manners and work ethic was symptomatic of this fear of a social group not yet integrated into the order of things. In this respect, male apprentices were the counterparts to that other group that the Georgians worried so much about: young, single women.

The most enduring artefact of this culture of suspicion towards apprentices is William Hogarth's great cycle of etchings, *Industry and Idleness*. It depicts the divergent life paths of two apprentices bound at the same time to a single London weaver. The Good Apprentice, Francis Goodchild, works hard, goes to church, marries the master's daughter, and so inherits his business, ending up a prosperous merchant who in the final scene parades through London in a carriage having recently been made Lord Mayor. The Bad Apprentice, Thomas Idle, shirks his duties as an employee and a Christian, finally running away to sea before returning to London to whore and carouse and, ultimately, commit murder, for which he is hanged at Tyburn in the penultimate plate.

Samuel Richardson was ever the Good Apprentice. 'I served a seven diligent years to it, to a master who grudged every hour to me,' he recalled of his apprenticeship. 'I took care, that even my candle was of my own purchasing, that I might not in the most trifling instance make my master a sufferer (and who used to call me The Pillar of his House).'

His apprenticeship to Wilde ended in July 1713. Two years later he became a freeman of the Stationers' Company. Moving from printer to printer, Richardson accrued experience as an overseer, compositor and corrector while searching for a patron. One of the printers he worked for was John Leake, and when Leake died in 1720 he took over his printing business in Salisbury Court, off Fleet Street. A year later, in 1721, he married his former master John Wilde's daughter, Martha. Now thirty-two, Richardson was finally established as a husband and businessman.

Salisbury Court was to be the base of Richardson's operations for the next four decades. Situated between Fleet Street and the Thames, the business was at almost the exact midway point between the old centre of London around St Paul's, and the fashionable purlieus of St James's. His immediate world was bounded to the west by the Temple Bar, the gateway that marked the boundary between Fleet Street and the Strand, between London and

Westminster, and whose elaborate façade was, as occasion required, decorated with the heads of Jacobite traitors. To the east, Fleet Street was separated from Ludgate Hill and the City proper by Fleet Ditch and the New Canal, the artificial tributaries that drained much of the human and industrial effluvium of the City into the Thames, and whose stench did little to hinder the brisk business done at the countless stalls selling fresh oysters that lined their banks.[12] In between these limits thrived a neighbourhood of tailors, lawyers, clerks, doctors and tavern-owners. There were also a significant number of printers and booksellers.[13] Conveniently for Richardson, Salisbury Court was equidistant between the booksellers of west London, like Andrew Millar, the greatest literary deal-maker of the day, based on the Strand, and those in the east, on and about Paternoster Row, such as Richardson's great friends and boosters Charles Rivington and John Osborn.

Richardson's timing was as propitious as his location. England in the 1720s was on the verge of a great explosion of printing activity. Literacy rates were approximately 60 per cent for men and 40 per cent for women. Rising education standards combined with economic prosperity and, for the most part, social stability created a ready market for the printed word. On the supply side, a bare minimum of government intervention in printing, improving legal protections for intellectual property, and an efficient postal service, all nourished the growth of the industry. Printers were kept busy by the three thousand unique titles being published each year by the 1740s – two-thirds of which were printed in London – and by the dozens of daily, weekly or thrice-weekly newspapers, journals and gossip sheets, not to mention the sleet of Grub Street pamphleteering that rained down continuously upon the capital.

Richardson's first big break in business came in 1733 when he was awarded a contract to print bills for the House of Commons. A decade later he won a second, considerably more lucrative contract to print the journals of the House of Commons. In between these two coups he continued to accumulate experience and trust in the book trade, his presses at Salisbury Court producing respectable tomes on history, geography, and various religious and moral matters. He engaged through his publications with some of the great intellectual debates and problems of the English Enlightenment. His presses took both sides of the fractious public discussion over Deism and demonstrated, through works like Daniel Defoe's *Religious Courtship*, an emergent interest in problems of love, romance and marriage. Many of his publications, such as the *Weekly Miscellany* and the *Daily Journal*, were fantastically dull, and his authors were little better. They did however provide Richardson with entrées into literary London – the author Aaron Hill became his great friend and supporter – and his correspondence with other, lesser figures provides us with crucial insights into his life in this period. In the mid-1730s he became a friend and correspondent with Dr George Cheyne, a quack doctor and nutritionist from Bath whose books on dieting and nutrition Richardson published.[14]

It is largely through his letters with Cheyne that we get our first idea of what Richardson may have looked like. Cheyne, who had been extraordinarily fat, detailed his obesity and its consequences in horrifying detail in his letters to Richardson (he wrote on one occasion of his 'putrified overgrown body . . . regularly the gout all over six months of the year, perpetual [retching], anxiety, giddiness, fitts and startings. Vomits were my only relief'), while extolling the merits of his 'strict milk, seed, and vegetable diet' and 'the necessity of frequent gentle vomits that cleanse the glands'. Richardson, it emerges, was himself sorely in need of this course of treatment. Cheyne berated him for his girth and prolific appetite, and his cowed friend agreed to slim down, thereafter boasting of his progress in his letters. By the time the first images of Richardson emerge in the 1740s we see a man with a pink, round, complacent face – like a gammon steak – and a simple white wig, who, if not vastly overweight, generously fills his breeches.

Richardson's struggles with his weight may have concealed a deeper personal torment. He was frequently ill throughout this period and at times hinted at psychological and physical exhaustion. Overwork likely accounted for some of this, but he was also haunted by familial tragedy. His marriage to Martha had produced six children – including three Samuels – none of whom survived infancy. Martha herself died in January 1731; four months later their last surviving daughter died too.[15] The next year he married Elizabeth Leake, the daughter of his former employer. Their marriage produced four daughters, Mary (Polly), Martha (Patty), Anne (Nancy) and Sarah (Sally), all born between 1735 and 1740. Richardson never had the son he hoped for, and it is quite possible that the profusion of women in his life sharpened his interest in the dynamics of courtship.

Richardson's failure to produce a male heir indirectly led to his first outing as an author. In the summer of 1732 he engaged as his apprentice his nephew Thomas Verren Richardson, perhaps with the intention one day of handing his business over to him. Worried for the young man's morals, Richardson took the occasion of Thomas's apprenticeship to set down his own thoughts on how an apprentice should conduct himself. The result was *The Apprentice's Vade Mecum*, printed from his own press in 1733. In its tone, content and rambling form, the *Vade Mecum* did but little depart from the conventions of the instruction manual. Beginning with the customary decrying of 'the degeneracy of the times, and the profaneness and immorality, and even the open infidelity that is everywhere propagated with impunity', it proceeded through a standard list of moral threats (women, the theatre, the tavern) that the pious apprentice would have to circumvent in the city. One of the few moments in which Richardson reveals his considerable descriptive powers comes during a critique of modern fashions, which he considered 'one of the epidemick evils of the present age', an especial threat to the young apprentice as it 'lifts up the young man's mind far above his condition'. What follows is an inadvertently hilarious description of the various modish affectations in dress that Richardson had observed in the streets of London ('fine wrought buckles, near as big as those of a coach-horse, covering his instep and half his foot'), before ending with a prayer that the 'ingenious Mr. Hogarth would finish the portrait' and 'shame such Foplings into Reformation'. There is a hard edge to Richardson's criticism of such pretensions. The dangers of material ambition haunt all his novels. The idea that status could be purchased rather than earned through moral example was repugnant to him, and he saw in that notion's prevalence the route by which men would be made work-shy and women would be sexually ruined.

The *Vade Mecum* never sold much, despite being supported by his bookseller friends and celebrated in various magazines and journals that Richardson had a hand in. But his book's commercial failure figured little in his larger fortunes. Richardson was prospering by this point and in 1738 he began to rent a country home in Fulham, a pile with three floors, a cellar, and a garden with a grotto. While he retained his quarters in Salisbury Court, Richardson now had the perfect writer's retreat in the countryside just west of London. No sooner had he taken up the lease than he was approached by his bookseller associates Rivington and Osborn with a commission to write a book of familiar letters. The concept – which conformed to a longstanding arrangement – was a book of letters sent from various stock characters (Mother to Daughter, Master to Servant, etc.) that doubled as a guide to letter writing and an exercise in moral instruction. Richardson agreed and set to work on these letters, to be written 'in a common style' for the use of rural readers. The first couple he wrote were 'letters to instruct handsome girls, who were obliged to go out to service, as we phrase it, how to avoid the snares that might be laid against their virtue'. In the writing, Richardson recalled a story he had been told decades before. It was about a beautiful girl from a

The plot of *Pamela* needs no embellishment – it does, indeed, resist it – but the novel's place in the history of seduction is better grasped with some additional context. First, *Pamela* helpfully demonstrates what kind of behaviour constituted 'seduction' at the dawn of the modern age. The first half of the book consists of Mr B—'s escalating attempts to claim his servant's body. Initially, his actions are relatively innocent. He gives her books, clothes and other small objects; he offers her additional sums of money to send home to her poor parents; he showers her with attention above and beyond what her lowly status in his household warrants; he flirts with her in private. When these gambits fail, Mr B— becomes more aggressive: he kisses her against her will; he gropes her bosom; he harangues her as a 'sauce-box', a 'bold-face', an 'artful young baggage', a 'little slut [with] the power of witchcraft'. Her resistance holds and his methods become truly Charterisian.[16] He hides in her room at night and surprises her while she sleeps. He kidnaps her and takes her to a private home where Mrs Jewkes, a London procuress, endeavours to corrupt her. Disguised as an elderly female servant, Mr B— enters the room Mrs Jewkes and Pamela share and tries to ravish her while his bawd holds her down. His rape frustrated (when Pamela faints, Mr B— desists), he tries to arrange a sham marriage in order to trick her into believing that they can now legitimately have sex.[17] This too, fails, and in a final throw of the dice Mr B— offers her a contract to become his kept mistress in exchange for 500 guineas, property in Kent, the use of all his servants, and 'two diamond rings, and two pair of ear-rings, and a diamond necklace'.

The variety, ingenuity and rapacity of Mr B—'s attempts on her leave Pamela rightfully despondent. 'This plot is laid too deep,' she laments at one point, 'and has been too long hatching, to be baffled, I fear.' It is also clear, though, that such behaviour was tolerated if not celebrated as appropriate for a well-born man to undertake in pursuit of a comely woman from a lower social class. Mr B—

approaches but never crosses the line of actual rape, which was a capital offence, albeit a rarely prosecuted one. As such, all his behaviour up to that point falls within the capacious eighteenth-century definition of 'seduction'.

In this context it is remarkable that Pamela is able to hold out at all. The forces of English society are arrayed against her and yet still she, a simple serving girl, is able to maintain her resolve. What guides her is a monomaniacal interest in maintaining her chastity, a duty buttressed by her parents in their letters to her. In their correspondence they impress upon her the impassable divide between the world of material wealth and that of priceless moral precepts. When they learn early on of Mr B—'s favours to her, they immediately warn her to be on her guard against him and remind her of the immeasurable value of 'that jewel, your virtue, which no riches, nor favour, nor any thing in this life, can make up to you'. Her parents ask her not only that she return to them to live in honest poverty rather than risk her virtue, but further that she prefer death to the loss of her chastity.

Pamela completely internalises these ideas. When Mr B— first kisses her and fondles her breasts, she writes that she 'would have given my life for a farthing' rather than succumb to his advances. There is an abiding significance to her refusal to sell or exchange her chastity. In an avowedly commercial age which celebrated and encouraged material wealth and accumulation, Pamela makes the claim that her virtue exists on a plane apart from the market economy. In the founding text of the modern literature of seduction, Richardson – no critic of the capitalist ethos – declares that questions of sex will not be subsumed into the rising tide of mercantile morality. The seduction narrative becomes the place where older Christian values survive the otherwise general triumph of the new values of the market and the merchant. There is a trap here, too. The elevation of virtue heightens the drama of its menace by a seducer. Things placed on pedestals have a tendency to fall from them, and the higher the column, the more devastating the impact. The counterpoint to the celebration of virtue was the loathing of its loss. 'Moral' men were equally comfortable venerating the virtuous and slandering the fallen. 'A Woman discarded of Modesty,' one book of manners advised, 'ought to be gaz'd upon as a Monster.'[18] Another author observed that if any man of worth and substance were to learn that the object of his affections had been previously seduced, then she would undergo an immediate and irreversible transformation: 'her beauty fades in his eyes, her wit becomes nauseous, and her air disagreeable'.[19] Consequently, virtue was a tightrope that all chaste women walked, ever aware of the chasm all about them. Henry Fielding's Amelia would later decry the bind in which the cult of virtue put women. 'Let her remember,' she tells her innocent female reader, that 'she walks on a precipice, and the bottomless pit is to receive her if she slips; nay, if she makes but one false step.'[20]

Richardson was well aware of the public fascination with the drama of that false step. From the outset he made it clear that his aim was to bait the hook of moral instruction with the worm of titillation.[21] He could not know how successful that formula would be. The first hint of his imminent success came from his wife. She read his proofs as he wrote them, and after a few weeks' work on *Pamela* she would come to his study each evening and ask, 'Have you any more Pamela, Mr. R.?'

It emerged upon publication that Mrs Richardson was not alone in her hunger for more of Pamela Andrews. First published in November 1740, *Pamela* went through an astonishing five editions in ten months. French and Italian translations were rapidly commissioned and were circulating on the continent within two years of the English publication.[22] In London, Horace Walpole recorded that 'the late singular novel is the universal, and only theme – Pamela is like snow, she covers every thing with her whiteness'.

An engraving from a scene in *Pamela*, where Mr B—
ambushes the titular heroine in the night

Pamela was originally published anonymously and as a nominally 'true' story. Only years later would Richardson coyly list himself as the 'editor' of the work. A mere handful of close friends knew that he was the author, though word soon spread through gossipy literary London. The rest of the public had to content themselves with open letters to the author published in magazines and periodicals or directed to the book's printer – who was, naturally enough, Richardson himself.

Whether he was named or unnamed, the rapturous reception of *Pamela* propelled Richardson to the front line of English literary life. His friends, perhaps predictably, showered superlatives on his novel, and their letters to him strain the norms of acceptable flattery. More revealing of the general adulation that the book received was the praise that ordinary people, either unknown to Richardson or ignorant of his identity as the author, laid upon *Pamela*. Clergymen wrote that his book would do more good for national morals than any number of sermons; writer and editor Ralph Courteville declared that 'if all the Books in England were to be burnt, this Book, next to the Bible, ought to be preserved'. Members of the public told how the novel had inspired them to seek the reformation of the rakes among their acquaintances, some even claiming success in the endeavour. Theatrical adaptations were written and performed; Hogarth, who a few years before had been praised by Richardson from afar, was commissioned to create a series of etchings depicting scenes from the novel.[23] *Pamela* was a cultural event that touched all classes. London society ladies proudly displayed their copies in public, while the villagers of Slough gathered at the blacksmith to hear the book read aloud and ran off to ring the church bells when their heroine finally married Mr B—.

Literary success seldom comes without controversy; *Pamela* bred critics as well as fans. These critics can be loosely divided into satirists and moralists. The former consisted of the writers, critics and readers who were sceptical of *Pamela*'s claim to realism. They saw in Pamela's rise from servant to lady of the manor a tale of canny social climbing, not the triumph of morality. Surely, they argued, if moral values were distinct from, and superior to, material values then rewarding the first with the second – which was what the book's subtitle seemed to celebrate – made nonsense of the novel's value system. The result was a chorus of scabrous criticism emanating from the capital's pleasure districts. In June 1741 Eliza Haywood, the best-selling female novelist of the age, published *Anti-Pamela; or Feign'd Innocence Detected*, which recounted in the original's epistolary format the rapid social ascent of Syrena Tricksy. Haywood's work came a few months after a more complete parody of Richardson's moralising: Henry Fielding's *Shamela*, whose anti-heroine is a courtesan on the make until she realises she can dupe Mr Booby into marriage instead. 'I thought once of making a little fortune by my person,' she writes to her bawdy mother. 'I now intend to make a great one by my vertue.'

Shamela and *Anti-Pamela* are but two examples among many. The satirical attacks on *Pamela* probed the holes in Richardson's worldview. They also demonstrated how opposing views of morality could cohabit in the same period. Richardson's morality, as we shall see, may have been ascendent but it still had to contend with the more permissive attitudes of Fielding and Haywood and their Covent Garden milieu. Any one sexual ideology rarely attains hegemonic status. The question is not which one triumphs but who attains cultural top billing. The rivalry between *Pamela* and *Shamela* is not simply an episode from English literary history but a permanent feature of the history of seduction.

As a printer and a longstanding participant in the London literary scene, Richardson could not have been surprised by the satirical attacks that came his way. Friends wrote to console him of the barbs hurled his way – the ever-faithful Aaron Hill prayed that some higher power might 'Deliver Pamela from these cold *Killers*, who assume a Merit in destroying her!'[24] – Richardson's occupation of the moral high ground was, however, impregnable and he could readily shrug off such attacks. More worrying were the criticisms of his work that came from fellow moralists. In works like *Pamela Censur'd* and *The Virgin in Eden*, Richardson was attacked by conservatives for writing little better than pornography. *Pamela*, they argued (and not without reason), was needlessly salacious and possessed of a wholly perverse moral lesson. It would doubtless corrupt more youths than it would save. They scorned the notion that this was suitable reading material for their daughters. The anonymous author of *Pamela Censur'd* went further, declaring that Pamela functioned as incitement to seduction:

The Advances are regular, and the amorous Conflicts so agreeably and warmly depicted, that the young Gentleman Reader will at the best be tempted to rehearse some of the same Scenes with some Pamela or other in the Family, and the Modest Young Lady can never read the Description of Naked Breasts being run over with the Hand, and Kisses given with such Eagerness that they cling to the Lips; but her own soft Breasts must heave at the Idea and secretly sigh for the same Pressure; what then can she do when she comes to the closer Struggles of the Bed, where the tender Virgin lies panting and exposed, if not to the last Conquest . . . at least to all the Liberties which ungoverned Hands of a determined Lover must be supposed to take?[25]

The passage inadvertently demonstrates the author's own criticism of *Pamela*. Writing about seduction, even for moral or instructive purposes, brings with it the unavoidable risk that the realistic portrayal of sexual collision will tip into salaciousness and pornography. The charge stung Richardson and he quietly modified the text in response to such criticisms.[26]

The controversies surrounding *Pamela* add to the sense that if Richardson's work cannot be confirmed as the first novel of the English language, then its publication must surely be considered the first great literary event in the history of the form. Its local and international popularity; the fervid debates it triggered; the parodies it spawned; the conversations and correspondences it informed; the sheer quantity of copies it sold: all militate towards the view that this was the moment when the Western world fell in love with the novel. Richardson courted his readers no less assiduously than Mr B— pursued Pamela, and in so doing acknowledged how the strategies of fiction mimicked the stratagems of the seducer. The novelist spins fictions to win an audience just as the seducer contrives to win his intended – and with much the same artistry. Richardson seems to nod to this symbiosis between real and fictional worlds in a brilliant passage put into the unlikely mouth of Mr B— shortly before he marries Pamela. Seeing his fiancée writing away, he expresses an interest in reading her letters and journals, and puns upon the similarities between reading, writing and courting:

I long to see the particulars of your plot, and your disappointment, where your papers leave off: for you have so beautiful a manner, that it is partly that, and partly my love for you, that has made me desirous of reading all you write; though a great deal of it is against myself; for which you must expect to suffer a little: and as I have furnished you with the subject, I have a title to see the fruits of your pen.

The passage could act as epigraph for *Pamela*'s enduring cultural resonance. Its publication was the moment that the fiction of seduction affirmed the seduction of fiction.

***

Before the publication of *Pamela*, Richardson was prospering; after it he was on his way to being rich. In Georgian England, wealth brought with it obligations to the poor and needy in one's extended social group, and a man in or above Richardson's position could expect a steady stream of petitioners and supplicants to make their way to his door. Early in 1743, one such indigent was directed to his offices at Salisbury Court by one of his clients, Dr Patrick Delany, an Irish cleric. Her name was Laetitia Pilkington and her life and career captured some of the vagaries of womanhood at the dawn of the modern age.

Born Laetitia van Lewen in either Cork or Dublin around 1710, Pilkington was the daughter of a Dutch doctor and an Irish Protestant mother. After a bookish childhood in Dublin, she was married in her mid-teens to Matthew Pilkington, a young clergyman with literary ambitions. Their courtship had been defined by mutual dissimulation as to the wealth and status of each family on the part of Matthew and Mr and Mrs van Lewen, and an understandable naivety, not to mention powerlessness, on that of Laetitia, matched by her husband-to-be's cynical persistence in an affair of the heart

that would not long detain him. The newlyweds' precarious prospects were reflected in the material belongings he brought to their
new home: a harpsichord, a cat and an owl, which 'were all his
worldly goods' at the age of twenty-five. Both Pilkingtons sought
literary recognition, a fact that might have given them common
cause and certainly gave them social access – Jonathan Swift became
a great friend to the couple and an enthusiastic supporter of
Matthew's work – but it also seems to have driven a wedge between
them, largely on account of Matthew's vanity. Pilkington would
later write, apropos of literary jealousy,

> And if a man cannot bear his friend should write, much less can
> he endure it in his wife; it seems to set them too much upon a
> level with our lords and masters; and this I take to be the true
> reason why even men of sense discountenance learning in women,
> and commonly choose for mates the most illiterate and stupid of
> the sex, and then bless their stars their wife is not a wit. But if a
> remark be true which I have somewhere read, that a foolish woman
> never brought forth a wise son, I think the gentlemen should have
> some regard to the intellects of those they espouse.

Her husband's true feelings towards her were revealed in 1732
when he obtained a year's posting in London, to be supplemented
by a commission from Swift to act as his agent in the capital.[27]
Laetitia was desperate to accompany him, but that September, as
Matthew prepared to leave, he told her quite frankly that 'he did
not want such an Incumbrance as a Wife, that he did not intend
to pass there for a married Man, and that in short he could not
taste any Pleasure where I was'. Laetitia was shocked; this admission was only the beginning of her marital woes.

Soon after his arrival in London, Matthew began neglecting his
clerical duties and instead devoted himself to the pleasures of the
West End. In Covent Garden he went to the theatre daily after

work and spent the night carousing with the fast set. Among his new rakish acquaintances was James Worsdale, a painter, poet, musician, wit and libertine with at least four illegitimate children, possessed of an immense and indefatigable charm, and who moved easily among the liberal-living aristocracy. Pilkington was soon to know all about Worsdale's charms. In 1733 she joined her husband in London, where she found him immersed in the nightlife: drinking, attending the theatre, and in hot pursuit of a Drury Lane actress (one Mrs Heron). 'I thought this but an odd manner of Life for a Clergyman,' she recalled. Matthew was by now convinced that he had to rid himself of the burden of a wife and set about trying to lure Laetitia into adultery. His first port of call, Worsdale, soon set about seducing his friend's wife. 'He did everything in his power to afford and encourage an amour between his friend and me,' Pilkington wrote of her husband. Matthew's efforts included the organisation of a romantic weekend trip to Windsor, the party consisting solely of Laetitia and Worsdale. After fending off her companion's hands for much of the coach ride there, Pilkington then had to barricade herself in the hotel bedroom at night in order to keep her suitor out. The evening's shenanigans made for a frosty morning's sightseeing. She made it back to London assailed but unconquered.

Pilkington was as frank as any of her female contemporaries about the existence of her own desires, and used the language and literary stylings of moral outrage more as a satirical device than as an actual expression of her private beliefs. She wanted love; she wanted intimacy. As an educated woman she knew that the costs of seeking either were infinitely greater than those faced by men. She was instantly aware that her husband's inducements to adultery could be lethal to her life fortunes. Women lost more in sexual adventure than men. They risked pregnancy and death and, at a minimum, pariahdom. ''Tis play to you, 'tis but death to us,' Lady Mary Wortley Montagu had said of seduction. This double standard was embedded in the law. Male infidelity within marriage was not apt cause for divorce; female infidelity was – and Matthew Pilkington well knew it.

At the end of 1733 the unhappy couple returned to Dublin. They were joined there by Worsdale, who became a leading figure in the Dublin Hell-Fire Club, an outfit that far exceeded its English model in its transgressions. Its members dined at a table with a seat left spare for the devil. Their mascot was a black cat who was served first at supper. Their womanising, drinking, and harassment of the subject local population soon passed into lore. As a divine, Matthew could not easily associate himself with such a group and had to content himself on its fringes. But he remained committed to losing his wife. Laetitia had to fend off the advances of a young poet named William Hammond, from whom she later extracted the following confession:

> Mr Pilkington described you to me, as a Lady very liberal of your Favours, and begged I would be so kind as to make him a Cuckold, so that he might be able to prove it, in order to [get] a Separation from you; promising to give me Time and Opportunity for it: he assur'd me, it would be no difficult Task; that I need but throw myself at your Feet, whine out some tragedy, and you would quickly yield.

After several years of such antics, Pilkington was by 1737 under-standably fed up with her husband's behaviour and admitted in her poems that she considered herself free of her marital vows. That summer she fell in love with a young surgeon named Robert Adair. An affair began, and at some point later in the year the two were disturbed in bed by Matthew, with posse concomitant, who having finally succeeded in proving his wife's infidelity broke out the wine, toasted their freedom, and kicked her out of the house at two in the morning. A divorce was granted by a Dublin court in February 1738; Adair vanished from her life soon afterwards. Unmarried, unsupported, and terrifyingly free, Pilkington made her way back to London at the end of the year.

Her journey to London was a taste of things to come. On the crossing from Ireland a wealthy rake propositioned her to be his kept woman. She refused. In the stagecoach from Chester to London a Welsh parson bought her food and then 'began to offer a little more of his civility than I was willing to accept of'. Spurned but not embittered, he 'made me a present of a ginger-bread-nut, curiously wrapped up in white paper'. The scene so amused their fellow passengers that they invited her to dine with them at a tavern in Barnet. There another man swooped down upon her, insisting that this 'little Hibernian nymph should dine with him', regaling her with tales of his wealth while she ate. She finally made it to London with three guineas to her name.

There her chief patron and support was Colley Cibber, actor and poet laureate, who set her up as the in-house wit and writer for the moneyed men of White's, the exclusive club (originally a coffee-house) in St James's. Pilkington lived for a period directly opposite the site, and played host to its members who came to enjoy her humour, partake of her conversation, or have her write love letters or political pamphlets on their behalf. This in turn funded her own literary outings, including the 1739 poem 'The Statues: or, The Trial of Constancy. A Tale for the Ladies'. Here she bemoaned the 'changeful' male sex, who

> in perfidy delight,
> Despise perfection, and fair virtue slight;
> False, fickle, base, tyrannick, and unkind,
> Whose hearts nor vows can chain, nor honour bind,
> Mad to possess, by passion blindly led,
> And then as mad, to stain the nuptial bed.

For all the outward glamour, Pilkington still existed from commission to commission and was always only a misstep from calamity. The crisis came in 1742, when an unscrupulous landlady lured her into accepting a trifling loan – forty shillings – and then had her arrested for debt. In October she began a three-month stint at the Marshalsea prison, where the costs of survival only exacerbated her financial crisis. Half-starved, she wrote to everyone and anyone for help. Cibber secured a guinea each from sixteen dukes. Her Irish acquaintance Dr Delany sent her twelve guineas, to be collected from his printer, Samuel Richardson of Salisbury Court.

Shortly after her release, Pilkington presented herself with some trepidation at the home and office of the author of the 'incomparable Pamela' – a work she had read and admired. She was impressed by Richardson's obvious wealth (his house, she reported, was 'of a very grand outward appearance') and his unfailing generosity. Richardson introduced her to his wife and children and invited her to stay for lunch and dinner. That evening he gave her the twelve guineas from Delany, as well as two of his own, and sent on her way with an encouragement to write to him. This she did, though only her portion of the correspondence survives.

Over the next few years, Pilkington would continue to experience setbacks and would return again and again to Richardson's generosity. When she needed a letter of credit to establish a print and pamphlet store she wrote to him. When her store was robbed and her home burgled, and her daughter Betty arrived on her doorstep penniless and heavily pregnant, Richardson sent money, linen and clothing. When her prodigal son appeared home from sea in rags, Richardson sent money to clothe him. When, at length, she decided to return to Ireland in 1747, once more it was Richardson who conveyed the money to make her final departure from London possible.

Richardson was a great collector of women – and of their stories, which he needed as the raw material for his books. In supporting Pilkington he was doing his duty as a man of wealth and Christian charity, but he was also accessing a world he would otherwise have known next to nothing about. But the literary transaction – though he did not know it – went both ways. For, back in Dublin, Pilkington did something both very innovative and very much of her time: she wrote her autobiography. *The Memoirs of Laetitia Pilkington*, published in three volumes from 1748, first in Dublin and then in London, was Pilkington's *magnum opus*, the work that, after a lifetime of impoverished scribbling, made her famous and financially stable.

The tone and style of the *Memoirs* is Swiftian but the content is Richardsonian. Pilkington's life in her telling was one long battle against the cruelties of a male world, made manifest time and again in the licence men displayed towards her body. She had seen 'the world from the palace to the prison' and the one constant was male rapacity to women. Clergymen were 'generally the first seducers of innocence'; one swinish aristocrat she met had 'devoted himself entirely to Belial' and then had 'the cruelty to attempt his virgin daughters'; the rakes of White's boasted to her of their conquests of girls' chastity ('a loss,' she knew, 'never to be retrieved'), while some lived lives of Caligulan debauch, like her acquaintance and client General Ligonier, who kept four adolescent mistresses in a single house in Mayfair. At the end of it all, women were discarded by their exploiters and shunned by wider society. The injustice was outrageous, Pilkington declared:

> Of all things in nature, I most wonder why men should be severe in their censures on our sex, for a failure in point of chastity: is it not monstrous that our seducers should be our accusers? Will they not employ fraud, nay, often force to gain us? What various arts, what stratagems, what wiles will they use for our destruction? But that once accomplished, every opprobrious term with which our language so plentifully abounds, shall be bestowed on us, even by the very villains who have wronged us.

Pilkington was far from alone in her diagnosis. The middle of the century saw an explosion in women's writing, and a recurring theme was the sexual wrongs women endured at the hands of licentious men. Memoirs that told of women's real-life struggles, like Teresia Constantia Phillips' *Apology* (1748) and the eponymous *The Narrative of the Life of Charlotte Charke* (1755) by the daughter of Colley Cibber, met with enormous public success. In 1744 veteran female writer Eliza Haywood established *The Female Spectator*, the first publication of its kind aimed at and written by women, and one whose early issues consisted almost entirely of tales of sexual entrapment. Many of the new female writers were friends, correspondents or clients of Samuel Richardson. His long-standing correspondent Sarah Chapone wrote a proto-feminist critique of English marital laws. His printers produced some of the later editions of Charlotte Lennox's brilliant burlesque of sentimental culture, *The Female Quixote* (1752), and supported satirical essayist Jane Collier's work from the outset. His dear friend Sarah Fielding (sister of Henry) published a long essay on his own work, and he encouraged and mentored a raft of aspiring female writers through his prodigious daily regimen of letter writing.

The 1740s and 1750s were a period when women discovered and rejoiced in what Thomas Seward (himself the father of a prominent female belle-lettrist, Anne Seward), in 1748, called 'the female right to literature' in a poem of the same name. Male writers and moralists understood the right of women to enter the literary space as of a piece with the expanding work of Enlightenment and as a hallmark of England's generous and far-sighted civilisation. The new chorus of female voices, and the tales of suffering and adversity they related, also inspired a revolution in sexual ideology. For centuries it had been taken for granted that men were morally superior to women. The Bible and the church fathers had said as much. In eighteenth-century England the exact reverse came to be widely believed: namely, that women were morally superior and that men were vicious, predatory and lustful.

Seduction narratives proselytised this new paradigm. Richardson had done his part with *Pamela*, but the long war to change perceptions and win new sympathy and respect for women could not have been won without the legion of new female voices. Male control of the cultural means of production, Samuel Johnson wrote in a typically perspicacious *Rambler* essay in 1750, had been a constant since antiquity, and as a consequence 'the reproach of making the world miserable has been always thrown upon the women'. But that stranglehold had now been broken. 'The pleas of the ladies appeal to passions of more forcible operation than the reverence of antiquity,' he wrote, and they were likely to win the day, he concluded, for 'they have stronger arguments'.

***

The arrival in some numbers of female writers with lived experience of womanhood might have been Richardson's cue to leave the literary field to those who knew better than he whereof they wrote. This, however, was not Richardson's way. No sooner had the final revisions to *Pamela* been completed than he plunged into a new and more ambitious work, ultimately published in instalments between 1747 and 1748 as *Clarissa: or, the History of a Young Lady*.

Clarissa and *Pamela* have much in common. Richardson claimed that his second novel was based on the same real-life tale of seduction that had inspired *Pamela*. Their basic literary and dramatic structures are very similar. Both are epistolary novels. Both involve pursuit, abduction, deception and assault on the part of their male characters, and virtue, eloquence and sublime forbearance on the part of their female ones. Where they part ways is in their endings. *Pamela*, for all its moralising, is essentially a comedy that concludes, in the Shakespearean mode, in marriage. *Clarissa* is a tragedy that ends in the death of its titular heroine. These conflicting finales reveal a major departure in Richardson's moral message. As explained by its subtitle, the story of Pamela Andrews is one of virtue rewarded. The humble servant is elevated in stature and ultimately in station by her unerring commitment to her moral principles. In practical terms Mr B—'s attempted 'seduction' of Pamela amounts to little more than severe workplace harassment. The disparity in power between seducer and seduced is so great as to deny the novel any great psychological depth. Richardson's decision to have *Pamela* end with Mr B—'s moral reformation and his marriage was probably necessary to make the book at all readable. If *Pamela* had ended with Mr B—'s rape of his servant and her subsequent death, then his novel would have been little more than an exercise in literary sadism.

Rape and death, however, are exactly what befall the heroine of his second novel. The first quarter of *Clarissa* follows Clarissa Harlowe's desperate attempts to avoid marrying Roger Solmes, a doltish local squire, whom her family insist she wed for his money. Her steadfast refusal to marry a man she loathes drives her into the arms of Robert Lovelace, a rakish aristocrat with designs on her heart and body. Lovelace engineers her escape from the Harlowe home and then sets about his epic attempt on her virtue. His pursuit ends neither with her capitulation nor in his reformation. Instead, after close to a million words of text, Lovelace transports Clarissa to a Hampstead bordello where he drugs and rapes her.

Despoiled but not ruined, Clarissa is transformed by Lovelace's rape into a martyr for virtue. She spends the rest of the novel dying, and in the process of her death becomes a kind of secular saint whose example illuminates the lives of those around her and succeeds in bringing about the reformation of Lovelace's best friend and fellow voluptuary, Jack Belford, who records her death and eulogises her 'unblemished virtue, exemplary piety, sweetness of manners, discreet generosity, and true christian charity: and these all set off by the most graceful modesty and humility; yet on all proper occasions, manifesting a noble presence of mind, and true magnanimity: so that she may be said to have been not only an ornament to her sex, but to human nature'. Lovelace himself is driven close to madness when he realises what he has wrought. He flees to Italy, where he is tracked down by one of Clarissa's relations and slain in a duel.

Clarissa's darker turn is legitimised by the relative social parity that exists between the Lovelaces and the Harlowes. The families are not perfectly equal – the Lovelaces are nobles and the Harlowes are not – but they are close enough in wealth and lifestyle to remove from the novel the tawdry class drama that underpins *Pamela*. Richardson was now free to explore the topic of seduction with more nuance. Lovelace and Clarissa are, in terms of breeding, education and social sophistication, peers. The drama of her seduction is not therefore one of power but of free will – a fact that Richardson helpfully (if somewhat elliptically) alludes to in the preface to the novel. There he writes that the goal of his novel is twofold, 'to caution parents against the undue exertion of their natural authority over their children in the great article of marriage: and children against preferring a man of pleasure to a man of probity, upon that too commonly received notion, that a reformed rake makes the best husband'.

The Harlowes' refusal to allow their daughter to marry a man of her choosing has channelled her towards Lovelace, a man she would have safely avoided if left to her own devices.[28] Once in his hands, her capacity to act rationally for her own benefit is further compromised by a social belief that a woman's mission is to rescue and reform wayward libertines. One of the many threads of *Clarissa* is the heroine's internal debate as to if and how Lovelace can be reformed. In Clarissa's mind, the prospect that Lovelace 'might be reclaimed by a woman of virtue and prudence' becomes her 'secret pleasure', a moral adventure analogous to the sexual adventure of seduction that Lovelace is bent on. For his part, Lovelace recognises from the outset that fostering the illusion that Clarissa's benign presence is bringing about his reformation is the key to winning her trust, her love and, finally, her body. 'Reformation shall be my stalking-horse,' he gloats to Belford. Again, Clarissa's free will has been imperilled by the false belief that her mission as a woman is to edify dissolute men.[29]

The roots of this belief were tangled up with one of the core concerns of the English Enlightenment. In *An Essay Concerning Human Understanding* (1690), John Locke had asserted that at birth the mind was like an empty room. His mission was to discover how it came to be furnished. The answer, he believed, lay 'in one word, from EXPERIENCE'. He continued:

> All our knowledge is founded; and from that it ultimately derives itself. Our observation employed either, about external sensible objects, or about the internal operations of our minds perceived and reflected on by ourselves, is that which supplies our understandings with all the materials of thinking.[30]

The key word is 'sensible'. Man was endowed with 'sensibility' – the capacity to perceive the world which, through cultivation, education and moral effort, could be expanded into a larger project of empathy, intellectual refinement and social sophistication. At a physiological level, Locke and his disciples (including Richardson's friend and client Dr George Cheyne) believed that sensibility operated through the nervous system. Medical research seemed to have demonstrated that women had more sensitive nervous systems and so had an innately superior capacity for sensibility compared to men. In a complete reversal of the ancient Christian belief that identified women with carnality, chaos and nature, the Georgians now understood women as the agents of a process of moral and social amelioration. Men were cast as coarse and brutish, and those denied regular contact with women (sailors, scholars, back-country squires) were deemed doubly so.[31] Men were encouraged to socialise with women in the hope that women's natural delicacy would rub off on them.[32] This so-called 'Cult of Sensibility' encouraged just the kind of risky heterosocial behaviour that could trap women like Clarissa Harlowe in perilous situations. Moreover, women with a surfeit of sensibility – as was thought to be rife among the educated middle and upper classes – were vulnerable to manipulation. Locke had warned in his *Essay* that humans were readily fooled by rhetoric and counselled that eloquent words 'are for nothing else but to insinuate wrong ideas, move the passions, and thereby mislead the judgment'.[33]

In the next generation, David Hume embellished the quandary. In *A Treatise of Human Nature* (1739–40) he famously claimed that each individual's experience of life was 'but a bundle or collection of different perceptions, which succeed each other with an inconceivable rapidity, and are in a perpetual flux and movement'. Reality was chaos. Resorting to reason was no guarantee, for it was 'and ought only to be the slave of the passions, and can never pretend to any other office than to serve and obey them'. Passions were primary to reason, in Hume's view, but they too could be 'founded on false suppositions' and so lead to fallacious beliefs and foolish actions. Locke and Hume moved our understanding of what guides human action away from old, inflexible theological categories of good and evil, sin and virtue, and towards a highly subjective, highly unstable vision of how humans interact with their environment and with one another. The explosion of seduction narratives in the same period situated sexual conflict within that new perceptual framework – and none did so with more care and psychological realism than Samuel Richardson's *Clarissa*.[34]

Seduction fascinates because it dramatises the conflict between reason and passion. Clarissa keenly feels within her the tussle between these rival forces. She proudly claims the 'right to a heart' – the freedom to feel and to love – while equally stating her pride in her powers of reason and perception. Her best friend and endlessly entertaining correspondent Anne Howe observes from afar the exact same contest, writing suggestively of how the 'throbs and the glows' of passion contrive to weaken women's resolve in the face of hardened how familiar these men-wretches grow upon a smile, what an awe they are struck into when we frown; who would not make them stand off? Who would not enjoy a power, that is to be short-lived?'

Clarissa's deepening tragedy is the realisation that she has emphatically lost this contest to Lovelace. She comes to realise that her own delicacy – her heightened sensibility – has led her into disaster. She fluctuates between emotional states, arrives at and discards any number of 'logical' conclusions, and is confused by competing passions towards her tormentor. Her own unstable personality – a word Richardson was the first to use in its modern sense in the novel that bore her name – is her greatest enemy. 'What strange imperfect beings!' she writes to Anne. 'But *self* here, which is at the bottom of all we do, and of all we wish, is the grand misleader.'

Lovelace has no such problems. A cold logician, totally amoral, utterly without sensibility ('What *sensibilities* must thou have suppressed!' Clarissa exclaims at one point), he expertly stage-manages his shifting personae and her corresponding responses to them. 'Ovid was not a greater master of metamorphoses than thy friend,' he boasts to Jack Belford, his confederate. Lovelace does not in the end succeed in technically seducing Clarissa – hence his need to resort to rape. Richardson, however, did succeed in articulating the dilemma at the heart of all post-Enlightenment seduction narratives. An examination of constellations of power in society at large can only go so far in explaining interactions among individuals. More pertinent, and infinitely more ambiguous, is the struggle between reason and passion that rages within and between each of us. These are finally questions of free will and its limits, questions which go unresolved from generation to generation even if each has its own prescriptions. Richardson's remedy was invariably some mixture of reformation for men and sequestration for women, as well as the generous admonition that all readers concerned for the virtue of the young ought to purchase his book, which had been written 'to warn the inconsiderate and thoughtless of one of the sex against the base arts and designs of specious contrivers of the other'.

***

Debut authors write in obscurity, untroubled by public interest; successful ones have to perform their duties in the spotlight, burdened by expectation. After the astounding success of *Pamela*, *Clarissa* was written under fierce scrutiny. Richardson's exertions were made all the more trying by the book's protracted gestation and long birth. *Clarissa* was begun shortly after the final editions of *Pamela* were released into the world. It was largely finished by the end of 1746, but even before the final manuscript was completed suggestions and complaints were pouring in from his various correspondents, many of whom demanded to see the proofs of the work he was labouring on. Consequently, well before the publication of the first two volumes in December 1747, Richardson was already being harried by critics. The interludes between the release of the third and fourth volumes in April 1748 and the fifth, sixth and seventh in December of the same year provided yet more opportunities for a now enlarged critical community to probe his plot, his characters and his parable. Rarely has an author had to defend a work before and during publication with such energy.

Given its now canonical position in English literature, it is easy to forget that *Clarissa* never sold as well as *Pamela*. It did, however, spark debate of equal intensity to its forebear and won Richardson new respect from the literary community. Lady Mary Wortley Montagu, who had damned *Pamela* as cheap trash fit only for her scullery maids, recorded how she 'eagerly read' *Clarissa*, sobbing over it, and felt transported by his art back to her own courting days.[36] Henry Fielding, who had gleefully mocked *Pamela*, was another convert to Richardson's work, writing at some length to him of his own emotional reactions to the novel, praising

Richardson's artistry and moral force, before concluding warmly: 'I heartily wish you Success. That I sincerely think you in the highest manner deserve it.'[37] Edward Young, a literary taste-maker almost as esteemed as Johnson, declared that the book's power confirmed the arrival of the novelist as an arbiter of moral norms and that 'the Bench of Bishops might go to School to the Writer of a Romance'.[38] Richardson had accomplished in *Clarissa* what he had not with *Pamela*: he had become a writer's writer.

Few, then, doubted Richardson's achievement. What was endlessly debated was his characters and the moral message they presented. Many questioned the need for Clarissa to die and interceded on her behalf. When Colley Cibber, an early reader of the manuscript, learnt from Laetitia Pilkington that Richardson had decided Clarissa was to perish at the novel's end, he could not contain his outrage:

> My heart suffers as strongly for her as if word was brought to me that his house was on fire, and himself, his wife, and little ones, likely to perish in the flame. I cannot bear it! had Lovelace ten thousands souls and bodies, I could wish to see them all tortured, stretched on the rack: no punishment can be too bad for him. . . . When I told him she must die, he said 'G—d d—n him, if she should.'[39]

Others took the opposite tack and chose to blame Clarissa's behaviour for her demise. Richardson displayed rare genius when, having received in the same mailbag one letter declaring Clarissa a prude and another a coquette, he replied by sending each correspondent the other's argument.[40]

Inevitably, much of the criticism focused on the character of Lovelace. As early as the autumn of 1746, when the novel was still circulating among a coterie of close friends, Richardson was having to defend his depiction of Lovelace to Aaron Hill, who thought it unrealistic that a character so evidently wicked would be able to ensnare the saintly Clarissa Harlowe. In a robust defence of his creative decisions, Richardson claimed that he had made Lovelace as dislikeable as possible to ensure that he did not inadvertently appear attractive in the eyes of impressionable young ladies. 'I once read to a young Lady part of his Character,' he explained to Hill, 'and then to his End; and upon her pitying him . . . I made him still more and more odious.'[41] Richardson was wise to stress the cruelty of his creation. Lovelace is easily the most enticing of his characters, something that was both a triumph and a quandary. Richardson was alive to accusations that he was of the devil's party without knowing it. This was one of the lessons learnt from the moral clamour surrounding *Pamela*. He sought to make Lovelace irredeemable and consequently impossible to love.

He did not succeed. In October 1748, while he prepared for the publication of the final three volumes, he received a remarkable letter from a female fan, who signed off as Belfour, a play on his fictional Jack Belford. After explaining at length why she believed the author should spare Clarissa, his anonymous correspondent made a frank declaration of interest in his great villain:

> . . . if I was to die for it, I cannot help being fond of Lovelace. A sad dog! Why would you make him so wicked, and yet so agreeable? He says, sometime or other he designs being a good man, from which words I have great hopes; and, in excuse for my liking him, I must say, I have made him so, up to my own heart's wish; a fault-less husband have I made him, even without danger of a relapse. A foolish rake may die one; but a sensible rake must reform, at least in the hands of a sensible author it ought to be so, and will I hope.[42]

The letter continued in this vein, by turns chiding and winsome, before concluding with the promise of a curse on the author should he see fit to deny his characters a happy ending. 'Now,' she concluded, 'make Lovelace and Clarissa unhappy if you dare.'

This was the beginning of a brilliant friendship. Richardson would respond and respond again, and his correspondence with 'Belfour' would turn into a friendship that lasted until the end of his life. For close to two years he and his circle would refer to this unnamed correspondent as his 'Incognita'. Her real name was Lady Dorothy Bradshaigh, the leisured wife of baronet (and fellow Richardson enthusiast) Sir Roger Bradshaigh. Richardson was almost sixty; Bradshaigh was in her mid-thirties. He would not know her true identity until February 1850, a full eighteen months after their first exchange of letters, and then only through the indiscretion of his friend, the artist Joseph Highmore. They met for the first time in Birdcage Walk, St James's, a few weeks after her unveiling, but this was one of relatively few meetings given the length and depth of their relationship. Theirs would never be a friendship of shared experience. Like his characters, they consumed themselves in writing to one another and those first crucial exchanges focused on the person of Lovelace.[43]

Richardson maintained to Bradshaigh that his fictional villain had to be an incurable case in order to prevent him becoming an excuse for male abandonment in the real world. If Clarissa had reformed Lovelace after all his wickedness, Richardson reasoned, then what would the lesson be to the everyday rake of Georgian England? He would conclude, Richardson reasoned, entering deftly into the mind of the debauchees he impersonated so well, that 'I [might] pass the Flower and Prime of my Youth, informing and pursuing the most insidious Enterprizes . . . As many of the Daughters and Sisters of worthy Families, as I can seduce, may I seduce, Scores perhaps in different Climates – And on their Weakness build my profligate Notions of the whole Sex.'

Such a view was the logical outcome of giving Lovelace an opportunity to atone. Clarissa's death was not Richardson's punishment of her, but her punishment of him and her parents. 'Whence my double Moral,' he finished grandly, 'extending to tyranical [sic] Parents, as well as to Profligate Men; and laying down from *her* the Duty of Children, and that whether Parents do theirs or not.'[44]

Shortly afterwards, Richardson sent Bradshaigh an advance copy of the fifth volume, which contained the infamous scene where Lovelace rapes Clarissa in Hampstead. The reading of it shook Bradshaigh's perception of Lovelace ('You have drawn a villain above nature,' she wrote) but did not break it. 'Blot out but one night, and the villainous laudanum, and all may be well again.'[45] By now the book was only weeks away from publication, and her prayers fell on ears deafened by the clatter of printers at work. At the beginning of the New Year she wrote again, shortly after reading the final volumes, 'You will hardly believe what Pains I have taken to reconcile myself to the Death of Clarissa, and to your Catastrophe.' She then proceeded to give a dramatic account of her reading of the last moments of Clarissa's life:

> Had you seen me, I surely should have moved your Pity, When alone in Agonies would I lay down the Book, take it up again, walk about the Room, let fall a Flood of Tears, wipe my Eyes, read again, perhaps not three Lines, throw away Book crying out Excuse me good Mr. Richardson, I cannot go on.
>
> . . .
>
> [My husband] Seeing me so moved, he beg'd for God's Sake I would read no more, kindly threatened to take the Book from me, but upon my pleading my Promise, suffered me to go on. That promise is now fulfilled, and am thankful the heavy Task is over, tho' the Effects are not. . . . My Spirits are strangely seized, my Sleep is disturbed, waking in the Night I burst into a Passion of crying, so I did at Breakfast this Morning, and just now again. God be merciful to me, what can it mean?

It meant that she was proving her sensibility, her delicacy, her worthiness as a woman fit to inhabit Richardson's worlds – fictional, moral and material. The letter signalled her submission, both to Richardson's fictional designs and to the exigencies of his moral outlook. No more would she champion Lovelace. Instead, Bradshaigh would go out of her way to demonstrate to Richardson how his art had transformed her own life. One sign of this came near the end of 1749, when she related how she had set out on an adventure of moral redemption of her own. She had come to know of a Cornish girl in her neighbourhood who, having been 'artfully seduced, and ruined' by her brother-in-law, was now shunned by her family and the wider community; he had gone unpunished. Having learnt of the sorry case, and inspired by the morals contained within Richardson's fiction, Bradshaigh determined to do something about it. She set about finding her ward honourable employment among good Christians, and harboured hopes for her long-term reclamation despite the loss of her virtue. Richardson encouraged her in these efforts, and joined her in execrating 'the inhospitable wretch, who could ensnare and ruin so young a creature'.[46]

Bradshaigh and Richardson both used the same word to describe this young woman: 'Magdalen'. Taken from the biblical figure of Mary Magdalene, a Magdalen was literally a reformed prostitute, but more generally a fallen but meritorious woman, like Bradshaigh's 'poor unfortunate' – or, indeed, Richardson's Clarissa – who had at no point actually prostituted herself but was no longer a virgin. The conflation of the two meanings in a single word is revealing. In stating an equivalence between former sex workers and unchaste women, moralists like Richardson and Bradshaigh merged economies of virtue with economies of value.[47] By drawing a parallel between the condition of prostitutes and the condition of seduced women they were identifying a community of women that shared a common feature: exploitation by men. This was one (of many) necessary and important precursor to recognising women as a group who needed special protections. It was a prototypical example of the feminist tactic of consciousness-raising. Though, as with many moral messages of the pre-feminist era, it cut both ways. If prostitutes were like seduced women, then seduced women were like prostitutes. The campaigning language of rescue and reform doubled as a device to police and constrain the behaviour of unmarried young women.

The example of the Magdalen shows how Richardson's fiction altered the lives of his readers. This was as he intended. Less predictable and, as it turned out, less palatable to Richardson was the influence his readers would have on his fictional output. Bradshaigh had been urging him to write another novel from the very beginning of their correspondence. In November 1749, he gave the first hint of what his new project might look like. Noting somewhat coolly 'the warm solicitude you so repeatedly express for my resuming my pen with a view to publication', he alluded in passing to the notion that he should write about 'a good man – a man who needs not repentance', before seeming to dismiss the idea and move on to other matters. His impetuous correspondent seized on these crumbs in her next letter, reminding Richardson what a service he would be performing for the cause of male reformation and noting in addition that his pursuit of such a project would 'let me have to brag, that I was instrumental in persuading you to do it'.[48]

By March the following year, Richardson had committed to the new book, which would in time become his third and final novel, *The History of Sir Charles Grandison* (1753–4). As with *Clarissa*, his work would be hurried along by the exhortations of his correspondents in England, but also of those in France and Germany. Richardson needed their support, for the novel did not come easily to him.[49] He complicated his own work by setting a decent portion of the action overseas, in Italy, where his titular hero goes to pay court to Clementina della Poretta in Bologna. Richardson had, of course, never left the British Isles, and in the preceding decades had barely travelled beyond a five-mile radius. He compensated for his total ignorance of Italy through diligent research and consultation with those who had travelled there – but the fundamental issue remained.

More prosaically, he had the deceptively challenging job of getting his character to Italy and back in a manner which made narrative sense. This perennial writer's problem was compounded by his usual ill-health. He wrote miserably to Bradshaigh that 'this is the worst of all my tasks, and what I most dreaded. Vast is the fabric; and here I am under a kind of necessity to grab it all, as I may say; to cut off, to connect; to rescind again, and reconnect.'

He persevered. By the summer of 1753 he had written much of the book and began to look ahead to publication.

Even in his own time, *Grandison* was not considered Richardson's finest work. But whatever its literary shortcomings, it fascinates because it reveals what Richardson thought an ideal man should look like – how he should behave, how he should talk, even how he should dress. The composition of such a man caused him as much trouble as any other part of the book. He wrote in April 1750 of the 'Difficulty of drawing a good Man, that the Ladies will not despise, and the Gentleman laugh at'. (He was, by the latter measure at least, not wholly successful. Colley Cibber laughed out loud when he was told that Grandison was a virgin upon marriage.) After three years of labour, the final product was a man worthy of the new English civilisation. Civility, manners, politeness – these are the words endlessly associated with Sir Charles Grandison. In an emblematic episode he talks the rakish Sir Hargrave Pollexfen – from whose clutches he has rescued Harriet Byron, his future wife – out of a duel. Grandison rejects duelling, as did many enlightened Englishmen, on the grounds that it was harmful to society and unbecoming of a man at ease with himself. Harriet understands his rejection of the feudal code of honour as a sign of his embrace of 'goodness, piety, religion; and to every thing that is or ought to be sacred among men'.

Grandison has arrived at civility because he has allowed his coarse masculinity to be curbed by feminine delicacy. He is thoughtful, empathetic, in touch with his emotions. His admirers note his 'feeling heart' and his endless capacity to 'speak feelingly' on any number of issues. He is, in other words, the ideal male product of the feminine culture of sensibility. His adaptation to feminine mores does not, however, render him foppish, unmanly or – that fatal word – unsexed. Grandison is decisive, plain-speaking, a man of action. He has simply internalised the merits of sensibility to just the right degree. Richardson's most well-travelled male character is consequently and paradoxically his most domestic one. 'I live not to the world,' he declares at one point, 'I live to myself; to the monitor within me.'

What Richardson was trying to achieve with *Grandison* can be best understood by reference to what he was writing against. It is no coincidence that the composition of his third novel was almost exactly coextensive with his bitter campaign against Henry Fielding. The two men's literary fortunes were intimately connected – *Pamela* had effectively launched Fielding's career as a novelist by inspiring him to write *Shamela* and then *Joseph Andrews* – but their personalities were poles apart. Fielding was an Old Etonian, a master of Greek and Latin responsible for a suspiciously didactic translation of Ovid's *Ars Amatoria*, and a bawdy writer who had made his name as a Drury Lane playwright. Spendthrift, genial and subversive, Fielding was an habitué of the Covent Garden scene and embodied its easy values. In a curious echo of Richardson's first novel, he had even married his former servant, Mary Daniel, following the death of his first wife. He was everything Richardson was not.

This did not necessarily mean that the two men were obliged to feud. After all, Fielding's sister was close friends with Richardson, and Fielding's glowing letter in praise of *Clarissa* could have been the start of an amicable correspondence. Richardson, however, chose to go to war. A year after Fielding wrote in admiration of *Clarissa*, Richardson savaged Fielding's masterpiece *Tom Jones* in a long and invidious letter to Lady Bradshaigh:

Nothing but a shorter life than I wish him can hinder him from writing himself out of date. The Pamela, which he abused in his Shamela, taught him how to write to please, tho' his manners are so different. Before his Joseph Andrews . . . the poor man wrote without being read, except when his Pasquins, &c, roused party attention and legislature at the same time.

Elsewhere in his correspondence he described *Tom Jones* as a 'dissolute book' and a 'profligate performance', and expressed satisfaction when he learnt it had been (temporarily, it transpired) banned in France. His friends rushed to confirm his opinions. Aaron Hill's daughters referred to the book as a 'rambling Collection of Waking Dreams'. David Graham wrote cloyingly that 'they who can listen to the dissonant jingle of Tom Jones, wou'd for ever be deaf to the Music of *your Charmer* [Clarissa]'.

Richardson maintained a posture of carefully curated scorn towards Fielding over the next few years. He revelled in the dismal reception of *Amelia* (1751), joking sourly to Bradshaigh that had Fielding 'been born in a stable, or been a runner at a sponging-house, we should have thought him a genius' for composing such a book, 'but it is beyond my conception, that a man of family, and who had some learning . . . should descend so excessively low'.[50] In 'A Concluding Note By The EDITOR', appended to *Grandison*, Richardson stated that his book was a riposte to the 'many modern fictitious pieces in which authors have given success (and happiness, as it is called) to their heroes of vicious, if not of profligate, characters'. 'The God of nature,' he continued magniloquently, 'intended not human nature for a vile and contemptible thing', and so he had written the book to show 'that characters may be good, without being unnatural'.

This was widely viewed as an attack on Fielding, who was by now near death – his body broken by gout, cirrhosis and other ailments, the fruits of a lifetime of hard living – and was obliged to leave England for Portugal in 1754 in a bid to improve his health. Fielding certainly regarded it as such. In his final work, *Journal of a Voyage to Lisbon*, he referred to *Grandison* as a 'tedious tale of a dull fellow', going on to call out Richardson by name and mock his oft-proclaimed belief that novels existed to instruct and that entertainment was 'but a secondary consideration in romances'.[51] He died shortly afterwards, but death brought him no respite. Thomas Edwards, a member of Richardson's circle, wrote to him apropos of the *Journal* of his surprise that 'a man who had led such a life as he had . . . should trifle in that manner when immediate death was before his eyes'.[52]

Richardson himself had the last word on their rivalry two years after Fielding's passing. In a letter to Sarah Fielding, he declared her brother a 'fine writer' before stating that 'His was but the knowledge of the outside of a clock-work machine, while your's was that of all the finer springs and movements of the inside.' Ostensibly Richardson was referring to the difference between Henry's and Sarah's writing. In reality he was describing the difference between Henry's writing and his own. The literary difference matters because the opposition between Fielding's fiction and Richardson's is inextricable from Richardson's conception of their opposition in moral outlook. Fielding's characters go out into the world and find adventure; Richardson's go out into the world and find disaster. The deep message of all Richardson's writings is that everything would be good if women simply stayed at home. The internal nature of his writings – the endless inner monologues, the endless examination of selves, the endless, endless writing of letters in rooms – reflects his belief in the merits of domestic values, which are the values of delicate, domestic women. When women stray from this norm they meet with catastrophe. This is why Clarissa on her deathbed blames herself for what has happened. 'Who was most to blame?' she asks. 'The brute, or the lady? The lady, surely! For what *she* did was *out* of nature, *out* of character, at least: what it did was *in* its own nature.'

Women can avoid seduction by staying at home as women should. Not only that, but by being totally domesticated, women can impart some of their domesticity to men, making them, like Sir Charles Grandison, men of feeling who will no longer contrive on women's virtue. Adherence to the moral code of domesticity created an actual virtuous cycle, the cost of which – and it was a cost, in Richardson's mind, well worth incurring – was that women had to retreat from the public world of men into the private world of the home.[53]

In praising Sarah Fielding for writing of the inside of human experience, Richardson was praising her for living up to this ideal of womanhood. This was in contrast to another group of women whom he judged to have abandoned their sex's norms, both in writing and in life. In the same period that he was inveighing against Fielding he was also busy slandering the reputations of certain female writers whom he believed were a discredit to the virtues he espoused. Specifically he singled out Constantia Phillips, Lady Frances Vane and Laetitia Pilkington. In a 1750 letter to Sarah Chapone, he notoriously referred to the trio as 'a Set of Wretches', and compared them to a previous generation of female authors (such as Eliza Haywood and Aphra Behn) who had also incurred his displeasure. It was the role of virtuous women, he told Chapone, to write against 'the same injured, disgraced, profaned Sex'. A few weeks later he repeated the message. 'Ladies, as I have said, should antidote the Poison shed by the vile of their Sex.'[54]

The critical attacks on Pilkington and the others were premised on the same set of beliefs that inspired his attacks on Fielding. The adventurous spirit had to be stamped out. Literature must turn inwards, and so must women. It was the only way to save virtue from seduction and bring about the general reformation of men.[55]

***

Richardson's moral system was by now heavily fortified and his faith in it unassailable. Even in his own lifetime, it was obvious that his ideas were growing in popularity. The values he evangelised in his books and private writings were increasingly the values of the ascendent middle classes. His novels were landmarks in the culture of sensibility and vital reference points for the resolutely dimorphic conception of gender roles that flowed from it. His was the vision of the proper sexual identities for men and women that would predominate in Britain until the end of the Victorian period. Nonetheless, it cannot be repeated often enough that for all its influence it was never an outlook without critics. Sexual ideology, like any ideology, is always a work in the making, an aspiration towards which we strive in a world marred by refusal, resistance and chaos. Richardson's triumphal march through the drawing rooms of the English mind was resisted every step of the way by satirists, pamphleteers, and hacks eager to put his preening worldview in the Grub Street pillory.

One of the most substantive demolitions of Richardson's *oeuvre* came in the spring of 1754, exactly halfway through the publication of *Grandison*. Written anonymously, but addressed directly to the author, *Critical Remarks on Sir Charles Grandison, Clarissa, and Pamela* was a gloriously unrestrained assault on Richardson's work and influence. Rambling, imprecise and unabashedly *ad hominem* ('Your success has farther corrupted our taste'),[56] the *Critical Remarks* nevertheless score some direct hits upon the citadel of Richardson's *Weltanschauung*. Women, he argues, are not the asexual figures that Richardson wishes them to be but individuals with the same range of desires, ambitions and appetites as men – and the same capacity for profligacy. 'Every woman is at heart a rake,' he writes, quoting Alexander Pope, and if they suppress their inner rake then they will seek to inhabit him vicariously.[57] This makes nonsense of Richardson's claim that his books exist to instruct the youth in Christian morality. However he rationalised it to himself, Richardson's focus exclusively on seduction resulted in novels that functioned to titillate rather than to castigate. His purported moral pedagogy was in practice a kind of primitive sexual education.

Approaching the apogee of his argument, the author continues with brilliant sarcasm that the literary preoccupation with matters of the heart popularised by Richardson would be more a spur to sexual activity than a bridle. A casual reader of the sentimental literature Richardson wrote himself and inspired in others

> would be apt to imagine, that the propagation of the species was at a stand, and that, not to talk of marrying and giving in marriage, there was hardly any such thing as fornication going forward among us, and that therefore our publick-spirited penmen, to prevent the world from coming to an end, employ'd all their art and eloquence to keep people in remembrance, that they were composed of different sexes.[58]

Such work, he noted dryly, was not only antithetical to the propagation of virtue but served to compound the existing work of 'provident nature', who had already 'implanted too many allurements, and has affixed too great a variety of pleasures to the intercourse between the sexes'.

The pamphlet, like so many others, made only a passing impression in Richardson's world, arousing the righteous anger of his correspondents and occasioning a few harrumphs from the great man himself. Richardson had seen off far worse, and by this point, well into his seventh decade, he could afford a certain diffidence in the face of lowly attacks on his celebrated body of work.

By the mid-1750s Richardson had arrived at the apex of his career as a printer-writer. His private business was flourishing. He continued to invest in his site at Salisbury Court, and his printers were kept busy by lucrative government contracts as well as the steady work of printing his own writings. Success brought recognition within his profession. In 1753 he completed his decades-long ascent of the Stationers' Company, when he was appointed Master of that body. Like Hogarth's Good Apprentice, he had scaled the heights of his profession from base to summit. His parallel conquest of the London literary scene brought him into the innermost circle of the cultural

elite, and won him the friendship of Hogarth himself, who occasionally attended the salons held at Richardson's Fulham pile.

James Boswell records a memorable incident at one such gathering in 1753. Over tea, Hogarth spoke approvingly to the room
of George II's recent decision to execute a Jacobite, Archibald
Cameron, for his participation in the uprising of 1745.

> While he was talking, he perceived a person standing at a window
> in the room, shaking his head, and rolling himself about in a strange
> ridiculous manner. He concluded that he was an ideot, whom his
> relations had put under the care of Mr. Richardson, as a very good
> man. To his great surprise, however, this figure stalked forwards
> to where he and Mr. Richardson were sitting, and all at once took
> up the argument, and burst out into an invective against George
> the Second, as one, who, upon all occasions was unrelenting and
> barbarous . . . he displayed such a power of eloquence, that Hogarth
> looked at him with astonishment, and actually imagined that this
> ideot had been at the moment inspired.[59]

The 'ideot' was in fact Samuel Johnson, who was a firm friend and
prolific defender of Richardson's literary project. Destined to
become the majestic centre of English literary life, Richardson
could not have wished to have a more prestigious critic in his
corner. Their alliance blossomed. Johnson savaged Fielding;
Richardson bailed Johnson out of debtors' gaol. Friendships with
such luminaries by this time came easily to Richardson. Hailed as
the 'great genius of Salisbury Court',[60] he now handled correspondence with some of the great names of his age. His fame crossed
borders and his fans travelled from far and wide to see him,
including the German editor who travelled several hundred miles
to kiss the inkwell that had given the world *Clarissa*. Richardson
responded to his celebrity with the unembarrassed satisfaction
that had won and would secure him the bitter resentment of his

detractors. 'Twenty years ago, I was the most obscure man in Great Britain,' he crowed, 'and now I am admitted to the company of the first characters in the kingdom.'[61]

Wealth, fame, and well-publicised moral positions brought Richardson in his final years into the budding world of Georgian philanthropy. Organised private charity was a relatively new phenomenon, but one that London's fashionable classes took up with enthusiasm. The rapid growth in number and scale of charitable institutions in these years was fuelled by the same trends that drove the obsession with Richardson's novels. The culture of sensibility had fostered an attitude of empathetic concern towards the poor and needy; the culture of moral reformation motivated moneyed (and concerned) elites to intervene in the lives of the working classes. The connection between moral panic and charitable sympathy was captured in the twin careers of William Wilberforce, whose anti-slavery campaign was premised on an identification with the suffering of others (the abolitionist slogan, 'Am I Not a Man and a Brother?', could never have been arrived at without the advance work performed by the cult of sensibility), but who was also the founder of the Society for the Suppression of Vice, a resurrection of the extinct Societies for the Reformation of Manners that Richardson had grown up with in Tower Hamlets.

Some of the new charities focused on the first- or second-order consequences of sexual immorality, and unsurprisingly they found a willing patron in Samuel Richardson. His first foray into philanthropy was his association with Thomas Coram's Foundling Hospital, to which he donated for several years and of which he became a governor in 1754. The Foundling Hospital was an orphanage that served to house and protect the unwanted offspring of fugitive sexual encounters. The children there were the bastard fruits of seduction, and some more cynical Londoners believed that the existence of such an institution would only encourage more fornication.[62]

The Foundling Hospital was an enormous success and became a

model for all future philanthropic empires. It also indirectly inspired the birth of another charity that came to represent in bricks and mortar what Richardson's novels had taught in paper and ink. In March 1751, Samuel Johnson's *The Rambler* contained an article written by a pensive 'Amicus'. On a recent walk the author had passed the Foundling Hospital, 'which I surveyed with pleasure, till, by a natural train of sentiment, I began to reflect on the fate of the mothers'. Why, Amicus wondered, did society protect the vulnerable infants spawned by seduction while it did not move to protect women from the predations of exploitative men? Prostitution was visible all over the city and Amicus believed, like a growing number of educated Georgians, that each woman he saw working the streets in rags and misery was a victim of seduction 'who, being forsaken by her betrayer, is reduced to the necessity of turning prostitute for bread'.[63] Prostitution was the consequence of circumstance, not of irretrievable individual corruption. Institutions existed to punish prostitutes, why did companion institutions not exist to reform them? The question was taken up the next month in *The Gentleman's Magazine*, when 'Sunderlandensis' wrote a response piece which laid out how such an institution might be run, and upon what principles. He referred to the example of convents on the continent as an imperfect image ('because they withdrew good people from general life') of what the refuge might look like and stated that while the focus should be on actual sex workers, 'the project could be extended to the seduced who had not yet become prostitutes'.[64]

These discussions in the press dovetailed with what Richardson had been saying for some years in both his novels and his private correspondence.[65] *Grandison* contained repeated disquisitions on the virtues of just such a proposed institution and made the same parallel to existing Catholic institutions.[66] As we have observed in his correspondence with Bradshaigh, Richardson had also internalised the equivalence between seduced women and established prostitutes.

In 1758 discussion gave way to action. That year the Magdalen

House was established in Whitechapel, east London, and accepted its first eight women, or penitents, as they were known. Richardson was soon involved as a donor and later as a governor. In 1759 he offered up his printer's in Salisbury Court to produce *The Histories of Some of the Penitents in the Magdalen House*, a book of narrative lives of certain penitents published with the end of attracting favourable publicity to the new institution. Richardson was doubtful that the book would sell but printed it anyway. 'It *must* appear,' he declared, 'for Virtues sake.'

The Magdalen Hospital in St George's Fields, Southwark, circa 1798.

The Magdalen House, like many London charities, was open to the public at certain times each week. Just as fashionable citizens went to the Foundling Hospital to see the orphans baptised, and to Bedlam to gawp at the insane, they went to observe the fallen women on their rocky road to reformation. On Sundays, the Magdalen's chapel was open for paying visitors for both the morning and the evening services. These became some of the most sought-after attractions in London, and tickets for them circulated at wildly inflated prices on the secondary market. The evening services, which for the first eighteen years of the institution's life showcased the florid preaching style of the notorious Reverend William Dodd, were a particular draw.[67] Richardson never went, but Bradshaigh did and wrote to him of her impressions: 'I was charm'd and mov'd with their behaviour, with their preachers, excellent, proper [illegible] drops of pleasing tears, glad I was, that you and your delicate nerves were at home. In short, I was in Love with the whole management, and regularity of the place, and I must observe, the psalm-singing was the sweetest of melody.'[68]

Bradshaigh took from her visit to the Magdalen the same lessons that she had taken from Richardson's novels. For her, the chapel of the Magdalen House was a place where Richardson's themes of seduction, abandonment, reclamation and repentance were acted out in real time. The place was a monument to and a buttress for the feminine values of delicacy and sensibility.[69] Her tears were appropriately shed.

Richardson's novels were torn between the rival impulses of moral instruction and prurient entertainment. So too were the services at the Magdalen. When the decidedly more rakish Horace Walpole visited in January 1760 (in a party of four coaches which contained, *inter alia*, Prince Edward, George II's brother), he provided a vivid account of the scene within the chapel:

At the west end were enclosed the sisterhood, above an hundred and thirty, all in grayish brown stuffs, broad handkerchiefs, and flat straw hats, with a blue riband, pulled quite over their faces. As soon as we entered the chapel, the organ played, and the Magdalens sung a hymn in parts; you cannot imagine how well. The chapel was dressed with orange and myrtle, and there wanted nothing but a little incense to drive away the devil – or to invite him. Prayers then began, psalms, and a sermon: the latter by a young clergyman, one Dodd, who contributed to the Popish idea one had imbibed, by haranguing entirely in the French style, and very eloquently and touchingly. He apostrophized the lost sheep, who sobbed and cried from their souls . . .'[70]

Afterwards the party went on a tour of the refectory where the Magdalens ate, hatless. 'A few were handsome,' Walpole noted, 'I was struck and pleased with the modesty of two of them, who swooned away with the confusion of being stared at.' His account reveals what was driving the great demand for tickets to such occasions. The Magdalen became a safari of seduction, where the rich and powerful could go and gaze upon the sullied but virtuous poor, striving so publicly for society's forgiveness. Georgian churches were one of the few places where unmarried women were regularly displayed. Places of worship became spaces of desire.[71] The Magdalen chapel, where the drama of seduction was performed for a paying audience of notables, was perhaps the most erotically charged religious space in the country.

The titillation of these services drove the charity's popularity and by the 1760s it was obliged to move to new lodgings. When it was finally completed, the new Magdalen Hospital, situated in Southwark, just south of the newly constructed Blackfriars Bridge, contained an expanded chapel that could seat five hundred visitors. Here, amid the modish crowds, in a room that smelled of warm bodies and cool stone, and which was brilliantly illuminated by the light that flowed in from the high windows, the Sunday visitor, with the sound of the preacher's exhortations ringing in their ears, could ponder their own moral reckoning with the example of the penitents before them.[72] In the new design the penitents were placed in the gallery, behind a latticed screen, only the silhouettes of their straw hats and pigeon-grey bodices visible through the woodwork. Invisible and present; secluded and displayed; confined from sexual life but considered as objects of sexual warning. For most of the audience, sitting in the naves and aisles, they were a spectral presence, hovering above the action in the church, heard only when they sang. But some lucky visitors were seated across from them in the gallery and could observe them up close. Glimpsed through the grille, and separated by only a few inches of wood, penitent and tourist beheld each other at an intimate remove, like Clarissa and Lovelace at that crumbling wall, and animated by the same forbidden sexual thrill.[73]

Richardson did not live to observe the scene. On 1 July 1761, painter Joseph Highmore visited him at home in Fulham for tea. Highmore had painted a number of works inspired by Richardson's books, including a celebrated series taken from *Pamela* and an iconic depiction of the moment Clarissa elopes with Lovelace. He had also been commissioned to do several portraits of Richardson, including one owned by Lady Bradshaigh that she hung in her closet, out of her husband's sight. He was sitting by Richardson's side when, while taking delivery of his third cup of tea, the author had a massive stroke 'and immediately faltered in his speech, and from that time spoke no more articulately'.[74] Richardson's condition rapidly declined and very soon he could no longer recognise his own family members. He died a few days later and was buried in St Bride's on Fleet Street, only metres from his printing shop in Salisbury Court.

Richardson had always insisted on the indivisibility of his moral and literary projects. This is a union that has lost credibility in each successive generation since his death. He is the most consistently (and acceptably) loathed author in the canon, largely on account of his overweening commitment to using literature as a vehicle for moral instruction. Most of his critics accept a grudging acceptance of his literary contribution as the admission price to a general rubbishing of his work. If we consider that to treat his literary achievements and moral outlook separately might allow a clearer-eyed evaluation of both, then we must nonetheless recognise the major part he played in the development of modern literature. In England his influence was comprehensive, and remained so well into the nineteenth century. His celebration in France by Rousseau and Diderot made him one of the most-read foreign novelists of the pre-revolutionary period. It was in French translation that he was read by many Russians, including Alexander Pushkin. When Tatyana in *Eugene Onegin* goes to bed with a novel beneath her pillow and dreams the dream that is to become the whole of modern Russian literature, it is Richardson's books she lays her head upon. Richardson was translated into Dutch, German, Danish and Italian in his lifetime. His novels circulated widely in the New World, and heavily influenced the first works of American literature. The size of his audience and the pleasure with which he was read were instrumental in popularising the novel as a format and introducing readers to the literary devices of modern fiction.

As for his moral project, Richardson stands at the head of one of the two great traditions in the history of seduction. One that worries; one that dwells on interiority; one that seeks redress for women and reformation for men. The subsequent chapters will show how, far from being particular to his time, Richardson's concerns about seduction, and the language and perceptual framework he drew upon to articulate those concerns, have served subsequent generations well. Anyone who has ever understood seduction as a problem of power, or as a quandary concerning the limits of free will, or as a social scenario that illuminates the discrepancy in condition between men and women, or as a battleground for competing visions of how enlightened citizens should behave towards one another – anyone who has ever considered such questions has lingered a while in Richardson's world. Seduction was a problem born of modernity, and Richardson was the first modern to recognise it as such.

Richardson's view of seduction was the perfect foil to the other great tradition in its history. One which rejected the conception of seduction as a problem to be pathologised, but rejoiced in the possibilities for personal and philosophical emancipation that it harboured. By his death in 1761, Richardson missed by two years the arrival in London of the itinerant Venetian musician, conman and *saloniste* who exemplified this rival vision of what seduction could be.

2

THE TRANSIT OF VENUS

The Grand Tour was a rite of passage for any well-born English rake. At the Tour's height in the mid-eighteenth century, hundreds of boorish young men left Dover each year for the continent. Their travelling schedules conformed to a norm: a sampling of French society, a dutiful survey of some of the westerly German states, then an ascent of the Alps into Switzerland, before a journey to Italy – the climax of any Englishman's foreign sojourn. Admired for its rich legacy of art, music and architecture, Italy, and Rome in particular, was the place where English parents and English tutors sent their English sons to gain some learning, some philosophy, and some sheen of culture.

For the young men on tour, Italy held other charms. She existed in the English imagination as a place of pleasure and passion, where Northern morals were thawed by Mediterranean seas. Travelling from Switzerland to Italy, James Boswell recorded a metamorphosis in his manners and constitution. 'The climate of Italy affects me much,' he wrote. 'It inflamed my hot desires, and now it keeps my blood so warm that I have all day long such spirits as a man has after having taken a cheerful glass.' The very air of Italy was intoxicating. No wonder then that English libertines misbehaved with more energy on Italian piazzas than they had even on the Piazza of Covent Garden. The effect of their homeland on their English guests did not go unnoticed by the locals. '*Inglese italianizzato,*' the proverb went, '*è un diavolo incarnato.*'[1]

The city most intimately associated with the scourge of Englishmen behaving badly was Venice. The Most Serene Republic was a place of pilgrimage for Europe's voluptuaries. Famous for her courtesans, her actresses, her bevies of scandalous nuns, and her expedient attitude towards matters of marital fidelity, Venice was the epicentre of a new sexual culture, her very name a gift to the punning poets of the *settocento*:

> *But chief her shrine where naked Venus keeps,*
> *And Cupids ride the Lyon of the Deeps;*
> *Where, eas'd of Fleets, the Adriatic main*
> *Wafts the smooth Eunuch and enamour'd swain.*[2]

When the lusty English swain disembarked at Venice, one of his first ports of call was the British embassy. From 1754 to 1766 the Resident in Venice was John Murray, one of the most notorious libertines in English diplomatic history. The son of a successful Manx merchant, Murray had won his sinecure through high-placed connections in Whitehall.[3] Set up in Venice, he acted as a paragon of dissolution to those English subjects that passed through his patch. The presence of his wife did not prevent Murray from maintaining a number of high-profile relationships with courtesans, nor later from fathering a second Italian family, four children strong, to whom he eventually left all his worldly possessions.

Lady Mary Wortley Montagu developed a strong aversion to Murray, memorialising him as a 'scandalous fellow, in every sense of that word . . . not to be trusted to change a sequin, despised by this government for his smuggling, which was his original profession, and always surrounded with pimps and brokers, who are his privy councillors.'[4] Others were less censorious, with many travellers grateful for his help in navigating that enigmatic city. He was well-liked among a portion of the Venetian population as well. One local friend recalled him as 'a handsome man, full of wit, learned, and a prodigious lover of the fair sex'. The same Venetian was well placed to affirm that last statement, for sometime in the spring of 1755, Murray asked him to accompany him on an errand that lay well outside his consular duties.

For many months Murray had been the principal lover of Ancilla, a celebrated courtesan. Ancilla had been sickly for many weeks. Friends suspected she had some kind of venereal disease, though this could not be true as Murray remained unafflicted. Lately, it had emerged that her body was wracked by a cancer that was corroding her throat, her neck and her beautiful face. She was now lying on her deathbed, and she summoned Murray to love her one last time. In healthier times both she and he had been exhibitionists who had welcomed voyeurs to their assignations. This time was no different. And so Murray's Venetian friend was brought along and installed in a secret viewing chamber, whence he could glimpse Murray's ministrations and Ancilla's final ecstasies. She died scarcely fifteen minutes afterwards. 'It was,' their secret sharer later wrote, 'one of the most striking spectacles I have seen in all my life.'[5]

If Venice is the capital city of seduction, it is in large part due to the man on the other side of that spyhole. There are several ironies to the phenomenon that was Giacomo Casanova, not the least glaring of which is that a man of whom we know so much on account of his twelve volumes of autobiography has been reduced to a single word, a magical invocation of seductive triumph, and has been in the process effaced, diminished, and denied a place in the material world that he so delighted in. The conundrum expands when we realise that Casanova, as indomitable a social climber as ever existed, would have rejoiced in this fate, a posthumous victory after life failed to properly reward his ambition.

A child of the stage, who matured in the stalls and reigned briefly from the boxes, Casanova understood better than anyone alive that the purpose of performance was to turn perishable reality into immortal myth. Actors, like all artists, seek to cheat death. Casanova was not an artist, but, driven by that same impulse to survive beyond his allocated years, he used the devices of art to sculpt his own existence. Casanova's was a life lived as a work of art.

Performance came easily to Casanova; introspection did not. His light touch on matters of ethics, morality and philosophy all vouch for his candidacy as representative of the second great strain in the history of seduction. If the classic seduction narrative discussed in the previous chapter was grounded internally – in the house, in the letter, in and between the heart and the mind – Casanova embodied the counter-narrative that roamed and gossiped and performed, that lived joyfully, carelessly out in the world. These two competing stories of seduction may have tipped in opposite directions – they still do – but they were also connected by a set of shared assumptions. Specifically, both took different sides of the great Enlightenment debate that pitted reason against passion. These were discussions in which Casanova eagerly participated, for, despite his reputation as a fop and a charlatan, he was, as this chapter will demonstrate, shuffled into the deck of the Enlightenment, even if only as a joker or a knave.

***

Giacomo Casanova was born in Venice in April 1725. His parish, where he was baptised and later tonsured, was San Samuele, remembered in a bawdy local ditty as a '*grande bordel*' where 'the men are all cuckolds and the women whores'.[6] The stereotype held true in the incommodious Casanova family home on Calle Delle Commedia, halfway between the Rialto and St Mark's Square.

Gaetano Casanova, who gave Giacomo his surname though most likely not his genes, was an actor-singer-dancer who some years before had courted Zannetta Farussi, a cobbler's daughter from Burano. The two married in Venice against her family's wishes, and Farussi became an actress. Her career soon outshone that of her husband. In Venice she was originally attached (as was he) to the Teatro San Samuele, owned by the Grimani family, members of Venice's closed patrician caste. As the Venetian theatres were closed for half the year, Farussi, like many actors, lived a nomadic lifestyle, travelling around Italy, Germany, England, France and Poland looking for work. Carlo Goldoni, the leading Venetian playwright of the eighteenth century, recalled her fondly as 'a very pretty and a very able widow of the name of Zanetta Casanova, who played the part of young lovers in comedy'.[7]

This description dates from after Gaetano Casanova died in 1733, but all the evidence suggests that Farussi had begun to wander from their marital bed many years before. Giacomo, their first child, believed that he was the actual son of Michele Grimani – and on his deathbed Gaetano formally entrusted him to the Grimani family's care. Francesco Casanova, their second son, was born in London and was reputedly the son of the Prince of Wales, the future George II. The paternity of Casanova's other three siblings (Giovanni, Maria and Gaetano) is unknown and largely irrelevant, given their nominal father's early death.

Farussi herself features only briefly in Casanova's early years as a sportive beauty, well aware of her charms, who embarrassed her son by flirting with his clergyman tutor, and who later worked every angle to get her children ahead in life. From 1737 these machinations were conducted from afar; that was the year Farussi moved to Dresden, where she took up a position as an actress in the court of the Elector of Saxony. She remained there for much of the rest of her life, while Giacomo was left in Venice in the care of his beloved grandmother.

Farussi did not initially have high hopes for her son. As a young boy, Casanova was sickly, prone to mysterious nosebleeds and periods of inanition where, in his own account, he 'was unable to apply myself to anything, and looked like an idiot'. Doctors thought the air of Venice was thickening his blood and making him simple. Farussi and Alvisi Grimani (the member of the Grimani clan deputised to watch over their ward) agreed on a course of action to have him sent to Padua to study.

On his ninth birthday, in April 1734, Casanova boarded a *burchiello* (a capacious barge, something like an outsize punt with two cabins) at midnight, crossed the lagoon in darkness and woke up as day broke on the Brenta Canal, the stretch of water and post road that connected Venice to Padua. Riding on one of the most dramatic waterways in Italy, Casanova would have glimpsed some of the many *palazzi* that lined the banks of the canal, with their English gardens, their twee little bridges, their concealed platforms where musicians could invisibly serenade *al fresco* dining parties. He would have passed the enormous building site that was in his lifetime to reorganise itself as the colossal Villa Pisani; he may have passed, unknowably, the Villa Foscarini where Lord Byron and Teresa Guiccioli would spend a blissful autumn eighty years hence; he was passing numerous sites that would later figure in his wild twenties, places where he duelled, danced and loved. For now, as a doltish child, he lay in bed watching the tops of the trees troop one by one past his window and asked his mother why the trees were walking past them. 'It is the boat that is moving, not the trees,' the despairing mother replied. 'Get dressed.'

Padua was part of imperial Venice's inland empire – what the seaborne Venetians knew with marine disdain as the *Domini di Terraferma* – and the crèche for Venice's privileged youth, who were sent to the university there to gain an education and to keep them from causing trouble in the capital. In the summer, all Venetians of any means decamped to Padua and its environs to escape the stench of the baking canals, and the spies and the sumptuary laws of the city's much-feared governing body, the Council of Ten. Padua was close to Venice in every respect. Still, the transition was a difficult one for the young Casanova. Adapting to living in a strange home was hard enough; negotiating his way through life in a rowdy student city forced certain realities upon him at a tender age.

Under the care of Doctor Gozzi, Casanova was soon recognised as a brilliant student, devouring Latin and Greek, demonstrating a nascent mastery of rhetoric and literature and a great love of medicine and chemistry – though ultimately he was obliged by his mother and guardians to study law – and learning to dance and to play the violin. Padua worked on his health and body, too. Away from the malarial lagoon he regained his appetite, slept well every night, and was soon growing rapidly. If the myth of Casanova centres on an effete courtier, the reality was of a strong, graceful man, over six feet tall, with thick Mediterranean features. He needed this new strength and new learning to survive the bustle of Padua. 'I made as many undesirable acquaintances as possible among the notorious students,' he recalled:

> The most notorious cannot but be those who are the greatest libertines, frequenters of places of ill repute, drunkards, debauchees, seducers of decent girls, given to violence, false, and incapable of entertaining the slightest virtuous feeling. It was in the company of fellows of this kind that I began to know the world by studying it in the harsh book of experience.[8]

It was one of the characteristics of Casanova's world that a familiarity with the bawdy demi-monde could aid the ambitious society man on the make. He records with some pleasure in his memoirs his first great success in polite society. It came at a supper in Venice held shortly before his mother left for Dresden and attended by his mother and other friends of the family. Among the party was a learned Englishman who decided to test the precocious student with a Latin riddle: 'Discite grammatici cur mascula nominea cunnus / Et cur femineum mentula nomen habet.'

To which Casanova replied, in perfect pentameter: 'Disce quod a domino nomina servus habet.'[9]

The room rocked with surprised laughter. Casanova was awarded a gold watch by the Englishman and the first taste of approval from his mother. One cannot help but think that this was the kind of humour a young boy could only have learnt among dissolute students. Whatever its provenance, its success made a great impression on him. 'It was my first literary exploit,' he recalled, 'and I can say at this moment that the seeds of my desire for the fame which comes from literature were sown in my soul, for the applause of the company set me on the pinnacle of happiness.'

Aged sixteen, Casanova was awarded a degree in law from Padua University and returned to Venice to pursue what everyone now agreed was a promising career in the clergy. Under the tutelage of Father Tosello in San Samuele he took minor orders, assumed the title of *Abate* (as in abbot or *abbé*), and became a regular at mass. Through Tosello he met and impressed with his quick wit a local patrician, Senator Alvise Malipiero. Malipiero took the young man under his wing – no small matter in a society as closed and jealous of its social borders as the Venetian oligarchy – and inducted him into the ways of high society, advising him how to converse, how to hold himself, what boundaries could be tested and which had to be respected. He encouraged the young man to philosophise, to advance himself professionally and socially, to cultivate his mind and his palate. A bachelor well past his active years but prodigious in his day, Malipiero also taught the young man about women, both by instruction and by inadvertent example. This elderly senator, whatever wisdom he dispensed willingly, gave Casanova a more profound lesson than he could ever have intended. For

Malipiero was in love with Teresa Imer, the seventeen-year-old daughter of an actor.[10] The home of Teresa's parents abutted the Malipiero pile; each day the voluptuous young woman would appear at her window to practise her singing, and each day Malipiero listened to her song and fell more deeply in love.

Learning of the senator's infatuation with her daughter, Teresa's mother began to take her to the senator's palace in the afternoons for closely chaperoned visits. There the senator would beg for her favours, only for the daughter to plead chastity while her mother harangued the pathetic old man with moral advice and dire warnings as to the security of his immortal soul. Once Malipiero was reduced to a state of impotent rage they would leave, and as the shadows grew long in the empty parlour he would philosophise with his young friend for hours at a time.

Nested within the otherwise joyful account of Casanova's coming of age, the melancholy remembrance of Malipiero's fading powers points to something larger in Casanova's literary project. Casanova's own memoirs were written in a quiet library in a silent castle in provincial Bohemia in his eighth decade of life, just as he discovered Malipiero's agony for himself. The Malipiero vignette is both a portent – a hazard sign tucked away in his heady youth – and the entirety of his condition. The ageing senator had sought to escape death through communion with young women, and now the ageing Casanova tried to escape death through immersion in his memories of the grand old man's humiliations – which were, he realises, fifty years too late, his own. A trail of ink and time and pain connects Casanova at his desk in sleepy Dux to the young man confounded by the spectacle of an old man immiserated by his own absurd passions.[11] The example of Malipiero is situated *mise en abyme* in the memoirs, inserted not as simply one more incident in a varied life, but as a belated recognition that fate had once tipped its hand, that the contours of his own life had been revealed to him in passing in the knowledge that revelation is wasted on the young.

The lesson was missed; the headlong charge continued. A few months later Casanova lost his own innocence in bed with Nanetta and Marta, two girls he had met through Father Tosello's niece.

The beginning of Casanova's amorous career at seventeen was marked by a series of rococo sexual escapades (a fumble with the blue-eyed courtesan Giulietta, a thwarted country romance with the maidenly Lucia, an encounter with a newlywed in a rattling carriage in a rumbling storm) and a betrayal. One day after lunch at Malipiero's, the old man went to have his siesta, leaving Casanova and Teresa Imer alone together. In his inimitably elliptic style, Casanova recalls 'sitting side by side at a small table with our backs to the door of a room in which we supposed our patron was sleeping, at a certain turn in the conversation it occurred to us in our innocent gaiety to compare the differences between our shapes. We were at the most interesting point of the examination when a violent blow from a cane descended on my neck.'

Hounded out of the house without his cloak or hat by the wrathful Malipiero, Casanova had both items returned to him later that day with a note informing him he was no longer welcome at the senator's soirées. Never one to hold a grudge, Casanova took this banishment in his stride and continued on his way. He had seized what Malipiero had to offer him at that stage in his life; he knew there would be other patrons in other *palazzi*. He would remain grateful for his worldly instruction for the rest of his life, warmly recalling the senator as 'M. de Malipiero, my first master in the art of good breeding'.

The breach with Malipiero came just as Zanetta Farussi had accomplished what she believed to be a considerable coup on her eldest son's behalf. In Warsaw, the sharp-elbowed Farussi, having charmed her way into circles of influence, had petitioned the Queen of Poland to have her daughter the Queen of Naples appoint Bernardo da Bernardis to the bishopric of Martorano in his native Calabria. She had done so by prior agreement with de Bernardis of a *quid pro quo*: that her son would be taken into his service once his appointment was confirmed.

This duly happened in May 1743, and in high spirits, the young man bought himself a new wardrobe and set out for Martorano. But as his rented carriage penetrated the Calabrian interior, his suspicions began to mount. The countryside was dreary and visibly poor. At Martorano the bishop's palace was in a state of disrepair and the food appalling. When Casanova asked if 'he had good books, a literary circle, or any good society in which to spend a pleasant hour or two', the old man merely smiled and said he had not so much as a newspaper to read.

This was not a tolerable state of affairs. 'Without a good library, a circle, a spirit of rivalry, a literary intercourse, was this a country in which I must settle down at the age of eighteen?' The final straw came when Casanova laid eyes on the congregation in church the next day. 'I saw nothing but brutes,' he wrote, 'who seemed to me positively scandalised by my entire appearance. What ugly women!' There was no future for him here. Asking the forgiveness of de Bernardis and requesting his release from his service, he received both, as well as a letter of introduction. Within three days of arriving in Martorano he was in a carriage to Naples, with his eyes set once more upon Rome.

'I was in Rome, with a good wardrobe, a fair amount of money, some jewellery, and a fair amount of experience, with good letters of recommendation, completely free, and at an age when a man can count on the help of fortune if he has a spark of courage.' Rome was a city built for the young Casanova, a place where a man 'must be a chameleon sensitive to all the colours which the light casts on his surroundings. He must be flexible, insinuating, a great dissimulator, impenetrable, obliging, often base, ostensibly sincere, always pretending to know less than he does.'

His youthful optimism was in this case vindicated by his possession of a letter of introduction to Cardinal Acquaviva, a man of much influence in the capital. At his audience with the Cardinal he was instructed to learn French, given his Eminence's hand to kiss, and told to report to the Palazzo di Spagna, where he held court, the next day. There he was given a job, a salary and an apartment. The young man marvelled at his good fortune.

Thereafter Casanova fell into an easy routine consisting of French lessons and clerical work for the Cardinal. Members of the Cardinal's circle occasionally took him into society, where he learned the ways of the famed Roman salons, or *conversazioni*. In his own time he was energetically pursuing a romance with Anna Maria d'Antoni Vallati (given the pseudonym Donna Lucrezia in his memoirs), with whom he had shared a carriage from Naples. Anna Maria's husband and sister had been travelling with her, but this had been no barrier to Casanova's initial advances. In Rome he courted her assiduously, with her husband's apparent indifference, but their budding romance was scotched time and again by sisters, mothers-in-law, priests and rival suitors. Finally, Casanova secured an outing to Frascati, two hours from Rome. There they lost themselves in the sylvan gardens of the Villa Aldobrandini, until they found themselves in a secluded spot, bound in shade, and with a prospect of the Roman plains, where they lay down together on a bed of grass. 'Here in the garden at Dux,' the older man interposes, 'I have seen an arbor of the same sort.' Then the fantasia continues:

> Standing face to face, intensely serious, looking only into each other's eyes, we unlaced, we unbuttoned, our hearts throbbed, our hands hurried to calm their impatience. Neither of us having been slower than the other, our arms opened to clasp the object of which they were to take possession. . . . At the end of two hours, enchanted with each other and looking most lovingly into each other's eyes, we spoke in unison, saying these very words: 'Love, I thank thee!'

Their affair produced a daughter, Leonilda, the first of Casanova's eight recorded love children.

Such frolics were not, however, compatible with the life of a serious young *Abate*, and at some point even the genial Cardinal Acquaviva decided that his protégé was not cut out for a life in the Church. Summoned to his rooms, Casanova was informed, with some regret, that he would have to leave his service and was offered a pay-off and letters of recommendation for a city of his choice. For reasons he never fully examined (or confessed to), Casanova chose Constantinople.

***

Constantinople turned out to be a dead end. Casanova's visit to the Sublime Porte was not dull – neither for him nor for the reader of his memoirs – but it was informative in shaping his cultural orientation. Given the chance to marry into the Ottoman elite by wedding Zelmi, the daughter of a rich old philosopher named Yusuf Ali, Casanova, after some weeks of reflection, declined. His decision reveals the breadth of his horizons at that stage of his life. Later, as a legendarily well-travelled man, Casanova would profess a thoroughgoing cosmopolitanism. Whether this was merely an affectation of middle age or something into which he genuinely grew with time, it was not evident when he was faced with the prospect of discarding his European inheritance and turning Turk for Yusuf Ali and Zelmi. He instead exhibited chauvinist attitudes typical of his day, mocking the idea that he would abandon 'fair hope of achieving fame among polished nations' in order to change his religion, sever his ties with his friends and family, and take up the study of 'a barbarous tongue'.

After several months in Constantinople, Casanova returned to Venice via Corfu, where he presented himself for military service and was assigned the role of adjutant to Signor D.R., the governor of the Galleasses. His days were spent in attending to his superior, his evenings in attendance on the card tables. The latter was immensely profitable, while the former brought him into the orbit of one Signora F., the eighteen-year-old wife of a galley commander, who immediately dazzled him with her beauty. The Signora, however, was not an easy conquest. Indeed, she ignored him altogether apart from the occasional contemptuous remark directed his way while he waited on the senior officers and their wives. Ever jealous of his *amour-propre*, Casanova was stung by her evident distaste for him. Unable to court her, he adopted 'the course of avoiding her, abandoning her to the stale gallantries of Sansonio, who had rotten teeth, a blond wig, a dirty complexion, and a stinking breath. But I remained chagrined and furious.'[12] He busied himself with his gambling and made good money playing faro at the local coffee-houses.

A curious and singularly Casanovian event proved to be the pivot upon which his romantic fortunes turned. On becoming an adjutant, Casanova had been assigned a French soldier as a servant. La Valeur was an illiterate peasant from Picardy, 'a scapegrace, a drunkard and a debauchee', ever at hand with a song or a funny tale.[13] Casanova was fond of the man, if only because he could practise his French with him. Then La Valeur fell ill, so ill that he was taken to hospital and given his final sacraments. Upon his death, the priest delivered a bundle of papers to Casanova saying he had been told by the dying man to ensure it was passed on to the highest authorities on the island. Opening the package, Casanova found a 'brass seal bearing a coat of arms surrounded by a ducal mantling, a baptismal certificate, and sheet of paper' upon which was written, in French, a confession that La Valeur's true identity was that of 'François VI, Charles Philippe, Louis FOUCAULD, Prince of LA ROCHEFOUCAULD'. Casanova immediately recognised this to be some variety of posthumous prank on the part of his deceased servant, as he had known some members of that family when in Rome serving Cardinal Acquaviva. His superiors, however, believed its authenticity and ordered the body to be accorded the proper respect demanded by his rank as an aristocrat.

No sooner had the dead La Valeur been transformed into the late Prince de la Rochefoucauld than news came from the hospital that the patient had undergone a miraculous recovery and was conscious once again. In no time at all, the revived Prince was up and about, and was being feted in the small world of the Corfu garrison. He was now a fixture in society, the guest of honour at every supper party and fawned over by the officers' wives. Casanova was adamant that the man was an imposter but was alone in his view. His refusal to recognise his servant's elevation came to a head at a dinner party where, in response to Casanova's declared assertion that his baptismal certificate was a forgery, the Prince cuffed Casanova about the face with the back of his hand. The young man left the house in a dignified fashion, waited in an alleyway for the drunken man to stagger out after dinner, and then had his revenge in the darkness, beating the Prince half to death with his cane. His honour restored, Casanova retired to the coffee-house, whence news arrived that he was wanted for assaulting an aristocrat.

Rather than face military discipline for what he considered a non-crime, Casanova absconded to the nearby island of Casopo where he lived the life of a glamorous outlaw. After some weeks of this a letter arrived from the French ambassador in Venice confirming what Casanova had declared all along, namely that La Valeur was a fraud. Both the Prince and the Picard had since vanished and the Corfu authorities were much embarrassed by the whole episode. He was now welcome back to Corfu without risk of punishment.

Casanova's vindication in this matter won him the admiration of Signora F. She now showed him signs of her favour and soon a romantic intrigue was afoot. Their affair is noteworthy less as a demonstration of Casanova's seductive prowess than as an example of a peculiarly Italian institution. For Casanova's entanglement with Signora F. did not conform to the pattern of his regular sexual escapades. At first it all seemed very promising: sentimental dialogues were had, gifts were exchanged, emotional confessions were made. Casanova felt final victory was near when Signor D.R. transferred him into the service of Signora F., and he was installed in her house in a bedroom not far from her own.

He now spent his days waiting on her: helping her in and out of carriages, dining with her when her husband was busy with military matters, caring for her when she was poorly. The performance of a sentimental courtship continued, but after a few weeks it became clear that he was little more than her servant. She teased him with displays of passion and promises of future release, but he was always and everywhere confounded. Perhaps out of pride, Casanova does not use the term to describe the position he was in, but as a Venetian and a man well versed in the ways of polite society, he could not but have known that he was not Signora F.'s lover but merely her *cicisbeo*.

The culture of *cicisbeismo* flourished in Italy throughout the eighteenth century. It was one of the most widely remarked upon features of Italian high society, and Casanova's reticence on the topic is curious given its ubiquity not only in foreign accounts of Italian society but also in Italian culture itself. The exact nature of *cicisbeismo* is contested, but in essence it was a kind of male concubinage whereby when a woman married, she took a man (in some accounts several men) as her *cicisbeo* (also referred to as a *cavalier servente*). This was done with the full assent of her husband, who according to custom was expected to tolerate the situation as a regular part of married life.

The origins of *cicisbeismo* are unclear, as is the etymology of the term. The exact parameters and the legal status of such an arrangement were hotly debated by contemporaries and remain so by historians. What is clear is that *cicisbeismo* was to be found throughout the Italian peninsula in Casanova's lifetime, and especially in Venice, which along with Naples was considered the seat of the phenomenon. In the former city, English traveller Samuel Sharpe observed in the 1760s, 'GALLANTRY is so epidemical . . . that few of the Ladies escape the contagion. No woman can go into a public place, but in the company of a Gentleman, called here, a *Cavaliere Servente*, and in other parts of Italy a *Cicesbeo.*' Sharpe went on to give the canonical description of what a Venetian *cicisbeo*'s life consisted of:

> This *Cavaliere* is always the same person; and she not only is attached to him, but to him singly for no other woman joins the company, but it is usual for them to sit alone in the box, at the opera, or play-house, where they must be, in a manner, by themselves, as the theatres are so very dark that the spectators can hardly be said to be in company with one another. After the Opera, the Lady, and her *Cavaliere Servente* retire to her *Casine*, where they have a Tete-a-Tete for an hour or two, and then her visitors join them for the rest of the evening, or night; for on some festival and jolly days, they spend the whole night, and take Mass in their way home.[14]

Sharpe is circumspect, as so many observers were, as to what went on during that time alone in the *casino* at day's end. The extent to which the relationship between lady and *cicisbeo* was sexual has been a subject of fierce debate for several centuries now, with the majority of reasonable observers reckoning that it would be naive in the extreme to believe that it was not. To be sure, the *cicisbeo*'s duties were not principally carnal. His main role, which never ceased to appal foreign visitors, was to *serve* his lady. This could involve anything from helping her dress, arranging her hair, playing cards with her, or ensuring she had something to eat and drink while she played cards with someone else. He was to be more uxorious than her actual, absent, and frequently far older, husband could ever expect to be.

The most famous *cicisbeo*, and the one who left the most complete account of the inner workings of the arrangement, was Lord Byron. While living in Venice in 1818, Byron met the eighteen-year-old Teresa Guiccioli, wife of Count Guiccioli, a wily politician from Ravenna well into his fifties. The two met at a Venetian salon and fell tumultuously in love. When Teresa returned to Ravenna and to her husband's house, she summoned Byron to join her there, and he soon found himself set up on a separate floor of the same *palazzo* as she, communications between the two being enabled, Byron caustically noted to a friend, by 'the aid of a Priest, a Chambermaid, a young Negro-boy, and a female friend'.[15] What followed was a crash course in *cicisbeismo*. Soon Byron was attending to Teresa at the theatre, ensuring her comfort at *conversazioni*, and making small talk with Count Guiccioli who, according to the edicts of *cicisbeismo*, had little choice but to accept the infamous English lord into his household.[16]

The arrangement pleased Teresa – and had its upsides for her husband, who was soon borrowing money from the wealthy poet upstairs – but it drove Byron to distraction. 'I feel – & I feel it bitterly – that a man should not consume his life at the side and on the bosom of a woman,' he wrote to his friend John Hobhouse in August 1819, 'and that this Cicisbean existence is to be condemned.' He begged Teresa to spare him the humiliation of *cicisbeismo* by eloping with him to some distant place, but she would have none of it and demanded he stay with her in the Romagna – which he did, albeit in a state of growing exasperation. A few months later he vented again to Hobhouse on the subject:

I am not tired of Italy – but a man must be a Cicisbeo and a singer in duets – and a Connoisseur of operas – or nothing – [here] I have made some progress in all these accomplishments – but can't say that I don't feel the degradation. – Better be an unskilful planter – an awkward settler – better be a hunter – or anything, than a flatterer of fiddlers – and fan-carrier of a woman. – I like women – God he knows – but the more their system here developes upon me – the worse it seems – after Turkey too – here the polygamy is all on the female side. – I have been a whoremonger, intriguer, a husband, and now I am a Cavalier Servente – by the holy! it is a strange sensation.[17]

Byron was not alone among otherwise forward-thinking men in believing that *cicisbeismo* travestied male dignity. Tobias Smollett, who witnessed the practice when in Italy in the 1760s, wrote that he 'would rather be condemned for life to the gallies, than exercise the office of a cicisbeo, exposed to the intolerable caprices and dangerous resentment of an Italian virago'.[18] Similarly, in his memoirs Carlo Goldoni recorded that he had 'long looked with astonishment on those singular beings called cicisbei in Italy, the martyrs of gallantry, and the slaves of the caprices of the fair sex'.[19]

The revulsion towards the practice on the part of so many men warrants further consideration. In the classical seduction narrative an unmarried woman was seduced and abandoned by an older, financially secure man. *Cicisbeismo* subverted all this. The woman was married, and so was financially secure – even more so (compared to England) in Italy, where marriage contracts often stipulated her personal income and the exact division of assets – and also socially secure. Furthermore, her *cicisbeo* served her – and who knows what more – at her pleasure, and hers alone. As it was not uncommon for girls to marry straight out of a convent, as Teresa Guiccioli did, and to marry a man much older than they, as Teresa did too, *cicisbeismo* was a humane way of allowing a young wife freedom, companionship, and some experience of the pleasures of sexual exploration without taking any risks as to her short-term respectability or long-term solvency.

This was why Teresa rebuked Byron when he begged her to abscond with him: that would have defeated the whole purpose of the arrangement. Byron might have found the system degrading and unsatisfying, but it clearly worked for Teresa. In asking her to elope, he was really asking her to prioritise his pride over her security. She was wise to refuse.[20] 'I am all for morality now,' a defeated Byron wrote ruefully to his friends, 'and shall confine myself henceforward to the strictest adultery.'[21] Byron and his like were used to a system of moral hypocrisy that served men. They could not abide a system of moral hypocrisy that served women.

Neither, it seemed, could Casanova. After playing *cicisbeo* to Signora F. for some weeks, he was in a state of near madness on account of a potent mixture of perceived humiliation and thwarted desire. After yet another encounter with the Signora that left him at a new pinnacle of sexual frustration, his resolve broke and he fled into the arms of Mesulla, a local courtesan. His few hours with her left him with a venereal disease whose existence he was obliged to acknowledge to Signora F., whereupon she promptly dismissed him from her affections. Soon afterwards his luck at the card table failed and he found himself without 'health, money, credit, good humour, consideration, wit, the ability to express myself, and with it, my power of persuasion'. Once more he found himself with neither connections nor prospects, and once more he decided to throw himself on fate. 'Not having abjured the goddess Fortune,' he explains in his memoirs, 'I thought that I could still count on her. I knew that she exercises her sway over all mortals without consulting them, provided that they are young; and I was young.'[22] He gave up his commission and returned to Venice.

***

Star student, failed cleric, decommissioned officer – by the age of twenty-one Casanova had been all of these things, and now, back in Venice without money or obvious direction, he returned to his roots in the theatre while he awaited Fortune's next play. Playing the violin in the pit of the Teatro San Samuele would, for some young men, have been an adventure in itself, and had he more respect for his parents' vocation he might have found in his new role a fitting tribute to Zanetta and Gaetano, who had walked those very boards he now sat beneath. But for the ambitious Casanova his lot was a deplorable one. He considered himself a failure and hid from Venetian polite society, where he was now remembered – if at all – as an also-ran, a youth who had failed to live up to the promise of his precocious boyhood. Exiled from the drawing rooms of the *beau monde*, he joined a group of hard-drinking pranksters who made merry and made trouble all over the city. He had, by his own measure, gone completely to the dogs.

In the spring of 1746 fate came to his rescue. When the scions of two great patrician families were wed in some splendour at the Palazzo Soranzo, Casanova was one of many musicians hired to provide a soundtrack to the occasion. On the third and final day of the festivities, he was making his way out after his shift ended when he found himself walking behind a man dressed in the red robe of a Venetian senator. As the cowled figure ahead of him was boarding his gondola, he reached for his handkerchief and unwittingly displaced a letter that fell onto the ground before Casanova's feet. Casanova hurried over to the senator before he could leave and handed him the dropped letter; in gratitude the old man offered him a trip home in his boat, and soon the two men were seated next to each other as his gondoliers picked their way through the packs of departing guests.

What happened next is unclear: the senator seems to have had a stroke of some kind, losing sensation in his arm and leg and experiencing uncontrollable facial contortions. Casanova quickly directed the gondoliers to a coffee-house, where he obtained the address of a local surgeon. As the gondola hastened back to the senator's *palazzo*, the surgeon bled him while Casanova tore apart his shirt to make an improvised bandage. He stayed with his new acquaintance while his friends, a doctor and a priest were found, and later, over dinner in the *palazzo*, learned the man's identity: he was Senator Matteo Giovanni Bragadin, a member of the patrician class, a prominent statesman known for the 'love affairs which had signalized his stormy youth', now long since past. He was also introduced to the two bachelors who lived with Bragadin, Marco Dandolo and Marco Barbaro, themselves both members of illustrious patrician families.

Inspired by either concern or cunning, Casanova stayed by Bragadin's bedside through the night. Before leaving, the doctor had strapped a compress containing a mercury ointment on Bragadin's chest. Sitting by the patient, Casanova watched with alarm as Bragadin's eyes fluttered and his breath became shallow. By midnight he was in the grip of a fever and Casanova, apparently without consultation, decided the compress was doing more harm than good and removed it.

Bragadin soon recovered and the next morning thanked the young man for saving his life, before firing his physician. In Casanova's telling, Bragadin, Barbaro and Dandolo identified in his timely appearance in the senator's life a portent, and they begged him to stay with them. They revealed that they were students of the esoteric and had surmised that Casanova had a gift. After some needling, Casanova confessed that yes, he was indeed well versed in the ways of the cabala, and he demonstrated his oracular powers for them. His favoured device was a numerological oracle, a system of numbers which, when organised in pyramids, could reveal the future. They informed him grandly that he was in possession of a great gift, at which point Casanova made an astonishing pronouncement. His oracle, he told them, had foreseen their meeting, an occasion he recounted in his memoirs:

actually living at the time. Whatever the truth of the matter, Casanova's elevation to the ranks of Venetian nobility was real. It is a matter of documented fact that he lived at the Palazzo Bragadin for much of the next decade and drew an allowance from the senator until the latter's death in 1767. By means fair, foul or felicitous, Casanova had made his way to the top of Venetian society, and his twenties would be spent in exhausting the sensual possibilities that money, rank and charm afforded a young man in Venice.

The world in which Casanova now immersed himself was one bathing in the immediate afterglow of a revolution in sexual manners. For centuries Venice had been associated with leisure, largely on account of the state policy of permitting, regulating and taxing prostitution which had helped spread the legend of the city as the Venus of the Adriatic.[23] However, the sexual licence she granted to professionals was not extended to the majority of women. On the contrary, Venice was similarly renowned for the virtual captivity in which unmarried girls and married women were kept. Well into the seventeenth century, travellers consistently reported on the custom. Englishman Fynes Morisson wrote that Venetian women were 'locked up at home, as if in prison'.[24] The very bricks of the city served to reinforce this idea that the home was a place of detention. Expecting to see one of the most splendid cities in Europe, many visitors were taken aback by the grim visages of Venetian houses, with heavy metal bars and wooden latticework (known as Gelosias – literally, 'Jealousy') laid upon the windows. Even when they were allowed out of the home, women were hindered by the requirements of fashion. Venetian zentildonne were long famous across Europe for their peculiarities of dress. They wore heavy zendale, a kind of all-encompassing shroud that hid their face and figure, and on their feet zoccoli, platform shoes so extravagant that they were essentially stilts, and so unstable that they required one or more servants to aid with movement.[25]

By the mid-eighteenth century, however, this culture of seclusion and concealment had been swept away. In Casanova's time, Venice was known for the expansive freedom enjoyed by her women. 'No women on earth are under so little restraint,' one visitor noted, 'and the word jealousy is become obsolete.' This new freedom was symbolised by new fashions: the *zoccoli* gave way to *scarpe*, infinitely more convenient flat-soled leather slippers, while the *zendale* morphed into something suggestive – so suggestive that a scandalised English visitor complained that 'the dress of their modest women is hardly more decent than that of our common prostitutes'.[26] Far from being shuttered indoors, Venetian women of means and fashion now maintained their own private apartments, or *casini*, where they could entertain their friends with cards, music and conversation, and where they could retreat with their *cicisbei* or anyone else they wished to spend time with unobserved. Women were now ubiquitous in public and could be found at the theatre, the opera house, gambling at the Ridotto (the state-run casino), taking chocolate and sorbet on St Mark's, or promenading around the gardens of the Giudecca. This transformation of the lives of Venetian women unleashed one of the great sexual revolutions of the eighteenth century, and Venice soon vied with Paris in the permissiveness of its sexual culture.

This turn from confinement to libertinism was so sudden and so pronounced that contemporaries, Casanova included, marvelled at it while having little understanding – apart from weary clichés concerning corrupted morals – of its origins. Venice is a fascinating case study for a revolution in mores precisely because of the sclerotic nature of the Venetian state. By design, very little changed in the Republic of Venice. The laws and the system of government had gone untouched for centuries. The geographic constraints on the island-state meant that the economy could neither grow nor seriously diversify, and in fact in this period the city was, if anything, depopulating and its economy shrinking. Revolutions in sexual manners are often associated with social, political and economic upheavals – none of these were present in eighteenth-century Venice, and yet it underwent one nonetheless.

What had changed, of course, was the Enlightenment. Venice was not, like Paris or London, a centre of Enlightenment learning and debate, but nor was it isolated from the consequences of the new ideas about man, the mind and society then circulating in Europe. Venice was the centre of the Italian printing industry and played host to tens of thousands of annual visitors, and so naturally imbibed some portion of the new philosophies. To be sure, the growing discourse surrounding individual liberties, the sustained attack on clericalism and religious superstition, and the nascent discussion of women's rights did influence sexual manners. However, it is easy to overstate the importance of Enlightenment *thought* in changing behaviour while understating the importance of Enlightenment *culture* in bringing about the same. For what united the disparate elements of Enlightenment Europe was a shared belief in the importance of sociability. After the horrors of the seventeenth-century wars of religion, there was a general acceptance that Europeans would be better served by a culture of amiability and leisure than one of confrontation and conflict. This new ideal was fostered in the court culture spawned by Louis XIV at Versailles and in his many imitators around Europe, and was simultaneously promoted in the public sphere – that enormous network of salons, academies, coffee-houses and correspondences that constituted the Republic of Letters, acting as a counterweight and occasional critic to those same absolutist monarchies.

At the same time European voyages of exploration, trade and colonisation led to encounters with a great variety of non-European, non-Christian peoples, forcing a philosophical conversation about what being European meant and a new self-consciousness about the distinguishing features of European civilisation. One consequence of these developments was the creation of a beachhead for female influence in an overwhelmingly male society. The new sociability took its cues from supposedly feminine values, and women – as *salonnières*, as patrons, as figures of fashion and admiration – were its social arbiters. Across Europe women came out of the home and assumed a public role as the agents of a new public culture. For thousands of educated and moneyed Europeans, the experience of Enlightenment was not predominantly one of studying the tomes of the *philosophes* but of learning civility, politeness and manners – what Montesquieu referred to as *moeurs douces* – by socialising with women.

As social norms softened, social life accelerated and attitudes liberalised, this new, heterosocial world created plenty of opportunities for carefree sexual adventure, which was understood within this new hyper-social paradigm. Looking back on his youth, Milanese playwright Giuseppe Compagnoni observed in the 1790s that in his lifetime 'society changed completely, and the long custom of staying together refined tastes, and introduced a culture of wit and good manners'. Part of this culture was a playful attitude towards sex and courtship:

> I regard European gallantry as one of the strongest social bonds: I attribute to it both the peaceful tranquility which reigns in our cities, and the esteem, respect, mutual assistance, which families and citizens have for each other. . . . Gallantry only has, as its general objective, a series of reciprocal actions, which, by their nature, are suited to increasing harmony and benevolence.[27]

In Italy, the new sociability collided with a new realism about the severity of the marriage market for women. Whereas in Protestant societies there was a shift towards conjugal marriage inspired by romantic love, in Catholic countries marriage was still frequently brokered by family patriarchs out of dynastic considerations. Many Enlightened Italians regarded the new sexual freedom granted to wives (through, for example, the culture of *cicisbeismo*) as just recompense for the mercurial way they were handled on the marriage market.[28]

Whatever the cause, the fact remained: no other city in eighteenth-century Europe enjoyed life like Venice. Prostitution and gambling were legal, summers were spent in the bucolic estates along the Brenta Canal (where aristocrats kept open house for months at a time, entertaining dozens of guests at ruinous expense), the masquerade of the carnival reigned for six months of the year, in turn attracting thousands of tourists. The cramped nature of city living in Venice forced activity out into the *calli* and *campi*, while the necessity of travelling by gondola (with their singing oarsmen, who helpfully doubled and tripled as both procurers and intermediaries between honest lovers) added a glamour to the most prosaic journeys. The city had Europe's first opera house, and seven theatres – more than either Paris or London – along with a staggering profusion of coffee-houses, wine shops and street stalls that were open at all hours of the day. The sheer exuberance of Venetian street life had no parallel in Europe. Goethe wrote of his experience of life on the lagoon:

The spectators are themselves actors, and the multitude is melted into one whole with the stage. All day long the buyer and the seller, the beggar, the sailor, the female gossip, the advocate and his opponent, are living and acting in the square and on the bench, in the gondolas and in the palaces, and make it their business to talk and to asseverate, to cry and to offer for sale, to sing and to play, to curse and to brawl. In the evening they go into the theatre, and see and hear the life of the day artificially put together, prettily set off, interwoven with a story, removed from reality by the masks, and brought near to it by manners. In all this they take a childish delight, and again shout and clap, and make a noise. From day to night, nay, from midnight to midnight, it is always the same.[29]

The musicologist Charles Burney had a comparable experience, though given his interests his senses were attuned to Venice's particular soundscape:

> The people here, at this season seem to begin to live only at midnight. Then the canals are crowded with gondolas, and St. Mark's square with company; the banks too of the canals are all peopled, and harmony prevails in every part. If two of the common people walk together arm in arm, they seem to converse in song; if there is company on the water in a gondola, it is the same; a mere melody, unaccompanied with a second part, is not to be heard in this city: all the ballads in the streets are sung in duo. Luckily for me, this night, a barge, in which there was an excellent band of music, consisting of violins, flutes, horns, bases, and a kettle-drum, with a pretty good tenor voice, was on the great canal, and stopped very near the house where I lodged; it was a piece of gallantry, at the expense of an inamorato in order to serenade his mistress.[30]

The intense sociability of Venetian life accounts for one of the peculiarities of Casanova's own memoir of his tempestuous life there. What is striking about Casanova's prose style is how visually and sonically flat it is. He has neither Goethe's eye nor Burney's ear. He has no interest in taking the reader through the dim and musky back-alleys with him, or in describing the brilliance of a flamingo sunset over the lagoon. For Casanova the only active ingredient of Venice was its social life. He forgoes a literary treatment of the sensory experience of Venetian life in order to absorb the reader in the labyrinthine ways of its social existence. Casanova faithfully records every hand of faro or basset, every scalding cup of post-coital coffee, every midnight passage across the water from *palazzo* to *casino*, every ball, every quip, every dance – for it was in these seemingly facile episodes that he found the vital essence of his age. For this was his time, as he recalls with that typical mixture of pride, pain and awe – since he was 'at no loss for money, endowed by nature with a striking exterior, a resolute gambler, a spendthrift, a great talker with a sharp tongue, completely without modesty, fearless, running after pretty women, supplanting rivals, and thinking no company good except such as amused me, I could not but be hated'.[31]

Venice was a bad place to be hated. For all its outward gaiety, the city was a police state, with powers temporal and spiritual gathered in the hands of the Council of Ten – the politburo of the city's patrician class – and total powers of investigation, arrest and punishment invested in the Council of Three, the much-feared Inquisition. This secretive body, peopled by incorruptible old men monomaniacally focused on maintaining their caste's grip on the Republic, retained a huge network of spies and informers whose task was facilitated by the cramped geography of the city and the talkativeness of its inhabitants. In Venice, Casanova remarks in his memoirs with as much accuracy as hypocrisy, libertinism was substituted for liberalism. His meteoric rise to social eminence and his cohabitation with Bragadin, Barbaro and Dandolo imme-diately marked him out for investigation by the Council of Three.

Although it lived among the rest of the population, the patrician class was hermetically sealed off from it by the continuity of its constituents' bloodlines. Every member of every patrician family had his or her name inscribed in the Golden Book, a ledger that contained the name of every Venetian descended from the Republic's founding elite. By Casanova's time the book had been closed to new entrants for centuries. No one could join it. If a patrician made a morganatic marriage, the children produced by it would be forfeit the rights of their patrician parent.[32] Moreover, as the patricians were obliged to govern the city, rule its colonies, and staff its army and navy, they were constantly under surveillance by the three state inquisitors for signs of corruption or rebellion. The social lives of patricians were closely monitored. At the extreme, the penalty for interacting with any foreign diplomat was death. But even their more casual friendships could be viewed with suspicion in the paranoid chambers of the Ducal Palace. Casanova's magical elevation to the trust and confidence of three of the city's most illustrious men could not be ignored by the Council of Three. His constant gambling, quarrelling and woman-ising, not to mention his occasional brushes with the courts, did little to endear him to the authorities. Less than two years after he had entered Bragadin's household, his new guardian advised him that he had better flee the city before he was arrested. Casanova went to Milan and Bragadin got to work smoothing out his young charge's legal problems.

For the next two years, Casanova roved the peninsula on the first of many tours. He visited Milan, Mantua, Cesena, Naples, Parma, Bologna and Ferrara. His activities were always the same – women, cards and opera – as was the company he kept: gamblers, noblemen, actors, soldiers and adventurers. It was in these months that Casanova laid the groundworks for his legend, putting in the anonymous hours of his apprenticeship to seduction, loving freely, passionately, and at times unsuccessfully. His affairs in this period – some of which brought him close to marriage – reveal him to be something more than a cynical libertine, if something less than an honest lover.

For Casanova, the pursuit of women was about more than the pursuit of his own pleasure. He was impelled by a boundless love of novelty, cruelly counterbalanced by a genuine love of individuals. Unlike many of the rakes and scoundrels among whom he moved, his earnest courtship of the women who fascinated him was normally devoid of the double-dealing he regularly employed on the rubes he encountered at the card table and elsewhere. Seduction was neither a purely rational exercise in manipulation, as practised by the classic Enlightenment libertine, nor the surrender to florid sentiment of the man of sensibility, but a game which both parties played and whose consequences both parties suffered. While he openly admits that he 'had no scruples about deceiving nitwits and scoundrels and fools', he argues that in the course of his affairs 'this sort of reciprocal deceit cancels itself out, for when love enters in, both parties are usually dupes'. Casanova grounded this philosophy in typical Enlightenment precepts, viewing men and women as rational agents who met – romantically or otherwise – on terms of parity. This was a presumption he seldom interrogated, though it is not hard to see how it might be challenged.

In early 1750, Bragadin sent word that Casanova was once more free to return to Venice. This he did, although he stayed barely long enough to make some money at cards before striking out for Paris. Casanova spent eighteen rather unremarkable months in France. In Lyon he became a Freemason and in Paris he describes himself as 'a candidate in the Republic of Letters'. He spent an enormous amount of time at the opera learning the code of high-society sociability and a comparable amount of effort perfecting his French – the language in which he would ultimately write his memoirs. His first forays into the networks of Enlightened society would stand him in good stead for many years to come, but at the time his eager attempts at penetrating the French court and his occasional lapses from polite norms marked him out as a callow outsider.

Eventually, legal woes and financial worries obliged Casanova to return to Venice, and to the protection and purse of Bragadin. The way home took him through Dresden, where he saw his mother for the first time in fifteen years, and Vienna, where he was appalled by the prudery of administration. 'Everything in Vienna was splendid,' he recalled, 'but there was great hardship for those who were votaries of Venus.' The devout Empress Maria Teresa considered gallantry a scourge and declared that her people did not 'have the devil in their bodies like the Italians'. This was inhospitable terrain for the twenty-seven-year-old Casanova and he was soon headed home. In May 1753, he returned to Venice.

View of the Brenta, near Dolo by Giambattista Cimaroli, late eighteenth century.

***

Casanova's homecoming coincided with the celebration of the Feast of the Ascension, the most extravagant of Venice's many public holidays. A cross between Valentine's Day and the Fourth of July, this was a time when young lovers exchanged gifts while the Doge reconsecrated the Serene Republic's commitment to the seas that had made her fortune by marrying the Adriatic at the Lido. For the period of the festivities, masking was permitted and the city's inhabitants abandoned themselves to leisure.

No sooner had Casanova reclaimed his rooms at the Palazzo Bragadin than his old patron declared his desire to leave the city to the young and retire to the peace of his country home outside Padua. Casanova accompanied him on the journey, dined with him at his estate, and then returned to the city by *barella*, a two-wheeled carriage that travelled along the post road that ran parallel to the Brenta Canal. As he passed through Oriago, his *barella* met a speeding cabriolet carrying an officer in uniform and a beautiful young woman. Ten metres or so before the two parties crashed into one another, the driver of the oncoming equipage swerved to avoid a collision and in the process tipped his vehicle riverwards. The lady inside was flung dramatically from her trap and landed perilously close to the edge of the canal. Casanova sprang out of his own carriage to help her, admiring as he did so the 'secret wonders' revealed in the disarray of her skirts. The coachmen quarrelled, the gentlemen reassured the distressed lady, and both groups went on their respective ways.

The next day was the scheduled date for the climax of the Ascension Day celebrations. That was when the Doge would make the annual pilgrimage across the lagoon from his palace to the cusp of the Adriatic in his fabulously gold, fabulously top-heavy barge of state, the *Bucentaur*, and fling a wedding ring into the sea, which he would claim as the city's faithful wife. It was customary for the nobility, foreign diplomats and other grandees to travel in the *Bucentaur*'s wake in their own craft. Casanova, naturally, was to follow the Doge in Bragadin's gondola. He waited for the appropriate hour on St Mark's Square, where he enjoyed a cup of coffee and watched the world go by. A masked woman came up to him and rapped him playfully on his shoulder with her fan. She said nothing; Casanova ignored her. Later, on his way to his gondola, he ran into her on a bridge accompanied by a masked man in an officer's uniform. He asked her why she had struck him with her fan, to which she replied that she was punishing him for his failure to recognise the woman he had so gallantly rescued the day before. He realised his error and invited the duo to ride with him in his gondola. Afterwards the group repaired to an inn near the Campo San Moisè, where Casanova declared his love to the mysterious woman. They went from the inn to a box at the opera and thence to another inn. Casanova took them home in his gondola, 'in which, under cover of the darkness, the beauty granted me all the favours which propriety permits a woman to grant when there is a third person to be considered'.

The next day, the officer appeared at Casanova's house and told him that he was Pietro Capretta and the woman was Maria Colonda, without specifying the exact nature of their relation to each other. Casanova was already suspicious of the couple's intentions, and suspected that Capretta was Colonda's pimp. The truth was in fact worse. Capretta explained that he had a contract to supply Hungarian beef to the City of Venice, but that cash flow problems were hindering his business. He asked Casanova – on the strength of a chance meeting, and an evening on the town together – to guarantee several bills of exchange on his behalf, taking his future cattle shipments to Trieste as collateral against non-payment. Casanova was left 'astonished by such a speech and such a proposition, which seemed to me chimerical and the source of continuous difficulties that I loathed'. He refused to be entangled in Capretta's financial machinations and sent him on his way.

This vignette – an upturned carriage on a post road, a serendipitous encounter during a festival, a fumble in a gondola, an artful escape from a financial swindle – is so typical of Casanova's world, yet it triggered a series of events that upended it. That traffic accident on the Brenta Canal was the fateful moment in his existence, one that led to his most beguiling love affair, to his criminal detention in wretched circumstances, and to the triumphant escapade that would become, in the fullness of time, the cornerstone of his legend.

For Casanova broke his promise to himself and did see Pietro Capretta again. The next day he called on the Capretta household as a courtesy. Pietro introduced him to his mother and his fourteen-year-old sister, Caterina. Casanova was ever exposed to *coups de foudre*, they were his stock-in-trade, and the ungenerous reader of his life might doubt the sincerity of his many infatuations. In this instance, however, later events would substantiate the feelings he claimed to have felt at once. Caterina fascinated him immediately. 'It took her no more than half an hour to enchant me by her bearing,' he recalled. 'What chiefly struck me was a lively and unspoiled nature brimming over with candour and ingenuousness, a gay and innocent vivacity, simple and noble feelings.' She had been well educated by her parents – both learned and pious people, whose library 'possessed no novels' – but had lived a cloistered existence. She was excited to meet an envoy from the world outside and peppered him with questions. When it came to leave, he did so with a heavy heart, convinced he would never see her again, and doubly convinced that even if he did he would never be allowed to marry her.

A remedy for his melancholy was near at hand. The same afternoon he called on a friend from his childhood, Signora Manzoni, who told him that his old flame Teresa Imer was back in Venice. Teresa had spent the previous decade on the road in Europe building her skill and fame as a singer, and had returned to the city for a short time in between stints in Bayreuth. The two spent the afternoon catching up and then went to the opera together in the evening. The next day he went to breakfast in her rooms, and finding her still in bed joined her there. The result was a baby girl whom he would not see until she was nearly six years old.

Teresa left for Germany shortly afterwards. No sooner had she gone than Pietro Capretta reappeared in his life, announcing the wonderful news that his sister was obsessed with him. Another trip to the Capretta household confirmed Casanova's affection for her, and hers for him, but it also stirred uncharacteristic misgivings. 'I examined the nature of budding passion,' Casanova writes, 'and I found it cruel. I could proceed with C.C. neither as an honourable man nor as a libertine.' He buried his doubts at the card table, losing extravagantly, but he could not shake off Pietro, who seemed intent on making the match between his sister and his would-be benefactor.

Casanova knew enough about the world to perceive that Pietro's matchmaking was inspired more by a love of his troubled cattle trade than of his little sister. Likewise, he knew enough about himself to understand that such ancillary schemes would not, ultimately, obstruct the ways of his heart. He allowed himself to be shepherded into a romance with Caterina. The two went to the opera together. They walked arm-in-arm through the *giardini* in San Biagio. They survived a lurid double date with Pietro and Maria Colonda.[33] Finally, falling ever deeper in love, and swearing solemnly that they should be married or elope, they took a *casino* on the Giudecca and shared a bed for the first time.

Casanova was as good as his word. While their affair continued, he now formally asked Bragadin to help him approach Caterina's father and broker a marriage with his daughter. The plan was delayed by Signor Capretta's absence from the city on business, but no sooner was he back than Bragadin arranged a meeting between the two older men. Casanova was sanguine; Caterina did not think her father would let her marry so young. Her pessimism was proved correct. Not only did Signor Capretta deny his suit, he declared that his daughter could not marry for another four years, and she would spend those four years in a convent on Murano.

The convents of Venice were one of the city's famed attributes, as much an attraction as its theatres and brothels. By the eighteenth century the lagoon was host to thirty-three nunneries that housed several thousand nuns.[34] Some of these were respectable educational and charitable institutions, a select few were elite music schools where all-female choirs and bands were trained to the highest standards; for the most part, however, the city's convents enjoyed an insalubrious reputation as hotbeds of dissipation. Passing through the city in 1739, the French visitor De Brosses reported stories of nuns fighting duels with poniards and three convents vying to provide the new papal nuncio with a mistress.[35] Carnival was celebrated within the convents as it was in the city more generally, as the exuberant, cacophonous depictions of the convents' visiting parlours at such times by painters such as Pietro Longhi, Francesco

Guardi and Giuseppe de Gobbis readily attest. The relative permissiveness of Venetian convents was accepted in recognition that women were placed in them for purely secular reasons: patrician families could not afford multiple marriages and the consequent dilution of their estates. The mazily named French diplomat Abraham Nicolas Amelot de la Houssaye argued in his contemporary account of the city that this accounted for 'the irregularity of the *Nuns*' of Venice, who were immured in their droves by parsimonious parents but then, perhaps out of guilt, were allowed 'to have some Entertainment in their Cloisters, and at least to be allowed the privilege of seeing their Lovers at a Grate'.[36] De la Houssaye's basic insight was correct. The convents were a product of secular needs, and made a healthy sum from the upper classes' need to shield their daughters from unwanted advances.[37] The money they extracted from their charges encouraged an indolent approach to matters of discipline, out of kilter with Italian nunnery norms.

The particulars of convent architecture revealed the Venetian way. One expatriate Italian, defending the Venetian system to an English audience, remarked that the visiting parlours of Venetian convents were more inviting spaces than was the case elsewhere on the peninsula:

> Both in the morning and afternoon they are allowed some hours of parlatory, as they call it. There they receive their visitors, and sit chatting with them through the iron-grate. This grate is double and very narrow throughout Italy. At Venice only it is not so: nay, the partitions there are so very large, that one may conveniently shake hands with them. But the largeness of the Venetian grates has ruined the reputation of the Venetian nuns.[38]

Questions of convent security were now foremost in Casanova's mind. Lover's bravado had first led him to believe 'that I could carry her off even if the convent were guarded with artillery'.[39] This was a chimerical aspiration; in the first instance he did not even know which convent Caterina was in. Even once he found out she was in a nunnery on Murano,[40] he could not access her, although a back channel was found by which the lovers could exchange letters. The correspondence revealed a problem far greater than a forced separation – Caterina was pregnant. One July morning, Casanova was woken up to receive a desperate letter from her. She was having a miscarriage and was haemorrhaging badly. The nuns were trying to help her as best they could, but she had not revealed her condition to them and they had not guessed it. She begged him to relay to her via Laura – their intermediary – materials to staunch the bleeding. 'I am scarcely dressed,' Casanova wrote, 'before I have another oar put to my gondola, and I go with Laura to the Ghetto, where I buy a Jew's whole stock of sheets and more than two hundred napkins, and after putting them in a bag I go to Murano with her.' In Murano, he set himself up in Laura's house while she went back and forth to the convent with illicit supplies of sheets and napkins hidden in her skirt. Having left with clean linen, she returned with a stash of bloodied cloth and the news that Caterina was close to death. 'When I saw the linen,' Casanova recalled, 'which she took out from under her skirt I very nearly dropped dead. It was sheer butchery. . . . I shuddered when the woman showed me a little shapeless lump in among the blood.'

Laura's traffic between convent and home continued for two nights. What she carried back in her skirt was a continual reproach to Casanova's careless ways. His moral system quavered and he began to doubt his whole way of life. 'I was really in despair. Seeing myself the murderer of this innocent girl, I did not feel that I could survive her.' He shunned female company, not even letting Laura's daughters wait on him. He realised that his uncontrolled passions had turned women into 'the instruments of my horrible incontinence, which had made me the executioner of an angel incarnate'.

Then Caterina recovered. Casanova returned to Venice and to his usual ways – though he moaned that 'without a real and satisfying love affair I could not be happy'. He did, however, receive news that he would be able to go and see Caterina in the convent. This he did, and learnt that he could also go to mass at the convent on feast days. Casanova was soon visiting the convent on every possible occasion, and Caterina wrote to him that his repeated attendance at their services had given rise to wild speculation as to his identity and motives.[41] There was no danger of his true purpose being revealed, and in any case, the two earnestly believed themselves to be married in spirit if not in fact – Casanova refers to Caterina as his 'dear wife' in this period. This being so, making such visits was the very least he could do amid the tragedy of their separation and her brush with death. Nonetheless, he was not a happy man. 'I was growing thin, I was wearing myself out; I could not long survive this sort of life. I was born to have a mistress and to live happily with her. Not knowing what to do, I gambled and I won nearly every day, yet for all that I was bored.'

1 November 1753. All Saints' Day. As Casanova left mass and made his way to his gondola, a woman dropped a letter in his path. When she saw he had collected it, she vanished. Once settled in his gondola, Casanova broke the seal and read the letter's contents. A long missive in French from someone claiming to be one of Caterina's fellow nuns, it contained a frank proposition and a number of scenarios as to how the two might meet. Casanova surmised from the style and tone of the letter that his anonymous correspondent might be the nun 'who was teaching C.C. French and who was beautiful, rich, and a flirt. . . . But I dismissed the suspicion precisely because it pleased me.' He decided to hedge, writing back that he would welcome a chance to meet her in the convent visiting rooms, in the company of a woman of her choice. The proposal was accepted and the necessary arrangements were made.

The following Sunday Casanova went to morning mass at the

convent as usual. That evening he returned to the entrance, masked and in the company of the designated woman. His escort 'asks to see M.M. The name astonishes me, for the bearer of it was celebrated.' With mounting excitement he was led to a private visiting room. M.M. (her real identity has never been uncovered) appeared at the grating, pressed a button which loosened four sections, allowing for the creation of a hole easily large enough for a man to pass through, stepped across the grille and embraced her friend. Casanova sat in silent rapture as the two conversed. M.M. was a 'rare beauty' in her early twenties,

> tall, so white of complexion as to verge on pallor, with an air of nobility and decision but at the same time of reserve and shyness, large blue eyes; a sweet, smiling face, beautiful lips damp with dew, which allowed a glimpse of two magnificent rows of teeth, her nun's habit did not let me see any hair; but whether she had it or not, its colour must be light chestnut, her eyebrows told me as much.[42]

The woman completely ignored him and, after an hour or so of conversation, returned through the grating without so much as a nod of recognition. This was more than enough for Casanova, who surrendered himself to the thrill of a nascent affair. He was fascinated by this beautiful, sophisticated woman, who had the ability to pass freely through the convent walls. Discreetly, he interviewed women who knew her, gathering a portrait of an enigmatic individual who had 'taken the veil when she is rich, highly intelligent, very cultivated, and . . . a freethinker'. She also proved an adept manipulator of male emotions. After the initial excitement of their nocturnal encounter in the visiting parlour, M.M. denied Casanova a meeting. Casanova was thrown off. At night he wrote her bitter letters and then destroyed them in the coolness of the morning. 'Such are the terrible moments to which a pursuer of women is exposed,' Casanova reflected, 'there is nothing more cruel.'

> They degrade, they distress, they kill. In my revulsion and humil-
> iation, my first feeling was contempt for myself, a dark contempt
> which approached the limits of horror. The second was a disdainful
> indignation toward the nun, on whom I passed the judgement she
> appeared to deserve. She was mad, a wretched creature, shameless.
> My only consolation was to think her such.

He wrestled with his wounded pride and the rattled emotions that
fluctuated between whimsical savagery and profound self-loathing.
He knew what reason demanded – 'I must pretend indifference'
– but he could not impose its sovereignty. After letting him dangle
for some days, M.M. came to his rescue, sending a consolatory
note that assured him she had not meant to humiliate him but
that a series of honest mistakes had kept them apart. Casanova
jumped at the letter, dashing off a florid response ('I cannot live
except in the hope of your forgiveness . . . I saw you, you dazzled
me,' etc.). The two quickly organised another meeting, *à deux*, at
the convent. There they had an honest exchange despite the inevitable Casanovian histrionics. He admitted that he had a lover in
the convent, 'but she has been torn from me. For six months I
have lived in perfect celibacy.' He still loved Caterina, 'but I foresee
that the seduction of your charms will make me forget her'. For
her part, she admitted she also had a lover, one of means and rank.
He was aware of her flirtation with Casanova and had made his
casino available for the two to use. They had their first, uncon-
summated, assignation there shortly afterwards. Casanova was
charged with organising their second, and his preparations for it,
and the philosophising that accompanied them, represent one of
the great intellectual excavations of the meaning of seduction.

A belief in the essential benignity of the reasoned pursuit of
happiness was at the heart of Enlightenment thinking. The aspiration for all civilised conduct was that rational individuals,
endowed with free will and moulded by polite society, could make

decisions designed to maximise their own pleasure and content-
ment without harming others, and, ideally, while benefiting them.
Enlightened pleasure was distinguished from animal gratification
by the inclusion of reason. Discussing his arrangements for his
assignation with M.M., Casanova observes that the three inherent
features of life are hunger, the sex drive, and the hatred of compet-
itors. Beasts and brutes can gain satisfaction from the fulfilment
of any of these three urges, but 'let us not call them pleasures . . .
for they do not reason about them'. He continues:

> Man alone is capable of true pleasures, for, endowed with the faculty
> of reason, he foresees it, seeks it, creates it, and reasons about it
> after enjoying it. My dear reader, I beg you to follow me; if you
> drop me at this point, you are not polite. Let us examine the thing.
> Man is in the same condition as the beasts when he yields to these
> three instincts without his reason entering in. When our mind
> makes its contribution, these three satisfactions become pleasure,
> pleasure, pleasure.

What has not been planned cannot properly be called pleasurable.
Casanova is distrustful of spontaneity for this reason. He knows
that the blind gratification of the passions leads to shame,
dishonour and injury. This is not to say that he never succumbs
to them, merely that he regards them as inferior to pleasures
more rationally won. Some portion of this preference is grounded
in a sincere belief that reciprocity is the key to genuine pleasure.
The amoral libertine is logical; the ebullient philanderer is impulsive. Both are concerned with smashing through the resistance
of their target. Jealous of their own pleasure, they pay scant regard
to that of the woman at hand. Casanova denies that this can be
the highest manifestation of enlightened love. The carefully
stage-managed seduction he prepares for M.M. is designed to
draw her willingly into the minuet. Delayed gratification is the

key. Just as 'we bear hunger in order to savour culinary concoctions better,' he writes, 'we put off the pleasure of love in order to make it more intense.'

Casanova's preparations for his second night with M.M. were an earnest testament to his philosophy of seduction. At short notice he found an expensive *casino* near St Mark's, containing a drawing room with a chandelier, mirrors, porcelain-tiled walls, an array of suggestive statuettes, a suite of matching sofas and armchairs. A second room was octagonal and mirrored from floor to ceiling, with counterposed looking-glasses that allowed the same object to be viewed from multiple perspectives. Adjacent was a hidden alcove that led to a spacious closet and thence to a chamber with a bed and a large bathtub, the panelling here embossed with ormolu and painted over with flowers and a pastiche of foliate Ottoman patterning. The *casino* came with a cook whom Casanova charged with finding suitable quantities of Burgundy and champagne, food for eight courses plus dessert, clean bedding, and candles for every room. He further ordered that he would have the meal that night which would be served to M.M. the next, to ensure the cooking met his standards.

The rooms were designed such that the servants' quarters and kitchens were structurally segregated from the front rooms. Successive courses were passed through a revolving dumb-waiter that allowed for no glimpse of the people on the other side. That evening Casanova solemnly consumed, plate by plate, a feast served on ornate Meissen crockery and then gave his notes to the waiting chef. 'Game, sturgeon, truffles, oysters, and perfect wines. I only reproached him with having forgotten to set out hard-boiled eggs, anchovies, and prepared vinegars on a dish. . . . I also said that another time I wanted to have bitter oranges to give flavour to the punch and that I wanted rum, not arrack.' The dress rehearsal took two hours, then he went to bed.

The next morning he rang for coffee, and before he left instructed his man to find fresh fruits and ices for their dessert that evening. With nothing to occupy his mind until the appointed hour, he went to the Ridotto and gambled until dusk. That evening his careful planning and exacting standards did not go unrewarded. M.M. was as impressed as he had hoped, and when she left in the morning to return to the convent the two were lovers.

Theirs was a quintessentially enlightened affair, and it represented something of a high-water mark in Casanova's career. There is little in the totality of Casanova's sex life that can be innocently defended. Even allowing for the disparities in norms and mores between his time and ours, it would require the most cynical partisan to make the case that numerous of Casanova's sexual endeavours were not something other than the meeting of rational, like-minded individuals, straying beyond the crooked boundary of the consensually transgressive, past the bogs and marshes of the tolerably deviant, and into the black valleys of sexual crime. His affair with M.M., however, perhaps because it was one which she managed more than he, is free of some of the doubts that trouble his other amours. She insisted that they use the best English-made condoms to ensure that she did not get pregnant. She tutored him in her free-thinking ways and made sure he read books from her library.[43] When she informed him that her lover wanted to be a hidden spectator to one of their assignations (concealed in an alcove behind a sofa, where flowers carved in relief in the wainscoting had unobtrusive spyholes cut out of their carpels), he assented without complaint.

M.M. made a mockery of the convent's security, moving freely in and out to visit Casanova in a *casino*, or to spend the night at the opera or gambling at the Ridotto. Casanova responded in style. At one point he learned from Laura that a masked ball was to be held in the convent's largest visiting parlour. Without first telling either Caterina or M.M. of his intentions, he attended dressed as the white-frocked clown Pierrot and danced a dozen *furlane* with a Harlequiness in pristine anonymity before a cheering crowd of nuns and day-visitors.

This was nothing compared to what M.M. did next. One evening, Casanova went to an assignation with her to find Caterina waiting in her place. The shock of Caterina's introduction into their affair initially caused a rupture, but M.M. was able to steer all involved back on to her intended course. Soon she had inveigled the three into a *ménage à trois*, which quickly expanded into a *ménage à quatre* when she brought into the circle her original lover, who was revealed to be François-Joachim de Pierre de Bernis, the French ambassador to Venice.

These were the golden days of Casanova's youth, and they could not last. Geopolitics initiated the unravelling of their coterie. De Bernis was summoned from Venice, where in truth he was doing very little, to Vienna to help negotiate an epochal diplomatic settlement between the houses of Bourbon and Habsburg.[44] The departure of her principal lover cast M.M. into a great depression and took from her some of the freedoms and privileges that the mistress of such a powerful man might expect to enjoy.

Meanwhile, Casanova himself was coming under ever greater scrutiny from the Venetian Inquisition. In late 1754 the Inquisition assigned him a spy, one Giovanni Battista Manuzzi, who was soon gathering information and producing reports chronicling Casanova's scandalous behaviour. In his telling, Casanova was a parvenu, a conman and a layabout who consorted with gamblers and atheists, had contacts with foreign agents[45] and had been the 'ruin of Bragadin, from whom he has extracted much money'.[46] While these allegations were swirling around him, Casanova managed to make an enemy of Antonio Condulmer, a patrician who in 1755 became a state inquisitor. Around the same time, he made the acquaintance of the aforementioned John Murray, the English Resident in Venice, and was soon sharing mistresses and making gossip with yet another high-placed foreign diplomat. Incidents began to pile up. Manuzzi approached Casanova directly concerning a chimerical diamond deal and, invited into Casanova's room, observed that he had heretical books and manuscripts relating to the cabala littered about. Lucia Memmo, a member of a distinguished patrician family, complained directly to the Inquisition that Casanova was teaching atheism to her son Andrea. Anonymous informants told the inquisitors that he was a magician, a devil-worshipper and a Freemason. Lurid rumours spread that Casanova had sold corrupted love philtres to one Countess Bonafede, who had subsequently gone insane and run naked about the Campo di San Pietro screaming his name.

It soon became common knowledge that Casanova was a marked man. As June turned to July, friends began to urge him to leave town. One morning, after a night spent restlessly walking the streets, he returned to his *casino* to find it had been raided by the guard. At Bragadin's, his old patron had a gondola and purse full of gold waiting for him; he implored his young friend to flee to Florence until it was safe to come back. Casanova refused. Misplaced pride kept him in the city. On the evening of 25 July 1755, he was arrested and taken to the Ducal Palace. He passed briefly before the tribunal, a formality under Venetian law which had no lawyers, no evidence, no witnesses, no real trial to speak of. In the archives his crime is listed as 'public outrages against the holy religion', but he was not informed of this. Nor was he told of his sentence: five years in the *Piombi*, the prison in the attics above the Ducal Palace.[47]

There were two dungeons in the Ducal Palace: the *Pozzi*, or wells, in the cellars, and the *Piombi*, or leads, in the rooftops. Both were objects of terror for the Venetian populace, though the dank *Pozzi* were lethal whereas the lofty *Piombi*, scorched in the summer and frozen in the winter, were merely very uncomfortable. As a relatively wealthy prisoner, Casanova benefited from being able to purchase a few luxuries for his cell, although these were pitiful recompense for the structural indignities of his detention. The ceiling was too low to accommodate his full height, so he moved about in a stoop at all times. The sounds of rats scurrying in the gables were constantly in the background, and were regularly joined by the booming chimes of the nearby clock tower of St Mark's. Sitting in his single wretched armchair, he was devoured by lice and drenched in sweat. Pretty soon he was in a delirium brought on by the ferocious heat and the equally ferocious boredom of his solitary confinement.[48]

When, at last, Lorenzo the gaoler brought him two books to read, they were as unappetising a selection as one might expect: a jesuitical work praising the heart and another religious text, a mystical work by a Spanish nun.[49] Neither provided much stimulus. Denied pen and writing paper, or even the company of other prisoners, and running low on money, Casanova was soon an enervated wretch.

Summer turned to winter, an event marked by a cataclysm. On 1 November, his cell began to quiver, the beams above bouncing out of position. For a few minutes the whole building threatened to jerk apart. The wardens ran about the corridors of the gaol in terror. Inside his cell, Casanova called out for God to collapse the Ducal Palace and release him from captivity. The prayer went unanswered, though two thousand kilometres away the city of Lisbon was near totally destroyed.[50]

The only exercise Casanova was permitted during his imprisonment was an occasional walk in the garret. This was a long dusty room, filled with junk abandoned by long-dead administrators who had worked in the palace below. In the first weeks of 1756 Casanova made two handy discoveries there. The first was a stick of polished black marble, the second a long metal bolt.[51] He soon realised he could use the marble as a whetstone to sharpen the bolt. These were to be the tools of his escape.

For the next eight months, Casanova dug through his floor in preparation for a nocturnal escape that would have begun in the Inquisitors' chamber, situated directly beneath his cell. Everything was in place when, a few days before he was scheduled to make his bid for freedom, he was moved to a larger, airier cell with a view of the city – a relief won for him by Bragadin's tireless advocacy on his behalf.

The sudden move came at an inopportune time and he had to start his plotting all over again. Due to various architectural hindrances arising from his new location in the building, he was obliged to draw other prisoners into his scheming. With the guards' blessing, he began sharing books with a man in another cell, Marin Balbi, an aristocrat and sometime monk. Communicating via messages secreted in the bindings of the books they exchanged, Casanova conspired to have Balbi start by digging through a ceiling into the crawlspace above the prison, and sent him his precious bolt – hidden in a bible and carried beneath a tray that carried two heaped plates of macaroni with butter and parmesan – to begin work. Once Balbi had done this he was able to break into Casanova's cell from above, and the two could then work on breaking through the lead-tiled roof. The target date was 1 November, when the Inquisitors and many other senior state officials left Venice for three days.

The scheme was almost abandoned completely when, in mid-October, a stool-pigeon named Soradaci became an inmate of Casanova's cell. After a few days of panic and despair, Casanova pulled himself together and in a hysterical display of his charismatic powers was able to convince Soradaci that angels were visiting his cell at night.[52] The angel was, of course, Balbi, who on the evening of 31 October emerged from the ceiling and into Casanova's waiting arms. They spent some time preparing the various items they would need for their escape, as well as attempting to borrow some money from fellow prisoners and having a last-minute shave. Then they ventured out onto the great roof of the building. After some hair-raising peregrinations around the slippery, fog-bound tiles (Casanova nearly died falling off, and spent two perilous minutes hanging from the gutter before he could right himself, a moment captured in a contemporary etching), the two found their way into one of the many offices above the Ducal Palace. Exhausted, Casanova now had a three-hour nap.

A 1787 engraving shows Casanova dangling from the roof of
the Ducal Palace during his escape from prison.

When he awoke he opened a window and recognised that they were directly above the San Marco quarter, where he had passed so many merry nights in *casini*. This was not, however, a suitable place to exit the building. They made their way in the darkness through the building until they came to a large, locked door. Using his spike, and heedless of the immense noise it made, Casanova smashed through the panelling until he had created a hole large enough to crawl through. They were now in a passageway which led to the principal entrance to the palace's interior – the Scala d'Oro, which led down to the Scala dei Giganti and thence to the Piazzetta di San Marco. When a new Doge was elected he would process in splendour up the Scala dei Giganti and at the summit would be crowned with his cap of state, the golden *corno*. Thereafter, the Scala d'Oro would be the official approach to his offices of state on the second floor of the palace. At the top of these stairs was an impassable door behind which Casanova and Balbi were now stuck. Casanova's bolt could do no more for them; the next step was in the hands of fate.

Casanova was by now in a total mess: smeared in grime, sweat and blood, wild-eyed from adrenaline and cortisol, covered in splinters, grazes, cuts, scrapes and bruises. He lay down and had an hour's rest. When he awoke the sun was about to rise. He took from his bundle a fine coat, white stockings, a lace-trimmed shirt, and a hat with golden brocade and a white plume. Having stashed his ruined clothes behind an armchair he went over to a window. In the courtyard some lackey saw a fine young man in the palace and assumed he had been locked in overnight. Balbi and Casanova stood at the door and listened to the jangle of keys as the porter made his way up the grand staircase. When the door opened it revealed a single man, unassuming and unarmed, now stunned as his brain made the necessary connections as to what he had just done. Casanova brushed past him wordlessly and walked down the Scala d'Oro, turned right and trotted past the two enormous sculptures of Neptune and Mars that bracketed the top of the Scala dei Giganti, descended those stairs into the porticoes of the Ducal Palace and out into the *piazzetta*, where, beneath a Tiepolo dawn, a few Grand Tourists were winding across the flagstones and the coffee shops were opening for a new day's business.

Balbi began to beg him to take them to the basilica, where they could claim the medieval right of asylum. Casanova, had he cast a glance in that direction, would have seen the twin ashen columns of the Pillars of Acre and beside them the freckled porphyry dish, *la pietra del bando*, where traitors' heads were displayed for three days and three nights. More likely he veered left without a second thought, passing the columns of St Mark and St Theodore, towards the quay where fishmongers were laying out their stalls beneath the watchful eyes of the cloaked and capped fishermen, fresh from the Adriatic, and a gaggle of *gondolieri* were making small talk.

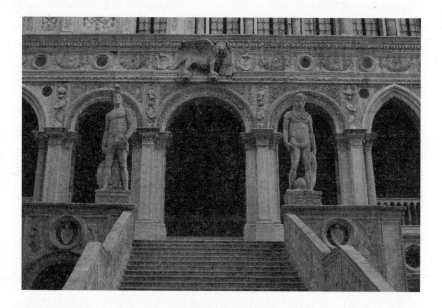

The stairs exiting the Ducal Palace that Casanova ran down on the final stretch towards freedom and exile.

He loudly cried out for a boat to Fusina, then halfway across the lagoon ordered them to take him to Mestre instead. There all was almost lost when Casanova was recognised by one of the Inquisition's spies while waiting for Balbi to finish flirting with a waitress in a coffee-house. They took a coach to Treviso – still within the boundaries of the Venetian state – and then left the town on foot, aiming for the independent Bishopric of Trento. Somewhere in the countryside Casanova gave Balbi the rest of his money, menaced him with his spike, and sent him on his way.

Alone, famished, thirsty and gloriously free, Casanova began his march towards the Alps.

***

In a characteristically ostentatious display of his classical education, Casanova describes himself as possessing *kerdaleophron*. In Homeric poetry, *kerdaleos* is an adjective used to describe the fox as cunning or tricky. The root of it, *kerda*, literally means 'profit' and the heart of the full word as Casanova uses it means something like profit-minded, self-interested, crafty. It is in this sense that Agamemnon hurls it as an insult at Odysseus, the famously sly Greek hero. Casanova's adoption of the word is a fascinating glimpse into how he imagines himself. For, following his departure from Venice in 1756, he did become something of an Odysseus in his wayward travelling existence, albeit an Odysseus without an Ithaca, scheming his way around Europe without end or purpose.

Casanova's peregrinations spanned the better part of three decades and defy easy summary. Travelling under the adopted title of the Chevalier de Seingalt,[53] he roamed freely around every part of the continent, rarely staying in any one place for more than ten months. Zooming out from the thickets of anecdote to consider the larger story he relates, it becomes possible to see Casanova's life in his account as something of a greatest hits tour of Enlightenment Europe. Following his flight from Venice he spent two years in Paris, where, with the aid of his old comrade from the convent, François-Joachim de Bernis, he became fabulously wealthy after organising the nation's first national lottery. In this period he also made the acquaintance of Rousseau, who did not impress him,[54] and the plutocratic dowager Madame d'Urfé, whom he conned with his cabalistic knowledge in order to better finance his extravagant lifestyle. In 1759 de Bernis sent Casanova on a mission to Amsterdam to sell French government bonds to help fund the ongoing Seven Years War. In Amsterdam Casanova ran into an impoverished Teresa Imer, accompanied by their daughter Sophie and her elder son Giuseppe. Imer persuaded Casanova to take Giuseppe back to Paris, where the poor boy soon became inveigled into a plot by Madame d'Urfé to obtain immortality by transferring her soul into the body of a child. Meanwhile, Casanova went on an extended tour of southern Europe, passing through Geneva, where he was thrilled to spend some hours in conversation with Voltaire, before passing leisurely through southern France and thence to Rome and Naples.

Returning to Paris in 1763, he received a summons from London. Teresa Imer had metamorphosed into Teresa Cornelys, the impresaria behind the ultra-fashionable Soho pleasure palace Carlisle House. She was at this stage – and admittedly only for a brief period – the wealthiest self-made woman in London, and she wanted her son back. Casanova crossed the Channel in June 1763 and was soon rooming in St James's, while making inroads into London society. He was a perfect match for Georgian London and records his visits to Vauxhall and Ranelagh, to the *bagnios* and coffee shops of Covent Garden, and to the various playhouses, attending the Italian opera – whose performers had once ranked his mother among their number – and the Drury Lane Theatre, where he saw David Garrick perform. At Carlisle House he caroused with the riotous aristocratic elite, and attending court he met George III and his wife. He discussed etymology with Samuel Johnson, met and refused the charms of the celebrated courtesan Kitty Fisher, and went before the court of the blind judge Sir John Fielding – brother of novelist Henry – who interviewed the suspect Venetian in perfect Italian.[55]

After London he went to Prussia, where he met, and flirted with, Frederick the Great, and then travelled on to Russia where he had several meetings with Catherine the Great. He met Augustus Winckelmann in Rome; he met Benjamin Franklin in Paris. For many of these meetings we have only Casanova's account – Voltaire, for example, barely makes mention of a meeting which takes up many exuberant pages in Casanova's memoir – although others left enthusiastic remembrances of this exotic exile. Not all were impressed. James Boswell met Casanova (whose name he Germanicised as 'Neuhaus') at a Berlin tavern in 1764, and recorded the devastating impression of 'an Italian, [who] wanted to shine as a great philosopher, and accordingly doubted of his existence and of everything else. I thought him a blockhead.'

Along the way there were many dalliances of varying degrees of seriousness and salubrity, though for the reader of Casanova's memoirs the endless sequences of affairs soon cease to beguile and begin instead to bewilder. The governing paradox of Casanova's literary project was that he was the greatest chronicler of a phenomenon that he lacked the self-knowledge to analyse. For even if Casanova failed to articulate it, there was a connection between sex, travel and Enlightenment, and it was forged in the final years of the 1760s, as Casanova skittered from capital to court at ever greater velocity, a ball on a perpetually spinning roulette wheel.

In 1767, Captain Samuel Wallis of the Royal Navy discovered the island of Otaheite, now known as Tahiti, in the South Pacific. It soon emerged that sexual mores on Tahiti were very different from those at home. The crew of Wallis's ship, the *Dolphin*, wondered at the beauty of the indigenous peoples and were taken aback by the forwardness of their women. English bashfulness was quickly overcome, and soon a thriving trade was under way, whereby sailors bought favours from local women using iron nails – something the locals coveted above all else – as currency. Soon the *Dolphin*'s crew were pillaging the ship for iron nails, spikes and rivets with such diligence that the captain feared the craft might disintegrate on open waters – as perfect a metaphor as can be imagined for the capacity of desire to destabilise complex structures. Such behaviour might only be expected from sailors, but the official Navy historian sat in judgement of Tahitian mores. 'Chastity does not seem to be considered as a virtue among them,' he wrote,[56] a judgement confirmed later that year when French captain Louis-Antoine de Bougainville arrived on the island. He observed many of the same habits that had shocked the English with a more gracious Gallic eye. 'These people breathe only rest and sensual pleasures,' he wrote, 'Venus is the goddess they worship . . . everything [in Tahiti] inspires sensual pleasure. And so I have named it New Cythera.'[57]

The association of Tahiti with Venus was confirmed in sentiment and in nomenclature in 1769, when Captain Cook arrived on the island. Cook was charged with conveying botanist and astronomer Joseph Banks of the Royal Society to Tahiti to document the Transit of Venus. Banks and Cook built their observatory on the shore and enclosed it in a palisade they named Fort Venus. When not engaged in astronomical work, Banks explored the island and marvelled at its sexual freedoms. 'Love is the Chief Occupation, the favourite, nay almost the Sole Luxury of the inhabitants,' he recorded in his journal, 'both the bodies and souls of the women are modeled into the utmost perfection for that soft science. Idleness, the father of Love, reigns here in almost unmolested ease.' Banks described and participated in 'Arreoy', gatherings of unmarried Tahitian men and women which involved wrestling, dancing and sexual orgies.[58]

News of an island in the distant Pacific whose inhabitants knew of no Christian God, seemingly lived in social peace amid a natural cornucopia, and enjoyed 'free liberty in love', exploded like fireworks in the imaginations of late-Enlightenment Europeans.[59] Explorations at the frontiers of the known world had seemingly endorsed the philosophical belief in the naturalness of desires and the healthiness of their free expression. Satirists, *philosophes* and polite conversationalists across the continent were soon writing and talking about Tahiti and the lessons it might hold for Europe. The most thorough treatment of the subject came from Denis Diderot, who in 1772 wrote 'Supplement au Voyage de Bougainville', an imagined dialogue between a Tahitian and a European which he used as a vehicle for a wide-ranging critique of French society and French colonial practices. One area among many where Diderot believed Europeans could learn from Tahitians was in matters of sexual morality. Speaking through his imagined Tahitian (named Orou), Diderot asserted that 'courtship exists in nature' and that the constraints on sexuality were unnatural contrivances: 'There's nothing natural in modesty; all the rest is convention. . . . The Tahitian would say to us,' Diderot continues, '"Why do you hide your body? What are you ashamed of? Is it wrong to submit to the most noble impulse of nature? Man, show yourself openly if you are attractive. Woman, if this man pleases you, receive him with candour."'

In a final flourish, Diderot declares that 'nowhere but in Tahiti will you find the condition of man a happy one, nor is it elsewhere even tolerable, apart from in a little backwater of Europe'. That place, another island in a smaller sea, was Venice, where 'morals are less artificial, and vices and virtues are less chimerical, than anywhere else'.[60]

Casanova's own sexual explorations were less replete with philosophical possibility. A typical encounter was the kind of glancing blow recorded in Paris. In pursuit of Camille, an actress, he shared a carriage with her and her occasional lover the Count de la Tour d'Auvergne. Squeezed in a two-seat trap, Camille sat on the Count's lap. In the darkness Casanova made the familiar move:

Full of desire, I determine to seize the opportunity, and, wasting no time, for the coachman was driving fast, I take her hand, squeeze it, she squeezes mine, I gratefully raise it to my lips, covering it with silent kisses, and, impatient to convince her of my ardour, I proceed as my state of bliss demands that I do; but just at the moment of crisis I hear La Tour d'Auvergne saying:

'I am obliged to you, my dear friend, for a piece of your country's politeness of which I thought I was no longer worthy; I hope
it is not a mistake.'[61]

Extracting meaning from such episodes is a mystifying endeavour,
made harder by the great number of them Casanova includes in
his memoirs and the comparative paucity of introspection with
which they are recounted. On this point, Byron once again offers
a useful approach. A man who knew as much as Casanova about
sex, transport and the intersection of the two, Byron also had a
more fully developed philosophy about the significance of such
experiences. Writing from Venice to Lord Kinnaird in London,
apropos of *Don Juan*, whose third canto he was then deep into,
Byron mounted a brilliant pre-emptive defence of his work:

> it may be bawdy – but is it not good English? It may be profligate
> – but is it not *life*, is it not *the thing*? – Could any man have written
> it – who has not lived in the world? – and tooled in a post-chaise?
> in a hackney coach? in a gondola? against a wall? in a court carriage?
> in a vis-à-vis? – on a table? – and under it?[62]

Intellectual capabilities aside, the two men had much in common.
The hunger for sensual variety described by Byron is found on
every page of Casanova's memoir, as is a corresponding, if implicit,
fatigue. Both men were exiles – Casanova from Venice, Byron to
Venice – and in exile both adopted a shallow cosmopolitan posture
that belied homesickness and wounded patriotism.[63] Sensualists
and travellers, rootless men in rootless relationships – between
the two we can scry the essential features of the heroic seducer:
a strenuous neophilia, a listless promiscuity and a naive cosmopolitanism.

***

On the evening of 29 October 1787, Casanova could be found in a box at the Nostitz Theatre in Prague waiting for an opera to begin. At sixty-two, he was a stiff old man in a short brown wig, dressed in fine if slightly faded clothes, looking on with well-practised hauteur at the tumult in the auditorium beneath him. For several hours crowds had been gathering before the theatre, eager to secure a ticket and a seat. The crush of carriages had created a mire of churned mud which fashionable ladies and their attendants had been obliged to pick their way through. Inside was chaos: the stalls and the parterre were packed; the gallery was so overwhelmed that spectators clung to the metal rods connecting the rafters, triggering concerns that the crush might collapse the roof. Adrift in the melee were vendors selling beer, sausages and lemonade. Shortly before seven the conductor entered the pit and received a thunderous reception, the crowd rising to its feet three times to show their appreciation. At last the uproar dissipated, the orchestra struck up, and the curtain lifted on the opening night of *Il Dissoluto punito, ossia il Don Giovanni* by Wolfgang Amadeus Mozart.

The tale of Don Juan had first been committed to paper in the early seventeenth century by a Spanish monk named Gabriel Tellez, who under the pen name Tirso di Molina wrote *El Burlador de Sevilla y Convidado de Piedra*. It was an instant hit and had become something of a dramatic and literary standard, reworked and reim-agined by authors and playwrights across the continent. The plot adhered to a norm: Don Juan Tenorio is a ruthless and cynical womaniser who at the beginning of the play seduces the beautiful Ana and then kills her upstanding father. Much of the action of the play consists of Don Juan escaping justice for his various crimes while seeking to corrupt an assortment of peasant girls and noble women. In the final scenes he encounters the shade of the man he killed and insouciantly invites him to dine that evening. The vengeful ghost accepts the offer, and once dinner has been served insists on returning the invitation by dragging Don Juan down into hell. In its various tellings, the tale of Don Juan was always meant to entertain, but it also contained a strong religious warning. Don Juan's crime is to make a mockery of the sacrament of marriage, a mortal sin for which he must pay with his life.

In the hands of Mozart and his librettist Lorenzo Da Ponte, the play took on a very different character. The basic plot structure survived but the moral message was overthrown. Don Giovanni struts across the stage not as a villain but an embodiment of liberty and libertinism. Donna Elvira is not a seduced maiden but a jilt jilted. We laugh at the uxorious Masetto and wonder at the true desires of his fiancée Zerlina. *Don Giovanni* shuns moralising in favour of a full-throated celebration of Casanova's world of leisure, travel and seduction. This was a milieu where sexual adventure was encouraged, and so it is only fitting that the orchestra approaches an ecstatic pitch as Don Giovanni's faithful servant Leporello recounts the conquests of his master:

> *Madamina, il catalogo è questo*
> *delle belle, che amò il padron mio;*
> *un catalogo egli è, che ho fatt'io.*
> *Osservate, leggete con me.*
> *In Italia seicento e quaranta,*
> *in Almagna duecento e trentuna,*
> *cento in Francia, in Turchia novantuna,*
> *ma in Ispagna son già mille e tre!*[64]

If Casanova was jealous of the Don's prodigality, he can only have approved of his justification for his liberal loving ways. 'I do it because I love them,' Don Giovanni explains to Leporello. 'Who is faithful to one is cruel to the others. I am a man whose heart is so large that I love all of them.'

Since the early nineteenth century certain people have claimed that it was no coincidence that Casanova was present at the first performance of an opera which, more than any other work of art, has come to represent one half of how Western culture has thought about seduction. It has been alleged that Casanova was not simply a passive onlooker in the theatre but a librettist admiring his work. The notion that Giacomo Casanova, semi-mythical seducer, had a hand in the composition of Mozart's *Don Giovanni* is so enormously perfect that it exerts a kind of gravitational pull on the imagination. The facts are more mundane, though nonetheless suggestive. Mozart's librettist for *Don Giovanni* was Lorenzo Da Ponte, a Venetian who had befriended Casanova during the latter's ill-fated return to Venice in the late 1770s. In his memoirs, Da Ponte speaks very highly of Casanova and specifically praises his writing abilities. In the winter of 1787 Da Ponte was working furiously on three separate librettos: *Don Giovanni* for Mozart, *Axur* for Antonio Salieri, and *Abore Di Diana* for Vicente Martín. He arrived in Prague from Vienna in time for the first rehearsals of *Don Giovanni* in early October, but was summoned back to Vienna to help Salieri rehearse for *Axur*, which was to be performed before Emperor Joseph II. Da Ponte's departure threw the preparations for *Don Giovanni* into well-documented chaos, culminating in the enraged theatre manager locking Mozart in his room to complete the opera. The theory goes that Da Ponte, who earlier in the year had run into his old friend while strolling around Vienna with Salieri, now summoned Casanova to Prague to help Mozart complete the libretto after he was obliged to return to Vienna to work on *Axur*.

The idea that Casanova could be drafted in to write a libretto at such short notice is not completely incredible. He was, after all, a published playwright, an accomplished violinist, and a man who through family, friendship and personal enthusiasm knew a great deal about the stage. Furthermore, the story of Don Juan would not have been new to him. Carlo Goldoni, who had written parts for his mother, had produced his own adaptation of the legend in 1736. More recently, librettist Giovanni Bertati's *Don Giovanni Tenorio, o sia Il Convitato di Pietra* had debuted at the Teatro San Moisè in Venice in February 1787 before moving on to Vienna. Additionally, Casanova knew the impresario at the Nostitz, Pasquale Bondini, as well as some of the troupe. The smoking gun is a few sheets of a draft libretto in Casanova's hand discovered in the 1920s. These seemed to show that Casanova had been tasked with assisting Mozart complete the libretto in the frantic final days before the 29 October debut. It is now conjectured that Casanova helped write parts of the second act, specifically an aria by Leporello in which he promises to reveal the crimes of his master Don Giovanni.[65] If true, there is a certain poignancy that Casanova – son of an actress, most eager of social climbers – should have written the part of a miserable manservant and not that of the Don.[66]

The true extent of Casanova's collaboration on *Don Giovanni* can never be known, nor can we know what thoughts were his when he watched his fictional counterpart descend into hell by way of the trapdoor of the Nostitz stage. Still fifteen years from his death in Castle Dux in 1797, perhaps he saw in Don Giovanni's end an intimation of his own, although his would be attended by neither crowds nor recognition. Maybe he glimpsed in it an allegory for the state of his beloved Europe – aristocratic, cosmopolitan, carefree, somewhat cruel – as it stumbled garrulously towards the French Revolution and the democratising impulses it unleashed. Venice might have come to mind, his impossible homeland sinking in splendour into the glittering lagoon. Most likely, however, this was but one more night's entertainment, and he thought of nothing.

3

AN UNSENTIMENTAL
EDUCATION

Shortly after Casanova arrived in Paris following his escape from the *Piombi*, a man named Damiens tried to kill Louis XV at Versailles. He barely managed to scratch the king but faced the full force of the law nonetheless. The punishment for the attempt on the king's life was a brutal death by torture, held in a public square.

On the morning of Damiens' death, Casanova and a mixed party of men and women went by carriage to the Place de Grève to watch the execution from an apartment window overlooking the scaffold. Space at the window was limited, so the three women stood in a row, their elbows on the windowsill, their feet on a little ledge. The men stood behind them, their feet sharing the same ledge, craning their heads over the women's for a glimpse of the bloody spectacle.

Damiens' death was an extensive, baroque affair. Bound to a bier at the scaffold, his body was pierced all over with red-hot pincers and then covered liberally with a boiling mixture of oil, resin, wax and molten lead. The hand which held the knife that cut the king was burned with sulphur. His body was to be torn apart by horses, one animal attached to each limb by a length of rope. This took so long to accomplish that eventually the executioners had to slash his joints and tendons with a blade; it worked, and the horses were finally able to detach his arms and legs from his body. The trunk and head was then thrown onto a fire. According to some eyewitnesses the jaw could still be seen moving amid the flames.[1]

Casanova watched some four hours of this butchery. At some point the sight of Damiens' agonies was so appalling that he averted his eyes in revulsion. Dropping his gaze, he noticed that the pair of friends to his side were seemingly unaffected by the execution playing out in front of them:

Tiretta kept Madame XXX so strangely occupied during the whole execution that it may have been only on his account that she never dared to stir or look around.

Being behind her and very close to her, he had raised her dress so as not to step on it, and that was all very well. But later, looking toward them, I saw that he had raised it a little too high; . . . I heard the rustling of the dress for two whole hours, and finding the whole thing most amusing I never swerved from the resolve I had taken. I admired Tiretta's appetite even more than his boldness, for in that respect I had often been as daring as he.

When at the end of the execution I saw Madame XXX straighten up, I turned too. I saw my friend as lively, fresh, and calm as if nothing had happened.[2]

By the time Casanova wrote these words, the Bourbon regime bequeathed by Louis XV to his son Louis XVI had been swept away by the French Revolution. The sensual world of Europe's courts and palaces was being replaced by an austere modernity with its own code of conduct and morality. The new world sat in harsh judgement on the sexual mores of the old. Casanova's account of fashionable aristocrats fornicating at the public quartering of a failed regicide encapsulated the connection drawn by many between tyranny and debauchery. In the revolutionary era of the

1790s, sexual questions would become political questions, while political rhetoric and iconography would be saturated with sexual imagery and gendered language. The sexual politics of the French Revolution would be parsed best by a writer who stood at another Parisian window in 1793 with a prospect on Louis XVI's voyage to face revolutionary justice. Mary Wollstonecraft's life and work would be a study of both the revolutionary and the reactionary potential of sex and seduction.

***

Wollstonecraft's long road to that window in Paris had begun in London's Essex hinterland, where she was born in April 1759, the second of seven children of Edward and Elizabeth Wollstonecraft. Her father had started out with a substantial fortune which he frittered away in pursuit of chimerical agricultural schemes that never returned the expected profits. The background to Wollstonecraft's childhood was her family's gradual descent from lower-upper-middle-class respectability to the most precarious of genteel poverties, a downwards social trajectory played out against ever-changing backdrops – London, the East Riding, London, south Wales, London – as her father dragged his family across the country on the hunt for his latest doomed scheme.

Edward had a furious temper and a taste for alcohol which combined in acts of attempted and realised violence against his wife. Some of Wollstonecraft's earliest memories were of trying to prevent this violence, going so far as to sleep across the boundary of her mother's door when she feared her father might come home drunk that night. These experiences, later reinforced by a Protestant taste for temperance in all things, gave her a lifelong appreciation for the evils of alcohol and a keen eye for the details of male slovenliness.[3] Her father's boorishness was made all the more grotesque by the social sanction he was granted (through no earned merit) as a man, a husband and a patriarch. The generational recurrence of this injustice was symbolised by the special privileges ladled out to Wollstonecraft's brothers, while the daughters were left largely to fend for themselves.

Denied any systematic education, Mary sought out her own, and from the earliest age showed an appetite for reading, writing, and the exchange of ideas and sentiments. Some of her earliest surviving letters – written when she was just fourteen – are poignant examples of this hunger for intellectual engagement. They also point towards her abiding interests, which she would carry with her from adolescence to adulthood. 'I have a heart that scorns disguise,' she wrote to her first friend, Jane Arden, 'and a countenance which will not dissemble: – I have formed romantic notions – I have been once disappointed: – I think if I am a second time I shall want only some infidelity in a love affair, to qualify me for an old maid.'[4]

These were prophetic words. Wollstonecraft's life was walked on a tightrope kept taut by the tension between her rational self and her passionate self, between the need for independence and intellectual achievement and her hunger for emotional attachments and dread of loneliness.

Wollstonecraft was a loyal sister and a constructive meddler in her siblings' lives, but the self-evident failure of the Wollstonecraft family unit made it clear to her that relationships born of mutual affection arrived at by rational decision-making were preferable to those imposed and sustained by gothic customs. Her first great experiment in new modes of social living was conducted in concert with Fanny Blood, whom she met in the mid-1770s while living in the village of Hoxton, on the outskirts of London. Hoxton was home to a large dissenting community, observant Protestants who worshipped outside the established Church of England and were at the forefront of commercial enterprise, progressive reform and political activism. The dissenting tradition emphasised personal improvement through formal education and private studies, and encouraged the thorough interrogation of established norms across every dimension of human experience. It was through connections made in Hoxton that Wollstonecraft was introduced to Blood, and the two were soon inseparable, Wollstonecraft travelling from Hoxton to her friend's home in Newington Butts, south of the Thames, whenever the opportunity afforded.

Wollstonecraft, who always wanted more from her relationships, claimed that 'to live with this friend is the height of my ambition', but life intervened. Her father moved them briefly to Laugharne in south Wales; less than a year later they were back in London, this time in Walworth, closer to the Bloods, but financial exigencies and the fierce need to flee her dysfunctional family home led Wollstonecraft, now nineteen, to take up a job as the companion to an elderly lady, based first in fashionable Bath and then in Windsor. She found the work both demeaning and stultifying, but it marked a necessary first foray into the outside world, and whenever she could she returned to London to spend time with Fanny Blood.

Near the end of 1781, Wollstonecraft's mother fell terminally ill, and Mary quit her work as a companion to tend to her through her long final sickness. Her death in April 1782 liberated her daughter to pursue a daring experiment in economic independence and female collaboration.

In February 1784 Wollstonecraft declared her intention to set up a girls' school. She raised money for the venture from within the dissenting community, recruited her sisters Eliza and Everina to staff it alongside Fanny Blood, and, after a false start in Hoxton, established their school in Newington Green. The school was on a perilous financial footing from the outset and remained so throughout its near three-year existence. For Wollstonecraft, however, whose twin needs were independence and usefulness, it provided a vital function.[5] It also brought her into close contact with the community of dissenters, radicals and writers who made their home in the area. She began attending the lectures and sermons of Dr Richard Price, a polymath, a quasi-Unitarian minister, and a prolific writer of tracts calling for reform. She befriended Mrs Burgh, the widow of progressive politician and activist James Burgh, author of the influential educational text, *Thoughts on Education* (1747). She met and bonded with the Reverend John Hewlett, an aspiring writer whose links with publishers and literary taste-makers in Paternoster Row would later serve Wollstonecraft well. Shortly before his death in the winter of 1784, someone in this milieu took her to have tea with an ailing Samuel Johnson.

Wollstonecraft's integration into this world was disrupted by her need to tend to Fanny Blood. In January 1785, Blood, who was suffering from consumption, travelled to Lisbon for treatment with her fiancé, Hugh Skeys. Without Blood, Mary's interest in the school waned; when she learned her friend was both pregnant and still persistently consumptive she decided her place was at her side. In a move she certainly knew would result in the school's closure, she borrowed money from Mrs Burgh and in November 1785 embarked for Lisbon.

These were tense, fretful times. Wollstonecraft was abandoning her community, her school and her sisters. She was borrowing money to attend to a quixotic sentimental mission. For all this, she was young and starting on an overseas adventure. 'When going to Lisbon,' she would later write, 'the elasticity of my mind was sufficient to ward off weariness, and my imagination still could dip her brush in the rainbow of fancy, and sketch futurity in glowing colours.' Not that she saw many signs for future hope upon arrival in Lisbon. She detested the sclerotic Catholic culture, disdaining Portugal as 'the most savage part of Europe, where superstition still reigns'. Characteristically, she saw the retrograde state of the nation reflected in its convents, places where women were imprisoned, deluded by religion and denied an education, where the 'rust of the mind' would accrue, layer by layer, never to be 'rubbed off by sensible conversation, or new-born affections of the heart'. Her unfavourable impressions were doubtless enhanced by the presence of personal tragedy. Wollstonecraft arrived in Lisbon as Fanny went into labour. Neither mother nor son survived, and after an illicit midnight burial in a Protestant graveyard, Mary returned to London.

The year that followed was one of depression and financial misery. The school was shuttered and Mary was harried by creditors. Out of this barren period, however, was born literary opportunity. Encouraged by Mrs Burgh and with the generous use of Reverend Hewlett's literary connections, Wollstonecraft won a princely ten-guinea advance from the illustrious liberal publisher Joseph Johnson for a commission to write a short book on education. The result was *Thoughts on the Education of Daughters*, published in early 1787. As an educational book by a woman for women, *Thoughts* was progressive by default. The substance of Wollstonecraft's argument, however, hinted at a germinating radical thesis that linked reason and passion, education and sex, independence and submission. At the heart of the book was a sustained critique of a model of female education that encouraged the development of a passing knowledge of peripheral subjects like music, art and geography and a dedication to wholly inutile interests such as cards, fashion and saccharine literature. What was missing from this education was the cultivation of reason. This was a fatal absence, Wollstonecraft wrote, because 'reason must often be called in to fill up the vacuums of life; but too many of our sex suffer theirs to lie dormant'. In contemporary society, little thought was given to that vacuum, as girls were expected to marry and then busy themselves with children and house-keeping. However, in the gap between her maturity and her marriage, a girl without an education was 'in great danger of being seduced', as there were plenty of men ready 'to take advantage of the artless tenderness of a woman who loves' but loves without logic.

It was not that Wollstonecraft disdained emotion, it was that she feared its power if left unchecked by the countervailing imperatives of reason. A woman who could not divine the difference between a sincere suitor and a cynical libertine faced ruin. The application of reason would filter out the rakes and allow for a more impassioned commitment to a good partner. 'We should always try to fix in our minds the rational grounds we have for loving a person,' she counselled.

Her book was a moderate success and, combined with her previous educational venture in Newington Green, established her as something of a pedagogue. This reputation, in conjunction with persistent financial need, qualified her for a job as governess to the daughters of Robert King, Viscount Kingsborough, the largest Protestant landowner in Ireland.[6] Lord and Lady Kingsborough were, by the standards of their class, progressive in their attitudes and attentive to the needs of their impoverished Catholic tenants. By the summer of 1787, when Mary accepted a position in their household at Mitchelstown, County Cork, they had produced close to a dozen children together, a fecundity which belied the strength of their marriage. A few years earlier, their household had been roiled by scandal when it was alleged that Lord Kingsborough's agricultural adviser, the famed agronomist (and later accidental chronicler of the French Revolution) Arthur Young, was courting Lady Kingsborough over the chessboard after dinner while the children's governess, Mrs Crosby, was carrying on an adulterous relationship with the Viscount himself.[7]

Their new governess was well placed to detect whatever traces of conjugal strife might have lingered when she arrived in the household after a painless crossing in October. For after a period of initial excitement, Wollstonecraft lapsed into a characteristic funk, and by the time she crossed the threshold of the fairytale her to one of the most important intellectual relationships of her career. By March 1788, the family had moved to Dublin and in her letters she was telling Everina that she had moved on to Rousseau's *Émile*. That Wollstonecraft responded positively to this initial encounter with Rousseau is noteworthy, as a general contempt for his *oeuvre* permeates her later writings: there is scarcely a work of hers that does not contain a snipe at the then revered Frenchman. Wollstonecraft mocked his 'fanciful state of nature', and abhorred his views on women's education and his biological determinism as 'wild chimeras'.[10] However contentious Rousseau's substance, his style was immensely influential on his contemporaries, even those who disagreed with him on everything else. Like Byron after him, Rousseau pioneered a certain personal aesthetic – independent, authentic, unabashedly emotional – that cast a spell on a generation of Europeans, including Wollstonecraft. I 'love his paradoxes,' she wrote to her sister, 'he was a strange inconsistent unhappy clever creature – yet he possessed an uncommon portion of sensibility and penetration.'[11] Her antipathy towards Lady Kingsborough and her admiration for Rousseau were united by a sense of her own burgeoning sensibility, a treasured aspect of her own personality and one which she thought went squandered in her loveless existence. In the same letter that she praised *Émile*, she lamented of herself that it was 'a sad pity that so sweet a flower should waste its sweetness on the *Desart* air, or that the Grave should receive its *untouched* charms'. She signed off, 'Yours an Old Maid'.[12]

During her time with the family, Wollstonecraft remained in contact with Joseph Johnson in London and worked on the manuscript of *Mary, A Fiction*. It was evident to her, however, that her literary ambitions were not about to blossom in the service of the Kingsboroughs, and her conviction that her intellectual potential as well as her sexual potential was going to waste made her an unhappy presence in the family. Her standing with Lady Kingsborough steadily diminished. When, in the summer of 1788, the family and their entourage went to England as part of a leisurely tour to France, Wollstonecraft was released from her service at Bristol after less than a year in the role. It was a setback and an opportunity. Aged twenty-eight, she now had no excuse not to pursue her vocation as a writer. Throwing herself on Johnson's generosity, she roomed in his home for several weeks until he had found her suitable, if very humble, lodgings on George Street, on the south side of Blackfriars Bridge.

Only twenty years before, the patch of south London she now called home had been open countryside, meadows that lay between Lambeth and Southwark. The area had been transformed with the construction of the original Blackfriars Bridge in 1769, and in a relatively short period of time had become a densely built, densely inhabited working-class neighbourhood. Poverty and precarity were visible and audible from George Street. The sounds of an organ grinder made their way into her letters, and the numberless beggars and crowds of unemployed mechanics invaded her political writings and her political consciousness.

In its short history, the neighbourhood had acquired a rough and ready reputation as the epicentre of the anti-Catholic Gordon Riots in 1780. It was also home to a significant number of philanthropic institutions, including two whose proximity to Wollstonecraft's new home must have resonated with her. The Asylum for Female Orphans in Lambeth, established in 1758 by Sir John Fielding, was little better than a workhouse; the treatment of its inmates appalled William Blake, who lived on the same street. A few streets south, down Great Surrey Street, was the Magdalen Hospital, the rescue house for seduced girls and women that doubled as a site of prurient entertainment for well-off Londoners; their carriages would have rattled past her window each Sunday.[13] For her part, Wollstonecraft was living in simple fashion. She had one servant and a very limited wardrobe. She scarcely ate meat and spent nothing on entertainments. A rather condescending account of her physical appearance that attests to her asceticism survives from this period: 'Her usual dress being a habit of coarse cloth, such as is now worn by milk-women, black worsted stockings, and a beaver hat, with her hair hanging lank about her shoulders.'[14] More generous chroniclers described a hale, passionate young woman with a thick mass of russet hair, and recognised her careless dress as part of her radical aesthetic. More precious than any of this was her arrival at a state approximating self-sufficiency. 'I must be independent,' she wrote to Everina from her desk at George Street, 'I am not without hope – And freedom, even uncertain freedom – is dear. . . . You know that I am not born to tread in the beaten track – and the peculiar bent of my nature pushes me on.'

Johnson published *Mary, A Fiction* to little fanfare in 1788 and was soon keeping her busy with translation work. She also became a prodigious reviewer for the *Analytical Review*, Johnson's monthly periodical with a radical bent. Over the next four years she would contribute hundreds of pieces, mostly short and pungent, on topics as diverse as boxing, bridge design and French history.[15] She enjoyed the activity and the place it secured her in literary circles, but the possibility of becoming little more than a Grub Street hack loomed large. As her husband would later note, 'this sort of miscel-laneous literary employment, seems, for the time at least, rather to damp and contract, than to enlarge and invigorate, the genius'. The writer whose work only serves the 'mere mercantile purpose of the day' risked being touched by 'the torpedo of mediocrity'.[16]

Wollstonecraft needed a larger canvas to work on. In the summer of 1789 a revolution in France provided one.

***

For much of 1789, the British establishment was cautiously opti-mistic about political developments across the Channel. The Prime Minister, William Pitt the Younger, initially greeted the revolution as an opportunity for 'good order and good government', continuing that 'France would stand forward as one of the most brilliant Powers in Europe; she would enjoy just that kind of liberty which I venerate.' Many statesmen agreed, choosing to draw parallels between events in France and those in England during the Glorious Revolution.[17] This sentiment held through the fall of the Bastille and a turbulent summer of riots, conspiracies and rural anarchy.

The event that led a good proportion of the British elite to oppose the French Revolution was an action by a group of Parisian women that autumn. On 5 October 1789 the fisherwomen of Paris, the famous *poissardes*, heard a rumour that the king's bodyguards were planning some kind of strike against the revolution. A huge crowd of them gathered at the Hôtel de Ville, where they looted weapons and then, dragooning in female bystanders as they went, marched from the city to Versailles. There they demanded a meeting with the king, skirmished with his bodyguard, and finally 'secured' the royal family and brought them back to Paris in triumph the next day.

A contemporary depiction of The Women's March on Versailles in 1789.

For some the Women's March on Versailles (as it came to be known) was one of the first great episodes of female agency in the French Revolution. For others it was a travesty, a subversion of gender roles and political norms. Edmund Burke was very much in the latter group. Burke was a writer and Whig member of Parliament, long admired by artists for his treatise on the sublime and by liberals for his defence of the American revolutionaries. It was well known that Burke was writing a response to events in France and his essay was much anticipated by liberals, who believed he would affirm the actions of French revolutionaries in a like manner to his warm support for those in America. This was not to be. Burke had been repelled by the anarchy he saw in France, which for him was encapsulated in the chaotic events of 5–6 October 1789. Similarly he was aghast at the gushing reaction to the revolution in English liberal and radical circles, whom he regarded as abandoning the finest traditions of the English constitution.

Burke's twin criticisms met on the occasion of a speech given by Dr Richard Price, Mary Wollstonecraft's friend and mentor from Newington Green, at the Old Jewry Meeting-House in London on 4 November 1789. Addressing the London Revolution Society, a political club that commemorated the political triumphs of the Glorious Revolution, Price reflected on the 'imperfect state in which the Revolution left our constitution' before declaring that first the American Revolution and now the French Revolution ('both glorious') had given him new hope for the possibilities of political change in England, in Europe, and all over the world. 'I see the ardor for liberty catching and spreading,' he concluded, 'a general amendment beginning in human affairs; the dominion of kings changed for the dominion of laws, and the dominion of priests giving way to the dominion of reason and conscience.'[18]

For Burke, Price's utopian reveries were 'unfounded, dangerous, illegal, and unconstitutional', an affront to tradition, law and civility. What angered him even more was the timing of Price's address.

Exactly a month after the Women's March, when, for Burke at least, all hope for a positive outcome in France was lost, Price had seen fit to praise 'these Theban and Thracian orgies, acted in France and applauded only in the Old Jewry'.[19] Burke went on to attack the march of the *poissardes* in gendered terms, conjuring up the image of 'the royal captives who followed in the train . . . slowly moved along, amidst the horrid yells, and shrilling screams, and frantic dances, and infamous contumelies, and all the unutterable abominations of the furies of hell in the abused shape of the vilest of women'.

The preposterousness of the revolution in France was symbolised by these women who dared to participate in politics. Sexual subversion and political subversion were now joined in a new rhetoric of reaction, one that saw in the politics of the French Revolution a universe where female 'sentiments which beautify and soften private society, are to be dissolved by this new conquering empire of light and reason'. 'The age of chivalry is gone,' Burke declared, 'all homage paid to the sex in general . . . is to be regarded as romance and folly.'[20]

The *Reflections on the Revolution in France* were published on 1 November 1790. Besides her anger at what she perceived as his betrayal of his earlier support for the rights and liberties of the American revolutionaries – which was widely shared in her circle – as well as his unrestrained assault on the benevolent Dr Price, Burke's words, especially as they touched on questions of gender, could have been little better designed to infuriate Wollstonecraft. In a white heat of wrathful inspiration, she took up her pen and within a month had written and had published – by Joseph Johnson, of course – a scathing response to Burke's polemic.

In its sheer vitriol, its naked *ad hominem* style, *A Vindication of the Rights of Men* was like nothing Wollstonecraft had written before or would write afterwards. Her attacks on Burke's person are by turns inventive and hilarious, though somewhat curious given their gendered nature, an interesting choice of rhetorical strategy given that the first edition of the *Vindication* was published anonymously but one that sits uneasily with her own intellectual project of dismantling sexual stereotypes. There are layers of irony to the use by a radical female writer of the shield of anonymity to treat a conservative male political theorist like a swooning girl, mocking his 'infantine sensibility', his 'pampered sensibility', and joking that she feared she might 'derange your nervous system by the bare mention of a metaphysical enquiry'. She was on firmer ground when defending the rights of the *poissardes*, whom she characterised, in the face of Burke's savage contempt, with both dignity and simplicity as 'women who gained a livelihood by selling vegetables or fish, who never had had any advantages of education'.

This stout defence led her argument back on to her favoured subject – the need to edify women through the illuminating powers of reason – where she welcomed the end of the cult of sensibility so lachrymosely lamented by Burke, declaring that it had turned women into 'vain inconsiderate dolls, who ought to be prudent mothers and useful members of society'.

The *Vindication* made Wollstonecraft famous, and its financial success relieved her of some of her financial woes, allowing her to move lodgings to Bedford Square and to buy a new dress. Its publication in December 1790 also marked the moment when English women manned the barriers of political debate. That month, two responses to Burke's *Reflections* were published, both by radical women – Wollstonecraft and Catherine Macaulay Graham. It was also the occasion for the publication of the first volume of Helen Maria Williams's eyewitness account of the French Revolution, *Letters Written in France*, in which she welcomed events in Paris as 'the triumph of human kind'. The presence of so many women in the political arena drew predictable scorn from conservatives, who mocked them as the 'Amazon Allies' of the French revolutionaries and as 'our *poissardes*' – some of the first outings of disdainful gendered language that would soon become widespread[21] – but it announced the arrival of women at the radical table. Quite literally in Wollstonecraft's case. In November 1791 she was invited to attend a dinner at Johnson's in honour of Thomas Paine, author of *Common Sense*, who was then in the midst of writing another reaction to Burke, *The Rights of Man*. Also present was Wollstonecraft's future husband, the radical philosopher William Godwin. Paine ate his food in silence as Godwin and Wollstonecraft sparred over subjects as various and divisive as 'monarchy, Tooke, Johnson, Voltaire, pursuits and religion'.[22] Wollstonecraft had found her political voice and would never again be silenced.

For all the attention it brought her, Wollstonecraft had misgivings about the substantiveness of her reply to Burke. She had written it too quickly and had made half-hearted attempts to stop its publication. Success mollified her, but the desire to offer the world a more complete and more considered declaration of her beliefs remained. Once again it would be events in France that moved her to take up her pen. Throughout the summer of 1791, the French National Assembly had been finalising the wording of the new constitution that would turn the country into a British-style constitutional monarchy influenced by the American model of the division of powers. This was the end of a two-year process of barter, negotiation and crisis.

French women had been closely following the framing of the new constitution. From the first days of the revolution women had been political agents, participating in protests, submitting petitions, and writing works of political theory and political journalism. Their demands were consistent. They wanted a resolution to the perennial shortages of basic goods (possibly accompanied by some kind of organised system of welfare), a programme of national education that would be open to women as well as men, and a reform of divorce laws. Women met to discuss these matters in political clubs like the Cercle Social, the Société fraternelle, the

Cordeliers Club and, later, in the Society of Revolutionary Republican Women. The more radical among them identified with the rough-and-ready street activists of the Parisian *sections*, the more genteel were allied with the Girondin faction within the National Assembly. Whatever their allegiance, politically engaged women had a stake in the outcome of the wrangling over the constitution and tried to influence the debates as far as they could. In the summer of 1791, as individuals and as part of clubs and delegations, women let the Assembly know what mattered to them. In one such address, Etta Palm called for marital reform and educational opportunities in language that chimed with many of Wollstonecraft's own thoughts on the matter. 'Conjugal authority should be only the consequence of the social pact,' Palm said; that pact ought to be a legal rather than a spiritual one, and so the law 'must give equal protection and maintain a perpetual balance between the two married people'. The protection of women's rights, she argued, was inseparable from the larger cause of French liberty:

> Abuse of liberty is a natural consequence of the oppressive regime of the indissolubility of marriage and of the dull and enervated education of the cloisters, haunts of ignorance and fanaticism which you destroyed in your wisdom. You will complete your work by giving girls a moral education equal to that of their brothers; for education is for the soul what watering is for plants; it makes them fertile, causes it to bloom, fortifies it, and carries the germ productive of virtue and talents to a perfect maturity.[23]

The constitution that was passed in September was silent about these concerns. The suffrage provisions assigned women the role of 'passive citizens', unable to vote. When Talleyrand submitted a report on education to the Assembly, he couched his argument for the separate treatment of men and women in the educational system in familiar Rousseauvian terms. Women 'ought not to aspire to exercise rights and political functions', he stated. 'One must seek their best interest in the will of nature.'[24] There was no move to institute divorce laws.

The betrayal of French women's political aspirations produced one of the first great feminist manifestos of the 1790s. Olympe de Gouges was an actress and political activist associated with the Girondins. Shortly after the ratification of the constitution she published her *Declaration of the Rights of Woman*, a blistering document that echoed the emancipatory proclamations of the American revolutionaries. Her pamphlet, 'a solemn declaration of the natural, inalienable, and sacred rights of woman', called for women to have the same rights and responsibilities as men. Like Etta Palm and Mary Wollstonecraft, she saw sex and education as being intimately linked, the central axis on which the condition of women turned. 'Woman, wake up,' she wrote, 'the tocsin of reason is being heard throughout the whole universe; discover your rights':

> Under the Old Regime, all was vicious, all was guilty . . . Reason finds other examples that are even more touching. A young, inexperienced woman, seduced by a man whom she loves, will abandon her parents to follow him; the ingrate will leave her after a few years, and the older she has become with him, the more inhuman is his inconstancy; if she has children, he will likewise abandon them. . . . Marriage is the tomb of trust and love . . . the way can be prepared through national education, the restoration of morals, and conjugal conventions.[25]

The French context is the key to understanding much of Wollstonecraft's thinking as she began work on her most famous book, *A Vindication of the Rights of Woman*. Written in the winter of 1791 and published in the new year, her second *Vindication* was framed as a response to events in France just as her first was framed as a response to Edmund Burke. This second, more substantial work was dedicated to Talleyrand, whom she met in London between the publication of the first and second editions of the *Vindication* (entertaining him at her flat, she served the famously sybaritic aristocrat wine in teacups), with the intention of dissuading him of the views on education that he had expressed to the National Assembly in his *Rapport sur l'instruction publique.*[26] What began over a debate concerning French education policy became a rich, idiosyncratic, and at times digressive text that resists easy classification. The core of her book was on the relationship between education and sex, the advancement of women and the concomitant advancement of humanity. 'Contending for the rights of women,' she wrote, 'my main argument is built on this simple principle, that if she be not prepared by education to become the companion of man, she will stop the progress of knowledge.'[27]

One of the main intellectual obstacles Wollstonecraft had to surmount in pursuit of this argument was the prevalence of physiological beliefs that women, by virtue of their biology, simply could not be educated to the same level as men. Consequently, some of her heaviest rhetorical salvoes were reserved for this kind of crude biological chauvinism and the men who expounded it:

> I will allow that bodily strength seems to give man a natural superiority over woman, and this is the only solid basis on which the superiority of the sex can be built. But I still insist, that not only the virtue, but the KNOWLEDGE of the two sexes should be the same in nature, if not in degree, and that women, considered not only as moral, but rational creatures, ought to endeavour to acquire human virtues (or perfections) by the SAME means as men, instead of being educated like a fanciful kind of HALF being, one of Rousseau's wild chimeras.[28]

However much she may have wished to, Wollstonecraft did not make the dismantling of essentialist views on sexual difference the cornerstone of her debate. The matter was of vital importance, but debating pseudo-science with pseudo-scientists was as sterile a pastime as it was ineffective. Wollstonecraft's watchword was usefulness, and the testimony of her own life experience was that women were best served by attaining an education and, through that, independence. As a result, large parts of the *Vindication* deal with the importance of education, pursued under 'the sober steady eye of reason'. She contrasts this continually with the facile miseducation of women under the influences of 'novels, music, poetry, and gallantry', which conspire to 'to make women the creatures of sensation'.

Within the prevailing social norms and structures of her day, this 'false system of education' could not but have sexual implications. It was a system, she wrote, that was more 'anxious to make [women] alluring mistresses than rational wives'.[29] This was foolish on two counts. First, ill-educated wives made for unhappy marriages. Female fripperies might be forgiven by a husband in the summer of youth, Wollstonecraft wrote, but 'the woman who has only been taught to please, will soon find that her charms are oblique sun-beams . . . when the summer is past and gone'. A woman with a well-stocked mind would be better placed to handle 'the more important years of life, when reflection takes place of sensation' and intimacy subsides into companionship.[30] More worrying yet were the risks of seduction faced by a population of women raised to be giddy *ingénues*. 'Men of wit and fancy are often rakes,' she wrote, 'and fancy is the food of love. . . . Such men will inspire passion. Half the sex, in its present infantine state, would pine for a Lovelace; a man so witty, so graceful, and so valiant; and can they DESERVE blame for acting according to principles so constantly inculcated?'[31]

To be sure, Wollstonecraft believed that seducers should be held financially responsible for the women they seduced and abandoned.[32] She was sceptical, however, of the sentimental trope that women should devote themselves to the reformation of men. Instead, she believed women were better protected from seduction and better served in life by seeking to elevate themselves through education. 'It is time to effect a revolution in female manners,' she declared, 'time to restore to them their lost dignity, and make them, as a part of the human species, labour by reforming themselves to reform the world.'[33]

***

The reader who comes to Wollstonecraft's writing in search of consistency is bound to be disappointed. Wollstonecraft had a questing mind, ill-disposed to dogma. She freely (though never casually) changed her mind as she accrued more experience of the world. There were, besides, too many conflicting strands to her own biography – her wretched, roving childhood, her precarious ascent to recognition, the rival influences of her dissenting faith and her free-thinking milieu, her intellectual pride and her material poverty – to permit her to perch too complacently on any one philosophical position. Permeating all this was her own keenly felt psychological volatility, the tug-of-war between reason and passion that she had felt since childhood and would tussle with until the end of her life. 'I am a mere animal,' she wrote to Johnson while at a low ebb in the autumn of 1792, 'emotions too often silence the suggestions of reason.'[34] Yet it was this awareness of the simultaneous attractions of contradictory attitudes that made her such a brilliant analyst of the human heart. She once defined love as 'the common passion, in which chance and sensation take place of choice and reason'. Love involved a loss of control; that was part of its thrill and its terror. Conversely, in Wollstonecraft's view, reason could always reassert itself, the logical mind stealing back ground from the tumultuous passions. The ideal state was a kind of equilibrium between the parts that produced neither a lustreless partnership nor a firestorm of uncontrolled ardours. These 'rational desires', as she termed them, held out the best hope for female love, free from subjugation and indignity.

Much of this nuance is lost in *A Vindication of the Rights of Woman*, which stakes out a vision of sexual relations that is far more ascetic and suspicious than Wollstonecraft allowed for in her own private life. Even as she was giving expression to the minatory streak in her sexual politics in the *Vindication*, Wollstonecraft was herself immersed in an experiment associated with the theory and practice of free love.

In the 1790s, notions of free love were neither widespread nor fully fleshed out. There was no key text on the subject, no recognisable groupings, no identifiable movement. The doctrines of free love, so far as they were even known, were treated as subversive and degenerate, the domain of cranks and madmen. Wollstonecraft had links to such a disparate network of sexual radicals. The 1791 edition of her children's book *Original Stories from Real Life* featured engravings by William Blake, another client of Joseph Johnson's. Blake was a radical's radical, and the extensive body of mystical poetry he produced was replete with obscurely phrased paeans to sexual liberation. In *Visions of the Daughters of Albion* (1793) he sang of 'Love! Love! Love! happy happy Love! free as the mountain wind!', a love unfettered by the bonds of law or custom. *The Captive of the Castle of Sennaar* (1798), written by Blake's friend George Cumberland, depicted a perfect community living on the fictional island of Sophis in the lake of Zambree, somewhere in the middle of Africa. Here a system of free love was practised, with no concept of marriage. When the narrator explains the English system of marital relations, the inhabitants recoil and tell him it is a 'brutal commerce' and a 'legal prostitution'. Instead every man and woman should be allowed to 'act freely; subject to no restraint while they *violate not the innocent will of another*'.[35] Such imagined sexual utopias were inspired by the apparently real ones discovered in the South Pacific, especially in present-day Tahiti.

The example of Tahiti inspired poets George Southey and Samuel Coleridge, who in 1793–4 planned to leave for America and set up a model society, the Pantisocracy, which would incorporate elements of free love into its organisation.[36] The Pantisocrats were also influenced by William Godwin, who in 1793 published his seminal work, *Political Justice*. The book's early editions included Godwin's condemnation of the institution of marriage, and a call for reformed sexual relations that was as close as the free love coterie came to having a catechism. In its pages Godwin attacked marriage as a despotic and irrational institution that captured in miniature all the failings of society at large. 'Marriage is law, and the worst of all laws,' he thundered, 'marriage is an affair of property, and the worst of all properties.' He proposed the abolition of marriage, the abolition of surnames, the free mingling of men and women, and the communal parenting of the children that were subsequently produced. In this condition, he believed, 'the intercourse of the sexes will in such a state fall under the same system as any other species of friendship'. Each man would 'assiduously cultivate the intercourse of that woman whose accomplishments shall strike [him] in the most powerful manner', and each woman would do likewise. If several men formed meaningful affections for the same woman, 'this will create no difficulty. . . . We may all enjoy her conversation; and we shall all be wise enough to consider the sensual intercourse as a very trivial object. This, like every other affair in which two persons are concerned, must be regulated in each successive instance by the unforced consent of either party.'[37]

The extent of Wollstonecraft's own participation in these utopian imaginings varied over the course of her life. Under the influence of Dr Price and the Newington Green dissenters she had been something of a prude. At the height of the revolutionary fervour in 1792 and 1793, she was an enthusiastic proponent of sexual liberation. Later, jaded by political and romantic failure, her attitudes would mellow into a qualified commitment to the principle of individual sexual freedom. She was throughout a consistent critic of existing marital arrangements and a convinced enemy of the stigmas that surrounded so-called 'fallen women' – the seduced, the abandoned, the ostracised. She wanted to believe in the possibility of a liberated sexual order, but struggled with the suspicion that it would degenerate into mindless sensualism and the further exploitation of women. It was a model that could only work among people with cultivated sentiments, a thorough education, and moral and psychological temperance. So many elements had to be present to ensure that free love could work that hers was ultimately an elitist vision of sexual liberation, practicable only by a small minority. 'Affection requires a firmer foundation than sympathy,' she wrote, 'and few people have a principle of action sufficiently stable to produce rectitude of feeling.' This is less a criticism of her thought than of her age, which bred radicalism out of what is now considered prosaic. All Wollstonecraft believed was that consenting men and women should be allowed to enter into voluntary sexual relations conducted on terms of equality, dignity and respect, and untroubled by social censure or legal intervention. If this seems banal today, then that speaks to the visionary simplicity of her thought. As Virginia Woolf observed, Wollstonecraft's 'originality has become our commonplace'.[38]

Wollstonecraft's own experiments with free love were almost exactly coextensive with the first phase of the French Revolution, and provided the emotional backdrop against which she encountered developments in France. Much like the revolution itself, her attempts to live out a new vision of sexual relations were a tale of boundless optimism turned to bitterest despair. It was a shared interest and enthusiasm for events in France that first drew her to Henry Fuseli, the brilliant Anglo-Swiss artist whom Wollstonecraft met at Joseph Johnson's dinner table not long after she arrived in London, and whom she began to pursue in earnest in the autumn of 1791 – just as she began composing A Vindication of the Rights of Woman. Wollstonecraft was thirty-two, famous, and approaching the acme of her radicalism. She had never had a lover. Fuseli was fifty; a short, irascible man with a strong German accent, who was wholly convinced of his own genius, his own career had taken off only recently, with a successful exhibition of Shakespeare illustrations in 1788, but he was undoubtedly one of the singular artistic talents of his age. His dramatic gothic compositions shared some of the physical drama of William Blake's (who distrusted Fuseli, describing him as 'both Turk and Jew') and much of the other-worldliness of Caspar David Friedrich's.

Neither his talents nor his interests were limited to art. Fuseli was fiercely proud of his republican Swiss pedigree and freely advertised his radical credentials around Johnson's table. He was a deep reader of the English literary tradition whose encyclopaedic knowledge of Shakespeare and Milton profoundly influenced his art. He was also a partisan of Rousseau and an obsessive reader of Richardson, who never failed to move this otherwise quite cruel man to tears. For Wollstonecraft, who knew nothing much of art, his political and literary passions provided some common ground with the man, who, whatever his failings – and there were many – she was perfectly primed to fall for. She was keen to love and drawn to genius.

For his part, Fuseli was a prideful man who enjoyed his fame and fancied himself something of a womaniser. He took a certain wicked pleasure in Wollstonecraft's pursuit of him. Well aware of the intensity of her passion, he would not respond to or even open and read her letters to him.

Whether she detected it in his art or in his person, Wollstonecraft seemed cognisant of Fuseli's sadistic streak. We gain a glimpse of this in a letter to the Liverpudlian lawyer and radical William Roscoe. Committed, as ever, to being useful, Wollstonecraft was dutifully helping to raise subscriptions for Fuseli's latest project, a series of prints inspired by Milton. In a letter to Roscoe in January 1792, she provided an update on Fuseli's artistic activities that was rich in suggestion:

Fuseli is going on with more than usual spirit – like Milton he seems quite at home in hell – his Devil will be the hero of the poetic series; for, entre nous, I rather doubt whether he will produce an Eve to please me in any of the situations, which he has selected, unless it be after the fall.[39]

The Fuseli imbroglio was made all the more wretched by the fact that he was married to a pretty young actress named Sophia. Consequently, Fuseli could encourage Wollstonecraft's pursuit when it took his fancy while rising above the fray by playing faithful husband when it did not, letting her embarrass herself with her passion for a family man. This was not a healthy cycle to be trapped in.

By the spring of 1792, Wollstonecraft's friends were well aware of her debilitating obsession with Fuseli. Johnson occasionally tried to goad her out of London and away from him; he worried about her mental health and her declining literary output. As rumour spread, Wollstonecraft slid deeper into debt and began to nurture ever more unlikely hopes about her future with Fuseli. In awe of his intellect, she began to harbour hopes for a purely platonic relationship where she might 'unite herself to his mind'.[40] This was not a realistic solution. As Godwin later observed, 'Mary was not of a temper to live upon terms of so much intimacy with a man of merit and genius, without loving him.' Even if she was, one can only imagine what Sophia Fuseli might have thought – had she been consulted – on the proposed inclusion of Wollstonecraft in her household.

As the affair began to spiral into scandal, Fuseli allegedly tried to reason with her and talk her out of her obsession. 'If I thought my passion criminal,' she is supposed to have replied, 'I would conquer it, or die in the attempt. For immodesty, in my eyes, is ugliness.'[41] The correspondence between the two did not survive, so the truth of Wollstonecraft's attachment to Fuseli is lost, the victim of burnt letters, partisan memoirs and incomplete archives. What we know glancingly, however, does suggest an all-consuming passion on her part and an equivocal interest in his.

The Nightmare (1781) by Henry Fuseli – one of the most disturbing and widely-reproduced depictions of Romantic sexuality.

The existence of this unequal and destructive dynamic made their next step even less explicable. On 20 June 1792, Wollstonecraft wrote to her sister Everina that she, Johnson and the Fuselis had planned a six-week excursion to Paris, where they hoped to meet their revolutionary idols, drink in the atmosphere and, in her case, bask in the success of the recent French translation of *A Vindication of the Rights of Woman*. France may have also afforded the promise of a new setting for her courtship of Fuseli. The date for their trip was set in early August. On the day, their party set out for Dover by carriage, only to learn at the harbour that events in Paris had overtaken them. On 10 August, Jacobin radicals and the Parisian *sections* staged a coup, resulting in a massacre of the royal bodyguard at the Tuileries Palace and the arrest of the royal family.[42] This was not a time to go sightseeing and the party turned back for London.

The disappointment of the French venture seemed to impress upon Wollstonecraft the need for a new frankness in her relations with Fuseli. She knew how she felt and she knew what she wanted. Reason dictated that she make her position clear to him. If the account of his biographer is to be believed, the critical moment came near the end of that summer:

> Mrs. Wollstonecraft appears to have grown desperate, for she had the temerity to go to Mrs. Fuseli, and to tell her, that she wished to become an intimate in her family; and she added, as I am above deceit, it is right to say that this proposal 'arises from the sincere affection which I have for your husband, for I find that I cannot live without the satisfaction of seeing and conversing with him daily.' This frank avowal immediately opened the eyes of Mrs. Fuseli, who being alarmed by the declaration, not only refused her solicitation, but she instantly forbade her the house.[43]

Thoroughly humiliated, Wollstonecraft apologised to Fuseli and swore off further contact. The chaos in Paris now looked preferable to the chaos in London, and Wollstonecraft fixated on travelling to France at the earliest possible date. The upheaval there was immense. On 29 August the French citadel at Verdun fell to the Prussians and the road to Paris was momentarily clear. Amid legitimate panic that the city would be put to the sword, the Jacobins orchestrated a bloody purge, murdering several hundred prisoners with knives and clubs on the night of 2 September. They also issued orders for the arrest and murder of the Girondin leadership. These went unfulfilled, but the fear of lustration now loomed large over that faction. Madame Roland, one of the leading female politicians of the day, wrote to a colleague that 'Robespierre and Marat have a knife to our throats.'[44]

The memory of the September Massacres, as they came to be known, was soon swept up in the torrent of events that followed. On 20 September the Prussian advance was halted by French artillery at the Battle of Valmy. The same day the National Assembly legalised divorce and decreed marriage to be a civil matter. On the 21st, the National Assembly abolished the monarchy. On 6 November, the French army defeated the Austrians at Jemappes, effectively ending the immediate military threat from outside powers and unleashing patriotic euphoria in Paris. Amid this riot of historical activity, Wollstonecraft composed an extraordinary letter to William Roscoe in Liverpool. 'I intend no longer to struggle with a rational desire,' she wrote, alluding to Fuseli, 'so have determined to set out for Paris in the course of a fortnight or three weeks; and I shall not now halt at Dover, I promise you; for as I go alone neck or nothing is the word.'

In her absence, she urged him to stay true to his radical beliefs, even as public sentiment turned against the French Revolution with news of the September Massacres. Displaying an astonishing indifference to the brutality of recent events, she joked that 'children of any growth will do mischief when they meddle with edged tools' and that he ought not to abandon 'immutable principles, because some of the mere instrument[s] of the revolution were too sharp'. Then, with a nod to the recent divorce law, she returned to romantic matters: 'At Paris, indeed, I might take a husband for the time being, and get divorced when my truant heart longed again to nestle with its old friends.'[45]

Desire and politics had merged. Whatever revolution was being forged in Paris would necessarily have sexual implications. She was soon to find out. A month later she disembarked at Calais.

***

Wollstonecraft arrived in Paris in mid-December with a cold. The days were short and the city was shrouded in an icy fog. Like all British visitors, she was appalled at the filthy streets and bewildered by the tangle of lanes and alleys, crammed full of teetering timber-framed dwellings, that constituted the medieval centre. Her own lodgings, on 22 Rue Meslay, between the recently rechristened Place de la République and the king's prison cell at the Temple, were far grander than she expected, six floors staffed by a troop of servants. Her hostess was absent and so she had the house to herself. Sick, lonely, and ill at ease being waited on in a stranger's house, Wollstonecraft was in no mood to strike out alone into the city.

Paris was not, in any event, at its most welcoming. On 10 December the National Assembly brought a formal indictment against the former King Louis XVI, known since the abolition of the monarchy in September as Citizen Louis Capet. When Wollstonecraft arrived, the trial of the king had begun in a paranoid atmosphere of invasion scares and royalist conspiracies. The streets were filled with soldiers recently returned from the front and tetchy National Guardsmen. The *septembriseurs*, the citizen-murderers of the prison massacres of late summer, mingled anonymously with the mob that Wollstonecraft had eyed sceptically as she entered the city.

As chance would have it, Wollstonecraft did not need to seek out history. The attic window of her tall home on Rue Meslay afforded a prospect over the road that took the former king from prison to courthouse. On 26 December she wrote a striking letter to Johnson in London describing her first encounter with revolutionary justice:

About nine o'clock this morning, the king passed by my window, moving silently along (excepting now and then a few strokes on the drum, which rendered the stillness more awful) through empty streets, surrounded by the national guards, who, clustering round the carriage, seemed to deserve their name. The inhabitants flocked to their windows, but the casements were shut, not a voice was heard, nor did I see anything like an insulting gesture. For the first time since I entered France, I bowed to the majesty of the people.

The dignity of the former king made a profound impression on her and his stoicism in the face of his reckoning filled her with foreboding:

> I can scarcely tell you why, but an association of ideas made the tears flow insensibly from my eyes, when I saw Louis sitting, with more dignity than I expected from his character, in a hackney coach, going to meet death, where so many of his race have triumphed. . . . I cannot dismiss the lively images that have filled my imagination all the day. . . . twice, lifting my eyes from the paper, I have seen eyes glare through a glass-door opposite my chair, and bloody hands shook at me. . . . I wish I had even kept the cat with me! I want to see something alive; death in so many frightful shapes has taken hold of my fancy.[46]

Voting began on Louis's fate in mid-January. The final tally of 361–360 was in favour of the death penalty – the deciding vote having been cast by Louis's first cousin the Duc d'Orléans, the richest man in France. Paris was shuttered the morning of 21 January when Louis was driven in a bottle-green carriage through thick fog to the guillotine at the Place de la Révolution. Wollstonecraft did not see his execution, nor did she see Louis pass through the streets lined with 130,000 soldiers, but sitting in her deserted house she would have heard the solitary, sepulchral drummer that went before his carriage as he travelled to his death.

It was the first of many executions during her time in Paris. Already in February she was wondering in a letter to Johnson whether 'the turn of the tide has left the dregs of the old system to corrupt the new'.[47] Around the same time she wrote this gloomy forecast, she was offered a place in a carriage back to London. She refused it. Whatever her doubts, she was committed to experiencing as much of the revolution as events would allow.

Britain declared war on France on 1 February 1793, effectively stranding Wollstonecraft in Paris for the foreseeable future. She was not alone in her exile. There was a large English contingent in Paris at the time, all enthusiasts of the revolutionary project. Wollstonecraft had connections to some of them through Joseph Johnson, and many of them would have been familiar with her through her writings. The British Club, based at White's Hotel, was home to Thomas Paine (who had fled the prospect of trial for treason in England in 1791 and was now a deputy to the National Convention, despite his not speaking French) and Joel Barlow, an American writer she had known in London, whose wife Ruth, whom she was friends with, would soon join him in Paris. Among the group was Thomas Christie, a colleague from the *Analytical Review* who, along with his wife Rebecca, hosted gatherings of expatriates.

Another expatriate hotspot was the salon of Helen Maria Williams, the chronicler of the French Revolution, whom Wollstonecraft met shortly after her arrival in Paris. 'Miss Williams has behaved very civilly to me,' she wrote to her sister Everina, 'and I shall visit her frequently, because I *rather* like her, and I meet French company at her house.' Williams was a committed supporter of the imperilled Girondin faction and the 'French company' that gathered at her house included many of its luminaries. There Wollstonecraft mingled with Jacques-Pierre Brissot, Madame Roland, Lazare Carnot and Nicolas Chamfort. Through Williams she likely met Madame de Genlis, the educational writer she had read and admired, who at that time was sporting a remarkable new necklace, a polished stone taken from the Bastille, studded with diamonds that spelt out *Liberté*.[48] Aside from the society she provided, she had much else in common with Williams.

Both were writers, both were committed activists who believed in the contribution women could make to revolutionary politics (Williams once wrote that 'whatever the imperious lords of the creation may fancy', women 'act in human affairs like those secret springs in mechanism, by which, though invisible, great movements are regulated'), and both believed that the revolution, in Williams's words, was 'an affair of the heart'.[49] Williams was engaged in a scandalous, if somewhat obscure, connection with another expatriate Englishman, John Hurford Stone, a merchant, a member of Dr Price's Hackney congregation, and a *divorcé*.[50]

Eager to forget the Fuseli fiasco in London, Wollstonecraft was keen to immerse herself in a revolutionary fling of her own. She had an inconclusive flirtation with another revolutionary tourist, the Silesian count Gustav von Schlabrendorf, who left a breathless account of Wollstonecraft at this time. 'There was enchantment in her glance, her voice, and her movement,' he wrote, she was 'the noblest, purest, and most intelligent woman I have ever met'.[51] She was fast losing any reservations about the proper place of desire in the brave new world of the revolution. Schlabrendorf overheard her brusquely inform a Frenchwoman that sexual pleasure was '*un défaut de la nature*'.[52]

The man upon whom her ardour alighted was Gilbert Imlay, a rangy and charming American whom she met at one of the Christies' gatherings on his arrival in Paris in April 1793. Imlay was a land agent by trade. He had written a widely read book on the opportunities available for settlement and cultivation in the American territories, especially in Kentucky. He had also written a sentimental epistolary novel, *The Emigrants*, that had made progressive noises about the need for divorce reform and the abolition of slavery while discoursing on other modish subjects such as the perfectibility of society, the merits of living close to nature, and the evils of excessive commerce.[53] There was no small irony in his proclaimed suspicion of commerce, for his novel as the revolutionary regime in Paris. In response the Convention introduced a slew of authoritarian measures through the month, expanding the number of capital offences, introducing the Revolutionary Tribunal to expedite trials, and ordering the creation of Surveillance Committees in every municipality. In early April, the Girondin General Dumouriez defected to the Austrians. Marat and Robespierre, operating through the recently organised Committee of Public Safety, now moved decisively against the Girondins. Many of those whom Wollstonecraft had met at salons and parties were fighting for survival. As the internecine warfare raged throughout April and May, many of her friends fled Paris, either for Switzerland or the provinces. Wollstonecraft herself moved to a cottage in Neuilly-sur-Seine, just north of the Bois de Boulogne. Here she worked on her latest project, a history of the French Revolution, ambled in the woods, and practised her French on the gardener. In the evenings she would meet Imlay, who had remained in Paris, for assignations at the Longchamp Tollgate at the city limit. The two were planning to emigrate to America, and she was consumed with visions of the blissful future that awaited them there. 'You can scarcely imagine,' she wrote to him late that August, 'with what pleasure I anticipate the day, when we are to begin almost to live together.'[57]

As summer turned to autumn, things fell apart, both romantically and politically. By September the first flush of their romance had passed and a new, sharper edge emerges in her letters to Imlay. 'Of late we are always separating. – Crack! – crack! – and away you go.' She was still utterly infatuated with him but was growing restive at the amount of time they spent apart and complained that he did not do enough to try and remedy the situation. Her concerns about his commitment increased further in November when she realised that she was pregnant. Sharing the widely held belief that a mother's emotional state influenced the health of the foetus, Wollstonecraft declared in her letter to Imlay informing him of the pregnancy that she aimed to be 'very attentive to calm my mind' to ensure the health of a child 'in whom we are to have a mutual interest'.[58]

This was to prove challenging. Imlay remained aloof in Paris until December, seemingly immune to Wollstonecraft's pleas and barbs. Shortly before the New Year, he moved to the Channel port of Le Havre. Plans to emigrate to America had been postponed. Imlay had spied a new mercantile opportunity born of the exigencies of war. The Royal Navy was now blockading French ports, leading to shortages throughout the country. Imlay set himself up as a blockade-runner, building connections with traders in neutral Scandinavia who would accept French silver as payment. Wollstonecraft loathed all this. She missed his presence; she shuddered at his commercial schemings. She wrote him scathing letters where she called him a tyrant, and then wrote additional letters pleading for forgiveness. The sexual confidence that had animated her less than a year before was dwindling, replaced by increasingly wretched bids for his affection. 'I do not want to be loved like a goddess,' she wrote to him on New Year's Day 1794, 'but I wish to be necessary to you.'[59]

Her relationship with Imlay faltered at the same time as disillusionment with revolutionary politics set in. In October 1793, as she was becoming aware of the first stirrings of her pregnancy, the political centre collapsed. At the end of the month, Imlay visited Neuilly with news from Paris. Brissot had been guillotined along with two dozen leading Girondins. A good portion of the glamorous French reformers among whom she had moved in her first hopeful months in Paris had been executed in one go. Their faces rose unbidden in her mind, 'but before she was conscious of the effect of the picture, she sunk lifeless on the floor'.[60] The Jacobins had finally triumphed over the Girondins; Robespierre was delivering on his promise to make terror 'the order of the day'.

The coming of the Terror was accompanied by a reconfiguration of the sexual politics of the revolution. The Girondins had been largely susceptible to the idea that the state could improve the lot of women through better educational opportunities and the extension to them of social and political liberties. The Jacobins held rather different ideas about the place of women in society. The principal influence on the new leaders of France was Rousseau, who had preached the merits of a stark sexual order. In Rousseau's view, the Bourbon state had been corrupted by the influence of women in the halls of power. The stew of mistresses, courtesans and unfaithful wives at Versailles had turned the politics of the Ancien Régime into a parlour game manipulated by women. The regeneration of the state and, by extension, of national morality, could be accomplished by simply banishing women from politics and confining them to the home. 'If women would only deign to nurse their children,' he wrote, 'morals would reform of themselves.' This insight led naturally to a new equation: sexual virtue equalled political virtue. Mistresses had corrupted the monarchy; mothers would renew the republic.[61]

This idea had been on the march since 1789. Any number of political figures had stated in unambiguous terms their opposition to female participation in public life. The 1792 constitution had cemented this principle by denying women the vote. Throughout, the pill of female exclusion was sugared with paeans to their superior virtue. Olympe de Gouges caustically observed that 'women are now respected and excluded; under the old regime they were despised and powerful'. The ascent of the Jacobins was merely the most extreme manifestation of this outlook. They were intent on purging women from politics and they relied upon a very crude, very gendered political rhetoric to do so.[62]

Ironically, the Jacobins were propelled to hegemony in the high summer of 1793 by just the kind of female political intrusion that they despised. On 13 July a Girondin sympathiser named Charlotte Corday travelled to Paris and murdered the Jacobin propagandist Jean-Paul Marat while he reposed in his bathtub. Marat's assassination and his prompt canonisation as a secular martyr to the revolutionary cause further brutalised Parisian politics, and further strengthened Jacobin resolve. It also bolstered the conviction that women had to be disbarred from political life. After a dramatic trial Corday was guillotined on 17 July. Her body was barely in the ground when women political activists began to notice a sea change in attitudes towards them. Claire Lacombe and Pauline Léon both noted in August that the fear that 'they might be designated as new Cordays' was being used to silence politically engaged women.[63]

These were prophetic words. What followed were months of murder and misogyny. At the trial of Marie Antoinette in October, the former queen's political meddling was constantly linked to her supposed sexual transgressions. The high water mark of the prosecution's campaign of prurient slander was the allegation that the queen and her lady-in-waiting had taught the Dauphin how to masturbate. These fantastical charges were wholly unnecessary in the pursuit of a guilty verdict – which was readily secured – but central to the rhetorical project of connecting sexual deviance to monarchical, counter-revolutionary sentiment.[64] She was executed on 16 October.

In the same period, many prominent women were either arrested or fled the country. Among them were several of Wollstonecraft's friends and acquaintances, including Helen Maria Williams, Madame Roland and Madame de Genlis. On 30 October, the National Convention outlawed clubs and popular societies for women, a move justified by recourse to the Rousseauvian language of impermeable sexual difference. Deputy André Amar, in explaining the need for the ban, alluded to standard tropes concerning the proper role of women in society. 'We believe,' he told the Convention, 'that a woman should not leave her family to meddle in affairs of government.' If women did involve themselves in revolutionary politics, the result would be chaos and corruption:

If we consider that the political education of men is at its beginning . . . that we are still stammering the word liberty, then how
much more reasonable is it for women, whose moral education
is almost nil, to be less enlightened concerning principles? Their
presence in popular societies, therefore, would give an active
role in government to people more exposed to error and seduction. Let us add that women are disposed by their organisation
to an over-excitation which would be deadly in public affairs
and that interests of state would soon be sacrificed to everything
in which ardour of passions can generate in the way of error and
disorder.[65]

A few days later, Olympe de Gouges, who in Article X of her
Declaration of the Rights of Woman had claimed for women 'the
right to mount the scaffold', herself went to the guillotine. She was
followed soon after by Madame Roland. The bloody enforcement
of the new sexual order was accompanied by the introduction of a
new iconography. In the new Jacobin France, the temptress of the
Ancien Régime and the street-fighting *poissarde* were comparably
subversive. 'Liberty is not a nymph from the opera, it is not a *bonnet
rouge*, or a dirty shirt,' one Jacobin orator proclaimed, 'liberty is
happiness, reason and equality.' Realistic portrayals of women as
actors and agents of revolution were replaced by bland allegorical
images that purveyed the Jacobin orthodoxy of the serene mother,
breast exposed, offering France the milk of liberty.[66]

Wollstonecraft was protected from the blood-letting by a typically
astute manoeuvre on Imlay's part. Early in September he had her
registered as his wife at the American embassy in Paris. This had
no legal force, and they were never married; it did however afford
her *de facto* recognition as an American citizen and kept her safe
amid the mayhem of the Terror.[67] Her relative security did not
conceal the fear and violence all about her. She visited her imprisoned friends in the overcrowded jails, haunted by the rattle of the

tumbril, and she witnessed with her own eyes blood running across the cobblestones after yet another execution. There is a judicious silence on such matters in her letters to Imlay – she was not so secure that she could risk expressing her revulsion in print – but the murderous atmosphere of Paris in those months stayed with her for the rest of her life. It doubtless contributed to her hunger for the stability of a domestic existence with Imlay and her rage at his departure for the coast.

The issue of geography was resolved in January, when she moved to join him in Le Havre. The following months passed in relative harmony as the couple established a household on the Rue de Corderie by the harbour and prepared for the arrival of their child. Fanny Imlay was born on 14 May 1794. In a letter to Ruth Barlow, Wollstonecraft reported that their French midwife, who was evidently on message, had quipped that 'I ought to make children for the Republic, since I treat it so lightly.' She continued that the 'little Girl begins to suck so *manfully* that her father reckons saucily on her writing the second part of the Rights of Woman.'[68] This period of family communion around the newborn child was painfully short-lived. Imlay's byzantine commercial dealings were consuming ever more of his time. He spent the summer going back and forth between Paris and Le Havre. Then, in September, he was obliged to travel to London in pursuit of information about a business deal gone awry. Rather than remain alone in the dreary coastal town, Wollstonecraft took Fanny to Paris, where the Jacobins had been crushed amid a final, chiliastic round of beheadings at the Place de la Révolution at the end of July. The city was safe now. The rounds of visits and gatherings resumed, albeit with the ranks of the radicals depleted and their confidence in their beliefs diminished. The passage of the Terror allowed each a moment of personal reckoning.

Wollstonecraft had now been in France for just under two years. Her belief in the merits of rational desires and uncertain freedoms had been tested beyond any limit that she might have imagined as a budding writer in London. France had given her love, a daughter and a wealth of experience, but at the expense of her idealism. Her experiment in radical love outside the bonds of marriage and the bounds of respectable society had forced her to confront some basic truths about human relationships. They could neither be rationalised nor managed. Freedom to love meant freedom to lose. Men could rove, but a woman with a child in her womb or at her breast faced certain constraints.

Imlay was now roving an awful lot. Confronted with the compromised state of her sexual beliefs, she nourished herself on Elysian memories of the first pangs of her romance. She wrote to Imlay that September:

> There is nothing picturesque in your present pursuits. My imagination then rather chuses to ramble back to the barrier with you, or to see you coming to meet me, and my basket of grapes. – With what pleasure do I recollect your looks and words, when I have been sitting on the window, regarding the waving corn!
>
> . . .
>
> If you call these observations romantic . . . I shall be apt to retort, that you are embruted by trade, and the vulgar enjoyments of life – Bring me then back your barrier-face, or you shall have nothing to say to my barrier-girl; and I shall fly from you, to cherish the remembrances that will ever be dear to me.[69]

This was mere bravado. Imlay was flying from her and she was perceptive enough to detect as much in their correspondence. She waited for him in France until the spring of 1795, subsisting on a starvation diet of false hope and pat nostalgia. In his letters to her, Imlay breathed faintly on whatever embers of mutual affection still glimmered, but he remained stubbornly in London. At the beginning of April, Wollstonecraft's patience finally broke and she resolved to return to England after a hiatus of two and a half years. On 7 April 1795, she wrote a curt letter to Imlay informing him to expect her and his daughter in Brighton within the week.

***

In London, Wollstonecraft learnt that Imlay had taken up with a young actress, and subsequently tried to commit suicide. The details of the attempt are unclear, though she did not succeed and word of her desperate condition reached Imlay, momentarily dragging him back into her affairs. His response was self-serving. He suggested that Wollstonecraft and Fanny might travel to Norway on his behalf to uncover the fate of a lost ship of his that had been engaged in running the British blockade.

Wollstonecraft agreed, and by early June she was in Hull awaiting passage to Gothenburg. The journey was repeatedly delayed by bad weather, and she peppered Imlay with letters to stave off boredom. In one such letter, she sketched a nascent theory of love which seemed to her to explain why their relationship had failed. Passion was the raw material of love, she wrote, and reason was the necessary cement. The problem was that 'the common run of men', which presumably included Imlay, had to 'have variety to banish *ennui*'. Lasting love, 'a unison of affection and desire', could only be achieved through the addition of a third ingredient: the imagination. The exercise of the powers of the imagination allowed the lover access to a higher state of romantic experience 'that renders every emotion delicate and rapturous'. Not all people could arrive at this state; it was 'the distinctive characteristic of genius' to be able to attain this superior kind of love. She was hopeful, though, that Imlay had the potential to reach it, 'which would open your heart to me. I would fain rest there'.[70]

These musings on the imagination stayed with her throughout her travels in Scandinavia. She arrived in Gothenburg on 27 June and embarked on a circuitous tour of the peninsula, which took her north up the coast, then across the Skagerrak strait to Risør, a remote coastal outpost in south-east Norway, and north-east to Christiania (now Oslo), before heading south through Gothenburg and thence to Elsinore, Copenhagen and Hamburg. Her journeys through the wild terrain of rural Scandinavia provided a kind of natural cure for her after months of trauma. She unspooled herself in the landscapes of Sweden and Norway. Communing with nature in the daytime, with only Fanny for company, she jotted down her impressions in the evenings, the polar nights so luminous that she could write without the aid of a candle. These notes in time gathered to become her greatest work, *Letters Written in Sweden, Norway, and Denmark* (1796), a strange and powerful piece of writing, structured as a series of letters to Imlay, who is never named and whose role in her life is never properly explained. Indeed, very little biographical exposition is provided, so that the casual reader is only faintly aware of the phantoms hovering above the page as she discourses on nature, politics, commerce and love.

There is a tidal quality to the *Letters Written in Sweden*. Wollstonecraft allows herself to range out into new waters, testing out ideas, considering images, exploring channels of thought; then the weight of personal tragedy tugs her back in towards familiar shores – the anxieties of motherhood, political disillusionment, heartbreak. A constant in the letters is the transformative powers of the imagination, which seem to offer if not an escape route from her troubles then at least a means of momentarily transcending them. The encounter with nature was the catalyst for these episodes of metaphysical release:

In the evening they also die away; the aspen leaves tremble into stillness, and reposing nature seems to be warmed by the moon, which here assumes a genial aspect. And if a light shower has chanced to fall with the sun, the juniper, the underwood of the forest, exhales a wild perfume, mixed with a thousand nameless sweets that, soothing the heart, leave images in the memory which the imagination will ever hold dear.

In the grip of these reveries her imagination was borne away to mystic territory. Wandering across the heath she heard the spectre of Fanny Blood calling out to her across the years. Walking among the groves of firs and pines at dusk, she seemed to sense their souls. Cruising down the coast from Helgeroa to Risør, she surveyed the barren shore and had a vision of the day when the world would be so overpopulated that even these blighted places would be crowded with humans:

> Imagination went still farther, and pictured the state of man when the earth could no longer support him. Whither was he to flee from universal famine? Do not smile; I really became distressed for these fellow creatures yet unborn. The images fastened on me, and the world appeared a vast prison.[71]

In their scope and lyricism, the *Letters Written in Sweden* represented a bound forward in Wollstonecraft's literary abilities. With her meditations on the role and power of the imagination, she was exploring poetic territory that would later be charted more completely by the Romantics – but the discovery was hers.[72]

'If ever there was a book calculated to make a man in love with its author,' William Godwin wrote of the *Letters*, 'this appears to me to be the book.' Nothing could make Gilbert Imlay any more disposed to love Mary Wollstonecraft. As she travelled south to Denmark, she tried to persuade him to meet her in Hamburg so that they could travel on to Switzerland as a family. When it became clear this was not going to happen, she accepted her lot with prideful resignation. 'I am content to be wretched; but I will not be contemptible,' she wrote from Hamburg in late September.[73]

She was at Dover by 4 October and in London soon afterwards. There she met Imlay and learnt that he had a new mistress.

All her hopes for the renewal of their love – it was now thirty months since their first meeting – were dashed. The crisis was insuperable. Wollstonecraft had been ideating about suicide for months now. At Hull she had considered the sea as a potential tomb for her worries. At a waterfall at Fredericstadt, she had felt the lure of the thundering water and had 'asked myself why I was chained to life and its misery'. She had always loved *Hamlet*, identifying with the lugubrious Dane, similarly unlucky in love and family and politics. In the end she played Ophelia, the tormented lover who took too much water in her grief. On the wet night of 10 October, she travelled by boat down the Thames to Putney where she walked up and down the banks until her dress was heavy with rainwater. Then she mounted the bridge and hurled herself into the dark swift river.

***

In April of 1796 Mary Wollstonecraft walked through the lush meadows from her new home in Islington to Somers Town, near King's Cross. Seven months after she had been fished out of the Thames and revived by a member of the Humane Society, Wollstonecraft was ready to experiment with love once more. She was heading to the house of William Godwin, the bachelor philosopher, to make a social call, unannounced and unaccompanied, in characteristic defiance of etiquette. At forty, Godwin was a stubby man with a lumpy nose and chin, as uninterested in social niceties as she was, though a little more prone than she to allowing dry philosophical disquisitions to intrude upon regular conversation. He shunned both the rococo clothing fashions of the day and the austere radical chic favoured by many in his circle in favour of the fusty, somewhat peculiar sartorial choices of a provincial eccentric – green coat, scarlet waistcoat and pointy red morocco slippers – which in several respects he was.

He had neither the natural charm nor the lanky good looks of Imlay. Still, Wollstonecraft and Godwin had much in common both socially and intellectually, as well as a shared past as supper guests of Joseph Johnson – not that these encounters had sparked anything like desire in either of them. In January the two had met at the house of Mary Hays, another female writer who had been courting Wollstonecraft's approval for some time. They had met on a couple of occasions since. Now, striding through the fields on the approach to his home, Wollstonecraft was consciously escalating the terms of their acquaintance.

Godwin's diary recorded his daily activity in telegraphic style ('Thursday 21st February 1793: Read the Amorous Cynic. Wedgwood's Concert: sup at Holcroft's'), and as of that January meeting Wollstonecraft had appeared in it only three times. After her April visit, the terse mentions of her presence rapidly increase, charting the rising pulse of their relationship. They struck up a correspondence which soon graduated from the literary to the flirtatious, and then to the amorous. 'It was friendship melting into love,' Godwin would later write,[74] a process which he nonetheless nearly scuppered by attempting to impose his philosophical precepts on their courtship. This was, nonetheless, the most rational desire either had ever entertained.

By the end of August they were lovers. By the New Year she was pregnant. As her condition began to show in the spring of 1797, they decided – with heavy radical hearts – to marry. Godwin thought the need for a ceremony ridiculous and 'contrary to the genuine march of sentiment'. Wollstonecraft was rather more concerned with the gossip it would give rise to. She had been going by the title of Mrs Imlay for several years now. Legally marrying Godwin would reveal that she had never been married to Imlay, had been nothing more than his mistress. Her fears were borne out. Following their April marriage several of their friends refused to be seen in society with them. There was much wagging of tongues besides about the union of two of Britain's most scandalous philosophers. 'You have not, perhaps, heard,' Henry Fuseli wrote to a friend, 'that the assertrix of female rights has given her hand to the *balancier* of political justice.'[75]

Conforming to convention, they now moved in together at Somers Town, but otherwise theirs was a most unusual marriage. They socialised separately or together as the fancy took them. Godwin rented another apartment in Somers Town where he would work from morning till evening, seeing his wife only at dinner. Godwin was also an affectionate stepfather to Fanny Imlay, refusing, in line with his principles, to indulge in the stigma surrounding bastard children. In his memoir of this period, Godwin was proud of their very rational domestic arrangements. 'We were both of us of opinion, that it was possible for two persons to be too uniformly in each other's society,' he wrote. By fragmenting the time they spent together while also keeping a traditional household they successfully combined 'the novelty and lively sensation of visit, with the more delicious and heart-felt pleasures of domestic life'.

It was during this new and welcome period of marital and domestic stability that Wollstonecraft began to write her most radical work, one that foreshadows the concerns of contemporary feminism far more than *A Vindication of the Rights of Woman*. The prescience of *Maria: or, The Wrongs of Woman* is made all the more remarkable given that it was never completed and contains a number of dead ends and fragmentary plot connections that she never had time to correct. For all this, *Maria* is a far more compelling read than her earlier novel *Mary* – yet another sign of her flourishing literary talents. The novel is set in a mad-house, where three characters – a man and two women – tell the tragic tale of their lives. Seduction lies at the centre of the life stories of the two women, Jemima and Maria, although the narratives told by each subvert in different ways the tradition of the seduction narrative.

Jemima is from a working-class background. Her mother was seduced and abandoned, and died less than two weeks after giving birth to her. Raised in the direst poverty, at sixteen Jemima went into service where she was raped by her master and, when she became pregnant by him, was evicted from his household. She had a back-street abortion and became a prostitute. Later she was taken into the house of a gentleman and became his kept woman. 'Fate dragged me through the very kennels of society,' Jemima says of her life, 'I was still a slave, a bastard, a common property.' The depiction of Jemima is innovative, for it was uncommon to use seduction narratives to focus on the plight of the poor, still less of poor women who were capable of coolly analysing the circum-stances of their oppression. For Jemima is a fierce and astute critic of British society. Whereas most sentimental heroines focus on questions of virtue and appeal to the reform of men through the inculcation of Christian morality, Jemima focuses on the structural problems facing women, especially economic ones:

> 'How often have I heard,' said Jemima, interrupting her narrative, 'in conversation, and read in books, that every person willing to work may find employment? It is the vague assertion, I believe, of insensible indolence, when it relates to men; but, with respect to women, I am sure of its fallacy, unless they will submit to the most menial bodily labour; and even to be employed at hard labour is out of the reach of many, whose reputation misfortune or folly has tainted.'[76]

The problems she faced, in other words, ran across more than one vector. The problems of poverty were made different by the fact of her gender. This was intersectionality two hundred years before the fact.

The unremittingly brutal world faced by women that Jemima describes makes Wollstonecraft's depiction of Maria even more remarkable. Unlike Jemima, she is from a respectable, well-off family. Her life arc seems to trace that of the typical sentimental heroine since *Clarissa*. As a young woman in thrall to romantic notions she has learned from novels, she is courted by George Venables, an apparently upright young man from a wealthy family. Little does she know, but 'in London, George had acquired habits of libertinism, which he carefully concealed from his father and his commercial connections'. She finds out his true nature too late. They are wed, only for Maria to discover that George is a boor, a drunk and an habitué of the meanest sort of brothels. 'Marriage had bastilled me for life,' Maria tells her friends.

Unlike most women, Maria decides to fight back. A woman of sensibility and reason, she decides that her marriage is effectively rendered void by her husband's coarse, unloving behaviour. In a brilliant passage she describes what her ideal partner would be like:

> A man of feeling thinks not of seducing, he is himself seduced by all the noblest emotions of his soul. He figures to himself all the sacrifices a woman of sensibility must make, and every situation in which his imagination places her, touches his heart, and fires his passions.[77]

She escapes her unhappy home and heads for London, where she meets and falls in love with Henry Darnford. The couple live together for a period, enjoying their outlaw passion, until her husband catches up with them. George sues Darnford for adultery and seduction. Under English law, husbands could sue men who intruded upon their marriage, often as a prelude to securing a divorce. Women were considered passive objects in these legal events, alluded to but not given voice.[78]

Maria chooses to upend this system by involving herself in Darnford's defence. She instructs his lawyers to plead guilty to the charge of adultery but to deny the charge of seduction. Forbidden by law to give evidence in person, she writes a testament which she hopes will be read out in court. In writing this document, 'she only felt in earnest to insist on the privilege of her nature', caring nothing for either the letter of unjust laws or the censure of a hypocritical society.

At the core of her argument is an attack on a 'false morality' that makes 'all the virtue of women consist in chastity, submission, and the forgiveness of injuries'. Maria insists on challenging the charge of seduction because she has exercised her own powers of reason to love Darnford of her own free will. She agrees that she was a victim of society in many ways, but refuses to go along with a legal fiction that assumes she could not make her own mind as to whom to leave and whom to love:

> I met the man charged with seducing me. We became attached – I deemed, and ever shall deem, myself free. . . . To this person, thus encountered, I voluntarily gave myself, never considering myself as any more bound to transgress the laws of moral purity, because the will of my husband might be pleaded in my excuse, than to transgress those laws to which [the policy of artificial society has] annexed [positive] punishments.[79]

This carefully modulated defence of free love was one of the last things Mary Wollstonecraft ever wrote. On 30 August she gave birth to a daughter, Mary Godwin. The birth initially seemed to have gone well. There were, however, hidden complications. Some sections of the placenta had become caught in her womb. After several days they began to rot, eventually leading her to develop septicaemia. She took ten agonising days to die.

Godwin tended her to the best of his abilities. In moments of lucidity she spoke to him of Fanny and Mary. Otherwise he busied himself with finding doctors and minding the children while she lay on the bed, wracked with fevers. The end came on the evening of 10 September, an event Godwin recorded with fearful brevity in his diary. '20 minutes before 8', followed by a long ellipsis.

Following his wife's death, Godwin decided to memorialise her in a biography. He immersed himself in her letters and manuscripts before setting about writing the story of her life. He worked at a furious pace. *Memoirs of the Author of A Vindication of the Rights of Woman* was published in January 1798. It was intended as a homage to a radical life. He did not shy away from any fact of her existence. Everything was included within its pages: her pursuit of Henry Fuseli, her extramarital affair with Gilbert Imlay, their false wedding in Paris, her illegitimate child by him, their separation and her two suicide attempts, her unusual courtship and premarital sexual affair with Godwin. He was unapologetic about the book's candour. 'There are no circumstances of her life, that, in the judgment of honour and reason, could brand her with disgrace,' he wrote. 'Never did there exist a human being, that needed, with less fear, expose all their actions, and call upon the universe to judge them.'[80]

Posterity may have arrived at the same conclusion, but in the short term his unbowdlerised account of her life was a public relations disaster of the first order. Even those well disposed towards Godwin could not understand why he would publish such things about his recently deceased wife. The poet Robert Southey wrote that Godwin exhibited 'a want of all feeling in stripping his dead wife naked'.[81] Joseph Johnson had pleaded with him not to publish it in its final form. For conservatives, his revelations about the private life of one of their most implacable foes were read with relish. Wollstonecraft's sex life was used to discredit her political principles.[82] In his poem 'The Unsex'd Females' (1798), the Reverend Richard Polwhele put Wollstonecraft at the head of

A female band despising NATURE's law,
As 'proud defiance' flashes from their arms,
And vengeance smothers all their softer charms
I shudder at the new unpictur'd scene,
Where unsex'd woman vaunts the imperious mien;
Where girls, affecting to dismiss the heart,
Invoke the Proteus of petrific art.

The 'unsex'd woman' was politically engaged and sexually liberated – both of which characteristics were to be feared and condemned in equal measure. As in France, now in England, sexual virtue was equated with political virtue. 'The moral sentiments and moral conduct of Mrs. Wollstonecroft [sic]', the *Anti-Jacobin Review* wrote in its review of Godwin's *Memoirs*, 'exemplify and illustrate JACOBIN MORALITY.' Wollstonecraft's travels to France and her early sympathy for the French Revolution were deemed comparable to her irregular relationships. Promiscuity and treason made easy bedfellows. In its index, the *Anti-Jacobin Review* listed her under 'Prostitution. *See* Mary Wollstonecraft.'[83]

The cruellest posthumous blow came not from the reactionary press but from the man who had loved her most. In later life, William Godwin disavowed much of his youthful radicalism, in particular the sections of *Political Justice* which dealt with free love. His *Memoirs* were also edited in order to tone down their sexual content. 'Is truth then so variable?' William Hazlitt wrote in a sketch of Godwin in 1825. 'Is it one thing at twenty, and another at forty? Is it at a burning heat in 1793, and below zero in 1814?'[84] Yet Godwin was not alone in growing conservative with the years. Many radicals of the 1790s made a similar journey towards the centre ground of British politics. Whether Wollstonecraft would have joined them there is unknowable. Nonetheless, their subsequent defection made her example look all the more anomalous and all the less encouraging. The prospects for the survival of her beliefs in the powers of reason, the pleasures of the passions, and the rights of individuals would reside in the next era.

Her shade would not have to look far. Though she and her daughter Mary had met only in passing at life's boundary, it was enough to ensure that the line of succession went unbroken. For whatever piece of the daughter lodged in the mother, a greater portion of the mother lodged in the daughter, and the questions that had animated her life were passed along to a new generation.

4

CIRCLING MARY SHELLEY

In May 1816, Mary Godwin, the only child of William Godwin and Mary Wollstonecraft, was staying in the Hôtel d'Angleterre in Geneva, waiting for a visitor from England. At eighteen, Mary was striking if not conventionally beautiful. Her curly brown hair was gathered in ringlets around her neck and pulled up around her temples to expose her most noticeable feature, the expansive, pear-white forehead that sat like a great tablet above the rest of her otherwise quite delicate face – an aquiline nose, soft, high dimpled cheeks, an unobtrusive mouth.

Even then there was an intensity apparent within Mary. Later, after tragedy, she would write that though her outward existence was solitary and monotonous, her inner life was wonderfully 'diversified by internal feeling'. This was characteristic modesty on her part. Mary's intelligence and energy had always shone through her natural reserve. Her large, hazel eyes at once hid and conveyed immense thoughts and fathomless analytical abilities. She was, after all, the daughter of the woman who had gone toe-to-toe with Edmund Burke, a girl hand-reared by one of England's greatest living political thinkers, and whose tutor, William Baxter of Dundee, where Mary lived from 1812 to 1814, was given simple instructions to raise her 'like a philosopher'.

It was following the completion of this task, and upon her subsequent return to London, that she met and fell in love with the man now by her side in Switzerland. Percy Bysshe Shelley was short, sickly, and frenetic with mental and creative energy when she met him in her father's drawing room in Clerkenwell. He was also married to Harriet Westbrook, whose charms had diminished for him once she became pregnant with their second child. Harriet saw the thumbprints of both of Mary's radical parents all over what followed. Her once faithful husband had turned 'profligate and sensual, owing entirely to Godwin's "Political Justice"'. With her target primed by her father's radical ideas, the daughter had then made her move. 'Mary was determined to secure him,' Harriet continued. 'She is to blame. She heated his imagination by talking of her mother, and going to her grave with him every day till at last she told him she was dying in love for him, accompanied by the most violent gestures and vehement expostulations.'[1]

Mary and Shelley did indeed have assignations in St Pancras Churchyard, where Mary Wollstonecraft was buried, though this was likely for convenience and privacy rather than an attempt on Mary's part to use her mother's sepulchre as a morbid prop for her seduction of Percy Shelley.[2] It also seems to have been here that the first declarations of love were made, though it is unlikely – as later chroniclers of their romance asserted – that their love was consummated atop the very grave of Britain's foremost feminist. But whatever had passed there between them, Harriet seemed to intuit early on that it could not be undone and that her husband was lost to her for ever. 'He cares not for me now,' she concluded in a despairing letter to Catherine Nugent, 'the man I once loved is dead. This is a vampire. His character is blasted for ever. Nothing can save him now.'[3]

Unpicking the politics from the passion in the youthful affair between Shelley and Mary was a hard task for anyone, let alone his spurned teenage wife. Likewise, judging the merits of any relationship from its beginnings is as myopic as judging it by its ending. But there was enduring significance to the torrid opening phase of Mary and

Shelley's remarkable relationship. Mary's whole life would be trian-
gulated between the shifting markers of romantic love, sexual
radicalism, and human – predominantly female – suffering. She never
forgot what had happened to Harriet. She came to believe it haunted
her. The thwarted promise and numerous pitfalls of sexual freedom
in a period of systematic and unabashed female subordination would
be a recurrent theme in Mary's life, writing and friendships.

William Godwin was indelibly linked in British minds with the
doctrine of free love. But the old radical's interest in the subject
had diminished considerably since the publication of the first,
infamous edition of *Political Justice* in 1793, to be replaced by a
fervid and abiding interest in staying out of debtors' prison. By
the time he became acquainted with Percy Shelley, the eldest son
of a well-to-do baronet, he was more concerned with securing a
large loan from his red-maned young disciple than with passing
on the torch to the next generation of radicals. Godwin acquired
the loan, with the intense romance between his lender and his
daughter thrown into the bargain. At this point all his philosophical interest in sexual freedom and free association vanished and
he expressed his opposition to the couple in unambiguous terms.

Undeterred, and enthused by the prospect of a Romantic adventure,
Mary and Percy planned an elopement to Europe. Aiding and abetting
their plan was Mary's stepsister Mary Jane Clairmont, the daughter
of Godwin's second wife. The date for their escape from London and
censure to Europe and liberty was set for 28 July. When the carriage
appeared at the agreed time and place, the two young lovers darted
in and – in a fateful last-minute addition – were joined by Clairmont.

The trip to the war-weary continent was a predictable disaster
and the trio were back in England in less than two months, the
principal product of their venture a pregnant Mary Shelley, scared
and only sixteen years old. She gave birth in March 1815 to a girl,
Clara, who did not live to see the summer. Mary would forever
afterwards associate spring not with hope and rebirth, but with

tragedy, and would date many of her later misfortunes to the original loss of that year.

The development of Mary's tragic sensibility coincided with her stepsister's transformation into a self-declared avatar of free love. Mary Jane Clairmont rebranded herself Claire Clairmont, daughter of liberty and roaming sexual spirit. She had arrived at this conclusion by a number of avenues: through intense readings of Wollstonecraft, Rousseau and other radicals; in an attempt to distinguish herself from her brilliant, sober stepsister; from her time spent in the orbit of Percy Shelley. There is good evidence to suggest that Clairmont and Shelley were romantically involved while Mary was confined during her ill-starred pregnancy, and some suggestion that she bore, then abandoned, Shelley's illegitimate child near the end of that year. What is clear was that there was some kind of intense rupture in the group in this period, one that, miraculously, seems to have been resolved by the beginning of 1816.

In January, Mary gave birth to a healthy boy, William, whom they referred to among themselves as Wilmouse, and by the spring the three were planning another trip to Europe. In May they set off for Geneva. There Clairmont hoped to pull off a *coup de théâtre*. In London, while Percy and Mary had been busy with their newborn, Clairmont had struck up an intimacy with a radical poet of her own – one even more notorious than her stepsister's. He was something of a reluctant lover and Clairmont had lured him down to Switzerland using her distinguished travelling companions as bait. They arrived a fortnight before him, and settled into the Hôtel d'Angleterre. In her letters Mary described in gorgeous prose the wonders of the natural setting – the boats that drifted into their moorings as dusk gathered over Lac Léman, the forbidding Jura mountain range that darkened into pitch as the sun fell behind it, the rolling lightning storms that at night illuminated the surface of the water and the flanks of the peaks. She was less impressed by the English tourists at the hotel. The 'haughty English ladies', she recorded, 'are greatly disgusted with this consequence of republican institutions, for the Genevese servants complain very much of their *scolding*'.⁴ The same haughty ladies disapproved of the scandalous poet and his two female companions, scandalous by association. They were shunned by their fellow guests and greeted with silence in the hotel's dining rooms and public spaces. Each day, meanwhile, their visitor from England drew closer.

***

The person they were waiting for was George Gordon Byron, 6th Baron Byron, poet, seducer, and now fugitive from English society and the scandals he had conjured therein. Byron's troubles had started in 1812 when he had first begun to consider marriage. That year he had published the first cantos of *Childe Harold's Pilgrimage*, and he and it had overnight become the talk of London. The poem was 'on every table', the Duchess of Devonshire wrote to her son in America, and its author 'courted, visited, flattered, and praised whenever he appears'.

One of those who put herself gently in the poet's path was Anna Isabella 'Annabella' Milbanke, a pious, intelligent and very serious young woman who had been sent down from the provincial north-east to find a husband. Her aunt was Lady Melbourne, wife of the 1st Viscount Melbourne, and one of the most politically engaged and influential women of the era. Under Lady Melbourne's auspices, Annabella was soon being courted by several eligible young men, including one of the Devonshires, and William Bankes, one of Byron's Cambridge friends, who lent her a copy of *Childe Harold*. The poem seized Annabella's imagination – as it had so many others – and she contrived to meet him.

Their first encounter, in March 1812, was a taste of things to come. Annabella noted his 'natural sarcasm and vehemence', his ill-concealed distaste towards society stalwarts, and his impatience with polite conversation. She also gleaned from gossips stories that 'indicated feelings dreadfully perverted' and that he was an atheist. She felt drawn to him nonetheless, sensing, it seemed, the possibility of a great moral adventure, ending with her redemption of the most infamous man in the country. For his part, Byron was impressed by Annabella's intelligence and the breadth of her reading. Like her, he had his reservations. He was frustrated by her twee Christian moralising – he would later describe her, rather perfectly, as having been 'systematically Clarissa Harlowed' – and her prim, awkward manner in social settings. Still, she was different from most of the respectable young women thrust his way in the London marriage market and he struck up a correspondence with her which resulted in a rather perfunctory proposal, which she wisely turned down.

Despite later allegations that Annabella's initial rejection inspired Byron to dedicate himself to her ruin, he seems to have taken the snub in reasonably good spirits. In any event, there were other distractions. For much of 1812 and 1813 Byron was consumed by a raging affair with Lady Caroline Lamb, a flighty, scandal-prone society beauty who was both two years his senior and married. Although he would later savage her in verse and disavow their relationship, they were, for a period, genuinely and completely infatuated with each other. 'You drew me to you like a magnet,' Lamb wrote to him, '& I could not indeed I could not have kept away.' Byron felt similarly entranced, later explaining to a friend that 'I am easily governed by women, and she gained an ascendency over me that I could not easily shake off.'[5] But shake it off he did. In the summer of 1812 he began to drift away from her, preferring instead the company of his half-sister Augusta Leigh, the 'autumnal charms' of Lady Oxford, and disposable nights with the actresses of Drury Lane.

Lamb responded to this attempted disengagement with legendary ferocity. She broke into his house dressed as a page and attempted to stab herself when Byron's friend and accomplice John Hobhouse hustled her out. She ambushed him at a society event, again with a knife, and slashed open her hand in the chaos that ensued. When she could not find her lord in the flesh, she contented herself with sending him a locket of her pubic hair in the post, accompanied with a note signed 'From Your Wild Antelope'. At length she fell silent, and Byron could continue on his Quixotic quest for marital bliss. But she had not forgotten him.

In late 1813 Byron and Annabella resumed their cautious courtship of one another. Both were torn between a perverse mutual fascination and the profound recognition that they were spectacularly ill-suited for life together. 'She requires time and all the cardinal virtues,' he observed, accurately, to one correspondent, 'I am one who demands neither.' Annabella was similarly sceptical, but they continued to draw closer: Byron inspired by a certain fatalism about the necessity of marriage and a particular cynicism about the financial security he (inaccurately) believed that Annabella would bring him; Annabella by Christian concern for the wicked lord's soul and a genuine passion for Byron which overrode her own better judgement. In 1814, Byron proposed again – by letter – and this time Annabella accepted. They were married in the living room of her parents' house in Seaham on 2 January 1815, and then were conducted by coach to Halnaby Hall, in Yorkshire, for their wintry honeymoon.[6]

Whatever doubts Annabella might have had about Byron were soon confirmed in Yorkshire. Her husband was not used to sharing a bed and would use any device to delay having to come up to their room. This meant in practice that he would get wildly drunk – something that Annabella had never been exposed to – and curse the servants. Once in bed his behaviour was not much better: he would scream in the night and have violent nightmares which woke him up; having awakened he would roam around the galleries armed with a pistol and dagger, muttering to himself. Their stay in Halnaby Hall did, however, succeed in getting Annabella pregnant.

The couple now moved to London and hoped to settle into a more routine family life. But Byron could not be calmed. The demands of married life grated on him. He was harried by financial woes that he felt he could not discuss with his wife. He remained socially and professionally involved in the literary scene of his bachelorhood – a world from which Annabella was excluded and which was replete with temptations for her husband. Whenever Augusta Leigh was present – and Byron seemed to hunger for her company – he would make astonishingly crude and suggestive remarks.[7]

Byron's cruelty and violence of temperament only seemed to intensify as the birth of their first child approached. He remained devoted to his wife in principle, but in practice she was the recipient of his harshest words and most deliberately devastating provocations. Byron was well aware of his volatile nature. He later admitted to Lady Blessington:

> As long as I can remember anything, I recollect being subject to violent paroxysms of rage, so disproportioned to the cause as to surprise me when they were over; and this still continues. I cannot coolly view any thing which excites my feelings; and, once the lurking devil in me is roused, I lose all command of myself. I do not recover a good fit of rage for days after. Mind, I do not by this mean that the ill humour continues, as, on the contrary, that quickly subsides, exhausted by its own violence; but it shakes me terribly, and leaves me low and nervous after.[8]

Annabella had an inquisitive, methodical mind. Confronted with the tempestuous Lord Byron and witness daily to his wild moods and erratic behaviour, she set out to diagnose him. As a child she had been trained in the sciences and was a great lover of maths (Byron nicknamed her the Princess of Parallelograms)[9] and now she put her formidable mind to work solving the problem of her husband.

On 15 December 1815, their daughter, Ada, was born. About the same time, Annabella's observations on her husband began to cohere into a persuasive hypothesis. She became convinced that Byron was mad, perhaps on account of water on the brain. A secret investigation of his letters and personal effects revealed some supporting evidence, to wit a copy of the Marquis de Sade's *Justine* and a bottle of laudanum, which was used, *inter alia,* to treat the insane.[10] She began to correspond with a doctor in the hopes of achieving a formal diagnosis. In the meantime she revealed her discovery to certain of her confidantes, who were quickly convinced of her reasoning. Quietly, Annabella began to plot a separation from her husband.

Byron was in the dark about all this. Wrapped up in his own affairs, he blithely assented to her request to travel to her parents' Leicestershire home with their newborn daughter. On 15 January 1816, Annabella bid farewell to her husband and left their London home with Ada. Byron would never see either of them again.[11]

At Kirkby Mallory, Annabella informed her parents of her findings concerning her husband's mental condition and, presumably, her suspicions about his relations with Augusta. Aghast, they agreed that she should immediately begin separation proceedings. Annabella's mother went to London to meet with lawyers, armed with a testimonial written by her daughter chronicling the story of their marriage. While she was thus engaged, the doctor Annabella had hoped would confirm her homespun diagnosis of madness contacted her. Lord Byron, he informed her, was not medically insane.

This was a turning point in the affair. Under English law, divorce was incredibly hard to come by. Parliament could issue divorces, but to do so was wildly expensive and very rare.[12] Husband and wife could agree by mutual consent to sign a deed of separation, but this could be difficult to engineer if the husband (who under the law held almost all the power) refused to cooperate; Byron was stubborn and could be relied upon to resist the separation with all his considerable energies. The final option was to go to court. Up until 1857 the Church of England ruled on marital matters through the ecclesiastical courts and permitted separations only in a few extreme scenarios. One of these was insanity, which was why Annabella had been so insistent on proving that her husband was mad. But now a doctor had diagnosed Byron as unstable but sane, she was forced to find even more radical means of ending their marriage.

In early February, Byron learnt of his wife's designs. His response was a mixture of disbelief, self-pity and cold rage. He made it known that he was eager to fight the case in the courts. In the meantime, Annabella's parents had redoubled their efforts on their daughter's behalf. Later that month, they presented their lawyers with evidence that Byron had had incestuous relations with Augusta Leigh. But here, too, there was a problem. Wives could not testify against husbands. Consequently, Annabella's statements on any matter – including incest – would be inadmissible in court. In an attempt to circumvent this stipulation, Annabella began to cultivate Augusta as a confidante and tried to obtain from her a written admission that her companionship with Byron had been extralegally intimate.

But London gossips operated without any such restraints. By March, scandal threatened to engulf completely all the parties concerned. Rumour was now rife that Augusta and Byron were lovers and that her daughter Medora, born in 1814, was their love child.[13] At the time, Augusta was living with Byron in Piccadilly. In an attempt to temper suspicions she moved to St James's Palace, where she had been made a lady-in-waiting to the queen. But stories continued to circulate. A siege mentality developed in the Byron household. Byron feared being hissed and mocked if he went to the theatre. He no longer attended to his lordly duties in Parliament lest he be insulted or ridiculed by his fellow aristocrats. Crowds sometimes gathered outside his house. Friends tried to fight the allegations on his behalf in public and to lift his spirits in private, but his situation was dire. It was in these circumstances that he responded favourably to a letter from a female admirer named Claire Clairmont. The two had a number of liaisons in his Piccadilly rooms. In the subsequent correspondence Clairmont encouraged him to join her in Switzerland, tempting him with the promise of meeting her distinguished stepsister Mary, and Percy Shelley, whose poetry he admired. Byron had never needed much excuse to travel and life in London was fast becoming unbearable. 'If what was whispered and muttered and murmured was true,' he later observed, 'I was unfit for England; if false, England was unfit for me.'[14]

Nevertheless, at this point he was still well positioned to fight a divorce suit. That all changed when a vengeful Caroline Lamb re-emerged in his affairs. Near the end of March she offered her services to the Milbankes as a witness against her former lover. 'I shall tell you that which if you merely menace him with the knowledge shall make him tremble—', she promised. Annabella loathed Lamb, but was eager to hear what she had to say. On 27 March, the two women held a lurid conference in the Milbankes' London home wherein Lamb revealed that Byron had told her he had long been 'in the practice of an unnatural crime',[15] one he had apparently been schooled in at Harrow and later mastered in Turkey.

Sodomy – 'the unnatural crime' – was grounds for divorce. Annabella was triumphant; Byron was now in a hopeless situation. It was not worth destroying his reputation for a court case he would surely lose. He acceded to requests for a legal separation and accelerated his preparations for a flight to Europe. Among these were the acquisition of a doctor to accompany him on his travels. John William Polidori was a young man recently graduated from Edinburgh University who came recommended by Sir Henry Halford, physician to King George. Another was the expenditure of the massive sum of £500 on a custom-made carriage, designed to be an exact replica of Napoleon's military carriage captured at Waterloo. This enormous navy and scarlet structure came with bullet-proof walls, a gold service set, a foldable bed, a dressing room, a library and all-weather blinds. On 21 April, Byron signed the Deed of Separation. Two days later, he and Polidori climbed into their Napoleonic carriage and rumbled off towards the Channel.

At Dover, as he went into exile in circumstances that would have made a pariah of anyone else, Byron's hold over the minds of English women persisted. Waiting to embark, a local doctor reported that the tavern Byron was staying in was besieged by 'many ladies accoutred . . . as chambermaids for the purpose of obtaining under that disguise a nearer inspection' of the most notorious man in the country. It was an outfit those ladies might have avoided had they known more of Byron's proclivities. After a short voyage, Byron and Polidori arrived at Ostend and checked into a hotel. 'As soon as he reached his room,' Polidori recorded, 'Lord Byron fell like a thunderbolt upon the chambermaid.'[16]

Only twenty years old, John Polidori had dark wavy hair, umbrous eyes and stormy features – an appearance more Byronic than Byron himself. Despite his professional background in medicine, Polidori had literary ambitions and was thrilled to be in the company of England's most celebrated living poet. His association with Byron had already helped further his progress in this area: John Murray, the poet's longstanding and otherwise loyal publisher had rather duplicitously contracted Polidori to write a record of his travels with Byron, to be published at some later date. He dutifully did so, recording his impressions of Byron and the local scenery as they trundled south through the Low Countries. The surrounding area still bore the marks of war and economic ruin: marks invisible in the landscape – when they visited the site of the Battle of Waterloo, less than a year after the fact, Polidori was surprised to discover only a few ploughed-over fields and some enterprising locals hawking souvenirs for visiting tourists – but evident everywhere in the poverty and exhaustion of the populace. Polidori noted the meanness of the villages, the drawn, unattractive women, the abominable roads, the crowds of beggar boys that ran alongside their carriage.[17]

Circumstances improved as they drew closer to Switzerland, though as they entered more mountainous terrain they found that their carriage now rolled like a galleon on the high seas as they made their way up hills and down valleys, and broke down repeatedly. On 19 May they finally entered Switzerland, and a little less than a week later, and exactly a month after they left London, Polidori glimpsed the peak of Mont Blanc. As was customary for English tourists, he tried his hand at capturing its beauty in writing:

> We saw Mont Blanc in the distance; ethereal in appearance, mingling with the clouds; it is more than 60 miles from where we saw it. It is a classic ground we go over. Buonaparte, Joseph, Bonnet, Necker, Stael, Voltaire, Rousseau, all have their villas (except Rousseau). Genthoud, Ferney, Coppet, are close to the road.[18]

This was by some distance the least celebrated account of Mont Blanc that the trip produced.

Shortly afterwards they arrived at Lac Léman. At the Hôtel d'Angleterre, an exhausted Lord Byron entered his age in the register as '100' and went straight to bed. The next day Polidori and Byron went for a swim in the lake. In his diary Polidori gloated over his comity with his noble employer: 'I *rode* first with Lord Byron upon the field of Waterloo; *walked* first to see Churchill's tomb *bathed* and *rowed* first on the Leman Lake. – It did us much good.'[19]

Claire Clairmont, along with every other English holiday-maker in the vicinity, had got word of Byron's arrival and sent him several letters requesting a meeting. These went unanswered. A few days after their arrival, the two men sailed across the lake to inspect a villa. On the return journey they spotted three figures walking along the shore where they were to disembark. They rowed over, got out and met Percy Shelley, Claire Clairmont and Mary Godwin.

***

The meeting of this variously strange, troubled and talented group of people on the shores of Lac Léman was consecrated by a bizarre climactic occurrence. In 1815 a volcano had erupted on the island of Sumbawa in modern-day Indonesia. The explosion at Mount Tambora was the largest of its kind in two millennia and put 140 billion tonnes of tectonic matter into the atmosphere, disrupting global temperatures and resulting in a volcanic winter. The effects were still being felt that June in Europe, producing the famed 'Year Without a Summer' that led to famine in some parts and ruined the holiday plans of well-heeled travellers in others. The weather in Geneva was damp, draughty and overcast – more Midlands than Alpine – obliging this band of young Romantics to spend more time inside than they might have preferred. Indeed, one of their first decisions was to move from the frosty Hôtel d'Angleterre to private lodgings across the lake. Byron and his entourage took up residence in the spacious, stucco Villa Diodati; Shelley and his in the more modest Maison Chapuis, a short walk away. Across the lake their fellow English visitors studied the fugitive poets and their female companions through a telescope, and rumours spread that the disgraced Lord Byron was leading a 'league of incest' on Swiss shores.[20]

But otherwise England and its judgements could no longer intrude upon their lives. After an initial, inevitable period of mutual circumspection Shelley and Byron were getting along like old friends. Shelley won the older poet's respect on the lake when their small sailing boat was caught in a storm. Shelley could not swim and Byron briefly feared for his life as their boat was pummelled by the waters, but was impressed by his companion's courage and calm under pressure. Theirs was the only relationship to deepen by waters of Lac Léman. Claire, who had been fantasising about her reunion with Byron for weeks, and who was now also showing the first signs of pregnancy as a consequence of their assignations in London in March, found herself largely ignored by her erstwhile lover. The bored lord did, occasionally, allow her into his chambers, but only for the most cynical reasons. 'If a girl of eighteen comes prancing at you at all hours of the night,' he explained to a friend, 'there is but one way.'

She was not the only one to feel jilted by Byron. Polidori had journeyed with him from London believing that this was the beginning of a great friendship between poets and equals, but now found himself displaced in his lordship's affections by Percy Shelley. Sidelined by the two other men, Polidori became stroppy and ingenuously malicious. On one occasion while out boating with the two, he challenged Shelley to a duel after the latter beat him in a sailing race. On another, he accidentally struck Byron's knee with the oar while rowing. When his employer remarked that this had caused him some great deal of pain, he seemed to revel in it. 'I am glad of it,' Polidori supposedly replied, 'I am glad to see you can suffer pain.'

Byron would later claim that only the presence of Mary in the boat had stopped him from tipping his impudent physician into the lake.[21] Even if this is true, it is unlikely that Mary would have much appreciated his gallantry. Byron was now just one more person preventing her from spending time with Percy.

Worse yet, with the two poets now away together, Polidori turned his scorned and winsome attentions on Mary. He noted in his diary small details from daily life that reveal a young man's first hopes for a burgeoning romance ('June 2. – Breakfasted with Shelley. Read Tasso with Mrs. Shelley. Took child for vaccination.'), but his ill-conceived infatuation quickly attracted Byron's expert bullying eye. On 14 June, after a rainy spell, Byron and Polidori were sitting on the balcony when they spotted Mary making her way up the wet slope towards the villa. 'Now,' Byron said to his lovestruck physician, 'you who wish to be gallant ought to jump down this small height, and offer your arm.' This he did, and duly sprained his ankle on the damp grass. In his diary, Polidori skates over the event, simply noting, 'After dinner, jumping a wall my foot slipped and I strained my left ankle.' Byron recorded the same in a letter to John Murray, noting that his doctor had injured himself in 'tumbling from a wall; he can't jump'. He could now only walk with difficulty.

A romanticised image of Byron at Villa Diodati. In reality he was massively overweight and spent the summer crash dieting.

Polidori's injury only magnified his feelings towards Mary, and a few days after the incident he made some kind of declaration to her. Mary, who had a largely philosophical interest in free love,[22] soon disavowed him of his notions. The young doctor recorded the moment in typically elliptical fashion: 'June 18. – My leg much worse. Shelley and party here. Mrs. S[helley] called me her brother (younger).'

The days that bore witness to Polidori's tumble and the hapless climax of his longing for Mary were also days of rain, confinement, ghost stories, and literary and philosophical investigations. Trapped together in Diodati on account of the appalling weather, the group began to discuss the latest developments in science. Polidori and Shelley talked 'about principles, – whether man was to be thought merely an instrument'. The doctor might also have told the party of the recent, and scandalous, lectures given by Dr William Lawrence in London. Lawrence, a surgeon and anatomist with atheistic tendencies who had at one point been Shelley's doctor, had electrified medical London earlier that year with a series of lectures at the Royal College of Surgeons. In these talks, Lawrence had attacked certain 'false notions in physiology' that sought to explain the origins of human life by reference to fashionable pseudo-scientific theories of vitalism, animal magnetism and mesmerism. He had deconstructed the various claims that there existed an 'independent living principle, superadded to the structure of animal bodies', concluding, as only a surgeon might, that no such principle could be 'discovered amid the blood and filth of the dissecting room'. Man was matter – nothing more. But the exact opposite was also discussed at Diodati. Mary recalled that they talked too about the work of Erasmus Darwin,

> Who preserved a piece of vermicelli in a glass case, till by some extraordinary means it began to move with voluntary motion. Not thus, after all, would life be given. Perhaps a corpse would be re-animated; galvanism had given token of such things: perhaps the component parts of a creature might be manufactured, brought together, and endued with vital warmth.

Galvanism referred to the work of Luigi Galvani, the Italian scientist who had pioneered the study of electricity. His nephew, Giovanni Aldini, had pushed his research to the limit in a grisly trial at Newgate Prison in London in 1803. There, Aldini conducted experiments on the corpses of recently executed criminals. His attempts to 'revive' the hearts and circulatory systems of the deceased were largely in vain, but he stunned his audiences nonetheless. The electrified corpses convulsed on the trolley. Eyes jerked and rolled in otherwise lifeless skulls. Arms crashed up and down violently. Chest and back muscles contracted with such force that they threatened to crush the rib cage.[23]

Over a decade later, this attempt to create life electrically had not been forgotten by England's poets. 'This is the age of oddities let loose,' Byron joked, as darkly as ever, in Canto I of *Don Juan*, where 'galvanism has set some corpses grinning'.[24]

Talk of science intermingled with literary creation. On the stormy night of 18 June, around about midnight, the group 'began to talk ghostly'. Byron read from a volume of German supernatural stories and then recited parts of Coleridge's 'Christabel', passages so haunting that Shelley fled from the room in hysterics and had to be treated with ether by Polidori – one of the very few occasions on which the young doctor applied his medical training to someone other than himself. Bored with simply reading ghost stories, Byron then suggested that each of them compose one of their own. They all spent a few days writing – except poor Clairmont, excluded once again – and regrouped a few days later to judge the fruits of their labours. It was not an impressive harvest. Shelley had 'commenced one story of his earlier life' but had become bored and abandoned the attempt. Byron had sketched the plot of a story involving two wealthy young friends on an ill-fated Grand Tour; then he, too, got bored, and left the story unfinished. Polidori's tale was slightly more complete but was, in Mary's telling, not much to behold, based as it was around 'some terrible idea about a skull-headed lady, who was so punished for peeping through a keyhole – to see what I forget'. The exception to this collection of botched and mediocre productions was, of course, Mary's own, which went on to become *Frankenstein*.

Mary's first novel would be published two years later, after a number of agonising rewrites and months of fretful editing. Nonetheless, it was recognisably the same tale that she began that June. Subsequently, there has always been the temptation to assume that the basic premise of the book – a monster constructed from body parts by a maniacal medical student and then given life by an electric spark – was a product of the pseudo-scientific conversations in which Mary had participated during those June days. Frankenstein's monster, in this telling, was built of those high-flown speculations and animated by the lightning that crackled over Lac Léman. There are a number of problems with this rather clean-edged narrative. Erasmus Darwin had never claimed that electricity could create life, and Mary was well aware of it. Similarly, it is hard to see how Dr Lawrence's intense materialism could readily inspire the heady theoretical speculations that undergird *Frankenstein*'s plot. Of course, Mary's genius was to take this melange of ideas and then 'to innovate upon their combinations'. The result was an astounding work of science fiction *avant la lettre*, a parable about the moral pitfalls of scientific creation that looked two hundred years ahead to the ethical dilemmas posed by cloning, robotics and artificial intelligence.

Such at least is the conventional telling of how *Frankenstein* came to be. But while the scientific explanation of its genesis is alluring, it also seems to miss an earthier, more proximate version of the book's backstory. *Frankenstein* is a book about the perils of reckless creation. However, Dr Frankenstein's generative powers are not unique to him but are common to all humans. Every man and every woman possesses the potential to create life. In an age before widespread contraception, this potential was not easily controlled. Sexual liaisons, consensual or otherwise, produced children. Seduction, which was defined as occurring either outside of marriage or in violation of existing marital bonds, produced illegitimate children – bastards.

No reader of *Frankenstein* can forget the moment of the monster's creation – the dreary November night when the young doctor animates his creature surrounded by the muck and filth of his makeshift surgery – but what he does immediately afterwards is equally important: Frankenstein runs away. He creates life and then absconds. He dodges responsibility for what he has made.

Later, when the monster finally confronts his maker on an Alpine summit above Geneva he speaks to him as an abandoned child to a father. 'I am thy creature', the monster tells Frankenstein, 'I ought to be thy Adam.' When Frankenstein cruelly disowns him, the monster's response cuts to the heart of the matter: 'You, my creator, detest and spurn me, thy creature, to whom thou art bound by ties only dissoluble by the annihilation of one of us. You purpose to kill me. How dare you sport thus with life?'

The moment in *Frankenstein* where the monster wakes up and his creator flees.

The double tragedy for bastards was both their rejection by their parent, usually their father, and their subsequent rejection by a society that held illegitimacy to be taboo. The illegitimate child became, like the monster, 'the scorn and horror of mankind'. This was a condition that Mary understood all too well. Her stepsister

Claire Clairmont was the illegitimate child of an absentee father who now bore a child who was destined to be illegitimate too. Her lonesome half-sister Fanny Imlay, the bastard child of the rakish Gilbert Imlay, would kill herself in October 1816, while Mary was working hard at the novel. Sleeping in his crib by Lac Léman while she wrote the first pages of the book was her treasured son Wilmouse, born out of wedlock. The desperate position of bastard children in English society was one of the reasons that Shelley had attacked the exclusionary institution of marriage in the notes to 'Queen Mab' (1813). 'Society avenges herself,' he wrote there, 'on the criminals of her own creation.'[25]

At the end of 1816, another tragedy born of the paranoia concerning the legitimacy or otherwise of newborns paradoxically gave Mary her route to respectability. At some point early that summer, Harriet Shelley, Percy Shelley's lawful and unloved wife, took a lover. His identity is not clear, though he is thought to have been an officer in the British army. Whoever he was, the man soon moved on and Harriet found herself alone, shunned by her family, abandoned by her husband, and living a solitary existence in London with little money. On 9 November she wrote a final letter to her family and then vanished into the night.[26] A month later her body was fished out of the Serpentine and an autopsy confirmed what was readily apparent: she was in an advanced state of pregnancy.

With Harriet dead, Mary was free to marry Percy. They were wed in London on 30 December 1816, and nine months later their daughter Clara Shelley – their first legitimate child together – was born. Clara's future seemed secure. But as 1817 drew to a close, the question of what to do with Claire Clairmont and Lord Byron's love child was becoming ever more pressing. Clara Allegra Byron, whom her mother lovingly called Alba, was born a few weeks after Mary became Mrs Shelley. For the sake of appearances, Mary had mingled Alba with the rest of the brood and raised her publicly as if she were her own, though Claire continued (to her frustration) to live with them. Mary had also considered incorporating Alba into the large and welcoming family of their friend and literary booster Leigh Hunt. This, ultimately, came to nothing. Then in 1818, with his health declining, Percy Shelley went to see his doctor, William Lawrence, who suggested that a move to warmer climes would be beneficial. The Shelleys (and Clairmont) began to prepare to relocate to Italy, where Byron was now based. Mary and Percy hatched a plot to deliver Alba to her father, who, they believed, would be able to provide for her future in a way that Claire never could. Byron had not shown the least interest in his daughter by Claire – he had refused, even, to come and visit the Shelleys when they settled in Lake Como that spring – but in April some caprice inspired in him a degree of paternal feeling and he ordered Claire to send their daughter to him in Venice, minus mother. Near the end of the month, one of Byron's servants arrived to collect the fifteen-month-old girl. Claire was herself only twenty but was now in a heartbreaking position. By law Byron had no automatic right to custody over his illegitimate child. But he was an aristocrat with an income; she, in her own words, 'a miserable and neglected dependent'. She loved and cared for their daughter, and she had every reason so suspect that he did not. It was a choice between some hope for her baby's future social and financial security and the certainty of a warm and loving childhood. With Byron's footman waiting to deliver the child to his master, she wrote a final, anguished note to go along with Alba:

> If I have been faulty I have suffered enough to redeem my error, my child was born in sorrow and after much suffering – then I love her with a passion that almost destroys my being she goes from me. My dear Lord Byron I most truly love my child. She never checked me – she loves me most she stretches out her arms to me & cooes for joy when I take her . . . I have wept so much to night that now my eyes seem to drop hot & burning blood.

The child left for Venice and soon afterwards their reduced party moved to Tuscany. Then in August two alarming letters arrived from Venice. Alba's nurse Elise, who had accompanied her charge to Venice, now wrote to them that life in Lord Byron's Venetian household was intolerable and that Claire needed to come at once to rescue her daughter. Stricken with worry, Claire immediately set out to reclaim Alba, taking Shelley with her, and leaving Mary, Wilmouse and a sickly Clara behind. Mary struggled to keep the house together by herself and was concerned with her daughter's fever, which she was powerless to treat in the ferocious heat of the Italian summer. In the midst of her worries, another letter arrived from her husband, instructing her to come to Venice at once. She was needed to take receipt of Alba, whom Byron refused to surrender to Claire under any circumstances.

On 31 August, despite all her forebodings, Mary left for the arduous trip to Venice accompanied by her son and her fading daughter. The four-day journey to Este, a day's travel from Venice, took them through the malarial swamps that then encircled the city and broke Clara's health. They rushed her to the city to consult with Byron's doctor, but it was too late. She died in Venice and was buried in an unmarked grave on the Lido.

Shelley, meanwhile, had been conducting his own investigations into Alba's circumstances and found nothing unduly amiss. Elise, it seemed, was more concerned with her own well-being, and, possibly, was seeking a way back into the Shelley household, as she had developed an attachment to their servant Paolo (whom she did, indeed, later elope with).

After a few days with her mother, Alba was returned to her father's care. Byron promptly entrusted her to Richard Hoppner, the British consul in Venice. Alba, or Allegra as Byron now renamed her, proved to be a handful and the arrangement with the Hoppners did not last long. After she had passed through several homes, Byron finally decided to send her to receive a convent education in Bagnacavallo, near Ravenna. Claire protested vociferously but her complaints went ignored.[27] At Mary's urging Shelley tried to intervene, offering to house Allegra in his own household in the circumstances of Byron's choosing. The proposal was met with threats that if Claire and the Shelleys did not cease meddling, Byron would move Allegra to a secret convent where they would have no access to her at all. 'No one can more entirely agree with you than I in thinking that as soon as possible Allegra ought to be taken out of the hands of one as remorseless as he is unprincipled,' Mary wrote to Claire, but in the meantime nothing could be done.[28]

Nor would it. As Claire had predicted, the climate at Bagnacavallo did not agree with Allegra. She would die there of typhus in April 1822. She was five years old.

A year after Allegra's death, Marguerite Gardiner, Countess Blessington, was travelling through Genoa and struck up a friendship with Byron, who was then living there. The two engaged in long, rambling conversations, which Blessington recorded and later had published in London. At one point Byron mused on how a death had a way of magnifying, post-mortem, his affections for those who he had found so tiresome to deal with in life: 'How did I feel this when Allegra, my daughter, died! While she lived, her existence never seemed necessary to my happiness; but no sooner did I lose her, than it appeared to me as if I could not live without her.'

The words of the monster on the mountaintop resound: *How dare you sport thus with life?*

***

The question of culpability – of who is the real monster – lurks behind every line of *Frankenstein*. Another book that also arose out of that summer by Lac Léman would make the question explicit and answer it in an incendiary fashion. In 1819, Byron, still idling in Venice, received a troubling piece of news from London. A scandalous novella had been published under his name, first in a literary journal and then as a bound volume. It was called *The Vampyre* and it told the story of the friendship between a wealthy orphan named Aubrey and the mysterious Lord Ruthven. The latter was an obvious stand-in for Byron: his name was an allusion to the antagonist of *Glenarvon*, a *roman-à-clef* by Caroline Lamb (a thinly fictionalised account of her affair with the poet that was also published in that turbulent summer of 1816), and his cold good looks and icy social manner were recognisably Byronic, in both literal and literary terms. Furthermore, the description of Ruthven dwells on his 'irresistible powers of seduction' and discusses at some length how the dark Lord shuns adventuresses, adulteresses and society flirts in favour of virtuous women and the most innocent young girls, whom he can then corrupt. This is abhorrent in itself, but what is even more appalling is the aftermath of Ruthven's seduction of previously chaste women: 'All those females whom he had sought, apparently on account of their virtue, had, since his departure, thrown even the mask aside, and had not scrupled to expose the whole deformity of their vices to the public gaze.'

Ruthven leaves a trail of destruction in his wake wherever he goes. Aubrey learns this the hard way after he foolishly agrees to go on the Grand Tour with his new friend. After a period he becomes disgusted with Ruthven's appalling behaviour and the two part ways. Continuing on alone, Aubrey soon arrives in Greece, where he falls in love with a local girl named Ianthe. She inducts him into the local lore concerning the 'vampyre', and in her description of the supernatural being, the lovestruck Aubrey dimly discerns 'a pretty accurate description of Lord Ruthven'. Ianthe is struck down by the monster a few days later. Plunged into grief, Aubrey enters a delirium. Ruthven visits his sickbed and the two resume their travels, only for the Lord to be killed by bandits during an ambush on their party. But when Aubrey returns to England he finds Ruthven alive, shape-shifted into Earl Marsden, of June. The two men had gone off alone on a mini-pilgrimage around sites associated with Jean-Jacques Rousseau. On the trail of his great novel *Julie*, they wandered together in stunned silence through the vineyards of Nerni, in awe of the beauty all about them. 'Thank God,' Byron suddenly exclaimed, 'Polidori is not here.' When, at the end of August, the Shelleys left and John Hobhouse arrived, Polidori's days as Byron's companion were clearly numbered. He was released at the beginning of the September and began work on *The Vampyre* shortly after. Polidori's only famous work was in a sense a high Gothic retelling of his angst-ridden relationship with England's most notorious poet, and a very modern parable about the dangers of meeting one's idols.

But *The Vampyre* is more than simply a fictionalised account of a friendship gone askew. It is also principally, and given the circumstances of its inspiration and composition perhaps ineluctably, a story about seducers and their 'serpent's art'. Hanging over the Villa Diodati was both the detritus from Mount Tambora and the wreckage that Byron had left behind in England. Each cast its shadow. Inside, the pathetic, pregnant figure of Clairmont and the mute and nameless Alba she bore were a palpable reminder that actions have consequences. Mary also posed a problem. Why had she wrecked the home and life of another woman, simply to traipse after an unstable and dissolute baronet's son, their own illegitimate child in tow? Added to the complexity was the fact that Polidori's own attempts at courting Mary had met with rejection and ridicule. His failure in this arena might have led him to speculate on why reckless – and sporadically wicked – men like Byron and, to a lesser degree, Shelley, were able to attract women while he could not. *The Vampyre* was also an attempt to solve the mystery of attraction. Hidden within it was a solution to that mystery, and it was an answer born of the same speculative science that infused *Frankenstein*.

In the final passages of *The Vampyre* Aubrey goes mad as he watches Ruthven charm his beautiful, chaste younger sister. As his mental condition declines, strange things occur. He hears Ruthven's voice in his ear and feels his presence about him at all times. Ruthven consumes his thoughts and exerts invisible but decisive control over his actions. Aubrey seems to hover somewhere between life and death. He is physically present in the world but practically powerless to intervene in it. He is living in a kind of suspended animation, having lost his free will but retained his normal bodily functions. Polidori conveys Aubrey's odd condition in a convincing manner, for it resembles a state he had studied extensively as a medical student: somnambulism.

In his final year at Edinburgh University, Polidori had submitted a thesis in Latin entitled *De Oneirodynia*, 'On Sleepwalking'.[31] The study of sleepwalking, or somnambulism as it was referred to, was an interesting and unusual choice for the young medic. Unusual because somnambulism was inextricably connected to mesmerism, which was among the most contested subjects of the day. Mesmerists were fascinated by somnambulism because it appeared to be an intermediate state between life and death. The somnambulist was physiologically alive but neurologically incapacitated in some way. The condition of the somnambulist seemed to demonstrate that the body and the will could be temporarily separated, that man could become an automaton.

Pseudo-scientists and quacks were not alone in this fascination. Somnambulism attracted the attention of serious scholars. Among this group the consensus was that somnambulism was, like most sleep disorders, a kind of insanity or mania. Sleeping and dreaming had long been associated with madness. When the body rested, so too did man's faculties. This was 'when monarch Reason sleeps', wrote one nineteenth-century doctor, quoting Dryden.[32] The association with madness explained why somnambulists seemed to do such strange things: attempting to climb walls and trees, shouting incoherent and nonsensical phrases, brandishing weapons. But what was truly unique to the condition was the curious pliability of somnambulists. They were totally docile, content to obey commands without question, and were thus ripe for manipulation. In Richerand's *Elements of Physiology* (1815) the French doctor observed that in somnambulism 'Sometimes one organ of sense remains open to impression, and then you can direct, at pleasure, the intellectual action. Thus, you will make him that talks in his sleep, speak on what subject you choose, and steal from him the confession of his most secret thoughts.'[33]

The mesmerists had noticed exactly the same phenomenon. But whereas the staid men of science believed that this strange state arose out of some kind of neurological disorder that could neither be controlled nor predicted, the mesmerists believed that they could induce the same condition. Starting with the pioneering work of Amand-Marie-Jacques de Chastenet, Marquis de Puységur, mesmerists began to experiment with 'artificial somnambulism', a precursor to hypnotism, whereby patients were put into a somnambulistic state through the (supposed) manipulation of their natural magnetic fields by a skilled mesmerist. In the years preceding the French Revolution thousands of such experiments were performed, often before large audiences. Joseph Deleuze, a contemporary scholar of the phenomenon, claimed that in the half century following Puységur's initial experiments in the 1760s as many as fifty thousand Frenchmen witnessed successful attempts at artificial somnambulism. He also stressed that 'there are prodigious differences between magnetisers, as to the power which they are capable of exerting', and that while 'some have frequently produced the state of somnambulism . . . others have made numerous efforts for that purpose, without obtaining such a result'. Those who possessed that special ability became powerful indeed, for their patients were 'subjected to the will of his magnetiser'.[34]

But with power came responsibility. Puységur had stated from the outset that his fellow magnetisers should 'fear the effects of animal magnetism in the hands of dishonest men' and was particularly concerned about artificial somnambulism being used to sexually exploit women.[35] His worries were soon borne out. In the 1790s animal magnetism as a field of study had been fatally discredited on account of its connection with certain unscrupulous men. Among them was Alessandro Cagliostro, the Italian conman, rival of Giacomo Casanova, and sometime resident of the Bastille for defrauding Marie Antoinette during the Affair of the Diamond Necklace. Cagliostro was also an occultist and 'healer' who dabbled in mesmerism. His abilities in this field had attracted a devout following in certain Parisian social circles, and Cagliostro then 'inflamed them with the desire of beholding extraordinary things; abused their credulity and seduced the imagination of females, whom he rendered instrumental to various deceitful purposes, without their even suspecting it'.[36]

A Practitioner of Animal Magnetism, a late eighteenth century engraving.

Things were not much better in England. There a certain Dr John Bell gave accounts of his many experiments in artificial somnambulism in his 1792 treatise *The General and Particular Principles of Animal Electricity and Magnetism*. The work reveals Dr Bell to be a first-rate fabulist but a scientist and ethicist of indeterminate rank. His reports are full of his deft exploitation of women in the name of science, including making them drink wine, remove their garters, break wind and, on one extraordinary occasion, be groped by a lunatic.[37] It was unsurprising, then, that mesmerism became connected in the public mind with underhand attempts to sexually control women.

This distrust seeped into popular perceptions of more reputable fields of research. When Humphry Davy conducted his famous experiments with laughing gas – another, more scientific attempt to put the human body into an intermediate state between life and death – he was ridiculed by London satirists who accused him only half-jokingly of putting women 'in a state of gas' for purposes less pure than the plain advancement of human knowledge. The anonymous author of *The Sceptic* (1800) claimed that a network of doctors pimped their patients to Davy, who treated them with gas and then 'in this insidious manner gained admittance to their lovely persons; he warms their snowy bosoms; blows up the latent spark of soft desire; explores each hidden source of human bliss, and unsuspected, riots in their charms!'[38]

'More than one fair patient,' the author scurrilously concluded, 'has become a mother in consequence' of Davy's experiments.

These new sciences were treated with all the more suspicion on account of their French origins. Horror, first at the revolution, and then at Bonapartism, inspired general revulsion at all things novel and French, and at that time one tended to be synonymous with the other. In a lavishly scatological cartoon from 1800, James Gillray depicted the Channel awash with excrement emanating from a huge dunghill in France. Napoleon floats foremost amid the ordure in his iconic bicorne, labelled 'First Horse Turd'. Lesser effluvia – Robespierre, Marat, Talleyrand – bob about him, while in the dunghill itself sit the names of other French agitators mixed in with their English confederates: Thomas Paine, William Godwin, and Joseph Priestley – a radical, a scientist, and the man who first synthesised laughing gas.[39] Among English reactionaries it was taken for granted that radical science and radical politics were dangerously intertwined. John Thelwall had lectured on Vitalism in 1793 and had spent 1794 in the Tower of London on charges of treason. In 1806 the *Anti-Jacobin Review* commented on a recent French work on universal fluid, in which Animal Magnetism was decried as a 'scandalous delusion' funded by Bonaparte. Artificial somnambulism was the target of the *Review*'s especial contempt, and its editors aligned themselves with 'the enemies of *somnambulism*' who 'exclaim, that all these pretended wonders are but impostures, the sport of delirious imaginations, the intrigues of silly mean women, the frauds of intriguers'.[40]

This, then, was the medical field that the precocious student John Polidori chose to specialise in while at Edinburgh. The study of somnambulism was sexually and politically subversive, indelibly linked to the French enemy, and treated with the greatest scepticism by reputable scientists. Polidori could not have been ignorant of these facts. Indeed, as the son of Catholic immigrants he must have been doubly aware of the subject's negative associations. But such considerations do not seem to have restrained his enthusiasm. Polidori remained fascinated by somnambulism even after he had graduated. In his journal from the summer of 1816 he records that he visited a certain Dr Odier in Geneva, 'who talked with me about somnambulism. . . . Odier gave me yesterday many articles of *Bibliothèque* – translated and *rédigés* by himself, and to-day a manuscript on somnambulism.'[41] This meeting with Odier took place only a few days before the night that gave birth to *Frankenstein*, and it may well be Odier's manuscript that was the basis for Polidori's conversation with Shelley on 8 June which, in his estimation, left Mary and Claire's 'brains whizzed with giddiness'.[42] Somnambulism was at the forefront of Polidori's mind that summer, where it mingled with his frustrations, his fantasies and his literary ambitions. It was there when he sat down to compose

The Vampyre, in which he used it as a device to explain Lord Ruthven's/Lord Byron's 'irresistible powers of seduction'.

Despite the botched circumstance of its publication, the success of *The Vampyre* made Polidori's name as a writer. But it did not cure his melancholy. A troubled, turbulent young man, he died in obscure circumstances in his rooms in Golden Square, Soho, in August 1821. He was buried in a Catholic graveyard, but all London knew that he had taken his own life, most probably poisoning himself with prussic acid. Polidori's death was but one of a wave that swept the male members of the party that had gathered by Lac Léman in 1816. A year later Percy Shelley would drown in the Gulf of Spezia, when his boat, the *Don Juan*, sank in a storm. Mary was left numb with grief, and it fell to Byron, Leigh Hunt, and a newcomer to the party – the leonine, ferociously Byronic Edward Trelawney – to burn the dead poet's body on the shores of the Tyrrhenian Sea, near Viareggio. Pouring out her misery in a letter to Maria Gisborne, Mary remarked parenthetically that 'Lord Byron has been very kind – but [his mistress] restrains him perhaps – she being an Italian is capable of being jealous of a living corpse such as I.'

If in tragedy she finally saw something to commend in Byron's character, she did not have much time to enjoy his company. Nine months later, Byron was dead in Missolonghi, struck down by disease as he fought for Greek independence. In a letter to Trelawney, Mary, clear-eyed as ever, noted that while Byron 'could hardly be called a friend', she had admired his poetry and had bonded with him at an intellectual and emotional level. She felt a pang when she saw his cortège pass beneath her window in Kentish Town on its way up Highgate Hill to his final resting place in Nottinghamshire. Not even little Wilmouse survived the massacre. He had succumbed to a fever in Rome in 1819 only a few months after the death of his younger sister, Clara.

Within a few years of *Frankenstein*'s publication all the men who had been present at its birth were dead. But the women they had known and loved and loathed, lived on – as did the problem of free love. Mary believed in free love philosophically even as she doubted it practically. In contrast to her stepsister, she had always been wary about the consequences for women of the free pursuit of their desires. Nothing she had experienced in the first twenty-five years of her life could have disabused her of this caution. The problem was not one of principles but of underlying structures. The terms of engagement in courtship were wildly skewed in favour of men. Men risked relatively little in seduction; women risked their reputation, their health, and the lives of their unborn children. This inequality was sustained by a series of interlocking systems of control and censure: some formal, others less so. Mary's parents had believed that these might be overthrown in a single motion, but by the 1820s the likelihood of a revolution in Britain was small. What was needed was tactical legal reform that would pave the way to lasting equality. What was also needed was a reformer with the will to make it happen. A decade after her husband's death, Mary met her.

***

Caroline Norton and Mary Shelley had much in common. Caroline was also the heir to a great literary and political tradition. Her grandfather was the great Anglo-Irish playwright and founder of Drury Lane Theatre, Richard Brinsley Sheridan, who was also a leading Whig parliamentarian. Like Mary's, this distinguished pedigree did little to materially improve the quality of her upbringing and she grew up in genteel poverty, the family surviving on a mixture of aristocratic patronage and royal charity. Consequently, though she never knew the kind of social ostracism that was the water Mary swam in, she could not depend, like most women of her class, on marrying or inheriting herself into financial security.

Her mother strove to win good matches for her daughters, but all she could secure for the flirtatious, playful, endlessly talented Caroline was the hand of George Norton, a dullard and a vulgarian with little money, a titled older brother, and a marked aversion to practising his chosen profession of lawyer.

As a result of Norton's reluctance to work, his bride was obliged to turn her childhood passion for writing into paid work. She published her first poetry collection, *The Sorrows of Rosalie*, to a warm reception in 1829 when she was twenty-one – almost exactly the same age as Mary had been when she published *Frankenstein* a decade earlier. Over the next forty years, Caroline would publish over a dozen novels, plays and volumes of poetry, and a number of profoundly influential political pamphlets; through her salons and dinner parties, as well as the journals she edited and contributed to, she helped shape literary and political life in London for a generation. This is a body of work and an enterprise that has now been almost totally forgotten, which is regrettable – for it was Caroline, just as much as Mary, who helped create the modern conception of the independent female intellectual.

It is not exactly clear when the two women met. There is good evidence to suggest that Mary wrote an 1831 profile of Caroline in the *New Monthly Magazine*. The sketch reveals a writerly appreciation of form and a preference for Norton's refined phrasing over the 'gaudy glittering sentences' of her rivals. It also shows a pronounced interest in her literary pedigree, 'in that long chain of hereditary talent . . . the rich cluster of genius and talent which is wreathed round her name she inherits'. This lineage fostered a childhood of scribbling, a *'furor scribendi'* that blossomed into adolescent precocity, and, by the time this piece was written, several works of poetry, some plays, and half a novel.[43]

The accompanying portrait shows a beautiful young woman with rich brown hair, thick eyebrows, and a Grecian aspect that recalled the Mediterranean temptresses of Byron's verse. In her own lifetime, Caroline was frequently compared to Byron – she was the 'Byron of poetesses' – but he was at least as Nortonian as she was Byronic.[44] The two shared an energy, an indefinable attraction, and a mastery of the written and spoken word that persists even at the distance of two centuries. Above all, they shared an unrivalled capacity for mischief-making. As a younger woman Caroline had been known simply as one of the 'strange girls' of the Sheridan clan, 'who swear and say all sorts of odd things to make men laugh'. But she soon came into her own as especially volatile company. In 1828 the Whig grandee Henry Edward Fox recorded in his diary how she teasingly declared her love to one John Talbot in front of her 'astonished husband before a roomful of people at Chesterfield House . . . The whole of it was a fiction; but such allusions are both dangerous and indecent for so young a woman. Her oddity makes her at present the fashion; and people admire her prodigiously.'[45]

By 1832 she was putting her considerable charms to nobler use, throwing herself into the effort to pass the Great Reform Bill. That year also marked the definite beginning of her relationship with Mary – the journal Caroline edited, *The Court Magazine and Belle Assemblée*, published a short story called 'The Pole' written by the 'author of "Frankenstein"'.[46]

By 1833 Caroline had borne her unloving and unlovely husband three sons – Fletcher (1829), Brinsley (1831) and William (1833) – and remained a source of fascination in society. A remarkable account of her effect on men survives in the diary of the society painter Benjamin Haydon, who was a regular at Caroline's salon in Storey's Gate that year. Haydon appears to have been a particularly easy mark, but his breathless account of her performance at a dinner party in July gives a flavour of the otherworldly effect she had on the men in her circle: 'Mrs Norton . . . lightened up at midnight, and gave us specimens of her exquisite humour. Her fine black eyes shone like Arsinoe's! Her Aegyptian mouth, her sublime head, looked quite inspired! It was a sight, & never to be forgotten!'

A few weeks later he entrusted to his journal more of the same florid prose:

> A more unaffected creature on thorough acquaintance does not exist. There she sat, looking like a Divinity, calm, self possessed. I could hardly trust myself to look at her! Grand Creature! . . . She told me she was fierce in her temper! Let her be. . . . She has beauty, Genius, & is not blue! which I abhor.[47]

Haydon, unsurprisingly, proved to be too insistent in his affections for Caroline and eventually had to be eased out of her circle.[48] But there were many more admirers waiting in the wings. In 1835, Edward Trelawney, Byron and Shelley's former accomplice and Mary's erstwhile suitor,[49] returned from a tour of America and re-entered London society. He soon encountered and was immediately bewitched by Caroline Norton. Known as 'Corsair Trelawney' in London social circles, the tall, lean Trelawney, his jaw visibly scarred from a gunshot wound to the face sustained during a failed assassination attempt in Greece, cut a piratical figure in London drawing rooms. But he was no match for Caroline. He was lavish in his pursuit of her, too much so, and within two years she was bored of this 'mysteriously awful, & vaguely sublime, but very fierce' man who, though fifteen years her senior, played the part of the lovestruck younger beau, made scenes in public, and ended the relationship with a rude, incoherent and faintly threatening letter.

While Trelawney had been making a fool of himself, Mary and Caroline became close friends. Mary participated in the London season of 1835 and had joined Trelawney on the social circuit. She followed Trelawney's courtship of Caroline with some amusement and no little encouragement – though whether this support was well-intentioned or otherwise is not wholly clear. In a letter sent that October, Mary dwelt at length on Caroline's charms, declaring that 'I never saw a woman I thought so fascinating. Had I been a man I should certainly have fallen in love with her; as a woman, ten years ago, I should have been spellbound, and had she taken the trouble, she might have wound me round her little finger.' She went on to praise in fulsome manner Caroline's wit, her beauty, her centrality to London social life.

Caroline Norton, sometimes known as the 'Byron of Poetesses'.

Perhaps she meant all this – she certainly repeated similar sentiments, in less rococo phrasing, on other occasions – but perhaps she was tempting Trelawney on in his vain endeavour, dangling before his hungry rake's eyes the prospect of an immortal conquest. The very next day she sent a letter to her friend Maria Gisborne. 'Trelawney is in England,' she wrote, 'he is enchained by Mrs. Norton – I do not wonder at the latter – she is a wonderful creation possessing wit, beauty and sweetness at their highest grade – They say a stony heart withal – so I hope she will make him pay for his numerous coqueteries [sic] with our sex.'[50]

In any event, Caroline and Mary's friendship proved genuine.

By April 1836, Mary was writing to Caroline for help with a delicate matter. That month, her father had died at the age of eighty. To prevent her stepmother from lapsing into abject poverty, she sought to have Godwin's modest pension transferred over to his widow. From the outset Caroline was willing and happy to help, though she was clear that Mary's chances would be significantly improved if she appealed directly to the Prime Minister, Lord Melbourne. In the letters that followed, Caroline demonstrated her familiarity with the British patronage system while also revealing her wit, her powers of social observation, and her vivid, antic prose:

> As to petitioning, no one dislikes begging more than I do, especially when one begs for what seems mere justice; but I have long observed that though people will resist claims (however just) they like to do favours. Therefore, when I beg I am a crawling lizard, a humble toad, a brown snake in cold weather, or any other simile most feebly 'rampante,' the reverse of 'rampant,' which would be the natural attitude for petitioning, but which must never be assumed except in the poodle style, standing with one's paws bent to catch the bits of bread on one's nose.
>
> Forgive my jesting. Upon my honour, I feel sincerely anxious for your anxiety, and sad enough on my own affairs; but Irish blood will dance. My meaning is, that if one asks at all, one should rather think of the person written to than one's own feelings. He is an indolent man – talk of your literary labours; a kind man – talk of her age and infirmities; a patron of all genius – talk of your father's and your own; a prudent man – speak of your likelihood of the pension being a short grant (as you have done); lastly, he is a great man – take it all as a personal favour.

Those last, intimate lines could not have been written at a more germane moment. A few months later, in the summer of 1836, the extent of Caroline Norton's relationship with Lord Melbourne would become the subject of a legal battle as well as a national fixation. It would also begin a heroic, decades-long struggle on Caroline's part that would result in the transformation of the rights of English women.

***

Under English law there were four civil actions available in the instance of seduction. Only one of these actions was open to women. This was the Breach of Promise to Marry tort, which allowed seduced women to seek damages in court if a man proposed marriage and then reneged on the offer at a later date. The tort for Seduction allowed fathers to sue the seducers of their daughters under a largely defunct but socially useful legal fiction of *per quod servitium amisit* ('whereby he lost services'), which held that a seduced daughter meant a loss of services for the father – anything as small as the making of his cup of tea at breakfast time – for which he was allowed to seek compensation.[51]

The final two actions were open only to husbands. The first was Alienation of Affection, which was open to any husband whose wife deserted him on account of the interference or meddling of another man. Alienation of Affection was distinct from the second charge in that it did not require sexual relations to have occurred between the defendant and the wife in question. That second, more serious charge, of Criminal Conversation (normally abbreviated to 'Crim. Con.'), provided for damages in the instance of adultery, with the court requiring reasonable evidence that a 'criminal intercourse' had existed between alleged adulterer and alleged adulteress.

The legal complication in Crim. Con. cases came in meeting the burden of proof. On account of spousal privilege, neither husband nor wife could testify in court against the other. As a consequence servants were called upon to stand in judgement of their masters' and mistresses' actions in a public space. The ensuing drama was always a source of public fascination. Whole magazines, such as *The Crim. Con. Gazette*, existed to feed the appetite for information about the sexual lives of England's rich and titled. But for all the shame involved in the public disclosure and society scandal that such cases brought with them, they remained a perennial temptation. The court awards could be enormous – the highest was £20,000 – and so the suit became a magnet for blackmailers, troublemakers, and those out to destroy the fortunes as well as the reputations of their rivals.

William Lamb, 2nd Viscount Melbourne, and twice prime minister of the United Kingdom (in 1834 and 1835–41), knew all about Crim. Con. cases. Had he cared to, he could easily have brought such a case against Byron when the latter cuckolded him quite spectacularly with his wife Caroline Lamb. But to do so would not have been in Melbourne's character. A raffish, charming, liberal gentleman, he had been raised in a permissive aristocratic atmosphere that regarded discreet affairs as the norm. Following Caroline's death in 1828, Melbourne had sought companionship in the arms of married women and had thought nothing of it. Husbands had thought otherwise. In 1828 a Crim. Con. case was brought against him by Lord Branden, the spouse of his mistress, Lady Branden, which Melbourne dodged only by means of a generous out-of-court settlement. In June 1836 he found himself accused again, this time by George Norton.

By the time that court case began in the stifling heat of Court of Common Pleas in Westminster, George Norton had known Lord Melbourne for over six years. The relationship was cordial and, for Norton, financially beneficial. In 1830 Melbourne (at Caroline's request) had secured Norton a lucrative job as a magistrate in Aldgate, east London, where he presided over the legal conflicts of London's working classes. What divided them was politics – Melbourne was a Whig, Norton the most reactionary kind of back-country Tory – and Caroline Norton. Caroline and Melbourne had become friendly during the great flurry of political activity that preceded the passage of the Great Reform Act of 1832. For much of the 1830s he was a regular at her salon and in her larger social circle. Melbourne was everything that Caroline sought in a man: powerful, intelligent, a great performer passionately involved in the issues of the day. Soon Melbourne was stopping by her home with great regularity on leaving work and was keeping up a daily correspondence with her.

While Caroline's relationship with Melbourne intensified, her marriage was falling apart. Norton was stupid, priggish and vindictive. He periodically beat her. In 1835 she moved to separate from him, but when he denied her access to her sons she submitted to a reconciliation. In the spring of 1836 there was another contretemps. Again she moved out of his house and again, when her sons were taken from her, she moved to mend fences. But this time Norton refused her. Spite and wounded pride almost certainly played their part, but it also seems that the prospect of trashing the reputation of the sitting Whig Prime Minister was too much of a temptation for him and his Tory handlers. A Crim. Con. suit was brought against the PM and *Norton v. Viscount Melbourne*, dubbed the 'Trial of the Century', was scheduled for 22 June 1832.

For all the hype, the trial lasted a day and a night and resulted in a victory for the Prime Minister. Norton failed to win any of the £10,000 he had sued for and went home in the identical condition to that which he had begun. Neither of the named parties in the suit had been present in the courtroom, though both had been represented by veteran barristers. The trial's real victim was Caroline Norton, who had neither been present nor represented. Crim. Con. cases were strictly clashes between men. The women they squabbled over were treated as collateral damage – and for Norton a great deal of damage was done. An array of servants – many of them clearly well trained by the prosecution's team of lawyers – had testified that they had observed 'familiarities and such things as would make you wonder' at Storey's Gate whenever Melbourne had come to visit Caroline. The star witness, the dipsomaniac, tragicomic figure of former servant John Fluke, readily admitted to having had a few drinks before taking the stand and went on to claim to have caught the couple *in flagrante*, with Caroline spread on a rug, thigh exposed, 'like a Spartan virgin'.[52] Caroline's letters to and from Melbourne, many of them achingly banal in content, were scoured for proof of lustful intention. Even though the jury (a diverse crowd of ten merchants, a banker and a retired admiral) found for Melbourne, Caroline's reputation in polite society could not survive such exposure.[53] She was forever afterwards associated with scandal, a point made clear when upon her accession to the throne a year after the trial, Queen Victoria refused to allow Caroline to appear at court – a rite of passage for all well-born men and women.[54] 'A woman,' Caroline wrote to Mary, a few days after the end of the trial, 'is made a helpless wretch by these laws of men.'[55]

For Caroline the most harmful legacy of the trial was her separation from her three young sons. After a period of initial uncertainty as to whether her estranged husband would allow her access to them, it became clear that he would not and that his refusal to do so was perfectly within the limits of the law. Confronted by unjust laws, she took up her pen and determined to change them. As she began her campaign in the latter half of 1836, the woman she turned to for support was Mary Shelley.

In between her humiliation in 1836 and her triumph in 1839 with the passage of the Custody of Infants Act, Caroline published no fewer than three pamphlets arguing for immediate reform of the law. Mary only worked closely with her on the first of these – *Observations on the Natural Claim of the Mother to the Custody of Her Infant Children* (1837) – but all three shared a common refrain, and Caroline's objectives and reasoning were laid out in a long letter to Mary in January 1837. The aim was simple: 'that children under the age of seven should belong, at all events, to the mother; and after that access dependent, not on the father, but on the Court of Chancery'. This, she noted, and which Mary must likely already have known, was simply extending to married mothers the rights afforded to the mothers of illegitimate children.

Her reasoning was twofold. First, there was a straightforward Enlightenment argument in favour of natural rights. The court-sanctioned separation of a mother from her children was a clear 'perversion of natural rights' that had to be corrected. The second argument attacked the organising principle of English common law: the sovereignty of property rights. She wrote to Mary:

> In this commercial country, the rights of property are the only rights really and efficiently protected; and the consideration of property the only one which weighs with the decision made in a court of justice. The great obstacle, in all the cases I have looked through, to the woman obtaining her child, or even obtaining that it should be in the hands of a third party as a proper guardian, has been the want of property to justify the interference of the law.

The radical nature of Caroline's reasoning can be easy to miss. Courts were unwilling to help mothers in her position – and vulnerable women in general – because 'the interference of the law' was usually premised on some kind of violation of property rights. By making a legal case premised on the violation of *natural* rights, Caroline was essentially arguing that the courts should concern themselves with questions of morality, not just property. This was revolutionary. Early nineteenth-century Britain was a modern(ising) society with a medieval legal system. The focus on property rights organised relations vertically. The fundamental question in the overwhelming majority of legal actions was one of who owned what. By injecting morality into the system, Caroline was calling for an equalisation of legal identities. Relationships would now be organised horizontally on the basis of rights, not upwards and downwards on the basis of ownership, tithes and obligations.

Working through her able and courageous parliamentary proxy Sir Thomas Talfourd, Caroline secured the passage of the Custody of Infants Act in 1839. The bill was the first feminist piece of legislation in English history. It identified rights unique to women and guarded them from abuse by men. In so doing it created a precedent that would reverberate throughout the English legal system.

But Caroline's victory was not without its ironies. In a letter of February 1837, she informed Mary of Talfourd's first attempt to introduce the bill to Parliament. 'I thought you would be glad to know this,' she wrote, 'both for the sake of the sex (whom you have not the clever woman's affectation of thinking inferior to men) and for me.' Here we see Caroline invoke a sense of sisterly camaraderie in pursuit of legal reform: they are two feminists working side-by-side for social change. The letter is revealing because everywhere else Caroline tended to distance herself from feminists, and in an 1838 letter to John Murray explicitly complained of scabrous political writers who 'erect an imaginary Mrs. Norton, something between a barn-actress and a Mary Wollstonecraft, and . . . hunt her down with unceasing persever-ance'.[56] Elsewhere she refuted 'the wild and ridiculous doctrine of [gender] equality'.

It is hard to know what Mary made of this dualism in her close friend. She had spent her whole life in the company of radicals who had achieved little, so she must have admired the practical Norton who said what was necessary to do the transformative. Nonetheless, given how much she treasured the memory of her father, her husband and, above all, her mother, she surely must have resented this disavowal of her family's radical legacy.

The most poignant irony was the fact that the new law did nothing for Caroline. Following its passage, Norton moved the sons to Scotland and into the separate Scottish legal system where the Act had no power. In the end, only tragedy reunited Caroline with her sons. In 1842 her son William fell from a horse, contracted complications from his injuries and died of septicaemia soon afterwards. The loss softened her husband's attitude and for the rest of her life she enjoyed more or less unrestrained access to her sons. The rapprochement had other welcome consequences. In 1848 she signed a legal deed of separation with her husband that guaranteed her an income.

The 1840s were a period of peace for both Mary and Caroline. The two women spent their time writing, travelling, and worrying about their sons. Their correspondence continued and they shared with one another the travails peculiar to women in their then uncommon position: single, self-supporting, intellectual. In an amusing letter from the time, chiding Mary for her lack of financial nous, Caroline joked about how she 'run about alone like a young bachelor'. Their lives were unconventional for their age, but their letters reveal very modern concerns. They fret over their sons' education, over securing payment from publishers, over finding suitable housing in London for a single woman.

In the wider world, political reform was gradually coming to English society. Ever since the Great Reform Act, women's rights had been a staple for parliamentary debate. The Custody of Infants Act had been a high water mark, but there was hope in other areas as well. Married women's property rights and divorce were two subjects of perennial discussion, as were seduction and prostitution. The rights of seduced women had been discussed during the debates surrounding the 1834 Poor Law, and were to come to parliamentary attention twice more in the 1840s. Throughout the decade, petitions flooded in to Parliament, calling for the greater policing of seduction and prostitution. The two phenomena were seen as fundamentally intertwined, as a seduced woman was not far from becoming a fallen woman. Seduction was a gateway to prostitution – the Great Social Evil, as it was known. In 1844, Henry Phillpotts, Bishop of Exeter, took up the issue. 'There were none so thoroughly Satanical as the seducer,' he told the House of Lords, 'and if it were possible for human laws to reach him, there was no punishment that ought to be forborne.'[57]

The bishop's concerns came to naught that year, but in 1847 the question was brought before the Commons when the Birmingham MP Richard Spooner introduced the Seduction and Prostitution Suppression Bill. Under the bill's provisions, men found guilty of seduction would face imprisonment 'with or without hard labour, in the common gaol or house of correction for any term not exceeding two years'. The bill was supported both by Tory moralists and by radical members such as the flammulously named Henry Galgacus Redhead Yorke, who growled from the floor 'that in his opinion it was the province of the House to put down every abomination that came under its cognizance, and, therefore, he came with the intention of supporting the measure of the hon. Gentleman opposite.'[58]

Despite these encouraging displays of bipartisanship, and the great support for the bill in the country at large,[59] its opponents in the Commons were more numerous and no less convinced of their cause. Members argued against the bill along legal lines that the offence was ill-defined, that the accused had insufficient avenues for appeal, and that the burden of proof would always be insufficient in such cases, and along moral lines that publicising lewdness in the courts would only aid its spread in the public at large. More worrying yet, men would be exposed to all kinds of new perils from scheming, cynical women. John Arthur Roebuck summarised the threat to British men: 'Under this Bill any man could be made the victim of the vilest conspiracy. . . . Under the provisions of this Act no one would be safe, from the Archbishop of Canterbury downwards – nay, not even the hon. Member for Birmingham himself.'

The bill was withdrawn. But once again a new fault line in British politics had been demarcated. Did the law exist to protect men or women, to guard morality or property, to buttress the existing order or to bring about reform?

These were big questions that touched every area of English life. But when the focus was narrowed down to issues of love, sex and courtship – and the potential of all those to impinge upon the law – then what was really at stake was the institution of marriage. Marriage was at the heart of English society. It was an event that everyone strove towards in the course of their own lives. It reaffirmed the bonds of law and religion that organised the nation and those of status and property that organised society. Marriage also entrenched sexual inequality. At the altar the woman ceased to exist. Her legal identity was subsumed into her husband's and the two became indivisible in the eyes of the law. This was the terrible significance of Miss Caroline Sheridan's transformation into Mrs George Norton. This was the principle of coverture, so called, as Blackstone noted, because while married the wife's existence was 'incorporated and consolidated into that of the husband: under whose wing, protection and *cover*, she performs everything'.[60] What made coverture so terrifying was the inflexibility of wedlock. Because a marriage could be dissolved only with great difficulty and at great expense, it acted as a one-way filter: one could enter but could not leave.

This immovable reality defined the sexual lives of all women. To follow their desires outside marriage was risky precisely because it threatened to preclude the possibility of security inside marriage. The pursuit of sexual freedom brought with it social ostracism, economic insecurity, illegitimate children; submission to marriage meant individual extinction and a life spent at the mercy of one's husband who could beat, rape and otherwise abuse his wife without 'the interference of the law'. Men, by contrast, faced none of these dilemmas and could be libertines within or without wedlock. For women, free love, or even enjoyment of the most prosaic of sexual freedoms, was chimerical while marriage remained monolithic. Nothing would liberate women more – legally, socially, sexually – than the liberalisation of marriage, and in the 1850s Caroline Norton achieved just that.

***

The near decade-long truce between George and Caroline Norton ended in 1851 with the death of Caroline's mother. In her will she left a bequest to her daughter and, knowing all too well of her son-in-law's covetous ways, she did all she could to ensure the money would go to Caroline and not to him. When Norton learnt of this he simply ceased to pay Caroline the money owed to her according to their 1848 legal separation. The money she inherited from her mother was less than the amount now withheld by her husband. Newly impoverished and once more enraged, Caroline turned the logic of the law upon itself. On account of her husband's vindictiveness she could no longer afford to pay various tradesmen for services already rendered, nor pay off her other creditors. However, under coverture she and he were indistinguishable. She did not exist, and all the debts she accrued were in his name and were liable to the legal entity known as Mr George Norton. Caroline simply ceased to pay and told the various bailiffs and debt collectors sent her way to seek payment from her husband.

This was an early and exquisite example of the tactic of heightening the contradictions. In August 1853 it resulted in a lawsuit, when one unpaid tradesman, the carriage-builder Thrupps of

Oxford Street, took George Norton to court for failing to meet his – meaning his wife's – contractual agreements. Caroline was called in as a witness and before a crowd of two to three hundred spectators the litigious couple sparred for several hours. Caroline was a child of the theatre, and if she did not exactly revel in the performative aspect of court proceedings, she well knew how to manage them to her own advantage. Before a rapt crowd who periodically burst into supportive applause, she chronicled how her husband had slandered her, taken the copyrights to her books, refused to pay his debts, private and public, and had kept her from her children. She concluded with a final, blistering assault on Norton's character:

> I know Mr. Norton can cheat me, and I have no doubt that my friends will assist me more than ever when they learn that the man who calls himself a magistrate, a barrister, and a gentleman, and who can also cheat poor tradesman, because I am called his agent, and it is not binding upon me. I do not ask for my rights. I have no rights – I have only wrongs.[61]

This final flourish was rhetorically devastating but not wholly true. It was Caroline's particular genius that she combined the ability to play the part of the wronged woman with that of the hard-headed political reformer. In the weeks after the trial she restated her complaints against the legal system in general and her husband in particular in a furious correspondence with George Norton in the letters pages of *The Times*. Then she took up her pen and wrote two powerful pamphlets – *English Laws for Women in the Nineteenth Century* (1854) and *A Letter to the Queen on Lord Chancellor Cranworth's Marriage & Divorce Bill* (1855). As the title of the latter suggests, Caroline was writing amid a revival of interest in the legal status of married women. While hers was only one voice among several arguing for reform, it was easily the most virtuosic. Her lines of attack were almost identical to those elucidated to Mary in 1837. Coverture, she argued, was a self-evident absurdity. It held that a married woman was 'non-existent in law' and no more deserving of legal protection than a slave labouring in the cotton fields of the American South. This was a clear violation of natural rights – not to mention of common sense and common decency. She simultaneously brought morality into play, condemning 'England's merchant spirit' where 'property, not morality, [was] the thing held sacred'. Caroline pointed out how morally injurious existing marital law was. Adultery was grounds for divorce for husbands but not for wives. Married women were held to the highest standard of individual morality, and rightly so, she argued, but married men could act the libertine without fear of legal rebuke. Caroline mocked the logic that the moral significance of a wife's adultery was magnified by the prospect of giving 'the husband a spurious son to inherit':

Truly: and the husband's adultery may give his friend, – into whose house he has crept like a thief, to steal faith and honor, – a spurious son to inherit. Or it may give some wretched victim of his seduction, a spurious son to drown or strangle. Or it may give him a spurious son, by some wanton, on whom he lavishes the patrimony of his legitimate sons. No matter! The wrong done by him cannot be measured by equal weight with the wrong done to him: for he is a man, and claims his right of exemption, by natural superiority.[62]

Unchecked male immorality within marriage resulted in damage to society at large. Creating avenues of legal redress for wives would benefit the institution of marriage and also protect public morality. Left unsaid was how new marital laws would change the choice architecture for unmarried men. Perhaps all men would start to rethink their behaviour towards women once they saw that not even husbands were invulnerable to legal challenge. Perhaps such reforms presaged an end to a legally sanctioned double standard and would hold men and women to the same ethical norm – what the next generation of women's rights activists would call the 'Single Moral Standard'.

Between 1853 and 1857 Parliament debated the topic of married women's rights in fits, their work impeded by the waging of the Crimean War. But in 1857 Lord Palmerston determined to have the proposed Matrimonial Causes Act passed that summer and the bill began its final passage through the Lords and Commons. Caroline was absent from the chamber but her voice was heard everywhere. Her closest proxy, Lord Lyndhurst, in effect quoted directly from her pamphlets, and even her erstwhile opponent Lord Brougham declared her *Letter to the Queen* to have been 'as clever a thing as ever was written' and decisive in shaping the terms of the debate. In the heat and stench of the London summer, when (according to *The Examiner*) 'men would almost give up Magna Charta itself to avoid another sitting' the new law was passed.[63] Four of the bill's clauses were included thanks only to Caroline's agitation and her vivid use of her own autobiography to illustrate the wrongs of the existing system.[64] Many of those clauses fatally undermined coverture and ensured its dismantling over the next generation. Both men and women could now sue for divorce on grounds of adultery and the process of divorce was simplified and handed over to a single, civil court. There had been 193 divorces in England from 1800 to 1857. By the end of the century there would be close to a thousand each year. Most pairings were still for life, but the institution was now a great deal more porous. With marriage less restrictive, love could be more free.[65]

***

Neither Mary nor Caroline gained much benefit by the new law. Mary, whose health was impaired in the late 1840s by crippling headaches, had died in 1851 from a brain tumour. By the time the Matrimonial Causes Act came into effect in 1858, Caroline's own marriage was so marred by legal complexity and procedural convolution that its benefits did not extend to her. She was only liberated by the death of the Right Honourable George Norton in 1875. In 1877 Caroline married again, the match this time far better – her new husband Sir William Maxwell-Stirling was a Scottish baronet, hispanist and writer – though their marriage was a short one, for Caroline died, at the age of sixty-nine, just a few months after the two took their vows.

By the end of the 1870s only one member of the original party that had gathered by Lac Léman in the gloomy summer of 1816 was still alive. Unwanted, neglected and systematically wronged, Claire Clairmont proved to be the great survivor, living to eighty, a life half a century longer than those of her great male antagonists, Lord George Byron and Percy Bysshe Shelley. For all her other theatrics, Clairmont had always made clear that she was not a writer. Although a lover of literature, she had never sought literary plaudits for herself. When the rest of the party sat around the Villa Diodati composing their ghost stories, she had sequestered herself away and occupied herself with more worldly matters. It was the final twist in the serpentine tale of the Shelley–Byron circle (that oddly named group whose principals died so soon) that it was Clairmont who would have the final word on the men she had known in her youth and whose poetry and radical doctrines she had admired. In the 2000s a fragment of a memoir Clairmont had written in her old age was discovered in the archives of the New York Public Library. 'I have to relate my recollection of two great Poets,' it began, 'on their account I hope this recital will awaken many profound reflections':

I will commit this sad tale to paper and finally to the public, it is with the intention of demonstrating from actual facts, what evil passion free love assured, what tenderness it dissolves; how it abused affections that should be the solace and balm of life, into a destroying scourge what . . . bitter tears [it] caused to flow, and what victims it immolated [the reader] will behold how the worshippers of free love not only preyed upon one another, but preyed equally upon their own individual selves turning their existence into a perfect hell.

Such will be the picture my recollections of two great poets S[helley] & B[yron] – will present; they were the fondest and most obstinate advocates and partisans and followers of free love . . . it appears to me that in the eternal interest of religion and morality of truth and right require a plain straightforward description of their opinions and conduct.

Under the influence of the doctrine and belief of free love I saw the two first poets of England . . . become monsters of lying, meanness, cruelty and treachery – under the influence of free love Lord B[yron] became a human tyger slaking his thirst for inflicting pain upon defenceless women who under the influence of free love . . . loved him.[66]

The age of free love was over.

5

OF MANN AND MEN

In 1902 a burly young man in worker's overalls ducked into a storefront in Los Angeles. He was there to see a fortune teller. The outfit he wore was a disguise. Jack Johnson was far from the zenith of fame that he would achieve within the decade, but he was still a recognisable figure. Wary of being identified by the fortune teller and drip-fed flattering forecasts, he had assumed the outward appearance of an ordinary working man to ensure his fortune was read fairly. 'But I did not fool her. She at once told me that I was a boxer, and recounted some of my past life with such accuracy that I was astounded':

> She proceeded to tell me many things concerning my future, some of them so fantastic and so improbable, viewed from the place I then occupied in life, that I departed from her presence feeling that she had drawn a highly imaginative picture of my life. She predicted that I would be the heavy-weight boxing champion; she told me of my forth-coming marriages and of various affairs that I was destined to have with women; she told me, almost in detail, of the adventures and travels that were to mark my later life [and] of my conflicts with the law.

Johnson did not give much credence to the woman at the time, but over the years all her prophecies were to come true. He did become the heavyweight champion. He did have many affairs with many women. Those affairs did bring him in conflict with the law. 'The Los Angeles fortune teller still looms conspicuously in my memory,' Johnson later wrote, 'and there are few developments in my life that do not in some way echo that incidental visit, many years ago, when I stood on the threshold of a life that was to be one of the most picturesque in American history.'[1]

Jack Johnson was prone to grandiosity, though his verdict on his own life is hard to dispute. For Johnson was no ordinary celebrity. He was black, and his race would be the single factor that tipped his remarkable career from the atypical to the extraordinary. His insistence on his right to pursue love affairs with white women, and his singular success in the field, brought him into direct conflict with prevailing racial mores. It also set him on a collision course with one of the great (and largely forgotten) American social experiments: the attempt to police seduction through the criminal justice system.

***

John Arthur Johnson was born in Galveston, Texas on 31 March 1878, fifteen years after the presidential decree that had freed his parents from slavery, and one year after the Corrupt Bargain of 1877 that threatened to return them, him, and all other black Americans to a kind of bondage. The first thirty years of Johnson's life were shaped by the failed attempt, known as Reconstruction, to heal the wounds of civil war and slavery. This Northern-led attempt to reconstruct the South was bitterly resisted and came to an end after the contested election of 1876. Thereafter, Southern white supremacists tilted the trajectory of their section towards what they called 'Redemption'. This aimed to put black Americans squarely back in their place and ensure that white rule would remain unchallenged in the South for generations to come. These were the years of lynching, the institution of the Jim Crow caste system, the informal disenfranchisement of a formally enfranchised people.

In his childhood, Johnson was partially protected from these bleak historical conditions. Reconstruction had created space for a small, besieged but tenacious business- and property-owning black middle class who had their own newspapers, their own schools and universities, and, most visibly, their own elected officials at both state and local level. The Galveston of Johnson's youth exposed him to these kinds of black success stories. Furthermore, his home town was one of the great Gulf ports, like Mobile and New Orleans, and tolerated a far greater degree of cultural and racial diversity than was typical in the vast Southern hinterland. Johnson grew up knowing of black politicians, playing with white street kids, and exposed to the great carnival of human folly that always accompanies the presence of large numbers of thirsty sailors on shore leave. His parents, Henry and Tiny Johnson, had a profound respect for education and ensured their children had access to as much schooling as their straitened circumstances allowed.

Johnson loved learning, and would remain an omnivorous autodidact, but he hated school and by the age of thirteen was working on the docks in Galveston. However positive his own memories and experiences of the city, he was still a black man living in a former Confederate state. The threat of violence always hovered about the edges of his experience. When Johnson was fourteen, a brutal incident in Texas was a stark reminder of the omnipresence of racial discipline in the Old South.

Near the end of January 1893, four-year-old Myrtle Vance was found murdered in the woods near Paris, Texas, a small city in the north-east of the state not far from the Oklahoma state line. The community was shocked by her death, and this shock was soon compounded by the spread of rumours that she had been raped during the assault. The sexual aspect to her murder gave it at once a racial dimension. Bishop Haygood, in an apology for what was to follow, described a community inflamed by the gruesome details of the attack on a white child. Vance, Haygood stated, had been 'first outraged with demoniacal cruelty and then taken by her heels and torn asunder in the mad wantonness of gorilla ferocity'. Later investigations would prove that she had not been so outraged, but the damage was done and the hunt was on for the necessarily black 'gorilla' who had raped and killed little Myrtle Vance.

Myrtle's father was a former policeman with a reputation for the rough treatment of those in his custody. Locals began to suspect that some former prisoner of his was avenging the father's sins upon the child. Their interest alighted upon Henry Smith, a mentally impaired black teenager who did chores and odd jobs for whites in Paris. For a few tense days the sinister attentions of the town's white citizens were concentrated on poor Smith. The twin facts of his innocence and his disability prevented him from readily understanding the horrifying position he was now in. When, at length, he realised what was alleged, he fled to Hope, Arkansas. A posse was formed and sent to fetch him, which they did. Upon learning of his capture, Ida Wells reported,

> News flashed across the country that the white Christian people of Paris, Texas and the communities thereabout had deliberately determined to lay aside all forms of law and inaugurate an entirely new form of punishment for the murder. They absolutely refused to make any inquiry as to the sanity or insanity of their prisoner, but set the day and hour [of his lynching].[2]

The nation had been given fair warning about what the citizens of Paris intended to do to Henry Smith, but the savagery with which they did it appalled even those long accustomed to intense racist violence. Back in Paris, Smith was met at the train station by a crowd of an estimated 10,000 people and was then paraded,

Mardi Gras-style, down 'Main Street to the square, around the square down Clarksville Street to Church Street, thence to the open prairies about 300 yards from the Texas & Pacific depot'. There, in a dismal field, a drab wooden scaffold with 'Justice' daubed in white paint on a plank on its front awaited Smith.

According to witnesses, he did not seem to understand what was to happen to him and had seemed cheerfully overwhelmed as he was led through the crowded, queerly jubilant town. It was only as he was being lashed to the stake on the scaffold in that field that the reality finally dawned on him. The town had now emptied into the field before him. The mayor had ordered schools and whiskey shops closed. Additional law enforcement had been called in to manage the crowds, but not to interfere with their purpose. Men, women and children, on foot, horseback and wagon, some with picnics, others with snacks and alcohol, watched as the men of the Vance family systematically tortured Smith with hot irons for close to an hour. They had come 'from every part of this section', one newspaper reported, they 'came from Dallas, Fort Worth, Sherman, Denison, Bonham, Texarkana, Fort Smith, Ark., and a party of fifteen came from Hempstead county, Arkansas, where he was captured. Every train that came in was loaded to its utmost capacity, and there were demands at many points for special trains to bring the people here to see the unparalleled punishment for an unparalleled crime.' Some turned away, but most looked placidly on as the Vance men went about their butchery:

> Every groan from the fiend, every contortion of his body was cheered by the thickly packed crowd of 10,000 persons. The mass of beings 600 yards in diameter, the scaffold being the center. After burning the feet and legs, the hot irons – plenty of fresh ones being at hand – were rolled up and down Smith's stomach, back, and arms. Then the eyes were burned out and irons were thrust down his throat.

According to some accounts Smith was still alive 'when kerosene was poured upon him, cottonseed hulls placed beneath him' and he was set on fire.

In the crowd was one Reverend King of New York state. He had known Smith and privately doubted that he was responsible for Myrtle's death. He attended Smith's *auto-da-fé* with the intention of silently praying for the condemned man. But once witness to the full horror of the spectacle, King could no longer contain himself. He begged the crowd to stop the torture, or at the very least to remove the children from the crowd of spectators.

King had gravely misjudged his audience. He was knocked to the ground with a rifle butt, beaten, dragged to his home, allowed to pack a travel bag, and placed on the first train north with a one-way ticket. Back home in the Empire State, a journalist for the *New York Sun* asked the reverend if he would ever return to Paris. 'I shall never go south again,' he replied. 'The impressions of that awful day will stay with me forever.'[3]

All racial politics are sexual politics, because all racists fetishise racial purity, and purity can only be sustained through the enforcement of a strict sexual apartheid. In the American South, lynching was the most infamous form of socio-sexual policing and is rightly remembered and memorialised as such. For all its variety and brilliance, Jack Johnson's own life would be played out in the shadow of the scaffold. Nonetheless, it was another form of sexual discipline that would ultimately ensnare him. For alongside the extra-judicial phenomenon of lynching existed a *de jure* system for the punishment of sexual transgressions.

The Americans had inherited from the English the four civil law actions – Criminal Conversation, Alienation of Affections, Breach of Promise to Marriage, and Seduction – that policed marriage, sex and courtship. In the United States they were referred to by the wonderfully saccharine name of the 'heart balm acts', a group of legal instruments that sought to salve wounded hearts with cash compensation. In the mid-nineteenth century these English legal devices were used as the basis for a peculiarly American exercise. Between 1848 and 1935 the United States embarked on one of the most ambitious, most expansive, and most intrusive judicial experiments in all its history: the attempt to regulate seduction by legal fiat.

Initially this involved the reform of the civil suit of Seduction such that women could bring suits against men on their own initiative.[4] The movement began in Michigan in 1846 and soon spread around the country. By 1913, eighteen states had enacted reforms liberalising the use of the Seduction tort,[5] leading to the development of a new language to describe sexual behaviour. Courts combined legal and moral principles to articulate what seduction was, who a seducer was, and who the law would identify as a victim of seduction. In the 1856 Iowa case of *Gover v. Dill*, the court held that evidence of active and organised misrepresentation was key to determining whether seduction had occurred. The victim must have been moved 'by some promise or artifice . . . by his flattery or deception'. Likewise consent, or failure to resist, or evidence that 'she had previously prostituted herself to the embraces of other men' could be a defence for the man. All men could be seducers; only certain types of women could be seduced. Using a variation of a phrase that would recur throughout the great American legal experiment in seduction, the Iowa court ruled that 'the person seduced must have been previously of chaste character – that she has yet preserved that priceless jewel that is the peculiar badge of the virtuous unmarried female'. This was a shift from an economic understanding of a woman's worth to a moral one; from an interest in a loss of services to a loss of moral standing. But it also created a new kind of moral economy – who possessed that priceless jewel? For if a court decided that a woman did indeed possess it, then the plaintiff could be in for a major windfall. Damages could run into thousands of dollars. The high water mark came with the 1915 decision in *Eller v. Lord*, where a South Dakota court awarded $25,000 to the plaintiff – $650,000 in 2019 terms.[6]

But this tinkering with civil suits was fairly minor when compared with the revolutionary decision to criminalise the tort of Seduction. Starting with New York in 1848, states began to threaten men with fines and imprisonment for what was deemed consensual but exploitative sexual behaviour. The text of the New York law was typical of what was to come. Seduction was a 'crime against society', and those found guilty of it could face a maximum of five years in prison and a fine of up to $1,000. Crucially, a seduced woman had again to be 'an unmarried female of previous chaste character'.[7] These laws were adopted throughout the country. By 1885, twenty-seven of thirty-eight states had such statutes; by 1921, the number was thirty-seven of forty-eight. These laws had common features. They all required that plaintiffs meet certain subjective moral standards. Lewd women, bawds and adventuresses were not welcome in courts, nor were prostitutes or 'immoral characters'. Most, but not all, states required that the women involved had to be unmarried, and some held that they had to be below a certain age. When it came to defining seduction, the majority of states understood seduction in relation to marriage, with twenty-two of thirty-seven state laws requiring that the 'prosecution must show either a promise of marriage or a feigned or pretended marriage'. More generally, seduction was understood as the 'Use of arts, persuasions, or wiles to overcome the resistance of the female who is not disposed, of her volition, to step aside from the path of virtue. . . . Any seductive arts or promises, where the female involuntarily and reluctantly yields thereto, are sufficient.'

In all but three states with these laws, the offence of seduction was classified as a felony and conviction could lead to a sentence of between one and twenty years in prison, as well as a fine. Some states allowed for men to avoid the jailhouse by marrying their victims, but women were by no means obliged to accept such legally induced proposals.[8]

The proponents of this legislation were largely married, middle-class women. They claimed to be acting in the interest of vulnerable unmarried girls, but the stories of those whom they looked to protect were far from flattering. The landmark New York statute of 1848 was the result of over a decade of sustained activism on the part of the New York Female Moral Reform Society (NYFMRS), a female-run association that by the 1840s had 50,000 members and hundreds of affiliate organisations. The women of the NYFMRS were deeply concerned about the moral dangers faced by young women coming from the countryside to seek work in the city. In their literature they dwell repeatedly on the threat posed to innocent provincials by the theatre, the dance hall, and other urban arenas where men and women met and mingled without parental oversight. The seduction of young women in such places would result in a fall from chastity to sin, followed by a life of spinsterdom, or worse, prostitution.

These fears were premised on a belief that women were by nature ingenuous and could be easily tricked into engaging in harmful behaviours. The female mind was so impressionable, these activists believed, that it had to be protected from all kinds of malign influences. They were particularly preoccupied with the threat posed to the young consciences by literature. All NYFMRS members had to pledge upon joining to 'discountenance all lewd books, poems, and pictures'. The organisation's journal, *The Advocate*, warned against 'the wondrous powers of fiction' which worked upon the female mind just as alcohol worked upon the male body. The works of Byron and Edward Bulwer-Lytton were singled out as being singularly pernicious. The characteristics of fiction – its artifice, its mastery of rhetoric and story-telling, its capacity to beguile the mind and suspend reason – were the same as the 'wily arts by which the young and unsuspecting are seduced and ruined'. Men who used flowery language or rhetorical trickery in conversation were to be avoided. The use of double entendre and wordplay by a man were a sure sign that he had ruinous intentions.[9]

The tropes of the successful New York campaign would be repeated across the country over the next seventy years. The forces of the law had to be mobilised to protect women who lacked the faculties to navigate the modern sexual market themselves. However, not all women were deemed worthy of protection. Courts and juries now had the right to choose who was worthy of legal protection by deciding whether or not a woman was of 'previous chaste character'. This meant that men now sat in judgment of women's character, even though those women came to court as plaintiffs, not defendants. Middle-class men tended to be much more magnanimous in their rulings when middle-class women were involved. Questions of moral standing inevitably collided with questions of social standing, and courts were haunted by the bourgeois presumption of working-class dissolution. Poor and working-class women who brought suits against their social betters were regularly smeared as whores and hussies. Race also came into play. There was not infrequently a correlation between the severity of a state's racial laws and the severity of its seduction laws.

The state of Alabama had some of the harshest laws in both spaces. The wording of the seduction statute was so open to interpretation that virtually all consensual sexual activity fell within its purview. Running parallel to the state's stringent seduction laws were its even more stringent laws on what was then known as 'miscegenation', or interracial sexual relations. Under Alabama law, 'any white person and any negro, or the descendant of any negro to the third generation' were not allowed to 'intermarry or live in adultery or fornication with each other'; they risked jail time or 'hard labor' if they were found guilty of so doing.

The laws regulating seduction and the laws regulating interracial love formally overlapped, as well. Seduction laws did not tend to mention race, but their companion laws governing racial love affairs had direct bearing upon who could and could not file a seduction suit. A black woman who wanted to bring such a suit against a white man in the state of Alabama faced two barriers. First, because interracial marriage was illegal, she could not realistically claim to have been tricked into sex by the promise of marriage. Furthermore, because interracial sex, or fornication, was illegal she would essentially be pleading guilty to a charge of miscegenation and would consequently be vulnerable to judicial persecution.

On the other side of the equation, black men were at constant risk of accusations of sexual impropriety made by white women. In a culture that granted white women a great deal of judicial freedom to bring suits against men on the grounds of sexual misconduct, allegations made by a white woman – inside or outside the courts – against a black man were almost never fact-checked and were almost always enthusiastically punished, though in those instances it was more often lynch law that predominated rather than any statute on the state law books. This was the case in the Texas of Jack Johnson's youth, which had strict seduction statutes on the book and a grim record of extrajudicial lynchings.[10]

***

Although it would later upend his life, the development of an elaborate legal structure to police seduction was remote from Johnson's life on the Galveston docks. The world of the Galveston stevedores was a harsh one, and his experiences there would set him on the path to the championship. His colleagues on the docks were 'some of the toughest and hardest-boiled men imaginable', he recalled. 'To them, fighting was one of the important functions of existence. They fought upon every occasion and on any pretext.

They shot craps and indulged in other forms of gambling with almost as much ardor as they fought.' Johnson's youth did not spare him from participation in these scraps and, confronted with their inevitability, he sought out boxing lessons in order to survive his workplace. Athletic, fast and powerful, Johnson quickly gained a reputation on the docks as a strong fighter and was soon taking on all comers.[11]

Even outside the rough-and-tumble world of the Galveston dockworkers, boxing in the 1890s was a very different sport from what it is now. Bare-knuckle boxing had persisted into the 1880s, and the first formal heavyweight title fight did not take place until John L. Sullivan fought Gentleman Jim Corbett in New Orleans in 1892. Even as it was being gradually formalised, boxing – or prizefighting, as it was commonly known – remained an astonishingly violent enterprise. Fighters wore no mouth guards, and the gloves were so small (customarily around 5oz) that they were no more than leather sheaths affording little protection. The average fight was scheduled for twenty rounds, forty rounds was the norm for title fights, and matches of as long as sixty rounds were not unheard of. Inside the ring there was no limit on the number of knockdowns a fighter could sustain and no neutral corner to which a boxer had to retreat in the event of one. There was no ringside doctor; fixed fights were so frequent as to be unremarked upon; it was not uncommon for referees, cornermen, and audience members to be armed with revolvers. Not a few fighters died in the ring.

As a consequence of all this, boxing was illegal in several states, including Johnson's native Texas. In 1895, Johnson's first formal fight – against a dockworker named John 'Must Have It' Lee – in Josie's Beer Garden in Galveston, ended up being fought on the beach after the police raided the original site. Johnson won the bout and the $1.50 in prize money that came with it. Spying a path to easy money, he sought to make boxing his profession, despite the plethora of legal, medical and social risks that accompanied the pursuit.

The gamble seemed to pay off. Johnson's abilities rapidly outgrew the opportunities on offer in the Galveston area and, aged nineteen, he decided to 'cast myself wholly into the lap of fate' and start riding the rails in search of fighting opportunities. Johnson's account of these early years is tinged with his customary good humour and love of sly understatement. A powerfully built young black boxer hoboing about the South in the last years of the nineteenth century could not expect a warm welcome in many towns. Life on the rails and on the road was lonely, financially insecure and unsafe. Johnson recalled the kind of reception he became accustomed to receiving in provincial America:

> [In] some of the smaller towns where a stranger was quickly discovered, police officers and constables manifested deep concern in me. In fact, they were generally so deeply interested that they often insisted that I remain as a guest of their town. On these occasions, I was introduced to the town Judge, who pried into my personal affairs and asked me embarrassing questions. Usually, after my meetings with the Judge, I was instructed to hasten out of town, which was exactly what I wished to do, and what I was trying to do when the police interfered. Sometimes I was detained, quarters being assigned me in the town jail.[12]

But he loved the freedom of a life on the move, and success and adventure came easily to the voluble young man.

In February 1901, Johnson returned to Galveston for a fight with a Jewish boxer named Joe Choynski. On the night, the two men stepped inside a ring in Harmony Hall, and in the third round Choynski knocked Johnson out for the first time in his professional career. At this point, with Johnson flat on the canvas and Choynski celebrating a quick fight and a fast buck, five Texas rangers entered the ring brandishing pistols and arrested both men for violating the state's ban on prizefighting.

Johnson's arrest and subsequent detention in the Galveston lockup was arguably the most propitious event in his long and celebrated career. The terms of the two men's confinement were less uncomfortable than they might have been. Sheriff Henry Thomas allowed both men to sleep at home but they had to spend the daytime in the prison compound. There, for the entertainment of law enforcement and curious locals, the two interned boxers sparred for several hours each day.

This was to be a formative experience for Johnson. At a time when most boxers, and most boxing fans, considered the essence of the sport to be the brute application of power along linear lines of attack, Choynski treated pugilism as an art form. He had studied its nuances, earned an appreciation for its delicacies, and in the process formed his own unique, evasive style that privileged an intelligent defensive method over a hard-charging offensive manner. Over the course of twenty-three days together, he imparted the secrets of the sweet science to Johnson. He taught him how to feint, dodge, slip; how to catch punches, how to counterpunch, how to manage his opponent around the ring. He taught him the dark arts of the clinch, where an opponent could be tied up and savaged with invisible but deadly body shots. Choynski gave Johnson the tools that would turn him from a good fighter into a great boxer. Johnson would scarcely lose a fight over the next fifteen years.[13]

Johnson's new-found style was the perfect match for his garrulous manner and teasing personality. A photo of him from the year of the Choynski fight shows a powerful, trim young man with shoulders like cannonballs and enormous, veined forearms. But what stands out is his head. Johnson shaved his head (he would later go bald, joking that this was on account of too much 'makin' babies'), and this, coupled with his large ingenuous eyes and soft

Thomas Rowlandson's *Road to Ruin* (1785) depicting a pair of overindulged Georgian rakes and their companions.

The Covent Garden Piazza – the meeting place of London's literary and leisure classes.

An episode from *Clarissa*, as painted by Joseph Highmore. Clarissa's family chastise their daughter (left) for her independence and self-proclaimed 'right to a heart' – a scene crucial in explaining how she ends up ensnared by Lovelace.

The chapel of the Magdalen Hospital in London. Society men and women paid to attend Sunday services and experience the thrill of sharing a space with the seduced and abandoned. The magdalens themselves are in the gallery, behind a screen.

Two paintings by the Venetian master Pietro Longhi that portray the social and sexual freedoms women enjoyed in the Venetian Republic.

A party in the visiting parlour of a Venetian nunnery during carnival. Note the size of the bars on the windows. 'The largeness of the Venetian grates has ruined the reputation of the Venetian nuns,' lamented one contemporary.

Jame Gillray's portrayal of the aftermath of the Women's March on Versailles in 1789 which led to a militia ransacking the palace and menacing the royal family. On the far-right Marie Antoinette can be seen fleeing down a corridor. On the far left, reverend Richard Price watches with pleasure in the company of a demon. The scene led Burke to famously complain that 'The Age of Chivalry is gone.'

Mother and daughter: Mary Wollstonecraft and Mary Shelley.

A satirical cartoon of Caroline Norton's adulterous affair with Prime Minister Lord Melbourne (christened William Lamb) whilst her husband, George Norton, looks on sporting cuckold's horns. The legal dispute that resulted from the affair led indirectly to the reform of women's marital rights – spearheaded by Caroline Norton.

A cartoon from a sensationalist book on the white slave trade. Seduction was depicted as the fatal first step towards sexual bondage.

"THE LOVE GAME."

A pander working "the love game," assumes the role of a banker's son seeking rest and fresh air. He hoodwinks the girls by stories of great wealth and position, the upper part of the picture shows the gay times promised.

Jack Johnson, heavyweight champion of the world, at ease behind the wheel. Over the course of his life he racked up an awesome quantity of speeding tickets.

An eighteenth-century depiction of animal magnetism.
Note the woman swooning in the bottom left hand corner.

A nineteenth-century depiction of Jean Martin Charcot's world-
famous experiments in hypnotism at the Salpêtrière hospital in
Paris. By the turn of the century hypnotism and seduction were
intimately linked in the popular consciousness.

A poster for the transatlantic bestseller, *Trilby*, featuring the most nakedly anti-Semitic illustration from the book, where Svengali hypnotises the helpless Trilby O'Farrell.

An anti-Semitic cartoon from *Der Stürmer*. The chimerical idea that Jews were trying to seduce 'Aryan' women en masse was directly invoked by Nazi legal theorists looking to justify the dispossession of the German Jewish community.

features, lent him an appearance that was not so much youthful as baby-faced. Johnson's great size and strength was made all the more eerie by these gleefully neotenous features and by his famously exuberant, eye-catching smile, enhanced still further by the gold-capped front teeth he had fitted once his finances allowed for the luxury.

The final component of Johnson's style was his permanent good humour towards the press and public, and the unaffected condescension with which he treated his opponents inside the ring. Johnson loved conversation and the back-and-forth of bar-room banter and saw no reason why it should stop inside the ring. The Johnson who marches spasmodically around the ring in surviving fight films from the period is constantly talking. Looming above his opponents, he laughs at their missed hits, applauds when they somehow land a blow, and smiles and shakes his head when they charge forward at him. In the clinch he would manoeuvre his opponent around the canvas, pausing to flirt with his girlfriends at ringside, taunt the opposing cornermen, or dispense thoughts to the assembled ring reporters. The effect was maddening, the jibes made unbearable to white boxers by the blackness of his skin.[14]

In 1898 Johnson had married a black woman from Galveston named Mary Austin. Not much is known about her, except for the fact that she left him in 1902. Johnson was fond of Austin and mourned her departure, but freed from the constraints of marriage he was now able to immerse himself in the sporting world. To be a sport, or a sporting man (or sporting woman), meant something quite significant in the first decades of the twentieth century. A sport could be an actual athlete like Johnson. It could also refer to someone who associated with sporting activities, like a racehorse trainer or boxing promoter. Furthermore, it could be applied to someone who enjoyed merely going to the races, or to a fight, or who liked to gamble on the outcome of either. A sport might be someone who simply sought the company of other sportsmen. Most card sharps, bookies, dandies and hustlers could be classified as sports. A sporting woman was often, but not always, a prostitute. A sporting house was a brothel. The capacious world of the sport was halfway between the violent world of the frontier and the sanitised world of celebrity. It had one foot in the underworld and the other in the headlines. At a time when sex, liquor and organised sports themselves were subject to a high degree of control, the sporting scene was one of relaxed social and sexual standards. Importantly, it was also a world where blacks and whites mingled much more readily than they did in the rest of society. As Johnson's boxing career took off, he became the uncrowned king of the sports and one of the great witnesses to one of the most decadent and unrestrained social scenes in all American history.[15]

In 1903 Johnson fell in with a new woman. Her name was Clara Kerr and she was most definitely a sport. Kerr and Johnson spent, by his account, two years of bliss on the road together as she dutifully accompanied him across the country in pursuit of fights. Money was tight at times – Johnson was still not earning large purses but was nevertheless spending prodigiously – but Johnson believed the relationship to be stable and loving.

Then, in Los Angeles in October 1905, a rival sport appeared in Johnson's household. His name was William Bryant. He was a horse trainer whom Johnson had known back east, and Johnson considered him an 'old and intimate friend' – intimate enough that he invited Bryant to share their home. But there was no honour among sports. While Johnson was not looking, a relationship developed between Bryant and Kerr, and one day Johnson returned home to find the two had vanished along with his money, his jewellery, and a good deal of his wardrobe. He informed the police and soon the two fugitive lovers were tracked to Tucson, Arizona. Kerr and Johnson made up, somehow, and then relocated to Chicago. But the move to the Midwest did little to mend their relationship or reform Clara Kerr. In September 1906, with Johnson low on money again, she absconded, taking with her the little he had. Once more Johnson came home to find his home ransacked and his lover gone. Once more he searched for her. But this time she had gone for good.

This second loss and doubled humiliation was too much for the prideful boxer. 'The world became a void for me,' Johnson recalled, a void he tried to fill with alcohol and hard living. Within weeks he was penniless, psychologically scarred and physically wrecked. Concerned friends lent him money and at length he decided to travel to New York City to seek out more fights. He was so poor that before he boarded the train a friend had to forcibly lend him a dollar to sustain him on the journey. Johnson might have had a single dollar to his name but he was still a sport, and he spent the money in fine style: 'Of this dollar I gave the train porter 50 cents; I bought two cigars with another quarter and the remaining quarter I tossed to a newsboy at the station when I arrived in New York.'[16]

If Johnson is to be believed, this second betrayal by Clara Kerr also resulted in a radical and fateful sexual decision. 'The heartaches which Mary Austin and Clara Kerr had caused me,' he wrote, 'led me to forswear colored women and to determine that my lot henceforth would be cast only with white women.'[17] From 1906 onwards he would never again be seen in public with a black woman by his side. There would be three legally recognised Mrs Johnsons, and a couple of others introduced with a wink and a smile. All of them would be white; this at a time when black Americans were regularly lynched for much less. Johnson knew the risks he was taking but he did not seem to care. Besides, his decision owed more to egotism than to provocation. 'I will never believe that he married his white woman just to spite white people,' one friend later wrote, 'I just think he did what he wanted to do because he wanted to do it.'[18]

Johnson's fateful decision to cross one colour line came just as he was figuring out his passage over another. By 1906, Johnson was confronted by a problem familiar to talented contenders. He was twenty-eight; he had won fifty-three of his fifty-six fights (as well as scores of undocumented bouts); he was in possession of a difficult, dangerous fighting style. It was both demeaning and unprofitable to seek matches with fighters of a lower calibre; his pugilistic peers – and they were few – did not want to meet him in the ring. What Johnson wanted, needed, and believed was already his was the title of heavyweight champion. But he could not have it. Ever since John L. Sullivan had been recognised as the first heavyweight champion in 1885, white boxers had drawn the 'color line'. Though most had fought black boxers on the way up, they considered it their duty once champion to keep the title in white hands. Jim Jeffries, the glowering ex-boilermaker who had watched from the sidelines as Johnson dismantled his younger brother Jack in 1902, was typical in this respect. Jeffries held the championship for six years from 1899, and during that time he would not defend it against a black man. 'I will never fight a negro,' he stated, 'back to the boiler works first.'[19]

But in 1905 Jeffries retired. There was nobody to fight, or at least nobody white to fight, he claimed, and so he would relinquish the championship and retreat to his California farm undefeated. The title then passed briefly into Marvin Hart's hands. Hart had fought Johnson only months before acceding to the title, but once champion he too drew the Color Line. Then, in February 1906, Hart lost the title to Tommy Burns in Los Angeles and Johnson had his chance.

Burns had stated that he would fight anyone of any race, creed or nationality to prove that he was the world heavyweight champion. This did not mean, however, that he was willing to fight Johnson straight away. A childhood of despairing poverty had impressed on him a thoroughly realistic attitude towards personal enrichment. He understood that the heavyweight title was a licence

to print money – but only while it was in your possession. A title
lost was worth nothing. If Johnson wanted a title fight against
Burns, he was going to have to find a way of making it worth the
champion's while.

It took many years and many thousands of miles on the road
to get Burns where he wanted him. As Burns toured North
America, Europe and Australasia, taking easy fights, participating
in vaudeville and variety shows, and generally cashing in on the
title wherever he went, Johnson was hot on his heels. He followed
Burns to his fights and heckled him from ringside. He spoke to
the press constantly, mocking the regnant champion and outlining
ad nauseam why he had earned the right to face him inside the
ring. Still Burns would not fight him. 'I virtually had to mow my
way to Burns,' Johnson said of these months on the warpath, '. . .
even King Edward of England was disgusted with Burns' tactics
and called him a "Yankee Bluffer".' Then an Australian showman
on the other side of the world came to his rescue.

Hugh D. McIntosh was an Australian businessman and impresario with a singular vision of how to profit from the confluence
of sports, race and naval power in Sydney Harbour in 1908. That
year, President Theodore Roosevelt's newly constructed armada
was scheduled to stop off in Australia as part of its two-year
demonstration of American sea power. The flotilla was known as
the Great White Fleet. Its mission served no formal military
purpose; its two-year circumnavigation of the globe was presented
as a gesture of fraternal goodwill to fellow Anglo-Saxon nations.
It was also a carelessly concealed challenge to would-be naval
powers. The imperialist logic of the day held that geopolitical
struggles were also racial struggles. The clash of great powers on
land and at sea was simply the Darwinian struggle for existence
writ large. It took a man with McIntosh's peculiar, cynical entre-
preneurial genius to see that in this perfervid atmosphere an
interracial heavyweight title fight was simply the same struggle for

existence writ small. The gate would be made by rowdy American sailors, Australians bloated with racial comity, and the promise of international film sales. McIntosh met Burns' demand for $30,000 and offered Johnson $5,000. Both men accepted. The fight would take place in Sydney on Boxing Day 1908.

'In Australia I was warmly received,' Johnson recalled, 'not withstanding the fact that Burns was the favorite in the betting, which was to be expected because of the racial element involved.'[20] As ever, he downplayed the extent of the animus displayed towards him. McIntosh's marketing plan was entirely premised on racialising the bout, and the global anglophone press was rooting for Tommy Burns on purely racial grounds. Not for the last time, both the press and the bookies allowed racial longing to obscure pugilistic judgement. The match was a mismatch. Johnson toyed with the smaller Burns for thirteen rounds before putting him out in the fourteenth. The police intervened to stop the filming seconds before the final blow landed; as such, the moment when Jack Johnson became the first black heavyweight champion was never recorded. Sitting at ringside was Jack London, then the most highly paid novelist in America, covering the fight for the *New York Herald*. 'There was no fight,' he told the *Herald*'s readers. 'No Armenian massacre could compare with the hopeless slaughter that took place today. The fight, if fight it could be called, was like that between a pygmy and a colossus . . . But one thing now remains. . . . The White Man must be rescued.'

The urgent need for white rescue would become apparent to all when Johnson returned to North America in the spring of 1909. After spending a few months enjoying himself in Australia, he steamed home, arriving in Vancouver on 9 March 1909. The press corps was waiting for him. When he appeared on the gangway, looking resplendent in a trilby and full-length double-breasted overcoat, the newsmen got their glimpse of the first black champion. They also made the acquaintance of a small, toothy woman, wrapped in furs and sporting a huge white plume in her hat. She was introduced as Mrs Jack Johnson, formerly Nellie O'Brien of Philadelphia. She was white.

Nellie O'Brien was in fact Hattie McClay of Mississippi, and she was not Johnson's wife. She was a sport and an all-round good-time girl who had fallen in with Johnson in New York in the summer of 1907. She liked to drink, dance and play music – the couple had entertained the press in Sydney by playing the fiddle together – and was endlessly tolerant of Johnson's caddish ways. McClay could not by any means be described as a great beauty, and it seems that Johnson enjoyed her company more than anything else. ('Hattie was a splendid gal,' Johnson sighs in his memoir, a description more cousinly than amorous.[21]) Not that such nuances mattered to the upholders of America's stark racial order. The apparent marriage of a white woman to the slayer of white manhood caused grave consternation. Galveston's planned homecoming celebrations were quickly cancelled, the authorities stating that Johnson would be arrested for violation of Texas's anti-miscegenation statutes if he entered the state with McClay. But Johnson had long outgrown his home town. He headed first to New York and then to Chicago, a city that he now knew well and that would become his home for the next four years.[22] With his winnings, Johnson set himself and his mother up in a house in the heart of the South Side's Black Belt, a community populated by tens of thousands of African Americans, and only a few blocks away from pleasure houses of the Levee, Chicago's vice district, where racial divisions were relaxed in service to the higher cause of making merry.

Sometime that spring, he met Belle Schreiber, a twenty-year-old from Milwaukee then working in the Everleigh Club, the most exclusive bordello in the Levee. Johnson quickly wooed her, at which point the proprietors of the Everleigh Club fired her for breaching their own strict rules governing race relations. Belle started touring the country with Johnson (and, at times, McClay). That October she was in the crowd when he devastated Stanley Ketchel, the middle-weight phenomenon and arch rake, in San Francisco.[23]

Less than two weeks after the Ketchel fight, Johnson was in New York, where he met a third woman at a Long Island racecourse. A cultivated woman from a privileged home, Etta Duryea was a sometime actress and former loving wife to a wealthy property developer named Clarence Duryea. By the time she met Johnson, she and Clarence were living apart and Etta was dipping her toes in the sporting scene. Johnson's courtship was swift. By the end of the year she was immersed in his world, spending Christmas with him and Tiny Johnson at their Chicago home on South Wabash Avenue. Also present were Belle Schreiber and Hattie McClay. It was not, by any account, a peaceful holiday period.

What white America made of the spectacle of a black champion cavorting around the country with several white women can be readily imagined. The white press endlessly editorialised against Johnson's very public flouting of the color line. The black press pleaded for modesty, lest Johnson's antics endanger the lives of his kinsmen. Death threats flowed in from all over the country. Johnson lived in full knowledge of white society's lethal disapproval of his interracial relations. During a tour of the Midwest in 1909, a taxi carrying him and Etta broke down in Minneapolis-St Paul. A mob quickly gathered and the couple were saved from harm only by police intervention.

***

Many whites craved to see Johnson cut down to size. Some wanted him lynched, and were happy to say so; but many more would settle for his lawful humiliation in the ring. In the undefeated Jim Jeffries, they had just the man for the job. Ever since Burns had hit the canvas in Sydney, the cry had gone up for Jeffries to return to the ring to defeat Johnson and redeem the championship. Jeffries resisted for some time. He was in his mid-thirties and grown fat from sitting on his farm and watching the alfalfa grow. He was also a legendary drinker, and years of whiskey consumption had dulled his reflexes. But he hated Johnson sincerely. He hated his 'yellow' fighting style. He hated his white girlfriends. He hated his black skin.[24]

For months the press did little but tout Jeffries' olympian strength and belittle Johnson's abilities. Journalists, former and active fighters, and concerned citizens had visited Jeffries on his farm to beg him to take up the mantle. Then, in November 1909, promoter Tex Rickard stepped up with an offer of a $101,000 purse. Avarice and misplaced racial pride won out over realism and a quiet retirement. That month Jeffries and Johnson met with Rickard in New Jersey to finalise the details. In December the contracts were signed in a public ceremony in Manhattan. The Fight of the Century was on.

The bout was set for 4 July 1910. The symbolism of the date was crude but compelling. This was to be the day when the white championship was liberated from black hands – a second Independence Day. Jeffries needed the time. He had been out of the fight game for five years. He had to regain his touch and shrink from an unwieldy 340lb (154kg) to his old fighting weight of 220lb (100kg). The task ahead of him was daunting; the pressure put upon him by an increasingly hysterical public intense. Johnson, meanwhile, had to straighten out his own affairs. McClay and Schreiber were being edged out by Duryea, and the two sporting women were more often than not living apart from the champion. This suited Duryea, but she found it hard to adjust to Johnson's peripatetic lifestyle and serial infidelities. She never would.

Whatever pain he caused her, and whatever her misgivings about their relationship, she was dutifully present in the crowd as Mrs Jack Johnson when he met Jim Jeffries in the ring in Reno that July. Jeffries had done what many thought was impossible and shed over 100lb (50kg) during training. He had sparred with

Johnson's old foe Joe Choynski, and his training had been supervised by revered former champions John L. Sullivan and Gentleman Jim Corbett. The press feasted on every trace of Jeffries' return to form and as the fight approached the betting odds began to widen in favour of the grizzled ex-champion. As the day drew ever nearer, white Americans succumbed to a kind of collective delusion concerning Jeffries' invincibility. The outcome of the fight was already known: Jeffries would whip Johnson, and whip him bad. The only problem was that Johnson was not behaving like a man about to be obliterated by a vengeful white fighter. The *Chicago Tribune* wrote of Johnson:

> The man is a puzzle. Physically, the greatest athlete the colored race has produced and mentally as keen as a razor in a sort of undeveloped way, he fiddles away on his bull fiddle, swaps jokes with ready wit, shoots craps, plays baseball, listens dreamily to classical love songs on the phonograph and is going to fight Jim Jeffries for the world's championship one week from tomorrow.[25]

Jack Johnson and Etta Duryea in Reno, Nevada, 1910, very shortly before his fight with Jim Jeffries.

This was not the countenance of a condemned man. The *San Francisco Examiner*, channelling, perhaps, submerged memories of Henry Smith's unwitting progress to the scaffold in Paris, suggested that Johnson's carefree demeanour was evidence of 'the same cheerful indifference to coming events [that has] marked others of the same race even while standing in the very shadow of the gallows'.[26]

Once again the press and the bookmakers had it badly wrong. The fight was scheduled for a gruelling forty-five rounds. Jeffries made it through fourteen, lurching forward repeatedly to get his man only to become tangled in Johnson's longer arms and then savaged in the clinch by vicious uppercuts. In the fifteenth Jeffries went down, and went down a second time; he was pulled to his feet by several cornermen, only to be knocked to his knees for a third and final time.

Victory in Reno made Johnson a rich man and the undisputed heavyweight champion. It also made him a hero to black Americans, many of whom took to the streets to show their appreciation. But nationwide celebrations at Johnson's victory morphed into nation-wide race riots as whites lashed out against jubilant blacks. Racial violence roared through the nation, afflicting provincial towns and major cities alike. In Roanoke, Virginia, 'a small race war' broke out, according to the local newspaper, on account of 'the word of a fresh Negro' on the subject of Johnson's victory. In Norfolk, Virginia, white sailors staged pitched battles against celebrating blacks. In Washington, D.C., marine units hunted down black soldiers seeking vicarious revenge for Jeffries. In towns as large as Atlanta and as small as Covington, Kentucky, the whole police force and reserves were called out to keep the peace. In New York, mobs of thousands of white men gathered in central Manhattan and attacked any and all black faces they saw. When the police waded in to rescue one victim they found him alive with a rope around his neck.[27] In his autobiography, Louis Armstrong recalled the day of Jack Johnson's victory as one of the most terrifying of his life. Armstrong was eight years old and working as a newsboy in New Orleans:

> That day I was going to get my supply of papers from Charlie, who employed a good many colored boys like myself. On Canal Street I saw a crowd of colored boys running like mad toward me. I asked one of them what had happened. 'You better get started, black boy,' he said breathlessly as he started to pull me along. 'Jack Johnson has just knocked out Jim Jeffries. The white boys are sore about it and they're going to take it out on us.' He did not have to do any urging. I lit out and passed the other boys in a flash.[28]

The knockdown that made Johnson a legend and a marked man.
His victory over Jeffries unleashed some of the most widespread racial
violence in America's modern history.

Such scenes were repeated in Cincinnati, Kansas City, St Louis, Omaha, Houston and Los Angeles. In Congress, politicians from both parties started to peddle the tendentious narrative that the race riots had been stoked by nationwide access to the film footage of the fight. A move was made to ban the interstate transportation of fight films – the same use of the Commerce Clause to control public morality that later underwrote the legal logic of the Mann Act – which ultimately led to the passage of the Sims Act in 1912.[29] The debates that initiated this piece of legislation introduced the nation to the florid racist rhetoric of Congressman Seaborn Roddenberry of Georgia. Speaking in support of the proposed ban, Roddenberry reached new heights of magniloquence:

> I call attention of the house to the fact that the recent prizefight which was had in New Mexico presented, perhaps, the grossest instance of base fraud and bogus effort at a fair fight between a Caucasian brute and an African biped beast that has ever taken place. It was repulsive. This bill is designed to prevent the display to morbid-minded adults and susceptible youths all over the country the representations of such a disgusting exhibition.[30]

It would not be the last time that Roddenberry invoked Jack Johnson in the House of Representatives.

For now, Congressional bloviating could not harm Johnson. Ensconced in Chicago's South Side, he was for the most part safe. But white America was now fixated on him. Unable to beat him in the ring, they sought to destroy him in the courts. The instrument of his destruction would be a law that passed with little fanfare two weeks before his meeting with Jim Jeffries in Reno: the Mann Act.

***

Technically known as the White-Slave Traffic Act, the Mann Act was the closest America came to having a federal seduction statute. It arose out of a campaign led by the Woman's Christian Temperance Movement (WCTU) and its formidable leader, Frances Willard, to bring about the end of the white slave trade – the melodramatic name given by Progressive campaigners to the alleged global traffic in young white women to feed the insatiable demand for prostitutes in the vice districts of all the major American cities. While it was conceptualised as an international phenomenon, akin to the actual global traffic in black slaves against which evangelicals had crusaded in the eighteenth and nineteenth centuries, the white slave trade was understood at street level as the mass seduction of white girls by unscrupulous men.

White slave narratives bore striking resemblances to the narratives employed during the earlier campaigns to criminalise seduction. 'Procurers and procuresses' had fanned out across the country to 'pursue their vile business of enticing young women and girls from the country, from railroad trains, from steamboats, and from their homes by false promises unmolested', one WCTU activist told a New York audience in 1901.[31] One of the most popular collections of white slave trade tracts was *Fighting the Traffic in Young Girls, or War on the White Slave Trade*, which contained a taxonomy of the methods by which 'Snakes Charm Canaries'. Some of these were typical employment ruses, but many were simply grotesque misinterpretations of contemporary courtship rituals, or even the wilful miscomprehension of the rudimentary components of normal social existence in turn-of-the-century America. In the hands of white slavery campaigners, almost every aspect of modernity became a way of entrapping women in sexual slavery. 'Women are also used to beguile other women for the trade,' one campaigner noted:

These infamous creatures sometimes go as agents for books, gramophones, or machines. A woman now in the penitentiary said she canvassed communities to sell toilet articles, for the purpose of finding girls. Victims are looked for in railroad depots, and trains are watched for young women traveling alone. General deliveries in post offices are watched where young women call for letters. Recruiting stations are found in dance halls, in the cities and amusement parks with drinking places as attachments. Ice cream parlors and fruit stores sometimes serve as spiders' webs for entanglement.[32]

Two images from the voluminous literature on the 'white slave traffic'. It was a standard technique of white slave trade activists to recast normal heterosocial behaviour as the gateway to sexual bondage.

The war on the white slave trade was really a war on certain disconcerting aspects of American modernity. What campaigners were truly concerned about was the uncontrollable dynamism and mobility of modern society. Trains, cars and transport depots loom large in white slave narratives because these were the means by which young women could move beyond parental control. They were also the means by which hundreds of thousands of non-white and non-Protestant men were moving into white American society. The rise of white slave activism coincided with the first wave of African-American migration north by train, and the arrival of hundreds of thousands of European immigrants by steamboat across the Atlantic. White slavers were almost always described as lying outside the traditional white, Anglo-Saxon, Protestant norm. French, Italians, Poles, Austrians and Russians were involved. 'All Europe, North America, Panama, South America, Egypt and other parts of Africa, India, China and Japan are the fields of operation of these atrocious men and serpentine women.' Jewish communities were the alleged ringleaders and were singled out as 'the backbone of the loathsome traffic in New York and Chicago'.

Activist concerns converged on Chicago, a city at the heart of the national railroad network and teeming with newly arrived blacks from the South, and Italians, Poles, Jews and others from Europe. Chicago was of course also home to the Levee, one of the nation's most notorious vice districts. In the first decade of the twentieth century the city became synonymous with the white slave trade. The *Chicago Daily Tribune* filled its pages with lurid stories from the slave markets in the city, warning its readers that beneath their very noses America's second city was 'becoming the "white slave" center of the world', and that the city's commerce in female virtue had become one of its 'great industries' alongside meatpacking, garment-making and construction. The apparent crisis in Chicago attracted the attentions of some of the most talented and determined campaigners in the country.

In 1908, United States Attorney Edwin W. Sims, fresh from a landmark anti-trust suit against Standard Oil, turned his considerable powers to solving the problem of white slavery in Chicago. He was horrified at what he found. 'In view of what I have learned in the course of the recent investigation and prosecution of the "white slave" traffic,' he reported, 'I can say, in all sincerity, that if I lived in the country and had a young daughter I would go to any length of hardship and privation myself rather than allow her to go into the city to work or to study.' Sims teamed up with District Attorney Clifford G. Roe, a prominent white slave activist and future author of the seminal text *Horrors of the White Slave Trade: The Mighty Crusade to Protect the Purity of Our Homes.* The two men believed that the problem warranted federal intervention and drafted a model law that made the transport of prostitutes across state lines a federal crime. This was a creative use of the Commerce Clause – a clause in the United States Constitution that arrogated to Congress the right 'to regulate Commerce with foreign Nations, and among the several States' – to deal with an essentially moral concern. Sims and Roe took the proposed law to Illinois Congressman James Robert Mann, a politician with impeccable Progressive credentials, who agreed to champion the law in the house. The law was introduced to the nation as the White-Slave Traffic Act, and in case there was any doubt as to whom it aimed to protect Mann defined the white slave trade as 'the business of securing *white* women and girls and selling them out-right, or of exploiting them for immoral purpose'. The bill won the support of President Taft and became law in June 1910. Henceforth, it would be illegal to

> knowingly transport or cause to be transported, or aid or assist in obtaining transportation for, or in transporting, in interstate or foreign commerce, or in any Territory or in the District of Columbia, any woman or girl for the purpose of prostitution or debauchery, or for any other immoral purpose, or with the intent and purpose to induce, entice, or compel such woman or girl to become a prostitute or to give herself up to debauchery, or to engage in any other immoral practice.

Those found guilty of violating the law that became universally known as the Mann Act faced up to five years in a federal prison and a fine of up to five thousand dollars. The law was described as a measure to combat prostitution and sex trafficking, but its focus on suasion, its expansive wording, and the lack of any definition of 'immoral purpose' meant it functioned as a federal seduction statute.

Those charged with executing the law were the zealous young agents of the Bureau of Investigation, the forerunner of the FBI. It soon became apparent that the young men of the Bureau were more interested in policing public morality than in monitoring the movements of professional sex workers. In no time at all the new law was catching out sexually adventurous young men throughout the country. In 1913 it ensnared the most sexually adventurous of them all: Jack Johnson, the first black heavyweight boxing champion of the world.

**

The Mann Act was the means; Chicago was to be the place. What was needed was a trigger. It came in the form of personal tragedy that hit Johnson in September 1912. In the months after the Jeffries fight, McClay and Schreiber had drifted further from the champion's interests and his relationship with Duryea intensified. In January 1911 they were quietly married in Pittsburgh, and that summer they sailed to Europe. Marriage had done little to dampen Johnson's appetite for the sporting life, however. In America, he maintained contact with courtesans and fast women – Schreiber included. In London and Paris he was besieged by female admirers, to Duryea's horror and disgust.

Back in America, Johnson struggled to find suitable fights and so busied himself with a new enterprise: the construction of a cabaret in the Levee where he would be owner, principal attraction and master of the revels. He poured his efforts into the Café de Champion, intending it as an embassy for the Johnson that he wished to project rather than the Johnson who was harangued and reviled in the press. Johnson spared no expense on decorating his club and freely displayed in it many works of art that he had collected over the course of his career.[33] Given pride of place were several large portraits of Etta and himself, intended as a monument to their marriage but also a statement of intent for the club itself.

The club opened in bacchanalian style in July 1912. Pretty soon, the Johnsons were living there full time: Jack entertaining special guests for hours in a private dining room upstairs; Etta confined to a top-floor suite with only a couple of maids for companions. As sports flocked to the café, the champion's infidelities increased commensurately. Johnson struck up affairs with Ada Banks, one of the in-house singers, and with eighteen-year-old Lucille Cameron, a white girl from Minneapolis, among countless others. Etta's mental health, which had always been fragile, disintegrated altogether.

Late in the morning of 11 September 1912, Johnson returned to the Café de Champion from the train station, where he had been organising tickets for a planned trip out west. Pulling up outside 41 West 31st Street, he saw the sidewalk was crowded with police vehicles. Worried, he entered his beloved cabaret. Inside,

> Friends told me to hurry upstairs that something had happened to Etta. Those ominous words gave me the worst fright I had ever had and I sped up the stairs not knowing but dreading what I was to find. She lay on the floor, her beautiful long hair hiding her face. Near her was a revolver. On one exposed bare arm was a red spot. I took courage and tried to convince myself that the shot had not been fatal. I gathered her up in my arms, and as I did so her hair fell back, revealing an ugly wound in her head. She died a few hours later.[34]

Earlier that morning, Duryea had asked her maids to pray with her and then sent them out of the room, locking the door behind them. On the first floor, singer Ada 'Bricktop' Smith was performing in the private dining room. On the ground floor the orchestra was in full swing. The noise was such that the band did not hear the single gunshot. Smith and others did, however, and they ran upstairs and broke down the bedroom door. Etta had shot herself through the head. She was thirty-one.

Johnson was distraught and plunged into a deep depression. His friends rallied to his side and plans were made for a funeral at St Marks AME in the South Side, followed by a fine burial in Graceland Cemetery.

The national press were less sensitive to Johnson's plight. 'MRS. JOHNSON TRIES SUICIDE. Pugilist's Wife, Tired of Being a Social

Outcast, Shoots Herself' was the *New York Times*'s reaction to Duryea's passing.[35] Tabloid coverage was yet more lurid, many papers dwelling at length on the alleged psychic consequences of interracial relations. Duryea, they declared, had clearly gone insane on account of shame: more evidence, not that any was needed at that time, that interracial love was unnatural and morally damaging. Others explored Duryea's ostracism from her family and her Long Island home town. The *New York World* recorded with some delight how her parents, siblings and extended family had severed all links with her as a result of her entanglement with Johnson. Few even of the wayward members of the Duryea clan would associate themselves with Etta, 'not even her cousin,' the *World* reported, 'Florette Whaley – who had eloped with the Rev. Jerry Cooke, the Long Island clergyman who deserted his wife in running away with the young choir girl – had sent her a word of condolence.' Duryea's mother, meanwhile, told the press that she hoped her prodigal daughter's death might warn off other girls who were considering love across the Color Line.

If the press were content to cover the tragic death of a depressed young woman in tones both morbid and flippant, they were still willing and able to scold Johnson for his romantic decisions. Johnson soon gave them an opening. Within a fortnight of his wife's entombment in Graceland, he had promoted Lucille Cameron from concubine to main squeeze. In October he introduced her to the press as the new Mrs Johnson. The resulting spasm of media outrage led to Lucille's mother, Mrs F. Cameron-Falconet, to come to Chicago to try and rescue her recalcitrant daughter from the heavyweight champion of the world. This short, fearsome woman was more than a match for Jack Johnson. Within a day of her arrival she had confronted him and demanded to see her daughter. When he complied, she ordered Lucille to come away with her. Her daughter stated that she loved Johnson and wanted to stay with him, where-upon Cameron-Falconet hired a lawyer and requested that the police arrest Johnson for abduction. She also began to mobilise public opinion against him. In a series of sensational interviews she begged the authorities to intervene and save her daughter – only nineteen – from the black boxer. She told the *Chicago Daily News* that 'Jack Johnson has hypnotic powers and he has exercised them on my little girl,' giving a vivid and macabre account of her confrontation with Johnson at his South Side home. There, in her version of events, she had pleaded with him to release Lucille from his hold. Johnson refused and then, allegedly, boasted of his immense powers of seduction: 'I told him I could not understand how she could be attracted by such as he, and he said he could "get" any woman he wanted. "I could even get you, too, if I wanted you."'[36]

Those words, that fictitious declaration, stirred something deep within the white psyche. The ensuing furore had been primed by many things: decades of sexualised racial rhetoric and racialised sexual legislation; the popularisation of 'white slave' narratives peopled by desperate white mothers, fallen white daughters and shameless, swarthy seducers; the raw wound of Jim Jeffries' defeat at Reno; the bitter-sweet memory of the racial violence that swept the nation after that fight; the limpic belief that only, if only Johnson could be destroyed then the White Man would be rescued. But that single phrase, *I could even get you*, represented the totality of white fears. The mask had slipped and fallen. Johnson was bent on destroying the foundations of the American order. He had to be destroyed in turn.

What followed had the dimensions of a national crisis and the details of a farce. Despite massive public pressure and intense institutional willingness, the police were unable to arrest Johnson for abduction, for the simple fact that in every interview she gave Lucille stressed that her relationship with Johnson was consensual. Confounded by legal facts, Captain Max Nootbaar of the Chicago police – a German migrant, a former cavalryman, and the legendary scourge of the Levee's bordellos – had Lucille arrested for disorderly conduct. 'I am doing this for humanity's sake,' he told the press. 'Legally, I have no right to hold the girl . . . but I believe the case warrants my action.' Johnson personally drove Lucille to the police station, where he was confronted by Nootbaar and Mrs Cameron-Falconet. Again they begged Lucille to hand Johnson over; again she refused. 'I would rather see you spend all your life in jail,' Lucille's mother said, moments before her daughter was led to the cells, 'than one day in the company of that nigger.'

Johnson hurried to the Café de Champion to get bail money. There he was greeted by a spurned and furious Ada Banks, who tried and failed to shoot him. Rumour soon spread that she had mortally wounded the boxer, leading a cartel of wealthy Southern racists to wire north an offer to fund her legal costs to the tune of $50,000.[37]

In the meantime, Cameron-Falconet and her lawyer succeeded in having a judge order Johnson's arrest for abduction. Johnson was briefly held and then released while he arranged the terms of his bond. Angry crowds now greeted him wherever he went – at the bank, at the courthouse, anywhere outside the Levee and the Black Belt. When he tried to hire private security, neither the Burns nor the Pinkerton Detective Agency would accept his custom.[38]

The black community's support for Johnson also started to slip. Some of the criticism from that quarter was more mordant than urgent, as with the *Philadelphia Port News*'s wry headline: 'Jack Johnson, Dangerously Ill, Victim of White Fever'. But much of it was damning. On 20 October, Booker T. Washington, who had long been wary of Johnson's ostentatious style, now denounced him publicly, telling an audience at the Detroit YMCA that 'undoubtedly Johnson's actions are repudiated by the great majority of right-thinking people of the Negro race'. Washington dwelt on the fact that Johnson's actions endangered the lives of his fellow black Americans. 'This man is harming himself the least,' he said. 'I wish to say emphatically that his actions do not meet with the approval of the colored race.' Washington's speech was met with acclaim in many bastions of black opinion, newspapers like the *Baltimore Afro-American Ledger* and the *Indianapolis Freeman*, which now also editorialised against the black champion.[39]

But whatever Washington might have believed, the threat of lynching was at this point directed principally at Jack Johnson. In Chicago, a large crowd gathered at Montrose and Clark – only a block away from where Etta Duryea Johnson lay freshly buried – and hanged an effigy of Johnson from a tree. On its chest someone had pinned a note reading 'This is the last of Jack Johnson'.[40] Against this hysterical backdrop Johnson went to the Appotomax Club in the South Side to defend himself before an assembly of black businessmen and community leaders. Before a largely silent audience, he began with a refutation of Cameron-Falconet's account of their meeting and proceeded to give a defence of his right to live and love in freedom worthy of any of the great Enlightenment champions of liberty:

> I want to say that I never made a statement attributed to me to the effect that I could get any white woman I wanted. I can lay my hand upon the Bible and swear that I never made such a statement. My father was a Christian and my mother is Christian, and I know what it means to swear by the Bible. I want to say that I never said anything of the sort about any woman of any color.
>
> I have been quoted falsely. The newspapers and the public have taken advantage of me because of my color. If I were a white man not a line of this would have reached the newspaper.
>
> But I do want to say that I am not a slave and that I have the right to choose who my mate shall be without the dictation of any man. I have eyes and I have a heart and when they fail to tell me who I shall have as mine I want to be put away in a lunatic asylum. So long as I do not interfere with any other man's wife, I shall claim the right to select the woman of my own choice. Nobody else can do that for me. That is where the trouble lies.[41]

A few days after this speech, the Chicago authorities, which thus far had been unable to legally detain Johnson, ordered that entertainment cease at the Café de Champion; two days later they effectively shuttered the business by revoking its liquor licence. This vindictive piece of bureaucratic warfare did substantial damage to the champion's financial position, but he remained stubbornly free.

In the course of their search for any legal pretext to arrest and hold Jack Johnson, the Chicago authorities called upon the Justice Department. Knowing Johnson's long and convivial history with prostitutes and prostitution and his nomadic lifestyle, they wanted to explore whether it could be proved that his relationship with Lucille Cameron was a violation of the Mann Act. The effort came to nothing. Such cases relied upon hard evidence of interstate traffic, and there was none in the case of Johnson and Lucille. Nonetheless, once this avenue of investigation was opened, the Bureau of Investigation became convinced that witnesses could be found from the sporting world who would testify that Johnson had engaged in such behaviour since the law came into effect in the summer of 1910. What followed was a kind of phoney war, as the Bureau combed through the various vice districts of the United States looking for people to turn state's witness on Johnson, while the boxer engaged in his own search to find and silence potential turncoats with cash and a ticket out of town. Then in early November, as the prospect of using Lucille Cameron to ensnare Johnson was rapidly diminishing, the Chicago office received an anonymous tip about a sporting woman whom it could be proved Johnson had shipped across state lines for 'immoral purposes'. She went by many names – Belle Gifford, Belle Baker, Belle Allen, Mrs Jacques Allen – but there was indisputable evidence that she was 'FORMERLY INMATE EVERLEIGH CLUB, CHICAGO, SAID TO HAVE BEEN ILLEGALLY TRANSPORTED BY JACK JOHNSON'. She was, of course, Belle Schreiber, Johnson's former lover, who had fallen out with him after he married Etta Duryea and was now eking out a precarious existence as a prostitute in Washington, D.C.

The Bureau's agents quickly tracked her down. She was a dream witness: eager to revenge herself on Johnson and in possession of a vast collection of letters, receipts and other such material that would furnish the infrastructure of a successful prosecution under the Mann Act. On 7 November, she was quietly taken to Chicago where she gave evidence before a grand jury. Within a matter of hours of her testimony, the jury had issued seven indictments against the black champion for violation of the Mann Act's prohibition on interstate traffic in 'white slaves'. Johnson was arrested that evening and briefly put in cuffs before being allowed to spend the night at home. The next day he went before a judge who refused to accept his request for bail. Johnson was sent to the Cook County Jail. They finally had him where they wanted him.

The case against Johnson was based on an incident in October 1910. At that time, Johnson had only just made Duryea's acquaintance and was still intimate with Schreiber. She had fallen on hard times and had contacted Johnson – who was flush after the fight in Reno a few months before – from Indiana asking for some money to set herself up as a prostitute. Johnson wired her $75 and told her to meet him in Chicago. When they met there a few weeks later, Johnson, a firm believer in independent living, suggested that she might establish and run her own brothel rather than simply tying her fortunes to another madam. Schreiber agreed and chose an apartment near the Levee. Johnson paid the first month's rent, helped her pick out furniture and organised a beer supplier. The furnishings alone cost close to $1,200. The champion had been generous to Belle Schreiber, and she could prove it because she had kept the receipts.

The occurrences of that October had all the makings of an open-and-shut Mann Act prosecution. In the event, Johnson would not have his day in court until the spring of 1913. Meanwhile he was out of jail and free to try and enjoy what he could of his shattered public and private lives. One diversion was his relationship with Lucille Cameron. Despite the most incredible pressure, she had remained by his side and she now asked him to marry her.[42] After some hesitation, Johnson agreed.

On 3 December, Lucille formally became Mrs Jack Johnson at a ceremony in Johnson's South Side house. Her despairing mother gave up and went home. 'MRS. CAMERON FALCONET HAS WASHED HER HANDS CLEAN OF THE WHOLE WHITE AND BLACK MESS', the *Chicago Defender* told its readers, 'AND HAS RETURNED TO HER HOME IN MINNEAPOLIS, MINN. IN UTTER DISGUST'.

Mrs Cameron-Falconet was not the only one to begrudge Johnson his hopes for marital bliss. News of his marriage to Lucille became public just as the National Governors Conference was getting under way in Virginia. From the podium, Governor Cole Blease of South Carolina called for Johnson to be lynched, asking 'if we cannot protect our white women from black fiends, where is our boasted civilisation?' He continued:

> In the South we love our women, we hold them higher than all things else, and whenever anything steps between a Southern man and the defense and virtue of the women of his nation and his states, he will tear it down and walk over it in her defense, regardless of what may be the consequences.[43]

A vocal and enthusiastic proponent of lynch law, Blease told the assembled governors that his position was that if the constitution forbade mob justice in defence of white female virtue, then 'to hell with the Constitution'.[44] Not to be outdone by his fellow Southerner, Seaborn Roddenberry once again brought his idiosyncratic oratorical style to the floor of the House of Representatives, this time calling for a constitutional amendment to ban interracial marriage:

> No brutality, no infamy, no degradation in all the years of southern slavery, possessed such a villainous character and such atrocious qualities as the provision of the laws of Illinois, New York, Massachusetts, and other states which allow the marriage of the negro, Jack Johnson, to a woman of the Caucasian strain. [applause] . . . Intermarriage between whites and blacks is repulsive and averse to every sentiment of pure American spirit. It is abhorrent and repugnant. It is subversive to social peace. It is destructive of moral supremacy, and ultimately this slavery of white women to black beasts will bring this nation to a conflict as fatal and as bloody as ever reddened the soil of Virginia or crimsoned the mountain paths for Pennsylvania. . . . Let us uproot and exterminate now this debasing, ultrademoralizing, un-American and inhuman leprosy.[45]

Such statements are obscene, but they reveal the unifying rhetorical power of the white slave narrative. The campaign to end white slavery crossed party and sectional lines. Progressives understood it as a policy project. Moralists viewed it as a quest for national purification. Racists grasped its versatility as a tool of racial control. In a country that within living memory had torn itself apart over the very real evil of black slavery, the crusade against a fictitious white slavery offered an opportunity to experience an alternative history where Northern white women were slaves, Southern white men, like Blease and Roddenberry, were abolitionists, and non-whites, like Jack Johnson, were slave masters.[46] In the context of the rolling back of Reconstruction and the reassertion of a *de facto* bondage in the South, the myth of white slavery in the North was also an excellent way of diverting attention from the failure of the North to change circumstances for former slaves and their children and grandchildren. Turning inwards was an escape.

Horror at the apparent spectacle of white slaves being traded in the streets of Northern cities became a way of redirecting the moral energies that should have gone into a proper reckoning with the condition of the post-war South. Perhaps Jack Johnson's greatest sin was to embody both the fiction of white slavery and the fact of Southern injustice in one very public person.

United States v. John Arthur Johnson began on 5 May 1913 in Chicago's monumental Federal Building. Federal prosecutors had originally tried to expand the number of charges to include the colourful and suggestive crimes of unlawful sexual intercourse and committing the crime against nature. There was no evidence for these charges, but they were a tactical ploy to further defame the black champion in the eyes of the jury. At the request of Johnson's lawyers, the judge threw out these supplementary indictments. The case was to be judged purely on the merits of whether Johnson had or had not violated the Mann Act.

In his memoirs, Johnson would decry the trial as 'a rank frame-up' – an act of judicial persecution against a black man who refused to conform to the racial order of the day. Historians have tended to take the same view. The Johnson case was so clearly politically inspired, so obviously motivated by racial prejudice and moral panic, that its outcome was never in doubt. This was a judicial lynching, not the impartial execution of the law. As much is evidently true. There was not a jury in Illinois that would have found Johnson innocent under these circumstances. The atmosphere in the courtroom was as poisonous as that in the press. Johnson was never going to get a fair trial; very few black men did in such cases.

Nonetheless, it is important to confront the case as Johnson, the jurors and the lawyers involved had to. They were dealing with the law as they found it, not as they might have wished it to be. To demonstrate his innocence, Johnson would have to prove that he had not transported Belle Schreiber across state lines for the purposes of prostitution. Johnson's defence was based on a stout denial of all the events described by the prosecution. In reality she was a prostitute, and he had always known that. Johnson might have seen nothing out of the ordinary in consorting with such women – it was all part of the sporting lifestyle – but to the average juror it would have been impossible to interpret their relationship as anything other than that of a prostitute and a client, or, if they were so inclined, a white slave and a white slaver. As a consequence, any evidence that Johnson and Schreiber had ever travelled together across state lines, or that Johnson had facilitated Schreiber's passage across state lines after July 1910, was evidence that the Mann Act had been violated.

Then there was the question of the apartment in the Levee. There were receipts for the purchases made in connection with it and the vendor testified at the trial that Johnson had paid for them. If this looked like Johnson establishing a brothel, that is because it is what he had, in essence, done. It was what sports were wont to do.

Johnson was ultimately a victim of the Mann Act's capacious wording. The law potentially criminalised all interstate travel involving sexually active adults. It was less a question of whether someone was guilty and more a point of whether there was the motivation to pursue a prosecution. Johnson had clearly violated the loose letter of the law and had certainly offended its puritanical spirit. That did not make the timbre of the trial any less distasteful, or diminish the fact that every aspect of Johnson's treatment was shot through with racism. Johnson was both guilty in law and guilty in colour. His infraction was legal; his crime was racial. As Sol C. Johnson of the *Savannah Tribune* observed: 'While it is true that he has done wrong, it is also true that he has been persecuted. The Negro-hating firebrands have had their inning. The prison wall yearns for Johnson.'[47] When the trial ended on 14 May, the jury quickly found Johnson guilty on all counts.

Johnson's conviction was met with the predictable headlines. Most were simply unadulterated expressions of *schadenfreude*. Some went further and foresaw that the case would be a spur to new and more invasive laws against interracial marriage. 'Jack Johnson Guilty Means Race Reforms', bellowed the *Cleveland Daily News*, 'Laws Prohibiting Intermarriage of Blacks and Whites Sure to Come. Black Pugilist Will Be Made An Example'. Black newspapers, whatever their view of Johnson as an individual, recognised that the case was a terrifying confirmation of the place of black Americans in white society. 'Every branch of the government is permeated with race prejudice,' said the *Richmond Planet* of Johnson's sentencing. It continued:

> There has been no colored man in the history of the country who has done more to injure himself in particular and the colored race in general than Mr. Johnson. He agitated the debilitating race question, this intermarriage of the races.
>
> There are sad hearts in the country today among the colored people. Their idol is shattered. It is painful to contemplate. There is mourning in the Southland.
>
> Farewell, Jack Johnson![48]

In the ring, Jack Johnson had been known for his elusive style and his mastery of feints and bluffs. But all his guile seemed to have abandoned him in the confines of the Federal Building. On 4 June the court handed down the sentence: a $1,000 fine and one year and one day in a federal prison. Johnson had two weeks to file an appeal. Confronted with the prospect of prison time, and utterly disenchanted with the justice system, Johnson rediscovered his old nimbleness. On 24 June, he slipped his police surveillance and drove to Englewood train station. There, as had been planned, he ran across the tracks and bundled aboard a train 'carrying a bag of bats and other baseball equipment' in his arms.[49] On board were

dozens of other athletic black men with baseball gear – the
members of an all-black baseball team called Foster's Giants who
were travelling to Canada for a series of matches. Johnson and an
associate jumped off in Hamilton, Ontario, and made their way
to Montreal where Lucille was waiting with tickets for a steamer
to Le Havre. As an alien in transit with paid tickets to a third
country, the Canadian authorities were unable either to detain the
fugitive boxer or enable his extradition. On Sunday 29 June, the
couple were aboard the liner *Corinthian* as it left harbour for
France. Jack Johnson was free.[50]

***

The American public might have met the particular prosecution
of Jack Johnson under the Mann Act, but doubts about the wider
application of the law were rife. The law did not deliver on its
promise of imprisoning packs of sexually voracious men. Instead,
many women were sent to prison for their involvement in the
sexual economy. The very first arrest under the law had been that
of Nettie Jenkins, a madam arrested while escorting five women
from Chicago to Houghton, Michigan. Furthermore, many of the
women being protected from apparent exploitation were willing
participants in the sex trade. This was true of the five women in
the Jenkins case. It was also true of Belle Schreiber and many other
sporting women. Bureau agents soon realised that many of the
women they were seeking to rescue neither wanted nor needed
their help. Moreover, the agents themselves had often signed up
to guard white virtue, not to intervene in the existence of women
who, in their eyes, were irredeemably lost to a life of vice. Such
prejudices were only compounded when the women involved had
a history of interracial relations. A certain Agent Lamarioux, inves-
tigating the case of Violet Hall in October 1911, informed his
superiors that Hall 'had one or more Jap lovers . . . [and so] can

hardly be classed as a white slave.'[51] The same was certainly true of Schreiber, who had been freely enjoying the champion's company for some years before turning against him in court.[52]

Doubts about who deserved protection under the Mann Act and who should forfeit it, hinged on that single ambiguous phrase: 'immoral purposes'. For agents and activists who were eager to use the law to police sexuality expansively, it was self-evident that immoral purposes encompassed a range of behaviours, from adultery to fornication and elopement. More conservative officials assumed that the purpose of the law was narrowly focused on the commercial dimension of the interaction. Inevitably, the two sides clashed, one alleging that the other was not enforcing the letter of the law and the other ridiculing attempts to micromanage the private lives of United States citizens. What was needed was clarification from a higher court; and in March 1913, as Johnson was preparing for his court date, the seeds of such an eventuality were sown in Reno when local police arrested two men for violation of the Mann Act.

The men concerned were Drew Caminetti and Maury Diggs of Sacramento, California. They were friends and scions of wealthy and politically connected Sacramento families. Caminetti was the wayward son of California state senator Anthony Caminetti, who in 1913 was nominated by Woodrow Wilson to serve as United States Commissioner for Immigration; Diggs was from a family of property developers and was himself a promising young architect. At twenty-seven and twenty-six respectively, both were married and both were having affairs. Maury was in love with Marsha Warrington, and Caminetti was involved with Lola Norris. The affairs were no secret: the men flaunted their younger girlfriends around town and even invited them to dinners where their wives were present. By March 1913, their behaviour was causing such a scandal that they began receiving threats from the outraged male relatives of all the four women involved. The local press started to take an interest, and Marsha narrowly succeeded in quashing an article on the foursome that was due to run in the *Sacramento Bee*. When the social scrutiny became unbearable, the men and their mistresses decided to flee to Los Angeles. They arranged to meet at a restaurant near the train station and travel to the city as a group. That afternoon, however, Caminetti got drunk and lost his wallet, and so was late to the rendezvous. By the time he arrived they had missed the train to Los Angeles and decided to take the next train out of town. This was going to Reno, Nevada, fourteen miles outside the California state line. In Reno the four found hotel rooms; Caminetti and Diggs then busied themselves with plotting divorces from their wives. But local police soon got wind of their presence in the city and arrested them under the Mann Act.

The men were shipped back to California and tried in a federal court. The affair soon became national news, Democrats alleging that the case was cooked up by Republicans looking to smear Anthony Caminetti and, by association, President Wilson. Nonetheless, the trial went ahead, proceedings beginning the day after *United States v. John Arthur Johnson* got under way, and the two men were duly found guilty. The *Sacramento Bee* welcomed the verdict on behalf of 'all good men and all decent women',[53] while South Carolina senator Ben Tillman called for the lynching of Diggs and Caminetti. Diggs vowed to appeal, telling the press that 'If I am a white slaver, 90% of men living are as guilty as I am.'

A substantial number of people agreed with him. It was one thing to use an expansive interpretation of the law to punish an upstart black boxer, quite another to use it to imprison two respectable, wealthy young white men. Neither Caminetti nor Diggs stood to gain financially from taking Marsha and Lola across state lines, making nonsense of the legal logic of the Mann Act as arising out of the constitutionally sanctioned right of the federal government to monitor interstate commerce. In other jurisdictions, judges had denied that the law applied to private romantic adventures. The same year that the two friends were convicted, a federal judge in Wichita, Kansas ruled that 'it was not the aim of Congress to prevent the personal escapades of any man'.[54]

With confusion spreading as to the scope of the law, press scepticism grew. As Caminetti and Diggs' appeals drifted from court to higher court, the newspapers began to uncover ever more cases of blackmail and extortion arising out of the Mann Act. Furthermore, the law seemed to victimise men – especially wealthy ones – but never women. In 1916 the *New York Times*, under the headline 'Uncle Sam, Blackmailer', noted caustically:

> If two immoral persons pass a state line in the course of their immoral proceedings the man is guilty of a crime but the woman is not. The result has been that this law has acted as a direct inducement to blackmail. . . . The law is in itself an absurdity, but that is less serious than its direct inducement to crime. It breaks up no 'white slave' traffic, but it does make the Federal Government the accomplice and instrument of blackmailers and facilitates their operations.[55]

The *Times*' editorial hinted at a sea change in public attitudes towards women, sex and the law. Implicit in its criticism of the Mann Act was that the law's exploitation by devious women was evidence that the moral premise of the law – namely, that women were meek and morally superior and needed special protection – was erroneous. That same year the Supreme Court accepted the appeal of Caminetti and Diggs and announced that a ruling would be handed down in 1917. This would provide legal clarity concerning the parameters of the law, but it would also serve as a unique opportunity to either halt or sanction the concept creep that had transformed a law designed to prevent the commercial trade in prostitutes into something more expansive and intrusive.

Just as the unhappy defendants of *Caminetti v. United States* were preparing to head to prison, the exiled principal of *United States v. John Arthur Johnson* was beginning to accept that a stint in an American jailhouse might be inescapable. Johnson's life had not been quiet since the *Corinthian* had steamed out of Montreal in June 1913. He was never one to languish in silence and misery, and if anything his exile transformed him from a mere celebrity into a mythic figure. No longer confined to the leisure districts of urban America, Johnson was now free by threat of imprisonment to live a peripatetic existence, full of adventure, disaster, pageantry and narrow escapes.

Johnson and Lucille arrived in Paris in July 1913 and spent much of the rest of the year bouncing around Europe. Paris and London were no longer as welcoming as they had been – the stigma of criminal conviction carried across the Atlantic – and the Johnsons found themselves drifting further afield, to Vienna and Budapest. At the start of 1914 they circled back to Paris, where Johnson hoped to earn some easy money in the ring. As ever, the chief problem was finding boxers of a suitable calibre to fight and promoters who could stump up the money that would motivate the Epicurean champion into the gym. A proposed fight in London with Sam Langford, a fellow black boxer from Boston, was rejected. The purse was only a couple of thousand pounds and Langford was a dangerous opponent. In a high-handed letter to the British sporting authorities, Johnson declared that he would not fight for less than $30,000.

Frenchman Georges Carpentier was another option, but the closest Johnson came to fighting him was when Carpentier refereed an uninspiring encounter between Johnson and the bruising but artless Irish-American fighter Frank Moran in Paris on 27 June 1914. The bout went the full twenty rounds. Johnson won on points but won no money: the earnings from the fight went straight into the pocket of a promoter Johnson had jilted earlier that year. The next day, Archduke Franz Ferdinand was shot and killed in Sarajevo.

As Europe's armies stirred to war, Johnson and Lucille were on a train to St Petersburg at the invitation of another extraordinary African American. George Thomas had risen from poverty in Georgia to become a successful restaurateur and society favourite in Tsarist Russia. Their progress east was repeatedly interrupted by special trains carrying troops; in Germany they observed from their windows reservists marshalling in stations and drilling in fields. 'The whole of Europe,' Johnson mused in his memoirs, 'would be under powder smoke before long.'

In the meantime, the preparations for war simply interfered with Johnson's latest money-making schemes. Thomas had been organising several lucrative theatre appearances for Johnson in Moscow and St Petersburg, scheduled for that July, but these now came to nothing. Exactly a month after their arrival, Germany declared war on Russia and the Johnsons fled to London via Warsaw, Berlin, Belgium and Paris, cutting an unlikely path through the chaos of mobilisation. Amid desperate scenes on the Channel coast, they secured passage aboard a boat to England; soon they were in London and, for the moment, safe.

Johnson was relieved to be back 'among English speaking people' and was laconically appreciative of the relative tranquillity that prevailed in London. But the organised violence of a general war obviated the need for organised violence in the ring. The era of liberal borders and nomadic sportsmen was now over.[58] Many patriotic fighters, such as Georges Carpentier and Bombardier Wells, were now serving in the ranks.

Johnson was adrift, until one day he bumped into promoter Jack Curley while walking his dog in Paddington. Curley had come across the Atlantic with a proposal: $30,000 plus training expenses to fight Jess Willard, the latest and largest of the Great White Hopes, in Mexico. Johnson agreed, and at the end of 1914 he and Lucille sailed to Argentina and onwards to Barbados, finally arriving in Cuba in mid-February. It soon became clear that the fight was not going to happen in Mexico. The country was in the throes of a civil war and the pro-American faction, led by Venustiano Carranza, made it clear that they would hand over Johnson to federal agents if he stepped foot in the parts of the country under their control. Peaceful, placidly corrupt, and close to Florida, Havana was fast emerging as the better location for the title fight. Near the end of February, Curley announced the location change. The fight was to happen on 5 April; it was scheduled for forty-five rounds.

Johnson was an admirer of Napoleon and saw in Bonaparte's rise from Corsican obscurity to European mastery a historical parallel to his own startling ascent. Napoleon's story had ended in a mire of defeat, betrayal and imprisonment, and Johnson had at times pondered whether his life would meet a similar end. But his confidence was at its usual high as he settled into his training routine in March 1915. He was not aware that the fight with Jess Willard, an overgrown farmhand from Pottawatomie, Kansas, would be his Waterloo. Johnson was now thirty-seven and he had fought only four times in the last five years. The championship had bred complacency; age brought arrogance just as it quietly sapped him of his strength, stamina and reflexes. Willard was younger, hungrier and perfectly conditioned.

After the fact, Johnson would claim that he had thrown the fight. One of the few moments in his memoirs where he forsakes his usual strident tone for a folksy, down-home manner is when he claims that he had planned to lose to Willard as part of a plea bargain that would allow him to go back to Chicago unmolested to 'again be with my folks' and 'settle down quietly and live in peace with my fellow man'. But on 4 April, Johnson certainly did not fight like a man who intended to lose. For the first fifteen rounds he gave the challenger a beating and at times came close to putting the lumbering, straight-punching Willard down for good. But Willard stayed upright and the fierce heat began to sap the champion's strength. As the fight entered the twenty-fifth round it became clear that Johnson had no answer for the fitter, stronger Willard. He was pummelled repeatedly during that round, one left hook knocking out Johnsons's two gold-capped front teeth. Rather than spit them out and let Willard and the crowd see that he had been hurt, Johnson elected to swallow them.

Johnson defeated by Jess Willard, the Pottawatomie Giant, in scorching heat in Havana, Cuba, 1915.

On his stool at the end of the round, he told his cornermen to get Lucille out of the audience. He did not want his wife to witness his downfall. But the end came seconds later, and Lucille was still in the crowd to see it. After a final devastating flurry Johnson was on the canvas, counted out under the fierce Cuban sun before an ecstatic white crowd. He had reigned for six years, four years less than his French idol.[59]

The fact that he was no longer the champion did nothing to change Johnson's legal status in the United States. He was still a wanted man. In May he returned via Spain and France to London, where he signed on with a theatre in Elephant and Castle. One night the performance was interrupted by a zeppelin raid. When the threat had apparently passed, Johnson fetched his white Benz and began to drive through the debris back home to Haverstock Hill.

> But the trip was not to be made undisturbed, for suddenly there came roaring out the black sky more bombs. The raiders had returned. Between blasts of bombs which were falling all around us, we could hear the whir and swish of the Zeppelin overhead. I speeded the car up in an effort to get outside of its bombing radius, but was surprised to learn that no matter how fast I traveled or in what direction I turned, the bombs were close upon us. It was then that I learned with considerable alarm that the Zeppelin was following us.[60]

At length Johnson arrived home, having been bombed all the way, and scrambled into his shelter. In his fanciful account the airships continued to bombard his house through the night, levelling the whole neighbourhood. He emerged the next morning to a scene of total destruction, his home ringed by smoking ruins. It is a glorious account, worthy of some of the more apocalyptic episodes found in Waugh or Fitzgerald – and equally fictitious. But the choice of the fiction reveals something of the man: his egoism (naturally, the bombing of London had to be all about him), but also his weariness at his persecution. Real or not, his pursuit by that zeppelin was the perfect metaphor for his condition.

The Johnsons soon tired of the deprivations of wartime London, and in the spring of 1916 they moved to Spain. In Barcelona Johnson's existence, which had always teetered on the edge of unreality, became surreal, both figuratively – he became involved in an advertising agency and did a few turns in La Monumental as a matador – and literally: in April 1916, he fought, and handily beat, Arthur Cravan, the nephew of Oscar Wilde and a Dadaist poet in his own right. He was still in Spain when the United States

If America seemed strange and unrecognisable to Johnson after a seven-year absence, it seemed increasingly foreign to those who had never left. It is perhaps only human vanity to believe that something as arbitrary and cosmically insignificant as the start of a new decade necessarily inaugurates a new stage in society's development. But in the Twenties America was transformed, and the contours of that transformation were described in a triptych of short stories published in May 1920 by a young F. Scott Fitzgerald. Physically, Fitzgerald was then in his lunar phase – he stares out of photos from the period pallid, even, and complacent, his face having yet to acquire the ruined grandeur of his bibulous majority – but his literary career was stellar. That March he had published *This Side of Paradise* to a rapturous reception, earning him a fair amount of money and guaranteeing higher prices for future works. Professional accomplishment translated into amorous success. In the spring, after a volatile year, Zelda Sayre of Montgomery, Alabama, finally accepted his proposal.[63] Zelda was Fitzgerald's great love and also the archetype for his female protagonists. She was the ur-flapper, a species America was becoming fast acquainted with that year and which Fitzgerald helpfully taxonomised in three stories published sequentially in *The Saturday Evening Post* in May: 'Bernice Bobs Her Hair', 'The Ice Palace' and 'The Offshore Pirate'.

The aesthetic profile of the flapper is well-known. The bob, the revealing, androgynous clothes, the chain-smoking, the drinking, the slang, the moody pose – best exhibited in the back of a speeding car. But in these stories Fitzgerald offered a more substantial philosophical perspective upon what she represented. The fundamental principle of flapperdom was a total rejection of the moral, and specifically sexual, values of their parents' generation. Flappers were bored stiff by the ladies of the WCTU and repulsed by their image of soft, Christian femininity. An episode in 'Bernice Bobs Her Hair', a brilliant account of one provincial girl's transformation into a liberated modern woman, captures the attitude perfectly.

erably divided by a body of water. The flappers and their male accomplices were not yet ready to overturn their parents' racial assumptions, which was ironic given that their parents regarded the new youthful fashions as worrying evidence of the negrification of white society. In fiction, Ardita's uncle calls her behaviour a reflection 'of the demi-monde'; in fact, the *Ladies' Home Journal* called for a legal prohibition on jazz dancing.[64] In truth, the new youth culture was an appropriation of the sporting culture of the pre-war era. (Ardita even takes her dates to see boxing matches.) But where the sports were rough, ready and defiantly interracial, the flappers and philosophers of the Jazz Age were safe, spoiled and exclusively white.

Jack Johnson had first-hand experience of this bleached and sanitised new vision of his former lifestyle. After getting out of jail in July 1921, Johnson bounced around Chicago and New York looking for fights, working the remnants of the vaudeville circuit, and taking jobs as a sparring partner for the new generation of heavyweight contenders. In 1923 he briefly became involved with a new cabaret called the Café de Luxe in Harlem. The venture was so successful that it was soon taken over by bootleggers and Johnson was cut loose.[65] Not that the former champion seemed to mind much. He had never liked jazz, preferring classical music. The club itself was an all-white affair and was gaudily decorated with the style and motifs of the Southern plantation manor. The black musicians on stage were instructed by management to play crude 'Jungle' jazz, to cater to the tastes and prejudices of the white clientele. It was a pastiche and an affront to the venerated memory of the Café de Champion.

Later, rebranded as the Cotton Club, it would become one of the cultural cornerstones of the Jazz Age and the concomitant Harlem Renaissance. Duke Ellington would make his name there; so too would Louis Armstrong, whom Johnson had indirectly terrorised as a child. Fitzgerald also drank there, and likely found in the decor a pleasing physical echo of the equally artificial vision of the Old South to which he repeatedly returned in his shorter fiction. It was a place that he describes in 'The Ice Palace' as a 'languid paradise of dreamy skies and firefly evenings and noisy niggery street fairs – and especially of gracious, soft-voiced girls, who were brought up on memories instead of money'. A place that never existed.[66]

For all its limitations, the sexual revolution of the Twenties was real and lasting, and did ultimately have progressive consequences. Furthermore, it was felt throughout the country rather than experienced merely in a few elite enclaves. The causes were many and familiar (urbanisation, secularisation, increased female participation in the workforce, increased mobility due to widespread automobile ownership, better information and access to healthcare, including birth control) and the symptoms were everywhere. Like all reformations in manners it proceeded gradually, unevenly, invisibly and for the most part unquantifiably – although some have tried to quantify its progress. Among them were the authors of a monumental 1930s report commissioned by the Roosevelt administration and entitled *Recent Social Trends in the United States*. A dour, statistical affair, its contributors studied magazines and journals from the preceding decade in an attempt to chart the rise of the new sexual morality. The report concluded:

Attitudes toward extra-marital sexual intercourse have undergone rather violent fluctuations since 1900, and particularly during the past 15 years. Correlated with attitudes on adultery, seduction and the like, have been those relating to sex 'thrill', promiscuous petting and the exposure of the human body.

The height of sentiment against traditional sex morals occurs between 1922 and 1929 . . . Particularly from 1923 to 1927 it was more frequently asserted than denied in these magazines that love, not marriage, was the only justification of sex relations, that sexual intercourse was a private matter in which society had no concern as long as children were avoided, that celibacy was abnormal and deleterious and the like.[67]

Changing attitudes were matched by changing behaviour. Another survey from the 1930s revealed that of women born after 1910 only 32 per cent were virgins at marriage, compared with 74 per cent of those born in the period 1890–1900. Kinsey report data showed much the same trend. Put simply, starting in the 1920s Americans started having a lot more extra-marital sex and were comfortable to admit as much to pollsters and social scientists.[68]

The paradox is that this sexual revolution coincided with the zenith of authoritarian moral, sexual and racial legislative activity. Virginia led the nation. In 1922, agitation by the WCTU and other women's groups resulted in the passage of an act that forbade the screening of any film containing 'obscene, indecent, immoral, inhuman' material or that might 'tend to corrupt morals or incite to crime'. In 1924, lobbying by the newly formed Anglo-Saxon Clubs of America (ASCOA) led to the Act to Preserve Racial Integrity, which criminalised intermarriage between whites and any 'colored' person including blacks, Asians, American Indians, Malays, or members of other 'non-Caucasian strains'. The Act also tightened the definition of whiteness, introducing the notorious 'one drop rule' where previously anyone with one-sixteenth or less non-white blood could claim legal status as white. Now 'no trace whatsoever of any blood other than Caucasian' was required. It was a quest for purity and segregation so radical that even the Nazis thought it too extreme.

In the same session the nation's first state sterilisation act was passed, allowing for state intervention in the bodies of those 'defective persons' who, if allowed to breed, would constitute a 'menace to society'. Interestingly, one of the supposed symptoms of such defectiveness was sexual promiscuity.

In 1926 the legislature passed the Public Assemblages Act, which forbade interracial gatherings of any kind in a public space, including theatres, cinemas, schools and university lecture halls. Walter Plecker, the director of Virginia's Bureau of Vital Statistics, later described total social separation as a means to an end of single woman into committing acts that broke the letter of the law. The *New York Times* reported on the case of Robert A. Torbillon (aka 'Dapper Don' Collins), a professional criminal who used the Mann Act as a vehicle for blackmail. It was claimed that he earned $200,000 through extortion rackets involving the Act. Similar frauds were conducted – by gangs and by opportunistic individuals – using Alienation of Affection and Breach of Promise suits. Numerous high-profile men were entangled in these schemes, including opera singer Enrico Caruso, the son of 1928 presidential candidate Alfred E. Smith, Frederick Gimbel, heir to the Gimbel department store fortune, plutocrat and playboy Cornelius Vanderbilt, and the boxers Gene Tunney and Jack Dempsey.[71]

The press was quick to point out that a new double standard had emerged: the law treated women as unimpeachably pure and chaste when they were, in fact, lascivious, scheming, and exploitative of the law's trust in their being otherwise. Lawyers declared the heart balm actions as 'instrument[s] of oppression, blackmail, and fraud', not tools 'for the righting of the wrongs of injured innocence'. It is no coincidence that the Twenties gave the world the word 'gold-digger', a term that captured the new cynicism associated with modern women and personified in Lorelei Lee, the protagonist of Anita Loos's best-selling 1925 novel *Gentlemen Prefer Blondes*. Largely unread today, Loos's book was one of the outstanding literary hits of its day – so popular, its author liked to boast, that James Joyce read it, despite his reading being strictly rationed on account of his incipient blindness. The plot follows Lorelei's fantastically successful attempt to marry into money by any means, fair or foul. Lorelei is glib, philistine, shallow and practically illiterate. She has her hair in a bob and wears slight, figure-hugging dresses. She drinks, dines and travels, and does it all on someone else's dollar. Yet for all her superficial superficiality, Lorelei demonstrates a remarkable knowledge of the law. At one point in the novel Lorelei is at a loss as to whether she should marry the plutocratic moral campaigner Henry Spoffard, who has confessed his love to her. She worries that Henry might be too attentive a husband, constantly busying himself with her private affairs. Nonetheless, Lorelei has him write her a letter containing his proposal and his declaration of love:

> So it is quite a problem and I seem to be in quite a quandary, because it might be better if Henry should happen to decide that he should not get married, and he should change his mind, and desert a girl, and then it would be only right if a girl should sue him for a breach of promise.

Elsewhere in the book, she refers in passing to the 'Man Act'. Lorelei might be vulgar and poorly read – but she knows her legal rights.[72]

American actress Ruth Taylor reading *Gentleman Prefer Blondes*,
Anita Loos's best-selling satire on America's hypocritical sexual mores.

Lucille Cameron knew hers, too. In 1924 she filed for divorce on account of her husband's serial infidelity. Despite its fractious ending, her marriage to Jack Johnson had been remarkable for its longevity. The couple had been thrown together in what was practically a shotgun wedding in the chaotic aftermath of Etta Duryea's death. They had spent twelve long, eventful years together, touring the world, witnessing war and revolution, experiencing the vagaries of celebrity. Johnson was married within a year of Lucille's departure to Irene Marie Pineau, whom he met – like Etta – at a racecourse. She too was white. In August 1925 she became the third Mrs Jack Johnson.

***

It was at around this period that Johnson starts to diminish in stature. Winnowed out of history, he begins shrinking from view. He had made a few attempts to get back into boxing after his release from prison. He made a show of going after Jack Dempsey, the new and genuinely terrifying heavyweight champion. To his enduring shame, Dempsey drew the color line and declared he would not fight a black boxer for the heavyweight title. As an older man, Dempsey would claim that he had used the color line as an excuse to dodge the still dangerous Jack Johnson. This seems like a gracious old man seeking pardon for the sins of youth. It was probably best that Johnson never met Dempsey in the ring. Johnson had taken twenty-six rounds to lose to Willard. Dempsey had taken three to destroy him, and did so with a ferocity scarcely seen again in a heavyweight title fight. In any event, the fight never happened. The closest Johnson came to Dempsey was when he served as one of Luis Firpo's sparring partners in the run-up to his shot at the title in 1923. He fought a few more bouts in the mid-Twenties and lost most of them. He was now over forty and his time had passed. There was a new era of fighters and new era of fight fans. Jack Johnson, once the most notorious man in the country, had been largely forgotten. At the height of the Depression he was to be found appearing in variety shows, available to be gawped at for a couple of cents, an exoticism with a golden smile from a vanished age.

By the mid-1930s, Jack Johnson was not the only aspect of the pre-war world that was beginning to look dated. In 1934, Roberta West Nicholson was elected to the Indiana state legislature. Born in 1903 into a prosperous, Republican Cincinnati family, Nicholson had married at the age of twenty-one into a wealthy Democratic family from Indianapolis. Her in-laws were fiercely progressive at a time when Indiana was controlled by the Republicans, and the Indiana Republican Party – everyone from the governor down – was controlled by the Ku Klux Klan. The Klan burnt crosses on Nicholson's father-in-law's lawn and sent her own father a hand-written note on his daughter's wedding day describing her as a 'nigger loving Jew'. First-hand experience of Klan hegemony turned her into a Democrat; a native Midwestern sense of independence and civic concern led her into progressive activism.

Though conservative in her actions, Nicholson had the liberal mind typical of her times. She had driven her first car aged twelve. She did not drink – though she had attended many Country Club parties where bootleg gin was served behind the bar and vomited up in the ladies' room – but she smoked, something unthinkable for a woman a generation before. She and her sister had been raised to be autonomous, adventurous, and the equal of their male peers. Her brother was a member of what she called 'the restless generation'. He had been shot through the throat at the Battle of Argonne, then gone west to be a stockbroker in California. Her life, milieu and outlook matched up exactly with those described in so many Fitzgerald plots, except that she was no ditzy flapper. In Indiana she threw herself into public life, first as an activist for the Women's Organization for National Prohibition Repeal and later as the founder of a branch of Planned Parenthood in Indianapolis – the first in the state. In 1934, following a scandal in the state Republican party, she spied a route to office and in the mid-term elections rode Franklin Roosevelt's long electoral coat-tails into the Indiana state capitol. There she legislated like a typical New Deal technocrat: she proposed a new insurance code; she helped pass an expansive new welfare bill (what one of her saltier colleagues called 'terrible communist social security'); she lent her vote to a (successful) measure to allow for the sterilisation of the criminally insane.

Then, in early 1935, she chanced upon an issue and made it her signature reform: the campaign to abolish the seduction statutes and their companion heart balm suits. Nicholson's campaign to pass what became known as anti-heart balm legislation was born of a deep sense of the laws' injustice. She later told an interviewer:

> My feeling about the law is that it just seemed perfectly silly to me, that from time immemorial, a female being engaged to be married could change her mind and say, 'Sorry Joe, it's all off'. But if a man did, and if he had any money, he could be sued. I thought it was absolutely absurd. I had no understanding whatsoever that I was bucking up against the basic tenet of English common law. . . . I thought it was undignified and disgusting that women sued men for the same changing their mind about getting married.

Nicholson began running a high-profile public campaign for the laws' repeal. It triggered first a state-wide and then a national debate about the place of seduction legislation in American society. Nicholson proved adept at courting publicity: her charge that female plaintiffs in seduction suits exhibited 'itching palms in the guise of aching hearts' drew laughter and applause throughout the nation. Suddenly, legislators who had long been silent on the issue found their voice. State Senator Wade called the legislation a boon to 'unscrupulous jackleg lawyers' and a disaster for everybody else; his colleague Senator McNabe challenged the very notion that lost virtue had a court-determined cash value. The press hailed Nicholson as the gold-digger's bane and portrayed her in cartoons as a shield against the depredations of vamps, temptresses and blackmailers adept at exploiting the law.

When debates on the proposed bill began in the state assembly, some expressed disbelief that women would want to lose these legal protections. 'Do you mean to tell me,' Republican Senator William P. Dennigan asked the floor, that 'you will help women by taking away their civil rights against philanderers and men who prey upon them?' Nicholson was nonplussed by such criticism. 'We have an opportunity to pass a piece of progressive legislation, in keeping with the times . . . Women do not demand rights, gentlemen, they earn them, and they ask no such privileges as these which are abolished in this bill.'[73]

Nicholson won the day. In the spring of 1935 Indiana passed the nation's first piece of anti-heart balm legislation. The law, known as the 'Gold-Diggers bill', abolished the heart balm actions of Breach of Promise to Marriage, Criminal Conversation and Alienation of Affection, and limited seduction cases in criminal courts to instances where the plaintiff was under twenty-one years of age. The legislation soon spread to other states. Six more passed legislation that year; another four would do so over the next decade.[74] In many states, as in Indiana, reform would be led by women, often from among the first generation of female legislators and often ardent feminists. Repealing seduction laws had become a feminist issue.[75]

Cupid celebrates the abolition of the seduction statutes in Indiana after a
campaign led by Roberta West Nicholson.

In retrospect Nicholson's victory was ambiguous and only half-realised. She understood her cause as a straightforward pursuit of equality before the law and an end to the implied condescension to women that she identified at the heart of seduction legislation. But many men clearly viewed the anti-heart balm campaign as a way of avenging themselves on the new women born of the 1920s. The language and imagery of the campaigning in the press – where men, not women, largely shaped the message – for the most part evoked modern, negative ideas of womanhood. Women were flappers, gold-diggers, blackmailers. At a deeper level, the repeal of protection for women in one arena represented a kind of revenge for their accrual of gains in others, most notably in the workplace and in the voting booth. Furthermore, even if it were true that anti-heart balm legislation was passed for good, progressive reasons then it only met with partial success. Of the twenty-three attempts to pass anti-heart balm laws in 1935, fifteen failed. Clearly a majority of states still believed in the old ideals of feminine meekness, chastity, and vulnerability before the seducer's wiles. This speaks to the incomplete nature of the social and sexual revolution of the 1920s. Snuffed out by the 1929 Crash and the Great Depression that followed, it failed to transform mores, serving only as a prelude to the thoroughgoing revolution of the 1960s and 1970s.[76]

What Jack Johnson thought of all this is unknown. By the mid-Thirties very few people asked his views on anything. He featured in the press, if at all, largely as a lone critical voice on the skills and prospects of Joe Louis, the new black heavyweight boxing sensation. Johnson had briefly attempted to bring Louis under his wing and when the younger man sensibly rebuffed him he went into opposition, critiquing Louis's abilities and loudly supporting his great rival, the German Max Schmeling. For his part, Louis, like many black contenders, was wary of Johnson. Since his Havana bout with Jess Willard, no black fighter had been allowed to challenge for the heavyweight title. Louis's management correctly surmised that the only way to get their man the shot he deserved was to market him as the Anti-Johnson. Louis was never seen drinking or gambling. He was never seen outside a church or out of a sober suit. He was never, ever seen with a white woman. Joe Louis had to play dumb – in both senses – to get the title that Johnson had won with a big mouth and a golden smile.

Nonetheless, it is highly unlikely that Johnson would have cared about the anti-heart balm laws. After all, heart balm acts and seduction statutes had never bothered him much when they were on the books and nothing had changed for him with their repeal. By comparison, both the federal Mann Act and the state miscegenation laws were still on the books, and both were energetically policed for the remainder of his life. It was no small irony that the United States went to war in 1941 with a Nazi racial state that considered American state racial laws too harsh for Hitler's Germany. There was perhaps no greater sign of Johnson's fundamental equanimity and graciousness that he would nonetheless appear at boxing exhibitions during the war to help raise money to fund a war for a government that had once waged war on him. His three marriages were still considered criminal in over half the states of the union on the night of 9 June 1946 when his speeding car flipped on a bend outside Franklinton, North Carolina, while travelling home from Texas to New York.

Johnson died as he lived, racing across state lines for no purpose other than his own. He would be laid to rest in Graceland next to Etta Duryea. Their marriage and their love would not receive universal legal recognition in America for another two decades. *Loving v. Virginia* – the Supreme Court ruling that both annulled all anti-miscegenation laws and served as one of the few occasions when legal shorthand rose to the level of cosmic poetry – was not handed down until June 1967, during the Summer of Love.

6

BLOOD OUT

The American mania for policing seduction was never fully embraced in Europe – though this was not due to a lack of interest in the subject. In Britain and continental Europe, the same sexual fears that loomed large in the American psyche were nourished by many of the same anxieties. If in the historical imagination late Victorian Europe slumbered in self-satisfied complacency, to its inhabitants it seethed with danger and novelty. The outward forms of industrial capitalism – filthy metropolises, mass migration, proletarian mobs, choking air and stinking rivers – were given a terrifying new significance by Darwinian theories that popularised the language of struggle, degeneration and extinction. As evolutionary theory begat racial theorising, so did social transformation beget gender trouble. Like their American counterparts, European cities were home to a flourishing public sex trade. They were also incubators for a new generation of feminist activists intent on upending the dominant sexual order. For conservatives, the rebellion of the 'New Women' of the 1880s and 1890s was directly connected to the new, racialised discourse that saw sexual permissiveness as the gateway to racial collapse. As in America, the panic over seduction was grounded in antagonistic and contradictory male attitudes towards race and gender.

In Europe these fears found expression less in the law than in a complex of cultural tropes that dredged up tales of the supernatural to give form to the anxieties of modernity. 'Witch-tales in this enlightened age!' marvelled the London-based occult guru Madame Blavatsky in the 1880s. 'You will have such witch-tales as the Middle Ages never dreamt of. Whole nations will drift insensibly into black magic . . .' Nowhere was this drift more in evidence than in the mind and milieu of one Londoner, operating out of a theatre in the city's West End.[1]

The first thing people noticed about Bram Stoker was his height. At a time when the army had by force of necessity to reduce the minimum height for prospective recruits from five foot six to five foot, Stoker was six foot two and muscularly built. Everything about him – his tidy russet beard, his ruddy cheeks, his legendary, booming voice – spoke of good health and vitality. Stoker's energy, good cheer and unthinking courage impressed everyone he met. On at least one occasion it also made the national press when, aged thirty-five, he dived into the Thames from a steamboat after witnessing the attempted suicide of a fellow passenger. Without a second thought, the papers reported, 'Mr. Stoker threw off his own coat, and pluckily jumped in after the drowning man, grappled with him, and succeeded in bringing him up to the steamer, where he was laid on the deck in an unconscious condition.' When he could not revive the man himself he took him back to his home in Chelsea so that his brother Thomas, a doctor, could have a go. The man died; Stoker seems to have survived his plunge in the rancid river unscathed. His wife, according to lore, was appalled when she came home to find a corpse laid out on their dining-room table.

Abraham Stoker was born in Clontarf, Ireland, in 1847, but spent almost his whole life until the age of thirty in Dublin where his father, also named Abraham, was a civil servant. His mother Charlotte was a respectable housewife who bore her husband seven children and involved herself in the charitable causes fashionable among middle-class women, which in her case meant an abiding interest in women's education and the rescue of poor, vulnerable girls from the streets and workhouses of Victorian Ireland.

The Stokers were Protestant, like much of the Irish elite, but their bourgeois status was hard-won. Abraham Sr was the son of an artisan and had raised his family's place in society by grinding his way up through the ranks of the colonial bureaucracy. The result was that his sons got the best education that could be hoped for, which in Ireland meant attending Trinity College, Dublin. Bram, their third child and second son, had been a sickly boy and a mediocre student but was transformed from the moment he arrived at Trinity in 1864, aged sixteen.

Trinity was an intensely competitive social and intellectual environment which consciously selected and shaped the future Irish leadership. Stoker's contemporaries were the sons of the elite and the fathers of Ireland's revolutionary generation. In ambitious company, Stoker stood out as being a high achiever with a hunger, easily worn, for success and recognition. There seemed no limit to the range of his interests and offices. He was president of the Philosophical Society and auditor of the Historical Society (founded by Edmund Burke), where he composed, read and discussed papers on everything from Shelley, Faust, Byron, and supernaturalism in literature to science, politics and racial theory. For his efforts in these fields he was awarded medals and certificates in history, oratory and composition, which sat alongside the dozen or so trophies he won for his athletic achievements in sports as varied as rugby, swimming, distance running, gymnastics, high jump, long jump, vaulting, slingshot and rowing. Years later his classmates would remember their friend's great strength, his flexibility, and his daring stunts on the rings and the trapeze.

He was also a presence on the Trinity stage – performing in productions of Richard Sheridan's *School for Scandal* and *The Rivals* – and a participant in student literary life as an avid if average short story writer. Alongside this packed schedule, Stoker also worked in the Dublin Civil Service for the final four years of his six-year stint at Trinity, a job to which he would apply himself with mixed interest until 1878.

Stoker formally left university in 1870 but remained intimately bound up in Trinity life, which was only to be expected given the university's dominant position in Dublin society. In 1871, already established as a local character and universally admired as an avatar of the Victorian values of thrift, industry and muscular Christianity, Stoker joined the *Dublin Evening Mail* as a theatre critic. There he reported to the *Mail*'s proprietors, Dr Henry Maunsell and Joseph Sheridan Le Fanu, the latter a descendant of the playwright and the author of the sapphic vampire thriller *Carmilla* (1872). He was soon ubiquitous in Dublin thespian circles, where he mingled with actors, playwrights, critics and managers, became a stalwart presence in the audience at the Theatre Royal, and grew easily into the role of assiduous networker – he started a correspondence (uninvited but happily received) with Walt Whitman, struck up intimate friendships with stage beauties like Genevieve Ward, and won the respect and attention of the dramatists who periodically came through town on tour.

One of the men drawn to Stoker would change his life. Henry Irving was one of the great Victorian freaks. Born in obscurity in the West Country, Irving had received little education – George Bernard Shaw liked to gossip that he was a virtual illiterate – but had acquired in his youth an obsession with the theatre. He began his dramatical career in the provinces, in Sunderland, and spent the better part of two decades perfecting his art and striving his way into London acting circles. A tall, stooping man with habitually hunched shoulders, Irving had thick hair, an expansive, bald brow, and a very large, very curious head, the great bulk of which began beyond the jawline as though it always sought to tip him downwards and conscious effort on his part was required to keep himself upright. On the stage Irving was known for his harsh, stentorian voice, his hypnotic eyes, and his bizarre incorporation of an affected limp that left one foot dragging after the other whatever character he played. Irving himself was an enigma, more comfortable playing a fictional persona than inhabiting a real one, but he was acutely aware of his capacity to enchant his audience.

Bram Stoker learnt of this up close during his first meeting with Irving in Dublin in 1876, after an evening at Trinity. By this stage in his career, Irving was one of the most respected British actors and commanded audiences wherever he went. Keen, perhaps, to bring this promising young man under his influence, he treated Stoker to a private recital of 'The Dream of Eugene Aram', a melo-dramatic narrative poem by Thomas Hood concerned with murder, guilt and gothicism. The poem was a well-known part of Irving's repertoire and one that Stoker was already familiar with. Nonetheless, when the famed actor launched into a rendition of the familiar lines after dinner at the Shelbourne Hotel in Dublin, something changed in Stoker for ever. 'There are great moments even to the great,' he later wrote, but

> That night Irving was inspired. Many times since then I saw and heard him – for such an effort eyes as well as ears are required – recite that poem and hold audiences, big or little, spellbound till the moment came for the thunderous outlet of their pent-up feelings; but that particular vein I never met again. Art can do much; but in all things even in art there is a summit somewhere. That night for a brief time, in which the rest of the world seemed to sit still, Irving's genius floated in blazing triumph above the summit of art. There is something in the soul which lifts it above all that has its base in material things. If once only in a lifetime the soul of a man can take wings and sweep for an instant into mortal gaze, then that 'once' for Irving was on that, to me, ever memorable night.

At the end of the performance Stoker collapsed to the floor in unmanly hysterics. It was the beginning of a great friendship.[2]

'Every Irishman who felt that his business in life was on the higher planes of the cultural professions,' George Bernard Shaw observed, 'felt that he must have a metropolitan domicile and an International culture: that is, he felt that his first business was to get out of Ireland. I had the same feeling. . . . [the] English language was my weapon, there was nothing for it but London.' Bram Stoker felt much the same way. He and Irving stayed in close contact after the night of 'Eugene Aram', and in 1877 Irving began to involve him in his plans to acquire a major London theatre, the Lyceum. When in November of that year Irving's designs for Stoker swam into focus, the younger man recorded in his diary three triumphant words: 'London in View!'

It would take another year to get there, but by December 1878 Stoker had resigned from the Dublin civil service, handed over his last review for the *Mail*, and was ready to sign on with Irving. The two met in Birmingham, where Irving was finishing a tour. Stoker visited Irving at his hotel in Edgbaston and later recalled that his new employer 'was mightily surprised when he found that I had a wife with me'.

Oscar Wilde once described Florence Balcombe as an 'exquisitely pretty girl . . . with the most perfectly beautiful face I have ever seen', and he was well-positioned to know. Were it not for Bram Stoker's mysterious appearance in her life, Wilde would likely have married her. Almost nothing is known about how Stoker and Balcombe met, how he won her, and how they lived together for the four decades of outwardly calm married life that followed. Very little is known about Mrs Stoker at all, except that she was exceptionally physically attractive, easily meeting the exacting standards of ethereal feminine beauty that the Victorians so coveted. Socially, she was a cipher. Biographers of her husband have had to survive on rumours and throwaway remarks to paint a picture of Florence Stoker as a frigid, vain, ambiguously cruel woman. The reality is that little is known of her except that she was sought after by painters and sculptors wanting to capture her likeness, and that she won the sympathy of London society after surviving a major maritime disaster in 1882, when the steamer *Victoria*, with Florence and her son aboard, hit rocks near Dieppe in the Channel, resulting in the death of 20 of the 120 passengers and crew and a public shaming of the travelling Italians who jumped into lifeboats reserved for women and children.

One interesting absence from the sketchy surviving portrait of Florence Stoker comes from the total lack of love for her evinced by her only child, Irving Noel Thornley Stoker, born on New Year's Eve 1879. Noel's memories of childhood feature his enormous bear of a father, who existed as if visiting from a fairytale on the periphery of his life, always dressed up and about to leave for Theatreland, but there is nothing about his mother. However, an image of Bram, Florence and Noel drawn by George Du Maurier that appeared in *Punch* magazine in September 1886 offers an unnerving public window into the Stoker household. It is a scene of late Victorian bliss: a garden party in the grounds of a fine country house; in the foreground the hulk of a dark-hatted, heavily bearded Stoker leaning forward in his wicker chair, a tennis racket at his feet; sitting a good metre and a half apart from him his wife, beautiful, glamorous and distant, looking down, either lost in her knitting or ignoring both the attentions of her husband sitting morosely across from her and her only child standing in boater and knickerbockers behind her, seemingly bemused by her refusal to play with him. The caption beneath reads:

FILIAL REPROOF

Mamma to Noel, who is inclined to be talkative, 'Hush, Noel! Haven't I told you that little Boys should be Seen and not Heard?'
Noel's reply, 'Yes, Mamma! But you don't Look at ME!'

It is an odd piece of Victorian sadism, inexplicable in its casual confusion of public and private.[3]

***

The portico of the Lyceum Theatre in 1881.

Within less than a year of their marriage in Dublin, the newly married couple found themselves plunged into the maelstrom of London life. Eventually the Stokers would make their home in and around Cheyne Walk, near the sleepy western end of the Thames Embankment, but in those first hectic years they lived only a few streets away from Stoker's new place of employment at the Lyceum Theatre, at almost the exact centre of London life. The Lyceum was and remains a large faux-Palladian structure situated at one of London's great meeting places. Perched on Wellington Street, just off the eastern tip of the Strand, the theatre's entrance was visible to the stream of Londoners and London traffic that travelled south to north across Waterloo Bridge each day and who could not have avoided the two huge illuminated signs that hung invitingly on the theatre's façade. The theatre also connected the eastern and western hemispheres of the city. Aldwych, which the Lyceum looked over, was the meeting place of the Strand and Fleet Street. The former was the great London thoroughfare that led to Westminster and thence to the wealthy districts surrounding Piccadilly and Hyde Park, before petering out in the bohemian villages of Kensington and Chelsea; the latter was the main route to the old City of London, whose course began as a tour of the great institutions of Victorian Britain – the Royal Courts of Justice, the Bank of England, St Paul's Cathedral – only to end in the scene of one of the nation's great shames: the teeming slums and rookeries of Whitechapel, Shadwell and Stepney.

The broader paradoxes of Victorian London were played out in the Lyceum's immediate environs. On the Strand, well-heeled shoppers rubbed shoulders with prostitutes, beggars and pickpockets. Clerks and dukes alike came to Covent Garden for the playhouses – as they had done since the eighteenth century – but also for the seedier pleasures of neighbouring Soho, a zone of gin shops, brothels and flophouses wedged uneasily between the more desirable districts of Mayfair, St James's and Bloomsbury. The contradictions to which the Lyceum bore witness were captured by Arthur Conan Doyle in *The Sign of the Four* (1890). When Holmes and Watson meet outside Irving's theatre on a mysterious errand for a client, they experience the strangeness of the West End, where the thick crowds 'of shirt-fronted men and beshawled, bediamonded women' spilling out of private carriages before the entrance to the Lyceum exist alongside a mass of undifferentiated humanity that 'flitted from the gloom into the light, and so back into the gloom once more'.

The gloom, smoke and smog that typified late Victorian London – and which was at its worst close to the river, where vapour from the Thames met with airborne effluent that gathered naturally in the water basin – was something that the Stokers would have noticed as soon as they arrived from Dublin. The period they lived in the city coincided roughly with the hey-day of the pea-soupers, the London Particular, the London Ivy – the infamous fog that defined the visual and olfactory experience of London living in this era. The yellow-brown miasma, that, depending on the light, the atmospheric conditions and the peculiar composition of local sources of air pollution could also shade into purple, vermilion, pale green and bog black, influenced and obstructed all life in this capital of global finance, industry and science. In December and January it regularly killed several thousand Londoners each month from respiratory disease. The fog also provided cover for crime and public disorder. The cast-iron London gaslights – those great symbols of rational civic planning – could not contend with the choking fumes, and in the shallow half-light moody crowds and groups of petty thieves could and did run riot with scant fear of the police. In 1886 there was a spate of such disturbances in Trafalgar Square and Pall Mall, on the Lyceum's doorstep.

More generally, the fog made mockery of Victorian pretensions to the conquest of nature and superstition by reason and investigation. A famous 1888 *Punch* cartoon depicted a hadean 'King Fog' accompanied by his imps sweeping over the British capital while the figure of Science lay defeated on the ground. The 'shores of Styx were bland matched with Fleet Street or the Strand', *Punch* declared, where 'a foul and foetid pall fell over each and all; its ingredients were mist, and muck, and smoke'. The 'ruthless reign of King Fog' had turned the citizens of London into ghosts – an image to which artists, journalists and writers would return repeatedly in those decades. Indeed, the whole city became a spectre, existing as the hostage of an unreal, unfathomable, wholly capricious haze that had neither source nor purpose. Oscar Wilde, who had moved to London at the same time as the Stokers and lived nearby, on the Thames side of the Strand, recalled watching the yellow fog roll up the river each winter morning until it consumed the whole city, leaving nothing in view but the dull white dome of St Paul's, hanging like a chandelier above the mustard cloudline. Victorian London was a nightmare waiting to be populated.

The Lyceum's role was to keep the nightmares out. Irving positioned it as a safe, conservative space that catered to the London elite and the aspirational middle classes. The selection of plays reflected this ethos. Irving rejected suspect new trends in theatre and playwriting in favour of lavish sets, high-end special effects and a focus on the classics. Over a quarter of the plays performed in the Lyceum under Irving were Shakespeare; the rest were for the most part historical pageants or tried-and-true audience favourites. Irving steered clear of the Ibsen revolution, an insistence which won him the disdain of the avant garde – especially Shaw, who, though a regular presence in the stalls, considered the Lyceum little better than a high-end music hall.[4] Irving did not care for such matters. A conservative by nature and by politics, he was interested in form and craft, and had little time for Shaw's socialist aesthetics, which were in any case philistine in the extreme.

Irving also needed to turn a profit. Before the curtain lifted on the first performance under his management, he and Stoker had already spent some £12,000 renovating the building. This included a complete structural and decorative makeover of the 2,000-capacity theatre; a retouching of the existing ornaments; the refurbishment of the dingy auditorium in more fetching shades of green and blue; and the commissioning of an entirely new act drop. The faithful green stage curtain was kept, and Irving's son would later recall how when the lights went down,

> and only the lower part of it was softly illumined by footlights, this green curtain seemed to fade into infinity – veiling, as Charles Lamb once said, a heaven of the imagination. It was the veil between the world of reality and of make-believe; when it rose the world before and behind the proscenium were blended; the illusory gained substance from the prosaic which in turn reflected something of the glittering image of the illusion.[5]

Stoker's specific role in the running of the Lyceum was that of acting manager. Irving and his stage manager, Harry Loveday, had complete control of the artistic direction of the theatre, of the conduct of the rehearsals, and of what was performed and who performed in it. Stoker had the arguably more complex role of mediating between the world of the stage, the world behind the stage and the world outside the stage. Most actors only had to play a handful of roles each year; Stoker had to shape-shift between countless roles each day. Outside the Lyceum he represented Irving's interests in court, in theatrical associations and cultural charities, on a few occasions in Parliament, and defended and promoted him and his work in the press. Stoker also had to handle the police, encouraging them to combat the petty crime that always threatened to make the West End unappealing to middle-class theatregoers and to crack down on ticket forgeries – a problem that repeatedly took him to Bow Street Court to testify on the matter. In front of house, Stoker was in charge of meeting the crowds who came to see the plays and ensuring that grandees, reviewers and Irving's mother were seen to their seats with all due care and courtesy. This was his most public function, and the sight of this rugged, smiling Irishman deftly marshalling the audience into position before each performance became a familiar and welcome fixture in London life.

Behind the scenes he would manage all the money that passed through Irving's theatres – over two million pounds over the course of his career – dealt with the salaries, gripes and idiosyncrasies of the several hundred actors, engineers and tradesmen in their employ, and otherwise ensured that the enormous operation that was the Lyceum Theatre ran smoothly and profitably.

From the outset Irving's venture was a magnificent success. The opening night of his first Lyceum production – *Hamlet*, with Irving in the lead role – on 30 December 1878 was a major society event, the audience numbering among it the Prince of Wales, former prime ministers and great rivals Gladstone and Disraeli,[6] poets Swinburne,

Tennyson and Wilde, the musical duo Gilbert and Sullivan, and painters – and later Chelsea neighbours of Stoker – Whistler and Millais. Irving went on to secure the enduring patronage of the Prince of Wales. The royal family would book boxes for the premieres of Irving's plays. Horace Wyndham would later write that in the last decades of the Victorian era an opening night at the Lyceum drew 'an audience that was representative of the best of the period in the realms of art, literature, and society. Admittance was a very jealously guarded privilege.' As master of the box office, Stoker was the gate-keeper to each first night at the Lyceum, and Wyndham wryly described how the proud Dubliner 'looked upon the stalls, dress circle, and boxes as if they were annexes to the Royal Enclosure at Ascot, and one almost had to be proposed and seconded before the coveted ticket would be issued'.[7]

Success in London gave Irving a licence to print money in the provinces. Starting in 1881, the Lyceum troupe began to tour regularly in northern England and Scotland, as well as Canada and the United States. To Stoker's mammoth workload was now added the logistical horror of having to organise the travel arrangements of several hundred thespians and workmen, along with their costumes, scenery and lighting equipment. For the Lyceum's first tour a separate train had to be booked just to transport the stage sets and lighting paraphernalia. But the profits were enormous. That tour netted £24,000; the nine tours of North America that Stoker organised between 1883 and 1904 brought in lesser but still considerable amounts.

It was on the road where Stoker earned his reputation for omnip-otence and ubiquity. On an 1893 tour of America he managed to negotiate a stage electrician out of jail after his arrest for violating immigration laws. On tour the actors of the Irving troupe learned to fear and obey their acting manager. Stoker disciplined any dram-atist who developed ideas out of step with Irving's aesthetic vision and personal preferences. An actor who tried to go on stage without wearing his make-up because he believed the foundation would run in the heat of the night was told 'to forget his theories and to go and get made properly up like everyone else'. Stoker's powers were almost uncanny. 'That devil Bram Stoker,' actor William Terriss told a colleague, 'he can see through a brick wall – God help you.'

This was only a little short of the truth. Ever in a hurry, Stoker did actually travel through a plate glass divider while moving at speed through the lobby of the Chestnut Street Opera House in Philadelphia, though, invincible as ever, he emerged on the other side without a mark on him.

***

After their 1884–5 tour of the United States, Irving and Stoker went home to the Lyceum. They returned to London in the summer of 1885 to find the city in a tumult. Moral outrage led to disturbances in the street. Newspapers editorialised, ministers sermonised, and social reformers agitated for change with new vigour. Committees of bishops and elder statesmen were formed, as were new alliances among previously fractious groups of nonconformist ministers, trade unions and bourgeois campaigners. Massive meetings in Hyde Park were discussed, organised and attended. Rumours of conspiracy, cover-up, even revolution abounded. Questions were asked in Parliament; dormant bills were revived and propelled through the two houses. By autumn English law and English democracy had been transformed.

The subject of the outcry was the sexual rights of English women. The source of the intense public furore was a series of revelations in the London afternoon daily, the *Pall Mall Gazette*. At the centre of it all was the *Gazette*'s editor, a professional acquaintance of Bram Stoker, William Thomas Stead.

With his dark three-piece suits and pocket chain, his full brown beard and piercing zealot's eyes, W.T. Stead was emblematic of a new force ascendant in late Victorian politics. Born in Northumberland in 1849 and raised in a Congregationalist household, Stead's three declared passions were 'Christianity, Cricket and Democracy', and his calling was as a campaigning journalist and editor. He had begun his career at the *Northern Echo*, England's first morning halfpenny paper and the champion of its restless working class. Initially a Gladstonian liberal, Stead had been converted to a jingoistic socialism by the late 1870s and believed in 'the duty of England as a civilising power among the weaker and more degraded nations of the earth'; he was frank in his acknowledgement that the 'Anglo-Saxon idea has gained possession of my brain'. At home in the provinces, where he corresponded with the great and the good in splendid isolation from London, Stead professed no desire to move to the corrupt and dissolute capital. He claimed that he had been to London once and had no desire to go again. 'If the Lord wishes me to go,' he declared, 'He will have to drive me thither with whips.'

The Lord did wish for Stead to go to London. In 1880 he was offered a job with John Morley, editor of the *Pall Mall Gazette*, based out of offices on the Strand, and he accepted. In 1883 Morley retired and Stead became editor himself. Under his authority the *Gazette* became an influential force in British life. Despite having a circulation of less than 40,000, the newspaper weighed in on the great issues of the day and not infrequently changed the course of events. Stead's advocacy helped send General Gordon to his martyrdom in Khartoum; his patriotic affront at the retrograde state of the navy resulted in a massive increase in the Admiralty's budget; a campaign against slum conditions moved the ultra-conservative Tory administration of Lord Salisbury to action on the matter. Then, late in the spring of 1885, Stead had a conversation which would change his life.

In 1880, Benjamin Scott, a committed social reformer and the Lord Chamberlain of London, had been appalled by a new book. That year, Alfred Dyer published *The European Slave Trade in English*

Girls, in which he declared the existence of an underground economy selling English girls into sexual bondage in the brothels of France and Belgium. In a bid to combat this threat, the London Committee for Suppressing the Traffic in British Girls was established, with Scott as its chairman. The committee included many reformist luminaries, such as Josephine Butler, the pioneering Victorian feminist and head of the Ladies National Association (LNA) – a group that lobbied for improved sexual protections for women. Scott's lobbying led to an investigation into white slavery by a House of Lords select committee, which reported in 1881 that British laws were insufficient to protect the bodies and morals of British women and girls.

The trade in British girls was symptomatic of a larger failing. British law sought to regulate vice rather than promote virtue. British women were vulnerable to sexual exploitation and social ruin, all too often ending up on the streets as the sexual playthings of debauched aristocrats.[8] 'In other countries female chastity is more or less protected by law up to the age of 21,' the Lords observed. 'No such protection is given in England to girls under the age of 13.' They recommended an increase in the age of consent from thirteen to sixteen; the introduction of penalties for indecent assault; criminalisation of the solicitation of women for employment in an overseas brothel; and tough new measures for those who aided and abetted the procurement and prostitution of minors. These formed the basis for a new Criminal Law Amendment Act, which lingered in Parliament for several years without ever becoming law. After another setback in 1884, an infuriated Scott decided that only a major scandal would secure the bill's passage, and so he went to W.T. Stead of the *Pall Mall Gazette* with a horrific story.

Scott told Stead that English virgins were being bought and sold in enormous numbers on the streets of London. Outraged, Stead sought the opinion of a retired senior Scotland Yard detective, who confirmed the story in no uncertain terms. Now thoroughly scandalised, Stead concluded that a conspiracy of silence – whose confederates were the press, senior politicians, and the capitalist and landlord class – was keeping the ghastly truth from the electorate. He was determined to expose the truth of the matter, and in June he embarked upon a journey into London's underworld.

Stead would later write of this voyage into the pit:

> I have been a night prowler for weeks. I have gone in different guises to most of the favourite rendezvous of harlots. I have strolled along Ratcliff-highway, and sauntered round and round the Quadrant at midnight. I have haunted St. James's Park, and twice enjoyed the strange sweetness of summer night by the sides of the Serpentine. I have been at all hours in Leicester-square and the Strand, and have spent the midnight in Mile-end-road and the vicinity of the Tower. Sometimes I was alone; sometimes accompanied by a friend; and the deep and strong impression which I have brought back is one of respect and admiration for the extraordinarily good behaviour of the English girls who pursue this dreadful calling. In the whole of my wanderings I have not been accosted half-a-dozen times, and then I was more to blame than the woman. I was turned out of Hyde Park at midnight in company with a drunken prostitute, but she did not begin the conversation.

Stead's elegy to the working girls of London spoke to his basic compassion towards women trapped in a life of prostitution. They were not to blame for their condition. On his travels through 'the maze of London brotheldom', Stead met the real culprits: the madams who groomed the nurses and shopgirls promenading in Hyde Park on the weekend; the professional seducers who corrupted girls and delivered them to brothels; the drunken mothers who sold their daughters for gin money; the trafficker who spoke in brisk, commercial terms of the slave routes that took London girls to continental brothels via Dover and Ostend; the employment agencies and servants' registries and bars and theatres whose business façade concealed a pernicious effort to corrupt and exploit working-class women.

At the heart of the labyrinth he met the men whose lust kept the market in existence, men almost exclusively from 'the very wealthy and the immoral idlers of the "upper ten."' These were aristocrats and capitalists, the sons and guardians of privilege. Somewhere along the way Stead also found the final proof of Scott's initial claim. A thirteen-year-old girl from west London, her virginity proven by a medical examination, had been sold by her sodden mother for five pounds, chloroformed, and delivered up to a wealthy gentleman in a Regent Street brothel.

Overwhelmed by moral revulsion, Stead struggled to find words to explain to the readers of the *Pall Mall Gazette* what he had witnessed in the capital of the British Empire. He raided Dante, Homer, even the Qur'anic accounts of hell to find parallels. In the end he settled on the myth of the Cretan Minotaur, who took as tribute the flower of the Athenian youth. London was the new Crete, its wretched and exploited women the sacrificial offering. Stead's series of exposés, including his ghastly account of the purchasing of a virgin, duly appeared in the *Pall Mall Gazette* over the course of the first ten days of July under the heading of the 'Maiden Tribute of Modern Babylon'.

In the first instalment of his exposé, Stead had emphatically denied that he was seeking a revolution in British sexual manners. 'However strongly I may feel as to the imperative importance of morality and chastity,' he wrote, 'I do not ask for any police interference with the liberty of vice. I ask only for the repression of crime.' Just three weeks later his tone had sharpened. In the intervening period his revelations had sent the country into a frenzy over women's sexual rights and this public outpouring in turn inspired Stead to raise the stakes. Parliament had hastily scheduled a third reading of the Criminal Law Amendment Act on 30 July. On 28 July the *Pall Mall Gazette* noted that MPs were now faced with a 'national uprising against the loathsome abnormities [sic] of sexual vice'. Parliamentary intervention was needed to forestall insurrection. 'If ever there is a social revolution in this country,' the *Gazette* warned, 'it will be over this very question.'

What Stead and his allies knew was that Parliament could not discuss the issue of prostitution and the alleged 'white slave trade' without also addressing the question of seduction: the two issues were inextricably linked in reformers' minds. The condition of England's prostitutes was understood to be the dark reflection of the glistening ideal of the 'Angel of the House'. Women either met a male standard of meek femininity and unquestioning submission to patriarchal authority or they were expendable outlets for unbridled male desire. It was no coincidence that one of Stead's greatest supporters in the struggle to pass the Criminal Law Amendment Act was Josephine Butler, Victorian England's lonely champion of women's sexual rights. Butler and the LNA had spent the previous fifteen years campaigning against the hated Contagious Diseases Act of 1867, which empowered police to detain any woman they suspected to be a prostitute and have her subjected to a forced inspection by a doctor to ensure that she was not a carrier of venereal disease. Those who campaigned against the Act loathed its partiality, its brutality and its ineffectiveness, but above all they recognised that alleged prostitutes' powerlessness before the combined spectres of 'medical despotism' and 'police despotism' was a dramatisation of every woman's impotence before an all-encompassing male despotism.[9]

For championing the cause of one of Britain's more despised and unsympathetic groups, Butler attracted little praise and a great deal of mockery. One of her critics once attacked her as 'an indecent maenad, a shrieking sister, frenzied, unsexed, and utterly without shame'. 'Unsexed' was the key word. The same word had been used to describe Mary Wollstonecraft, and it referred to a specific idea of womanhood. Butler was 'unsexed' because she contravened the norms of her sex – understood quite literally as referring to her genitals. In Victorian medical literature, women were portrayed as 'the Sex', hostage to their wombs (hence prone to hysteria), sent temporarily mad during menstruation, and finally ruined by menopause. Their biology determined the roles they could play in life: either as 'an instrument to the convenience and lust of men' (through a life of prostitution) or as the mute, submissive bearer of children within marriage.[10]

Victorian feminists and their allies knew that the only way they could make progress on major issues – women's education, employment, and voting rights, among others – was to escape a framework that viewed them purely as sex objects. But paradoxically they had to do that by talking about sex. Women had to sexualise politics in order to desexualise themselves. Butler perfected this sinuous rhetorical strategy. One of her most powerful devices was an attack on the double standard of sexual morality. Why was it, she famously asked, that while society mindlessly indulged male libertinism, 'we never hear it carelessly or complacently asserted of a young woman that "she is only sowing her wild oats"?' Men and women should be held to the same standard.

This ostensibly banal assertion contained a radical germ. Implicit in the argument was the assumption that women were *already* abiding by this superior standard and that only men had to change in order to meet it. Female purity was constantly juxtaposed with male dissolution. Butler and her fellow activists encouraged a view of women as essentially innocent and men as essentially rapacious. Male allies like Stead came to share wholeheartedly in this opinion. 'Girls, and I say this emphatically, are not seducers,' he later wrote. 'They have innate delicacy and refinement. I say honestly that I do not believe that one woman in 10,000 would cast herself at the feet of lust except under duress or under the force of circumstances.' Female perfection required radical male change in order to meet the same standard.

Another of Stead's allies, Edward White Benson, Archbishop of

Canterbury, founded the Church of England Purity Society; it later merged with Ellice Hopkins's British White Cross Army (established in 1885) to form the White Cross League, an organisation which encouraged single men to take public vows of chastity until marriage and to wear a white ribbon on their lapel to identify themselves as embodiments of the new morality. But individual change was not enough – the law had to protect the special needs of women in this area. Prostitutes had to be protected, but so too did girls, mothers and wives – all women.[11]

The staid members of Parliament were wholly unprepared for the complexities of the reformers' arguments and methods. Gathered together at the height of summer, many were perplexed by the fact that a law apparently meant to deal with the problem of underage prostitution actually aimed at the total reformation of sexual norms. Members were not unduly troubled by the request to raise the age of consent from thirteen to sixteen – albeit the few that grumbled about the risks of blackmail for teenage boys – though that measure did not meet the hopes of some feminists who had argued for an age of twenty-one. Similarly, proposed new measures to combat sexual assault and to tackle those who enabled juvenile prostitution were not seriously challenged in the chamber. What did cause consternation was the language used to describe procuring. The law defined a procurer as 'Any person who procures or attempts to procure any girl or woman under twenty-one years of age, not being a common prostitute, or of known immoral character, to have unlawful carnal connexion, either within or without the Queen's dominions.' Those found guilty of procuration faced a two-year prison sentence.

The problem was that this looked a lot like a seduction law. The description of 'not being . . . of known immoral character' seemed to mimic American seduction statutes that spoke of 'previously chaste character'. An 'unlawful carnal connexion' was defined as 'sexual intercourse is unlawful where no valid marriage exists', which seemed to revive the old crime of fornication. Finally, the additional crimes of procuration 'by false pretences or false representations' echoed the language of suasion commonly associated with seduction and courtship, not sexual enslavement. Confusion reigned as to whether the bill actually criminalised seduction or not. The attorney general, Sir Richard Webster, stated it did; Lord Bramwell – one of the most senior jurists in the land – declared that it did not. In between lay every shade of opinion. Many members observed the injustice that the new protections applied only to women and girls, and put men and boys of the same age at legal disadvantage. Others stated that the door was now open to blackmail and extortion.

Edward Lyulph Stanley, Liberal member for Oldham, called for a clarification of what 'false pretences, false representations, or other fraudulent means' looked like in practice. He suggested that, as in American seduction statutes, a promise of marriage ought to be the benchmark for a false pretence that resulted in sex. In any event,

> There ought to be some illustration given to show what kind of false pretences would be punishable. It would be too much for a woman to induce a man knowingly and willingly to go with her, and then to turn round and give him two years' imprisonment on the charge that she had been influenced by the false representations made to her. . . . That would be carrying the Criminal Law to a dangerous length.

But no clarification was forthcoming in the final bill. Many parliamentarians clearly believed that the bill acted as a *de facto* seduction statute and that it was open to abuse and exploitation by cynical women and 'vicious girls'. Outside Parliament, there were those who agreed with them. 'This Act of Parliament,' complained a columnist in the radical publication *The Anarchist*, 'places the power of irreparably injuring the character and prospects of innocent men, into the hands . . . of rash and meddling philanthropists . . . The bill,' the anonymous writer continued, 'opens a wide door for . . . fraud and intimidation.'[12]

But such concerns could not now prevent the passage of the Act. Public pressure and media scrutiny was too intense. The bill passed the Commons on 7 August and the Lords on 10 August. As promised, Stead hosted an enormous public protest in support of the new measures in London at the end of August, shortly before the bill was signed into law by the Queen.[13]

W. T. Stead in prison uniform.

Shortly after this triumph, Stead suffered what most would consider a painful personal setback. It transpired that the man he had described in his reporting who had paid five pounds for a virgin was none other than Stead himself. Working through a network of former prostitutes and madams, Stead had arranged for Eliza Armstrong's delivery to that hotel in London's West End. Keen to play the part of the pederast rake convincingly, Stead, who was a teetotaller, drank a bottle of champagne before making his way to the hotel, where he paid the money and then burst into the room where the drugged and thoroughly terrified Armstrong lay in a stupor. Then, in order to prove that the transnational trade in girls was a going concern, he had her transported to France where she was taken into the care of the Salvation Army. When the facts of Stead's behaviour emerged, he was promptly put on trial and sentenced to three months in jail. A farcical end to a farcical enterprise, but in fact from Stead's perspective it was a triumph. Not only had he succeeded in changing the law but his martyrdom was providential proof that he was fighting the good fight.[14] Stead had also ruptured the complacent calm of high Victorian England. His dispatches from Babylon had revealed another London – a filthy, fogbound world bubbling over with perversion and sexual danger. A world of monsters.

Stoker knew W.T. Stead. One of his duties was the management of the Lyceum's relations with the press, and the *Pall Mall Gazette* regularly reviewed their productions. Stoker also knew the many politicians, journalists and Establishment worthies who gathered after hours in the Lyceum's Beefsteak Room to discuss the issues of the day with Henry Irving. That summer talk must have turned from time to time to the antics of W.T. Stead and those whom Irving's circle knew dismissively as 'the psalm-singing mob'.[15] More prosaically, the wild scenes outside the *Gazette*'s Strand offices that July – the huge crowds, the ranks of policemen – would have obstructed Stoker's morning commute to work and naturally drawn comment from the Lyceum's employees.

For the women of the Lyceum, Stead's reports would have had a special resonance. In the public mind, actresses had long been interchangeable with prostitutes, an association that Stead reinforced again and again in his journalism that summer.[16] All actresses had to live with this stigma. Ellen Terry, the Lyceum's leading lady, was all too familiar with it. The daughter of strolling players, as a teenager Terry had been an artist's model for George Watts, a painter associated with the Pre-Raphaelites.[17] Despite a forty-year age difference, Watts and Terry had married in 1865. In their subsequent divorce papers, Watts had claimed that he had wed Terry 'to remove an impulsive young girl from the dangers and temptations of the stage'.[18] By 1885, Terry was twice divorced, had two children out of wedlock, and was among the highest-salaried women in the country, earning a massive £200 per week as an actress. Although she largely toed Irving's ideological line at the Lyceum, in her intellectual, creative and financial independence Terry was something of a harbinger of the New Woman, and would later become a patroness of the suffragist movement. Even the placid confines of Irving's theatre were not completely removed from the torrid sexual politics of late Victorian London.

***

In the summer of 1888, when he and his company departed London for an extended tour of the provinces, Irving leased out the Lyceum to an American actor-manager named Richard Mansfield. It was to prove one of Irving's few missteps – one that let the violence and despair of London's dark places on to his hallowed stage, puncturing the veil of reality and make-believe once and for all.

Mansfield's production was a stage adaptation of Robert Louis Stevenson's *Dr. Jekyll and Mr. Hyde*. Published in 1886, Stevenson's novel had been rapturously received and quickly became a best-seller. In a long, effusive review, *The Times* declared the story a *tour d'esprit*, Stevenson Edgar Allan Poe's better and George Eliot's equal, and the book 'a finished study in the art of fantastic litera-ture'.[19] But the newspaper did not regard *Dr. Jekyll* as simply a work of fantasy. The reviewer understood its plot – the gradual uncov-ering of the schizoid split between the avuncular, Anglo-Saxon Dr Jekyll and the malevolent, simian Mr Hyde – to be taking place on 'strictly scientific grounds'. Stevenson's work was of a piece with the latest biological and psychological research, specifically that unleashed in the wake of Charles Darwin's two masterpieces: *The Origin of Species* (1859) and *The Descent of Man* (1871).

Darwin's theory of evolution by natural selection initially took an optimistic view of biological development. 'As natural selection works solely by and for the good of each being,' he wrote in the famous closing passages of *The Origin of Species*, 'all corporeal and mental endowments will tend to progress towards perfection.' But in the 1880s this whiggish view of evolution was called into question. Ray Lankester's *Degeneration: A Chapter in Darwinism* (1880) had argued that if the conditions of life softened then organisms would cease to elaborate in response to threat and instead undergo 'a gradual change of the structure in which the organism becomes adapted to less varied and less complex conditions of life'. Degeneration was the 'stippression [sic] of form, corresponding to the cessation of work'. Parasites were the classic example. Once a parasite found a way of living off the life essence of another organism, its genetic development eschewed all evolutionary 'work' irrelevant to the improvement of its parasitic existence.[20]

Lankester's two great scientific influences were the German biologists Anton Dohrn and Ernst Haeckel, pioneers in the field of embryology. Haeckel had become known for his embryological theory of recapitulation, whereby a foetus in the womb passed through its species antecedent stages as it developed from a scattering of simple cells to, in the case of humans, a fully developed baby. Along the way, he postulated, the future organism climbed its own family tree. En route to personhood a future human was a group of cells, then a fish, then a primate, and finally a human. As Haeckel and his acolytes endlessly explained, 'Ontogeny Recapitulates Phylogeny.' As the embryonic organism underwent this process, it developed and then shed the features of its species' previous incarnations. Human foetuses at one point have a monkey-like tail, but they have lost it by the time they are born. But, Haeckel argued, it was possible that these traits would not be lost – that vestigial traits, or atavisms, could persist in otherwise fully developed individuals. However it found expression – phys-iologically, psychologically, anatomically – an atavism was the equivalent of a human infant being born with a prehensile tail.

Cesare Lombroso observed atavistic humans everywhere – or, to be more precise, everywhere he looked, which was in prisons and penal colonies. Lombroso was an Italian criminologist, and an acolyte of the Darwinian theories expounded by Haeckel and others. In the 1860s, while examining the skull of the deceased Italian brigand Vilella, he had what he described as a revelation. Criminals were not like the rest of the population. The criminal was in fact 'an atavistic being who reproduces in his person the ferocious instincts of primitive humanity and the inferior animals':

> Thus were explained anatomically the enormous jaws, high cheek-bones, prominent superciliary arches, solitary lines in the palms, extreme size of the orbits, handle-shaped or sessile ears found in criminals, savages, and apes, insensibility to pain, extremely acute sight, tattooing, excessive idleness, love of orgies, and the irresistible craving for evil for its own sake, the desire not only to extinguish life from his victim, but to mutilate the corpse, tear its flesh, and drink its blood.[21]

As this (partial) list of traits and features demonstrates, for Lombroso physical and behavioural traits were co-morbid in the biological criminal. Behaviour and biology were intimately linked. In the process, causation became hopelessly confused. Lombroso readily embraced both hard theories of heredity and softer environmental explanations. 'The aetiology of crime,' he wrote, 'mingles with that of all kinds of degeneration: rickets, deafness, monstrosity, hairiness, and cretinism, of which crime is only a variation.' This was, of course, music to the ears of social conservatives and connoisseurs of decline throughout the West. Although his works were only translated into English in the very last years of the nineteenth century, his ideas soon gained currency outside his native Italy. His breakthrough work, *L'uomo Delinquente* (*Criminal Man*), was published in 1876. By 1881 the *Pall Mall Gazette* – which published Stoker's short fiction and reviewed the Lyceum's plays – was discussing the Italian's writings in its columns, concluding gravely from it that 'savagery is always very close to our civilization, and that the criminal and indolent easily glide back into the manners of Australians and Red Indians.'[22] A few years later, in 1887, the *Gazette* uncritically told its readers: 'Lombroso asserts that no less than 40 per cent. of prisoners are born, or habitual, criminals, whom no house of detention, no penal servitude will change, and to whose existence the public had better accustom themselves, adjusting their minds to the existence of this latest natural phenomenon.'[23] In England, the novel notion that there existed a criminal genus mingled easily with a pre-existing belief in the existence of a sociologically defined 'criminal class', not to mention a general phobia of the poor and a concomitant and lurid fascination with their moral, social and domestic condition – as Mansfield's adaptation of Stevenson's novel, and the appalling historical backdrop to its run at the Lyceum, would soon demonstrate.

Like Lombroso's biological criminal, Mr Hyde is both physically and behaviourally different from the upstanding Dr Jekyll. Jekyll is tall and hale; Hyde is decrepit. Both Hyde's appearance and his actions are described in relation to monkeys – animals lower down the evolutionary scale. Jekyll, as a physician, a gentleman and a man of culture, represents the apex of civilisation. Hyde mocks his learning by scrawling obscene marginalia in Jekyll's books. Stevenson used London's geography to symbolise the distance between the two men. Jekyll lives in a large, clean, spacious home with a garden, previously owned by a well-known surgeon. When Utterson, the narrator, tracks Hyde through the 'great chocolate-coloured pall' of the London fog his pursuit leads him to Soho, 'a district of some city in a nightmare':

> As the cab drew up before the address indicated, the fog lifted a little and showed him a dingy street, a gin palace, a low French eating house, a shop for the retail of penny numbers and twopenny salads, many ragged children huddled in the doorways, and many women of many different nationalities passing out, key in hand, to have a morning glass; and the next moment the fog settled down again upon that part, as brown as umber, and cut him off from his blackguardly surroundings.

Jekyll is home, hearth and a well-stocked library; Hyde is gin, foreigners, and fog.

Mansfield's great stunt was to play both Jekyll and Hyde at once. In the famous promotional photo advertising the play he is depicted in both guises simultaneously, the wretched figure of Hyde double-exposed over the dapper Jekyll, an image which visually recalled Darwin's famous illustration in *The Descent of Man* of the monkey loping upwards into *Homo sapiens*. All these theatrics, and all the knowing nods to contemporary science, could not help Mansfield. The play opened on 4 August 1888. From the outset it underperformed both critically and commercially. The failure of an intensely psychological novel to translate on to the stage might be no great surprise. But circumstance dictated that Mansfield's misfortune be of a different order altogether. *Dr. Jekyll and Mr. Hyde*, as *The Times* had insisted, was meant to be an entertaining fantasy but the city determined to turn it into something horrifically real.

In the early hours of 31 August, Mary Anne Nichols was found dead in Buck's Row, Whitechapel. A week later the body of Annie Chapman was discovered in Hanbury Street, Spitalfields. There was a hiatus of three weeks before two women, Elizabeth Stride and Catherine Eddowes, were murdered in the same hour on the night of 30 September, one in Whitechapel and the other on the eastern edge of the City of London. There was then another, longer break in the violence until 9 November, when the appallingly mutilated body of Mary Kelly was found in her flat in Spitalfields. All the victims were allegedly prostitutes; all lived in London's East End; all had been subjected to varying degrees of savagery and dismemberment by an unknown killer.

The Jack the Ripper killings, or the Whitechapel Mystery as it was known in the press of the period, gripped the nation at the exact same time as Richard Mansfield was staging *Dr. Jekyll and Mr. Hyde* at the Lyceum. The media descended on Whitechapel and its environs, and their coverage of the crimes and their setting was inflected by the same social anxieties and Darwinian theorising that ran through Stevenson's novel. In a famous series of *Punch* cartoons on the murders, the denizens of London's East End were portrayed as little more than animals – hunched, bestial, idiotic – living in an environment as degraded as its inhabitants. Echoing W.T. Stead, *Punch* compared the lattice of streets, alleys and courtyards in the East End with the Minotaur's lair; echoing Lankester, Lombroso and the rest of the Darwinian declinists, it asked: 'Held Dante's Circles such a dwelling-place? Did primal sludge e'er harbour such a race?' Whitechapel was the monster lurking within an otherwise civilised London; the Hyde to the capital's Jekyll.

The connection between what was going on in the streets of the East End and what was being played out nightly on the Lyceum's stage (only two miles from the sites of the murders) was not lost on the press, the public or Richard Mansfield. On 2 October, the *Pall Mall Gazette* offered its readers a summary of the various theories concerning the identity of the murderer. Among them was 'The Jekyll and Hyde Theory. – that the murderer lives two lives, and inhabits two houses or two sets of rooms.' On 5 October, the City of London police received an anonymous letter alleging that Mansfield was himself the Ripper. The author had apparently seen the Lyceum production, and though he had a 'great liking for acters', upon seeing Mansfield in the role 'I felt at once that he was <u>the Man Wanted</u> & I have not been able to get this Feeling out of my Head.'[24] This was not, presumably, the kind of audience response Mansfield had been hoping for.

Touring in Scotland, Stoker and Irving looked on with some concern as negative publicity accrued to their theatre and ticket sales plummeted. Pressure mounted on Mansfield to cease performing his play and to switch to less controversial fare. Mansfield decided to do just that. In mid-October the *Daily Telegraph* approvingly reported that the production was being abandoned. 'There is quite sufficient to make us shudder out of doors,' the paper noted, 'few will regret Mr. Mansfield's determination to show us, before he leaves England, a pleasant side of human nature in contrast to the monsters he has conjured up.' Hoping to win back public favour, and perhaps allay questions as to his personal culpability, Mansfield announced that he would give the receipts from an evening's performance of the comedy *Prince Karl* to the Refuge Fund for the Poor of the East-end of London.[25]

Nothing, however, could save Mansfield now. The abject failure of *Dr. Jekyll and Mr. Hyde* left him in a disastrous financial position: the rent on the Lyceum went unpaid and he had to borrow money from Irving to return to the United States. The fiasco served to confirm 'Irving's distaste and suspicion of contemporary authors'; the next Lyceum production would be a dramatical stalwart: *Macbeth*.

Stoker, as the man in charge of the theatre's finances, would have been intimately familiar with the fiscal problems arising out of Mansfield's woes.[26] But Jekyll, Hyde and Jack the Ripper also resonated with him artistically. The killings and the mysterious powers of their mysterious perpetrator would linger in his mind and re-emerge in the novel he was just starting to plot.

***

While *Punch* was content to portray the Ripper killings as the work of an atavistic brute, other, more perceptive observers noted that the reverse was likely the case, namely that the culprit was charming, socially intelligent, and capable of winning over scared and suspicious women. The *Spectator* argued that judging by his 'success in pacifying the women', the murderer must be 'respectable, and even gentle in appearance' and manner.[27] The notion that the killer was physically and socially attractive seems, judging by the weight of contemporary evidence and modern research, substantially true. In this way, the Whitechapel Mystery reaffirmed the Victorian narrative that connected seduction, prostitution and male rapacity. It also added, or rather emphasised, a new dimension to the sexual dangers English women faced: Jewishness.

British anti-Semitism had always been an odd phenomenon, defined by the absence of its object rather than its presence. In 1290 Edward I had banished all English Jews from the country, and it was not until the seventeenth century that they were permitted to return. By the mid-nineteenth century there were only around 30,000 living in the country. For the vast majority, Jews were an exoticism – spoken of but never seen. Many Englishmen saw a Jew in the flesh only when they went overseas. In this period, Jewishness in the English imagination was normally associated with the Sephardic Jews who lived on the Mediterranean littoral, and tended to be part of a prospering mercantile caste rather than a segregated ethnocultural one. Henry Irving's encounter was typical. He spent the summer of 1879 yachting around the Mediterranean with some wealthy friends. Boating from port to port, he found his attention at every harbour drawn to the local Jewish population, many of whom conducted business at the quayside. These majestic, rather romantic figures confounded the native stereotypes he had grown up with. The crystallising moment came, according to his son, in a port on the Maghreb:

He had seen a Jew in Tunis, beside himself over some transaction, tear his hair and his clothes, fling himself upon the sand writhing in rage, and a few minutes later become self-possessed, fawning and full of genuine gratitude for a trifling gift of money. Picturesque in his fury, having regained his composure, the Jew had stalked away with kingly dignity behind his mule team.[28]

Irving now had his way into one of the most controversial and, to his mind, misunderstood figures in dramatical history: Shylock. Upon his return he revealed to Loveday and Stoker his plans for a radical reinterpretation of *The Merchant of Venice*, and on 1 November 1879 the play opened at the Lyceum. Irving's performance as the title character won him widespread acclaim and was considered a watershed moment in anglophone depictions of Jewishness.

Irving could not have known it, but his portrayal of Shylock came at a pivotal moment in the history of English Jewry. Between 1881 and 1905 approximately 100,000 Jews came to Britain, driven overseas by persecution in the Russian empire. Jewishness ceased to be a distant phenomenon and became a component of urban life in many of England's great cities. Thousands went to Liverpool and Manchester, but the overwhelming majority gathered in relatively small parts of east London. Forty thousand lived in Stepney, where they constituted a quarter of the population. Whitechapel and Spitalfields played host to much of the rest, but communities sprang up all over the East End, in Goodman's Fields, Mile End, Shadwell, Cable Street, Dock Street and elsewhere. The shock of mass Jewish immigration into these neighbourhoods was compounded by their hitherto relatively stable demography – the populations of many East End neighbourhoods were over 70 per cent London born – and the inescapable fact of the newcomers' difference.

The complexion of English Jewry had previously been defined by the cosmopolitan, business-minded Sephardim, but the Russian and Polish Jews were Ashkenazim. Their world was defined by claimed that though Jews committed a lower percentage of crimes compared to other groups, their criminal activities were concentrated in 'fraud, forgery, libel, and chief of all, traffic in prostitution.'[31] Among rabid anti-Semites it was taken as writ that Jewish wickedness found gleeful expression in the immiseration of gentile girls. For many more it was simply a lazy conclusion drawn from the geographic coincidence of poverty, prostitution and Jewish arrivals.

Moral campaigners had often associated the rise of prostitution with the demise of traditional morality and the incursion of alien faiths. During his early forays into the field, W.T. Stead had characterised the haunts of sex workers as 'colonies of heathens and savages.'[32] Established English Jews responded vigorously to these allegations. In 1886, the Jewish Ladies' Association for Preventative and Rescue Work issued its first report on the matter, and sent representatives down to the docks to help prevent newly arrived women from falling into the hands of 'Men-sharks, and female harpies of all descriptions' set on entrapping them into sexual bondage. In 1888 the *Jewish Chronicle* described East End prostitution as 'a blot upon our community at large', and the Chief Rabbi Hermann Adler voiced concern about alleged Jewish involvement in white slavery.[33]

The association would prove hard to shed, for the simple reason that it blurred so easily into the belief that Jews possessed the special ability to influence and seduce the gentile mind. 'Intellectual superiority, Oriental subtlety, and the training of sorrow,' English anti-Semite Arnold White wrote in *The Modern Jew* (1899), 'accredit the Jews with a complex and mysterious power denied to any other living race.' This had been a trope of English anti-Semitism since the Romantics and had gained widespread credence with the rise to power and pre-eminence of the uniquely suave and winning Benjamin Disraeli.[34] The idea that Jews had ill-defined magical abilities was, of course, centuries old,[35] but it fused perfectly with the late Victorian mania for the occult. Hypnotism, mesmerism and telepathy remained stock subjects for scientific debate and fictional embellishment. The notion that hypnotism could be used to seduce women persisted, albeit as a hotly contested subject, among true believers in the practice.[36] Its connection to the Jewish community was merely an extension of old prejudice to new circumstance which long survived the immediate crisis surrounding the Whitechapel Mystery.[37]

In the 1890s the trinity of Jewishness, hypnotism and seduction was consolidated in one of the first modern literary blockbusters. For much of his life, George Du Maurier had been a draughtsman and cartoonist working for London magazines. Since the 1860s he had found regular employment at *Punch* – in 1886 he had contributed the strange Stoker family scene mentioned above – and other popular publications. But in the 1890s his sight started to fail him and he switched from drawing to writing. His first novel made little impression. Then, in 1894, he published *Trilby*.

Set in certain bohemian neighbourhoods of 1850s Paris, *Trilby* tells the story of Trilby O'Ferrall, a beautiful if uncouth Irish laundress and artist's model who falls under the influence of a musician and impresario known only as Svengali. Svengali is a Jew, and is repeatedly described in the crudest terms. He is a 'filthy black Hebrew sweep', 'a big hungry spider' with 'bold, brilliant black eyes, with long, heavy lids, a thin, sallow face, and a beard of burnt-up black which grew almost from his under eyelids'. He bullies, cringes, borrows, hides, spits, performs, insults and manipulates the whole novel long. Attracted by Trilby's beauty he brings her under his sway through mesmerism, takes her as his mistress, and uses his hypnotic powers to turn her into the most sought-after singer in Europe, making himself fantastically wealthy in the process. When he suddenly dies mid-performance, Trilby's musical abilities disappear and she too withers and dies, used, consumed and discarded by her Jewish controller for whom she has been 'a flexible flageolet of flesh and blood – a voice, and nothing more.'[38]

An illustration from *Trilby* (1895), George Du Maurier's best-seller that featured one of the most pernicious anti-Semitic portrayals in modern literature: the predatory Jewish super-villain Svengali.

Trilby was a sensation on both sides of the Atlantic. Du Maurier's novel sold two million copies in the first two years. Trilby-mania resulted in innumerable commercial spin-offs (of which only the eponymous Trilby hat survives in common parlance). Stage adaptations proliferated. At one point twenty-four separate productions of *Trilby* were touring the United States, among them a burlesque of the novel performed at the Garrick Theatre, New York, by Richard Mansfield.[39] When it was announced that Paul Potter's acclaimed production was coming to England, there were high hopes that it would be staged at the Lyceum. 'It would be a pity if the Lyceum company did not secure the English rights,' one commentator opined, 'for Mr. Irving would make an inimitable Svengali, and Ellen Terry would be Trilby without trying.'[40]

Irving and Stoker had good reason to be optimistic – after all, Trilby was directly compared to Ellen Terry in the text of the novel[41]

– but it was not to be. Potter's *Trilby* went to the Haymarket Theatre in Piccadilly, run by actor-manager Herbert Beerbohm Tree. Its run at the Haymarket lasted three years and 260 performances, making Tree so much money that he could afford to buy and rebuild a whole new venue, Her Majesty's Theatre, across the road. The Lyceum management team's chagrin can be readily guessed at.

By the mid-1890s Bram Stoker had arrived at a crossroads in his career. He had been at the Lyceum for the better part of two decades. A known and respected member of London society, he had travelled the world in partnership with Irving, meeting statesmen, artists and magnates along the way. Still, Stoker wanted more from life. Many of his friends and associates had already achieved recognition. Hall Caine was a millionaire novelist, as were George Du Maurier and Arthur Conan Doyle. George Bernard Shaw's career was rapidly picking up steam. Henry Irving's long reign at the top of London's theatrical world was crowned in 1895 when he was knighted at Windsor Castle by Queen Victoria, the first actor ever to attain the distinction. Some of his contemporaries had risen so far, so fast they had already experienced collapse and ruin. The same day that Irving's knighthood was announced, Oscar Wilde was sentenced to two years' hard labour for gross indecency. The law he had violated was the Criminal Law Amendment Act of 1885, section 11, which had criminalised homosexual sex.

Stoker's restlessness had led him down a number of avenues. In 1886 he stunned his colleagues by announcing his interest in training to become a barrister, an endeavour which seemed scarcely possible given his enormous responsibilities at the Lyceum. Nonetheless, he quietly did the work and was duly called to the Bar at Inner Temple in 1890. In 1891 he invested alongside Arthur Waugh, Hall Caine and others in an ambitious European publishing scheme. This went awry and a great deal of money was lost. He had continued to write, publishing several novels between 1890 and 1895. None made much of an impact in a crowded literary marketplace. Yet he persisted. In 1896 he borrowed money from Hall Caine, took time off from the Lyceum, and went to Cruden Bay in Aberdeenshire to put some serious work into writing the novel that had bubbled away in his mind for five years. The commitment paid off. On Friday 28 May 1897, *The Times* announced in its 'Publications To-Day' column, amid a list that included such timeless works as *His Dead Past* by C.J. Wills, *An Exile From London* by Colonel R.H. Savage and *A Frisky Matron* by Percy Lysle, the release of 'DRACULA. By Bram Stoker.'

***

There was no single reason why Bram Stoker should have chosen to write a vampire novel. He had some personal connections to the genre – his former employer Sheridan Le Fanu had written *Carmilla*, one of the major books in the vampire canon, and his friend Hall Caine was very close to Dante Gabriel Rossetti, John Polidori's nephew[42] – but by the 1890s it was familiar territory for writers and dramatists. Stoker was writing for honest reasons: he needed the money. It seems probable that he identified the vampire narrative as a suitable vehicle for the kind of middlebrow mystery-thrillers so popular at the time. It was also a literary genre that lent itself to engagement with many themes and interests of the day. Reading *Dracula* in light of the larger trends and concerns of late Victorian England it is striking how many he involved in the plot. Mesmerism, immigration, urbanisation, racial theory, imperialism, Jewishness, feminism – all are present in his book. But *Dracula* is more than a simple *gemischt* of topical issues. It is clear from Stoker's very earliest extant notes for the book that he intended it to be about sexual danger.

In its essentials *Dracula* is a seduction narrative. The Count is the seducer; he pursues friends Lucy Westenra and Mina Harker, seduces them by means of his hypnotic powers, uses and corrupts their bodies, and then abandons them. Lucy and Mina's contrasting sexual personae mimic those of the conventional morality of the day which, as of 1885, had been embedded in law. Mina is the model woman: Christian, domesticated, almost pathologically disposed to supporting her husband. It takes all the Count's wiles to ensnare her and their encounter amounts to rape.[43] Lucy is a pampered aristocrat, who speaks suggestively of her appetites and is desirous of male attention. She craves her assignations with the Count, sleepwalking from her bed each night in Whitby and making her way up to meet him at the abbey on the cliff. There she swoons on a bench overlooking the sea while Dracula feasts on her throat. When Mina notices Lucy's somnambulism she locks her doors and windows, only to observe her trying to escape through them at night in order to meet with her vampiric lover. As a result of her corruption by the Count, Lucy becomes a sexually predatory vampire herself, though it is implied that this is not so much a perversion of her true self but a vindication of the old belief that 'blood will out'. Lucy was primed for immorality and was lewd and vicious before the Count arrived – he simply revealed her. Mina, even after her assault, remains a redemptive figure and eventually helps bring about his destruction and her own rescue.

Nothing here departs from the basic literary model handed down from the eighteenth century. The modern spin Stoker puts on it – and *Dracula* is a very modern book – is that of race. The men arrayed against Dracula – Mina's husband Jonathan Harker, the English peer and Lucy's fiancé Arthur Holmwood, the American adventurer Quincey Morris, the English doctor James Seward, and the Dutch vampire slayer Abraham Van Helsing – are all Anglo-Saxon. The Count is from Transylvania, a place that loomed large in the Victorian imagination as a disconcerting goulash of tribes, creeds and ethnicities.[44] 'Its population,' the *Spectator* declared in 1888, 'is a singular mixture of nondescript Wallachs, Aryan Teutons, Turanian Huns, Semitic stragglers, and Hindoo nomads, who have existed side by side for ten centuries without the least claimed – both physiognomically and behaviourally. Dracula is associated with the primordial past, the Hobbesian world of the virgin forest, his behaviour unimproved by contact with civilisation. Holmwood, Harker and the rest embody the virtues of that civilisation and use its strengths to destroy the Count. Rational planning, moral force, and above all the judicious use of cutting-edge technology are their weapons. They represent the apex of Victorian civilisation. The Count's powers, by contrast, are of a cruder order. As a blood-sucker, Dracula is literally a parasite. Like any parasite he has highly developed feeding faculties, but his other functions have atrophied. Given that he feasts on women and uses mesmerism to access their bodies, his seductive powers are paradoxically a feature of his biological degeneration. The racialised seducer is not simply a parasite or even an ethnocultural other, but a destabilising force that threatens progress itself – evolutionary, social and moral – and does so by corrupting the Anglo-Saxon woman.

That the Count uses hypnosis to seduce his targets is significant. The history of seduction is the history of the post-Enlightenment tension between reason and passion. To the racist mind it was impossible to accept that Anglo-Saxon women might rationally choose to partner with their racial inferior. Sexual panic and racial panic met in a discourse that imagined the racial 'stock' of the West being overwhelmed or 'swamped' by lesser races. Naturally, such a discourse only made sense if Anglo-Saxon women were actually breeding with these racial outsiders; and if they were – and were doing so consensually – then the very cornerstone of Victorian gender ideology, namely that women were meek, submissive and faithful, was called into question. Hypnosis helped explain away this quandary. The mesmerised subject has their reasoning faculties suspended; some hypnotists argued that the mesmerised individual was in a state of hysteria, lost to their emotions. Either way, they could no longer be held responsible for their actions. The cultural trope that connected seduction, hypnotism and race thus worked to salvage the myth of Victorian womanhood, while reinforcing the belief that 'undesirable aliens' were subversive inferiors possessed of atavistic sexual powers.[52]

The dark heart of *Dracula* is the unspoken fear that those precious women may in fact desire the outsider, the alien, the Count. This anxiety is connected in the novel to a trend at large in late Victorian society – the spectre of the New Woman. Between the passage of the Criminal Law Amendment Act and the publication of *Dracula*, the place of women in Victorian society had been transformed. A series of new laws had granted married women new rights. The movement for women's suffrage was gaining momentum. Women's access to and enrolment in higher education had boomed. A quarter of British women now participated in the workforce, and a number were beginning to make incursions into the hitherto exclusively male professions. These developments met with suspicion, and that suspicion was expressed in the figure of the New Woman.[53]

In so far as she existed at all, the New Woman was a bridge between the fusty world of high Victorian sexual role-playing and the more relaxed gender order of the 1920s and 1930s. She was looking ahead to a post-suffrage world and beginning to experiment with how women would be after basic civil rights had been won. The New Woman was engaged, passionate and independent.

To her detractors she was little less than a harbinger of social collapse.[54] The reformulation of gender roles, male critics warned, would lead to chaos. These fears were explored on the stage. The 1880s and 1890s saw a deluge of New Woman theatre. In Sydney Grundy's *The New Woman* (1894), the Colonel complains, 'Why can't a woman be content to be a woman? What does she want to make a beastly man of herself for?' and suggests that the New Woman is 'a sex of their own . . . They have invented a new gender.' The drive towards greater independence, often defined against the institution of marriage, was associated with a perversion of biological norms. 'No, to be a woman trying not to be a woman,' the protagonist of Arthur Wing Pinero's *The Notorious Mrs. Ebbsmith* (1895) declares, 'that is to be mad.'[55] These New Woman plays tended to share a common, and comforting, narrative arc. An allegedly emancipated woman toys with gender-bending behaviour (smoking, flirting, intellectual activity, employment), then falls in love with a masculine man, realises the errors of her ways, and is won back to the feminine 'norm'.

Stoker would write a novel, *The Man* (1905), which conformed exactly to this model, and had as its protagonist the New Woman archetype Stephen Norman, a woman with a man's name. Stoker's domestic life reflected his gender politics. When Walter Osborne's rococo portrait of Florence Stoker was exhibited at the Royal Academy in 1895, the press noted how pleasingly she conformed to classical femininity. *The Era* intoned:

> Mr Osborne has evidently taken pains to give a correct idea of the intellectual features of the lady, we might say, with Hood, that everything about Mrs Bram Stoker is 'pure womanly' according to the old-fashioned notions respecting the sex. One has no impression of the 'new woman' in the fine intelligence, the lady-like dress, and refined manner, the artist has depicted. Mrs Bram Stoker appears in white, the folds of the gown being arranged with simplicity and artistic taste.[56]

If his home was safe from the New Woman, then by the 1890s Stoker's workplace was not. In 1890, Ellen Terry's daughter Edy Craig joined the Lyceum's troupe of actors and actresses. She was the very embodiment of the New Woman, who had turned down Girton College, Cambridge to pursue a career on the London stage. If the Lyceum resisted dramatical modernism in all its forms, Edy Craig immersed herself in the new modes of theatre and acted in productions – then considered radical – of dramatic works by

Ibsen and Shaw. A passionate feminist, she would later establish theatre companies devoted to publicising the suffragist cause.[57] Edy worked alongside Stoker in London for seven years, and toured America with him in 1895. Exactly what he made of her is not known, though if *Dracula* is anything to go by his views on the New Woman were dim indeed.

Central to the attempt to pathologise female independence was a boorish caricature of the emancipated woman as slatternly and sexually aggressive. Male-on-female courtship was the respectable norm; female-on-male seduction was an abomination.[58] George Bernard Shaw explored this theme in his play *Man and Superman* (1903). In the preface, Shaw explained that the idea for the project had arisen out of a suggestion from a friend that he produce a play based on the legend of Don Juan. Shaw complied, after a fashion, but made it clear in the preface that 'my Don Juan is the quarry instead of the huntsman'. The inversion of roles reflects what Shaw saw around him. Women, he wrote, were now 'Aggressive, powerful: when women are wronged they do not group themselves pathetically . . . they grasp formidable legal and social weapons, and retaliate.'

They asserted this new power in all areas of life, including sex. 'As a result,' Shaw concluded, 'Man is no longer, like Don Juan, victor in the duel of sex.' Independent women were sexually voracious and their lust could dominate men. The vampire was increasingly an image applied to women, not men, as a metaphor for the sinister new appetites women were supposedly exhibiting.[59] The same year *Dracula* was published, there was a major public contretemps over the exhibition of Edward Burne-Jones's *The Vampire* at the Royal Academy. Burne-Jones was a friend of Stoker's who had done design work for the Lyceum and had also sketched Florence Stoker. His painting is an inversion of Henry Fuseli's *The Nightmare*, and depicts a voluptuous, bare-armed woman astride a slumbering, bare-chested man. In *Dracula* almost the exact same scene is portrayed in print. From the very beginning of the novel Lucy Westenra is linked to the New Woman.[60] In a letter to Mina she boasts that three men (Holmwood, Morris and Seward) have proposed to her on the same day. 'Why can't they let a girl marry three men, or as many as want her, and save all this trouble?' she complains. This outrageous wish is realised later in the book. With her blood drained by the Count, Holmwood, Morris and Seward all volunteer their veins to provide urgent transfusions into Lucy's own. 'Then this so sweet maid is a polyandrist,' Van Helsing thinks aloud.

In death, Lucy becomes a vampire and stalks Hampstead Heath. When the men trace her to her den in Highgate Cemetery, she attempts to seduce her former fiancé: 'She still advanced, however, and with a languorous, voluptuous grace, said: – "Come to me, Arthur. Leave these others and come to me. My arms are hungry for you. Come, and we can rest together. Come, my husband, come!"'

Van Helsing intervenes in time and Lucy is driven back to her grave. There her sexual transgressions are punished in horrific fashion. Holmwood plunges a stake into her heart; Seward and Van Helsing saw off her head and stuff her mouth with garlic; her butchered corpse is then sealed in a lead coffin, like some kind of radioactive material. The savagery with which Lucy's cadaver is treated might leave us to wonder who or what is being punished: a fictional vampire or a very real, independent, and sexually awakened young woman.[61]

The New Woman's sexual aggression was chimerical, a useful fiction invented by her male critics.[62] In reality, many *fin de siècle* feminists were themselves sceptical of sexual liberation. Sexual freedom was often countenanced in theory; in practice women often recoiled from it. 'We none of us know what exactly is the sexual code we believe in,' Beatrice Webb observed, 'approving of many things on paper which we violently object to when they are practised by those we care about.'[63] While there were feminists who staked out a radical position premised on the merits of free love and sexual experimentation,[64] they were always a minority and were frequently regarded as a harmful distraction from the serious work of securing reform.

Most women simply wanted to experience freedom, to see 'with our own eyes, and not, as the women of the past have done, with the eyes of men', as one pamphleteer eloquently put it.[65] They wanted at least the prospect of a life lived without reference to men, even if only for a period before marriage. Many centrist feminists sought neither to destroy the institution of marriage nor to live outside it in perpetual libertinage; they simply desired its reformation. Marriage ought to be made more accommodating of female independence. This could be achieved in part by legal reform; in part it had to be brought about by voluntary changes in male behaviour. In riposte to the patronising image of the New Woman, they proposed instead a New Man, who would welcome and support female autonomy in education, the workplace and the home. The partnership between New Man and New Woman would usher in a new sexual order that would 'exemplify reciprocity and cooperation'.[66]

The more battle-hardened among them were, however, doubtful of the prospects for the New Man. They argued that sex was a trap laid by men and inherently degrading to women. It was better, they declared, to refuse to play the game. To live independently of men, sexlessly if necessary, was better than to flirt with subjugation. This vestal vision of committed feminism was encapsulated in Margaret McMillan's motto 'Marriage is bad and Free Love is worse'.[67] Christabel Pankhurst went further, calling for a total rejection of heterosexual sex until feminist victory had been declared on all fronts. Her rallying cry was immortal: 'Votes for Women and Chastity for Men'.[68]

These nuances are lost in *Dracula*, which should be no surprise. Stoker's novel is essentially one of male anxiety, not a condition tolerant of complexity. Stoker embodied Victorian values, and *Dracula* manifests Victorian fears. The notion that Jews were hypnotising gentile women was as absurd as the notion that marginally less oppressed women were now sexually harassing men. Nonetheless, change was afoot in English society. Immigration was changing the complexion of the country and, in the racial terms of the day, the make-up of the national stock. New gender norms were ascendant and a growing number of women were living increasingly independent lives. Feminism seemed to be subverting the gender order just as immigration threatened the racial order. In the minds of the male establishment, the two phenomena were closely connected: rebellious women shirked their reproductive duties, leaving the nation open to 'swamping' by racial inferiors.[69] Foreign men, meanwhile, stood by to capitalise on their host's weakness and the availability of English women. The quandary was that the impulse to protect women – measures like the 1885 Criminal Law Amendment Act – only seemed to embolden the women's movement further. The apparently hopeless position of English men is captured in the dynamic at work in *Dracula*. Van Helsing and his team spend the first part of the novel keeping Lucy alive by elaborate means and the second part hunting her down and elaborately butchering her body – as good a metaphor as any for Victorian attitudes towards women.

***

Bram Stoker died in April 1912 – the same week that his friend W.T. Stead perished aboard the *Titanic* – but his most famous creation lived on. Following his death, Florence Stoker became his literary executor and the guardian of his royalties and copyrights. By the 1920s all her late husband's works ceased to generate an income, with the exception of *Dracula*. In straitened circumstances following his death, Florence was understandably proprietorial about Bram's vampire tale and was enraged when she learnt in April 1922 that an unlicensed adaptation of *Dracula* had premiered at the Berlin Zoo the month before. Through lawyers in London and Germany, Florence established that Prana-Film had commissioned director F.W. Murnau, who had recently produced a German-language version of *Dr. Jekyll and Mr. Hyde – Januskopf* (1920) – to make a free adaptation of Stoker's *Dracula*. Murnau's film had a number of differences. Count Dracula became Count Orlok; the action was moved from London to Bremen; the *dramatis personae* was dramatically reduced. But these changes were not enough to save the Germans from Florence's wrath. The plot of the film was clearly her husband's and no permission had been obtained from his estate to use it. From her flat in Knightsbridge, Florence orchestrated a legal campaign – it would last many years – to receive compensation from Prana-Film. When the film company went bankrupt, she demanded in lieu of payment the destruction of all copies of the film. Her wish was finally achieved in July 1925 and *Nosferatu*, considered the apogee of German expressionist film-making, was consigned to oblivion.[70]

Murnau's Count Orlok was not the only vampire to haunt the imagination of the Weimar Republic. German screens and German novels were filled with tales of the supernatural. Films like *The Cabinet of Dr. Caligari* (1920) and *Dr. Mabuse the Gambler* (1922), and books like Hanns Heinz Ewers's *The Vampire* (1921)[71] and Arthur Dinter's *The Sin Against the Blood* all blended racial and sexual panic and featured Jewish or quasi-Jewish villains in prominent roles.[72] The presence of esoteric themes in Weimar culture was a continuation of a pre-war fascination with the occult; their proliferation, however, was the consequence of the tectonic shocks that German society had experienced in 1918 and 1919.[73] For thousands of *völkisch* mystics, far-right demagogues and disillusioned veterans, defeat was not simply a national trauma but an eschatological event, a fissure in reality that had unleashed monsters on Germany.[74] 'Yesterday we experienced the collapse of everything which was familiar, dear and valuable to us,' Rudolf von Sebottendorf, founder of the mystic right-wing Thule Society told his followers on 8 November 1918. 'In the place of our princes of Germanic blood rules our deadly enemy: Judah.'[75] In 1919 members of the Thule Society formed the *Deutsche Arbeiterpartei* (DAP), which upon the rise to prominence of one of its more compelling speakers, Adolf Hitler, became the *National Sozialistische Deutsche Arbeiterpartei* (NSDAP) in 1920.

For the hard right, the vampire was the perfect metaphor for the Jewish threat they saw all about them. In his monstrous person met the competing fears of sex, race (specifically, blood) and biological degeneracy. It was no surprise, then, that when Hitler sat down in his cell in Landsberg Prison in 1924 to pen his personal and political testament *Mein Kampf*, the language and imagery of vampirism mixed readily in his prolix diatribes against the Jews. Hitler returned repeatedly to the vampire metaphor, referring to Jews as the 'eternal blood-sucker', as 'parasites'[76] always on the hunt 'for a new feeding soil for his race', lamenting the 'blood-sucking tyranny' of 'Jewish' financial interests and darkly predicting that the Jewish 'vampire' would die soon after 'the death of his victim'. Such epithets mixed freely with the familiar associations made between the perils of seduction and the menace of the racial other. Recalling the Vienna of his youth, Hitler writes that 'in no other city of western Europe could the relationship between Jewry and prostitution, and even now the white slave traffic, be studied better'.[77] The Jews were the 'seducers of our people', who had degraded modern ideas of health and beauty – through, of all things, their alleged control of the fashion industry – to allow 'for the seduction of hundreds of thousands of girls by bow-legged, disgusting Jewish bastards'. Such language was common among Nazi demagogues. Julius Streicher's *Der Stürmer* endlessly mixed demonic and vampiric imagery with frenzied allegations of Jewish sexual predation. In a 1926 edition of the paper, he claimed that Aryan girls subjected to street harassment by Jewish men could ward off their pursuers by the prominent display of nationalist icons, like the Iron Cross, on their persons – just as a vampire could be scared off with garlic and crucifixes.[78] In *The Riddle of the Jew's Success* (1927), Theodor Fritsch declared that the 'Hebrew displays the features of the parasite' and did not 'derive his means of existence directly from Nature . . . but only by means of an intermediary system of living, the essential members of which he sucks dry'.[79] Fritsch married his disgust at the Jews' physical condition with a perverse admiration for their seductive powers. 'One is also inclined to assume the presence of some hypnotic power,' he noted, 'when one observes how even old and ugly Jews render young females docile and submissive to their desires.'[80]

Upon their ascent to power in 1933, Nazi lawyers quickly went about laying the groundwork for a new set of racially inspired laws that would protect Germany from this imagined Jewish threat. In September 1933 a group of Nazi lawyers, including the future head of the People's Court, Roland Freisler, issued a legal manifesto known as the Prussian Memorandum. The Memorandum laid out a vision of Nazi race law that would supplant the liberal laws of the Weimar Republic. Just like the Americans of the Progressive era, Nazi racial thinkers in the 1930s were obsessed with racial mixing – what Hitler had called 'race-poisoning' – and wanted to use the law as an instrument to protect the purity of the German race. To this end the authors of the Memorandum proposed the creation of a new crime: race treason. 'Every form of sexual mixing between a German and a member of a foreign race', they wrote, 'is to be punished as race treason, and indeed both parties are to be subject to punishment. . . . Particularly deserving of punishment is the case in which sexual intercourse or marriage is induced through malicious deception.' Their judicial model as to how to implement this new law was the United States, the home of inventive and expansive laws on race, sex and seduction. 'It is well known,' the Memorandum continued, 'that the Southern states of

North America maintain the most stringent separation between the white population and coloreds in both public and personal interactions.' Here was a system that the Nazis could emulate.

In 1934 Nazi lawyers, Freisler again among them, met once more, this time at the Commission on Criminal Law Reform, to discuss how to legislate into existence the Nazi racial utopia. At the forefront of their minds was sex, specifically how to introduce an 'effective quarantine separating the racially foreign elements in Germany from the people of German descent'. First to speak was Fritz Grau, a member of the Academy of German Law, a future SS colonel and future Nuremberg trial defendant. The American example, Grau said, was laudable but the Commission had to consider the difference in condition between the black American in the Jim Crow South and the Jew in Nazi Germany. It was all well and good to go down the 'path of social segregation and separation' but the sexual threat posed by Jews could not be mitigated so long as the latter held economic power within the German state. 'As long as they have the most beautiful automobiles', Grau told his colleagues, 'the most beautiful motorboats, as long as they play a prominent role in all pleasure spots and resorts', they would exist as a temptation to German women.[81] The answer was in the first instance 'positive statutory measures that forbid absolutely all sexual mixing of a Jew with a German, and impose severe criminal punishment', but also, Grau suggested, economic dispossession.[82]

A year after this meeting the Nuremberg Laws were instituted. Echoing the exacting racial and sexual laws in place throughout the United States, the Nuremberg Laws forbade marital and extra-marital relations between Jews and those 'of German or related blood'. Furthermore, Jews were forbidden to employ as domestic helpers 'female subjects of the state of German or related blood who are under 45 years old' – a preventative step against the mythical white slave trade, which German anti-Semites had long believed the Jews controlled.

Nor was Nuremberg the end of the Nazi campaign against the Jewish-Vampire-Seducer. As the 1930s wore on, anti-Semitic legislation intensified, with a host of exclusionary laws, injunctions and regulations put in place to further deny German Jews a place in the society of their birth.[83] In 1938, Fritz Grau's dream of destroying the economic power of German Jews was realised when new statutes were introduced that forbade Jews from operating businesses and engaging in the trade of goods and services of any kind. They were also to provide the state with details of their bank accounts and declare all wealth in excess of 5,000 Reichsmarks.[84] No longer would Jewish-owned cars and speedboats tempt the racial honour of German women.

A year later, as the Third Reich prepared for war, Nazi theorist and Himmler protégé Gregor Schwartz-Bostunitsch published *Jew and Woman: The Theory and Practice of Jewish Vampirism*. The book reinforced the connection between Jewishness, vampirism and racial pollution through sex just as the Nazis were about to become sovereign over the largest concentration of Jews in the world. The successes of the 1939 campaign against Poland and Operation Barbarossa against the Soviet Union would ultimately bring some ten million Jews under Nazi control. This inevitably posed a distinct problem to the Nazi mind. If, after all, the Jews were a supernatural force, an 'eternal blood-sucker', a vampire forever thirsting for German blood, then the most radical solutions to the 'Jewish Question' had to be entertained. At the Wannsee Conference in Berlin in 1942, fifteen men gathered round a table and planned the Final Solution. Among them was Roland Freisler, the lawyer who had spearheaded anti-Jewish racial and sexual legislation throughout the 1930s. That same week, also in Berlin, a Nazi screenwriter penned a memo about Weimar-era cinema for the Party Education Office entitled 'Superstition in Film'. There was much decadence in the German cinema of the pre-Nazi period, Hans Fischer-Gerhold declared, but some films from the time did contain political and racial messages that the Nazis could make use of. One such film was *Nosferatu*, F.W. Murnau's unauthorised retelling of *Dracula*. Fischer-Gerhold praised *Nosferatu* as the story of a 'vampire of Slavic origin' who preys on innocent Aryan blood. The message of the film was clear. Only one race could survive the confrontation: 'either the German or the Jew'.[85]

A Nazi cartoon from 1930's Germany linking seduction, prostitution and anti-Semitism.

SEDUCTION REMAINS

Among the first wave of refugees following Hitler's rise to power was a German-Jewish philosopher with a compelling explanation as to how Europe had succumbed to fascism. Herbert Marcuse had been born to a prosperous Berlin family in 1898. A bookish young man, he had been conscripted in 1916 but was spared front-line service due to his poor eyesight. He was in Berlin in 1918 when the Hohenzollern regime and the German war effort collapsed amid mutiny, revolution and incipient civil war. Already a committed Marxist, Marcuse manned the barricades as fighting broke out between right-wing paramilitary groups and communist insurgents. The nascent revolution was crushed, right-wing factions either co-opted or indulged by the new government, and a disillusioned Marcuse moved to Freiburg and studied Hegel.

As the 1920s wore on, the National Socialists grew in political influence and Marcuse began to search for academic positions outside the Nazifying German university system. In the early 1930s this led him to an association with the Institute for Social Research, a coterie of heterodox Marxist thinkers gathered around philosophers Theodor Adorno and Max Horkheimer. Marcuse joined the institute in Geneva in 1933 and the next year followed it to America, where it found shelter within Columbia University in New York City. A passionate opponent of the Nazi regime, Marcuse did not hesitate in offering his assistance to the Americans during the Second World War. He was given a position in the Office of Strategic Services (OSS), a forerunner to the CIA, as an analyst focused on parsing the dynamics of German society. At the war's end he returned to academia, taking up a succession of posts at Columbia, Harvard and Brandeis.

Marcuse's entire adult life had been shaped by the Nazi catastrophe. In the immediate aftermath of the war, he sought to turn his formidable intellectual powers to explaining how it had come about. To do so he would depend on theories of human sexuality grounded in Marxism and Freudianism. From the Marxist tradition, Marcuse drew upon a long-established set of beliefs about the relationship between capitalism and sexuality. In *The Communist Manifesto*, Marx and Engels had argued that capitalism led to the commodification of all social ties. In every aspect of intimate life – in the family, in courtship rituals, in the bedroom – they observed the influence of exploitative sexual relations that mirrored exploitative economic relations. The revolution they envisioned would necessarily transform sex as much as it would economics. They looked forward to the abolition of the family, the demise of prostitution, and the extinction of seduction itself. All these phenomena were relics of a corrupt bourgeois sexual culture ripe for destruction.[1]

Subsequent Marxist intellectuals took up this sexual theme. In *Women and Socialism* (1879), August Bebel imagined the 'woman of the future' as being 'socially and economically independent':

She is no longer subjected to even a vestige of domination or exploitation, she is free and on a par with man and mistress of her destiny. In choosing the object of her love, woman, like man, is free and unhampered. She woos or is wooed, and enters into a union from no considerations other than her own inclinations. . . . Under the proviso that the satisfaction of his instincts inflicts no injury and disadvantage on others, the individual shall see to his own needs. ... No one is accountable for it to others and no unsolicited judge has the right to interfere. What I shall eat, how I shall drink, sleep and dress, is my own affair, as is also my intercourse with a person of the opposite sex.[2]

Socialism would liberate women, and in so doing liberate sexuality. One corollary of the emancipation of women would be the obsolescence of seduction. Men and women would now meet on terms of parity. Sexual partners would be chosen frictionlessly on the basis of mutual attraction. This was a recurring theme in socialist literature, popularised in best-selling books such as Edward Bellamy's *Looking Backward* (1888) and William Morris's *News from Nowhere* (1890).[3] Following the implementation of Marxist precepts in Russia after 1917, Bolshevik politician and feminist theorist Alexandra Kollontai foresaw the emergence of a 'communist morality' that demanded an end to 'the buying and selling of caresses'.[4] The end of seduction, along with the abandonment of other manipulative and exploitative sexual practices, would be but one of many happy side-effects of the new socialist order.

What interested Marcuse was why capitalism depended upon this repressive sexual order. It was here that the writings of Sigmund Freud became relevant. In *Civilisation and Its Discontents* (1929), Freud had argued that repression was central to the entire enterprise of human civilisation. Each individual was a seething cauldron of appetites and desires which, left to their own devices, would preclude the possibility of collaboration in pursuit of a larger, more harmonious social order. The solution was to prevent the individual, by coercion where necessary, from realising their own selfish, chaotic impulses and instead divert their energies into productive and peaceable activities. Marcuse sought to challenge Freud's pessimistic prognosis by reference to Marxist theory. It was surely the case, he reasoned, that modern industrial economies were capable of producing enough goods and services for their populations, yet humans were obliged to work harder than ever. Marcuse suggested that Freudian repression was indeed going on in these economies, but that this repression was in excess of what was needed to meet the material needs of the workforce. Echoing the classical Marxist theory of 'surplus-labour', he referred to this phenomenon as 'surplus-repression'. Marcuse believed that surplus-repression was a feature of the capitalist economic order and that it was having disastrous effects on the collective psychology of those trapped within it. 'Suppressed sexuality', he wrote, leads to 'hideous forms [of release] so well known in the history of civilisation; in the sadistic and masochistic orgies of desperate masses, of "society elites," of starved bands of mercenaries, of prison and concentration-camp guards.'[5]

By marrying Freud and Marx, Marcuse believed he had identified the sexual origins of fascism that lurked within all capitalist societies. The delusion of the capitalist system was that there was no alternative to this system of repression – that human progress and civic order depended upon it. Marcuse argued that this was not the case and that 'the possibility of a non-represssive civilization is predicated not upon the arrest, but upon the liberation, of progress'.[6] He imagined a new kind of civilisation, socialist and sexually liberated, where 'no longer used as a full-time instrument of labor, the body would be resexualized':

> The regression involved in this spread of the libido would first manifest itself in a reactivation of all erotogenic zones, and, consequently, in a resurgence of pregenital polymorphous sexuality and in a decline in genital supremacy. . . . This change in the value and scope of libidinal relations would lead to a disintegration of the institutions in which the . . . interpersonal relations have been organized, particularly the monogamic and patriarchal family. . . . The process just outlined involves not simply a release but a transformation of the libido: from sexuality constrained under

genital supremacy to the eroticization of the entire personality. It is a spread rather than an explosion of the libido.

These theories were outlined in his *magnum opus, Eros and Civilization*, published in 1955. Marcuse did not use the phrase 'sexual revolution' (although he was familiar with, if disdainful of, the work of Wilhelm Reich, a fellow Jewish émigré with overlapping research interests, whose corpus included the 1945 book *The Sexual Revolution*), but with the publication and popularity of this book he would be forever associated with it. This tall, dour man, with his pipe and widow's peak and old-world manners, became the unlikely hero of a generation of student activists, radical intellectuals and exponents of sexual liberation. In charting the relationship between the economic and the sexual spheres, Marcuse unleashed a discussion about the political significance of sexual behaviour that reverberated around the Western world. As the Fifties gave way to the Sixties, his reputation as the prophet of the sexual revolution continued to grow. In 1965 he moved to California to teach in the edenic surroundings of UC San Diego. There this unassuming old man with his rich German accent, who could be found most afternoons smoking a cigar in his La Jolla garden or walking hand-in-hand with his wife beneath the cliffs on Torrey Pines Beach, became the epicentre of the culture wars that wracked the West. Styled the 'angel of the apocalypse' by the *New York Times*, he received death threats from the Ku Klux Klan, and an offer from the American Legion to pay his salary on the condition that he never teach again.

His supporters were no less ardent. His books were read from Oakland to Bonn; student protesters in Paris and Frankfurt marched with signs that read 'Marx, Mao, Marcuse'; he was credited (probably apocryphally) with the slogan 'Make Love, Not War'; he counted Angela Davis, Shulamith Firestone, and Kathy Acker among his disciples; students flocked to his classes in such numbers that loudspeakers were rigged up to broadcast his words to the crowds gathered outside the lecture hall. When, in the summer of 1967, the Summer of Love, he told students in Berlin that 'we have to develop the political implications of the moral, intellectual, and sexual rebellion of the youth', he announced himself as the intellectual idol of a generation intent on proving that the personal was indeed political.[7] At the heart of this fascination with Marcuse were his passionate insistence on the centrality of sexual questions to political affairs and his original insights into how intimate matters were correlated to economic structures.

Herbert Marcuse lecturing in Berlin during the Summer of Love.

***

One young person whose early life seemed evidence of the radical promise of sexual liberation was Janine Ceccaldi. Born in colonial

Algeria in 1926, Ceccaldi belonged to a firmly bourgeois family. Her father was a prosperous functionary of the Third Republic; her mother an elegant housewife. Despite the conservatism of her surroundings, Janine quickly emerged as a precocious daughter. She was a brilliant student at school, and her intellectual curiosity led her to literature – Dostoevsky and Thomas Mann in particular – and to Marxism. Aged fifteen when Hitler invaded the Soviet Union, Janine's communist sympathies were a rebellion against the stifling circumstances of her upbringing but also an act of individual courage. France was occupied by the Germans, and the Vichy regime actively persecuted left-wing groups. She involved herself in the communist underground in wartime Algiers and got herself excluded from school for a term for calling her anti-communist philosophy teacher 'a lackey of capitalism and colonialism'. Janine tested the limits of her society in other ways, too. From her early teens, her parents worried about her apparent sexual permissiveness. She also rebelled against the spiritual norms of a uniformly Catholic society by showing an adolescent interest in mysticism and the occult.

Shortly before the war ended, she took her Baccalauréate and looked to attend university. Characteristically, she was drawn to the two degree courses she considered the most masculine: law and medicine. Her parents considered the latter the more appropriate for a woman and she took up the gruelling course of studies, eventually specialising in anaesthesiology. All the time, she maintained her communist sympathies, participating in 1944 in the first conference of the Algerian Communist Party when it was formally reconstituted after several years underground. There she marvelled at the sight of Jews, Muslims and Christians, French and Arabs working together and 'expressing in many languages the same dream of fraternity'. After qualifying as a doctor in 1948, she left Algeria for Slovakia, where she helped 'build socialism' as part of a volunteer brigade working on the railways. Once that project was completed she attended a communist youth conference in Budapest.

Back in Paris, she found herself at the Gare de l'Est, without a job or a home but free to live her life as she wished. She took a job as a medical adviser to the Social Security bureau responsible for working-class districts in suburban Paris. In 1951, while on a trip to the forest of Fontainebleau, she met René Thomas, a casual labourer from Clamart, a solidly proletarian neighbourhood in south-west Paris. The couple cohabited for two years before moving to the French Alps, where René hoped to get a job as a ski guide. They moved around from Chamonix to Albertville (where they married) before settling in Pralognan-la-Vanoise; there she got a job as doctor at a ski station and he found work on the mountains.

In 1955, Janine's contract expired and she accepted a posting on an anti-tuberculosis project on the island of Réunion in the Indian Ocean. While she waited for her husband to join her, she had an affair with a local diver, whom she referred to as her 'dolphin'. When René arrived a few months later, the afterlife of the affair did little to improve the state of their marriage – already afflicted by the tension between her impassioned bourgeois communism and his pragmatic working-class upward mobility – but she became pregnant shortly afterwards. They spent those months awaiting the birth of their child, nursing exotic travel plans. They would kayak down the Nile, scale the peaks of Africa, drive from one end of the continent to the other.

When their child, Michel Thomas, was born in February 1956, they decided that they should not let him interfere with their travel plans. Aged only five months, Michel was entrusted to his paternal grandmother Henriette in Clamart. At their farewell in Réunion, Janine took a final look at him, said goodbye with '*l'oeil sec*' and went off on the long-planned African adventure.

At the end of their trip, in 1957, René and Janine separated. Janine returned to Réunion and practised medicine. Single, and working long days at the hospital, she decided she could not raise Michel herself, but was uncomfortable with his upbringing in Clamart and insisted that he be transferred to her mother's care in Algiers. Algeria was then in the midst of a brutal insurgency against French colonial rule. During his first few years there, Michel's own life was blissfully unaffected by it. His grandmother lived in an apartment of five or six light-filled rooms, down whose corridors and balconies he rode his tricycle. At a young age he was clearly an intelligent child, reading by the time he was three and inventing elaborate games at the age of four. There was little time to get comfortable in Algiers. He was four and a half when his parents formally divorced – still something of a rarity at that time in France – and only five when his grandfather died of cancer and his father came to Algiers, escorted by two parachutists, to rescue his son from a city that was fast becoming a permanent war zone.

Once again he was sent to his grandmother's home on the periphery of Paris. Michel would be raised by Henriette, his loving surrogate mother, with her reliably working-class ways and reflexive communist beliefs. He would see his parents on holidays – hiking or skiing with his father in the Alps, the occasional trip to Réunion to see his mother – but otherwise they were absent from his upbringing. His father prospered as a mountain guide, travelling around the world for work: there were expeditions to the United States, to Chile, to Nepal, two trips to Afghanistan. His mother remained in Réunion but travelled a great deal too, sometimes for work, sometimes for pleasure. As time passed she drifted away from communism and passed through several phases of belief – Hinduism, Islam, Christianity, New Age – what her son would later disdain as 'spiritual channel-hopping'.

In his teenage years, Michel also had a spiritual awakening of sorts. Although his childhood was largely happy, thanks to his adoring grandmothers and the permanent cast of aunts and uncles, his own worldview took a pessimistic turn in his mid-teens. A bright, bookish boy, he read Baudelaire and listened to Pink Floyd. The turning point, in his telling, came during a school trip to Bavaria in 1971, when he was fifteen. There he first read Blaise Pascal's notoriously gloomy *Pensées*. It was a transformative experience. 'There must have been some *secret flaw* in me,' he later wrote, 'that I tumbled, feet together, offering not the least resistance, into the abyss that Pascal opened up beneath my feet.' From Pascal it was a natural progression into Nietzsche, The Velvet Underground, Kafka, The Stooges, Dostoevsky and Schopenhauer.

This anxious philosophical turn took place against the backdrop of the turbulence of France in the Sixties and Seventies. The tremors of 1968 were felt even in his exurban *lycée*, and his formative years were played out amid the disintegration of the values of his childhood – the values of his grandmothers. Michel came to believe that his experience of abandonment and family breakdown was somehow symptomatic of the new world born in those decades. 'In a sense,' he later commented of his parents' decision to transfer him out of their care, 'this was a precursor of the vast movement towards the dissolution of the family which would follow. I grew up with the clear awareness that a great injustice had been committed towards me.'

His parents were too old to be *Soixante-Huitards*, but he judged them as the necessary 'precursors' to that generation, two canaries in the coalmine of the post-war West. The world he would mature into would be populated almost exclusively by people like them: hyper-mobile, sexually free, unashamedly individualistic. It was a world defined by unending interpersonal conflict, what he termed *la lutte*, the struggle. The world of the struggle was far removed from what he remembered as the tranquil, loving world of his childhood, of France in the Fifties and early Sixties. Many years later, in his second novel, he would refer to this world as the 'Lost Kingdom', whose values were embodied for him in the figures of his grandmothers. In tribute to them, and in homage to that lost world and those lost values, Michel took as his *nom-de-plume* his grandmother Henriette's maiden name, Houellebecq.

∗∗∗

One of Michel Houellebecq's contentions about the post-1968 world is that rampant materialism, consumerism and individualism have effectively attenuated experience to the extent that it would be naive to consider individuals as having something so dramatic as a unique biography. Furthermore, the 'progressive effacement of human relationships' means that individuals cannot even orientate their lives in relation to those of others. Westerners live within a spiritual and emotional void; as such there is no narrative arc to their existences, simply a period of growth, consumption and decay lasting several decades.[8] Consequently, outside the circumstances of his early childhood and the immediate family drama triggered by his wayward parents, Houellebecq's own life sheds little light either on the themes of his writing or on the history of seduction. This is, however, completely in line with his intuition that this crisis in personal history mirrors a larger stalling in Western history – that the societies he has lived in and describes in his writing are simply spinning their wheels. It was appropriate, then, that his literary debut should have occurred in the 1990s, the vaunted decade of the 'End of History' described by American political theorist Francis Fukuyama.

Yet in terms of Houellebecq's own analysis of the cause of this societal crisis, occasioned by the so-called sexual revolution, a different thesis of Fukuyama's is more instructive. In 1999 Fukuyama published *The Great Disruption*, an attempt at explaining some of the centripetal social forces he observed at work within the developed world. Fukuyama argued that the trends associated with the sexual revolution – the collapse in the fertility rate, the demise of traditional marital norms, the deterioration of the family unit – should be understood not as a consequence of a revolution in values but as the result of a revolution in economic structures. What happened in the 1960s and 1970s, he argued, was a transition in advanced economies away from manufacturing and towards services. Physical labour lost its primacy and was replaced by intellectual labour. This levelled the labour market for men and women. In aggregate, men might enjoy a natural advantage over women in physically demanding jobs in heavy industry. There was no such advantage in service roles that relied on intellectual and interpersonal abilities. The onset of the much-trumpeted Information Age effectively ended centuries of male economic advantage. Female participation in the labour force soared; the wage gap narrowed. A stratum of economically independent women sprang into being, their ranks growing with each passing year.[9]

This economic narrative runs counter to the popular narrative that foregrounds the cultural dimension of the Sexual Revolution. John Updike's couples, frolicking in their 'post-pill paradise'. Alexander Portnoy's complaints. Isadora Wing travelling from New World to Old in search of the 'zipless fuck' in Erica Jong's *Fear of Flying*. Brigitte Bardot – who claimed she was the 'first to demonstrate that a woman could very well lead a man's life without being a prostitute' – taking the role of the historically male ur-seducer in *Don Juan 1973 ou Si Don Juan était une femme*. Serge Gainsbourg and Jane Birkin's 'Je t'aime . . . moi non plus'. James Bond and the Bond girls. The landmark obscenity cases over *Lolita*, *Howl* and *Naked Lunch*. Jim Morrison telling reporters, 'We make concerts sexual politics. The sex starts with me.' The list goes on: Twiggy, *Alfie*, *Deep Throat*, Mick Jagger, *Hair*, Hugh Hefner, Helen Gurley Brown, *The Graduate*, Janis Joplin, *Oh, Calcutta!*, *Last Tango in Paris*, *Les Valseuses*, *Emmanuelle*, hippies, Haight-Ashbury, the Latin Quarter, Swinging London, mini-skirts.[10]

The cultural map is, however, a poor guide to the terrain of the sexual revolution. Entertaining as the output of these years was, and stark the contrast it provided to the bland offerings of the 1940s and 1950s, it was not in historical terms a unique explosion of transgressive creative expression. The 1920s was a remarkably fertile period for cultural iconoclasm and was by a number of measures a more progressive era than the decades that immediately followed it.[11] As discussed in earlier chapters, Venice, London and Paris had been hotbeds of cultural and sexual experimentation throughout the eighteenth century. (It is telling, on this point, that *Fanny Hill*, or *Memoirs of a Woman of Pleasure*, the text at the centre of a number of obscenity cases on both sides of the Atlantic in the 1960s, had been written in England in 1748, the same year that the first volumes of *Clarissa* were published.) The cultural manifestations of the sexual freedoms of these years were brilliant, but they were not new and they were not decisive. By contrast, the transition from a labour-intensive economy to a knowledge economy was without historical precedent.

There are two critiques that might be made of this line of argument. The first is political. Many of the transformations of the 1960s and 1970s occurred because of legislative action. Changes to the law helped liberalise social norms regarding, for example, divorce, but also had economic implications. In West Germany, for instance, married women could not take jobs outside the home without their husbands' permission until the law was changed in 1957; similar laws (the so-called Marriage Bar) persisted in the United States into the 1960s. Likewise, well into the 1970s English women could not get loans or mortgages without a male guarantor on their applications. In Britain these and other economic inequities were not challenged until the passage of the Equal Pay Act (1970) and the Sex Discrimination Act (1975). In other words, the economic revolution of the Information Age was still constrained by antiquated laws. The fact that these were eventually abolished had less to do with pure economics than it did with the fact that women had been enfranchised earlier in the century and were able to mobilise to bring about legislative reform. In this narrative, it was suffrage, not economics, that sparked the sexual revolution.

The second, connected criticism relates to contraception and abortion. The 1960s and 1970s saw a wave of landmark legal rulings and legislative events that transformed women's control over their bodies. The development and popularisation of oral contraceptives ('the pill', marketed under the brand name Enovid) in the 1960s was feted as one of the greatest technological breakthroughs in human history. In the next decade, the incremental successes of the pro-choice movement granted women even greater sexual freedoms. For feminists, it was taken as writ that sexual freedom was born of contraceptive rights. 'It is no longer possible to deny that we face the certainty of a sexual revolution,' Margaret Drabble wrote in 1971, 'and that this revolution, which much affects the institutions of marriage and parenthood, is caused largely by the development of contraceptive techniques.' This focus on contraception was a motif of much of the literature of the sexual revolution. One of the few things that really shocks Alexander Portnoy is the discovery that the prostitute he sleeps with in Rome has neither diaphragms nor oral contraceptives. Much to her dismay, he gifts his girlfriend's supply of Enovid to her. Likewise, the whole plot of *Fear of Flying* hinges on Isadora's easy access to, and generous use of, contraception.[12]

Taken together, the political and contraceptive cases for the sexual revolution constitute potent criticisms of the economic argument outlined above. The shortcoming common to both is the outsized emphasis both place on events within the particular decades of the Sixties and Seventies. In the United States, for instance, the campaign for contraceptive rights dated back to the 1920s. This scored major successes in the pre-pill era. By 1955, 70 per cent of white married women aged eighteen to thirty-nine had used some form of contraception at some point in their lives, a figure that had risen to 80 per cent by 1960. Furthermore, the uptake in usage of the pill was a lengthier process than is typically granted in the more breathless accounts of the sexual revolution. Due to state laws, racial and economic disparities, and information deficits, the pill did not become truly widespread in the USA until the 1970s. The situation was even starker in Europe. In France and England the pill was not totally legalised until the late 1960s and not made available from state health services until the 1970s. The circumstances surrounding abortion were even more diverse. Sweden legalised abortion in 1938; Ireland in 2018. In America, *Roe v. Wade* has been constantly attacked and circumscribed at a state and national level since 1973.[13] The point is not that contraceptive and abortion rights are peripheral to questions of sexual freedom, but that the accumulation of these rights has been far more piecemeal and contingent than is normally articulated in narratives of sexual liberation. Zooming out, it is clear that while the struggle for these rights was integral to the sexual revolution, local and national circumstances were paramount in deciding their success. In contrast, the economic story was the same across the West. In those decades, in a wide variety of countries with a range of social policies, manufacturing as a share of economic activity declined, female participation in the workforce increased sharply, women flooded into the professions, and female incomes rose. This 'quiet revolution' in the economy grabbed fewer headlines but underwrote all the other changes that occurred in public and private life.

There is space for a synthesis of these competing yet interconnected arguments. Again, it is the language of economics that comes to the rescue. In 2004 economists Roy Baumeister and Kathleen Vohs published a groundbreaking theory of sexual behaviour that they termed 'sexual economics'. For most of history, they argued, women had exchanged sex for male resources. Denied full or fair participation in the economy, and unpaid for domestic and care work, a woman's 'value' lay in her sexuality. In contrast, male sexuality had a very low value but men could 'trade' non-sexual goods for access to female sexuality:

> Men will offer women other resources in exchange for sex, but women will not give men resources for sex (except perhaps in highly unusual circumstances). In any event, the bottom line is that sexual activity by women has exchange value, whereas male sexuality does not. Female virginity, chastity, fidelity, virtuous reputation, and similar indicators will have positive values that will be mostly absent in the male.[14]

At the heart of sexual economics is the notion that female sexuality is a 'good' with a 'price'. For much of history that 'price' had been kept very high. Baumeister and Vohs argued that the pressure to keep the price high explained a number of tropes and taboos of Western sexual discourse, most notably the double standard which held a promiscuous woman to be worthless but a promiscuous man to be worthy of admiration. Furthermore, they noted that in the absence of alternatives women were incentivised to police sexuality in their own ranks, as the collective could not afford to allow the actions of one individual to 'lower' the price of all female sexuality.

The language of sexual economics can come across as cold and dehumanising. Nonetheless, its insights closely correspond to those of the Marxist critics of bourgeois sexuality who had claimed that capitalism had commodified all interpersonal relationships. Socialism, they believed, would liberate women by allowing them to share equally in the fruits of the economy. As discussed above, this was a recurrent theme in socialist literature. In *News from Nowhere*, William Morris showed how gender roles and sexual expectations would be upturned by the restructuring of the economy under socialism:

By far the greater part of these in past days were the result of the laws of private property, which forbade the satisfaction of their natural desires to all but a privileged few, and of the general visible coercion which came of those laws. . . . Again, many violent acts came from the artificial perversion of the sexual passions, which caused overweening jealousy and the like miseries. Now, when you look carefully into these, you will find that what lay at the bottom of them was mostly the idea (a law-made idea) of the woman being the property of the man, whether he were husband, father, brother, or what not. That idea has of course vanished with private property, as well as certain follies about the 'ruin' of women for following their natural desires in an illegal way, which of course was a convention caused by the laws of private property.

In sexual-economic terms what Morris is saying is that under socialism the 'price' of sex would fall. Women would no longer depend on men for resources and would no longer need to suppress their sexual desires in order to maintain their 'value'. A 'low' price for sexuality is indicative of improved gender equality. Women no longer have to depend on men and marriage for survival; they need men, as the feminist quip went, like a fish needs a bicycle. ('We had more in our lives than just men,' Isadora Wing declares in *Fear of Flying*, 'we had work, travel, friends.') One way of understanding the sexual revolution of the twentieth century is to consider it as a sustained reduction in the price of female sexuality brought about by increased economic independence, improved contraceptive rights and expanded legal protections for women. In this low-price sexual-economic market, expressions of sexuality proliferated because they were no longer attended by the same risks they had been in the past. Love did not become free, it became cheap.[15]

It was not at all clear what this meant for seduction. Feminist thinkers were split on the issue. In her essay 'Seduction and Betrayal' (1973), Elizabeth Hardwick argued that the sexual revoin particular the writings of his graduate student Angela Davis, Marcuse began to develop a theory to explain how capitalism had been able to adapt so readily to women's liberation and the spread of sexual freedoms. His argument foreshadowed Fukuyama's, made twenty-five years later. 'Under the impact of technological progress, social reproduction depends increasingly less on physical strength and prowess,' Marcuse wrote, 'either in war or in the material process of production, or in commerce. The result was the enlarged exploitation of women as instruments of labor.' The transition towards a knowledge economy more welcoming of women's contributions, as well as the success of the Western democracies in meeting women's political demands and contraceptive needs, had unleashed a revolution within the capitalist order that did not challenge its basic structure.[18] 'These liberating tendencies,' he continued, 'are made part of the reproduction of the established system. They become exchange values, selling the system, and sold by the system. The exchange society comes to completion with the commercialization of sex.'

The sexual revolution he had prophesied in *Eros and Civilization* had arrived, but it was decidedly capitalist in its characteristics.[19]

While Marcuse fretted about the fate of the sexual revolution from his sunny perch at La Jolla, a group of French intellectuals in Paris published a series of books that described with eerie prescience the post-sexual revolution world. In 1970 Pierre Klossowski published *La Monnaie vivante* (*Living Currency*), a brief, dense work of critical theory in which he described how in advanced industrial economies sexuality, intimacy and emotion were becoming increasingly commoditised. This ran counter to the predictions of several generations of socialist intellectuals, who having identified 'erotic enjoyment' as one of 'the most vital human needs . . . decided to extend the "communization" of all goods to the living objects of voluptuous desire'. In reality, Klossowski observed, sex had been privatised, not collectivised, and so it was better to think of modern sexuality in capitalist terms as something that was marketed, bought and sold, something that circulated like currency within society.

Klossowski's ideas were developed by Jean-François Lyotard in his 1974 work, *The Libidinal Economy*. Written during a period of disillusionment with Marxism, *The Libidinal Economy* was a paean to capitalism's immense energies. Far from depending on the repression of sexuality, Lyotard wrote, capitalism was riven with 'libidinal intensities' and was more sexually liberating than socialism. Jean Baudrillard drew upon the work of both Klossowski and Lyotard in the composition of his 1980 book *Seduction*. Baudrillard, like the other two, accepted that the sexual revolution had happened but was essentially capitalist in nature. The exercise of one's sexuality, he reasoned, was now conducted along entre-preneurial lines. 'As a mode sex takes the form of an individual enterprise based on natural energy, to each his desire and may the best man prevail (in matters of pleasure). It is the selfsame form as capital.' What interested Baudrillard was the role seduction would play in this new order. Socialists had imagined that seduc-tion would be abolished along with private property. Now, with the triumph of sexual freedoms alongside the survival of private property, some argued that seduction was an anachronism that would vanish in the face of women's liberation and permissive sexual mores. Not so, Baudrillard declared. 'Revolutions and liber-ations are fragile,' he wrote, 'while seduction is inescapable.' The fallacy common to both notions was that sexuality was simply something that could be transacted. In reality this was not the case. 'To believe in sex's reality and in the possibility of speaking sex without mediation is a delusion.' Outside prostitution, sex cannot simply be purchased. ('In the last instance, a purely sexual statement, a pure demand for sex, is impossible.') In this respect it is different from other 'goods'. Sex occurs between individuals after a period of mediation. Seduction is that mediation. Although

liberated sexuality behaves in all other ways like any other liberalised market, in this respect it is unique. Sexuality responds not
to impersonal market mechanisms, but to what Baudrillard calls
the 'poetry of desire'. By unleashing sexual freedom, the sexual
revolution had greatly multiplied the number of potential sexual
encounters occurring between individuals. In the process, far from
being abolished, seduction became ever more important to the
lives of sexually liberated peoples.[20]

***

In the early 1980s, Michel Houellebecq got a job in the exemplary
profession of the new data-driven economy – he became a
computer engineer. He loathed his profession ('Computers make
me puke. My entire work as a computer expert . . . has no
meaning'), but it did give him an early prospect on the digital
revolution and how vast flows of information, enabled by computers,
would upend society. More unusually, Houellebecq connected this
technological transformation with the sexual revolution. In his
first published work, a long essay on the horror writer H.P.
Lovecraft, Houellebecq wrote scathingly of modern capitalism, in
words that recalled Marx and Engels' famous passage in *The
Communist Manifesto*:

> The reach of liberal capitalism has extended over minds; in step
> and hand with it are mercantilism, publicity, the absurd and
> sneering cult of economic efficiency, the exclusive and immod-
> erate appetite for material riches. Worse still, liberalism has spread
> from the domain of economics to the domain of sexuality. Every
> sentimental fiction has been eradicated. Purity, chastity, fidelity,
> and decency are ridiculous stigmas. The value of a human being
> is measured in terms of his economic efficiency and his erotic
> potential.[21]

This was to be the philosophical launch pad for his first two novels: *Whatever* (1994, published in French with the more explicitly Houellebecqian title *Extension du domaine de la lutte*) and *Atomized* (1998), two books that by virtue of their subject matter and their bitter, brooding tone might be considered as the first two novels of the twenty-first century. Both dealt with the condition of men and women in the post-sexual revolution era and both considered the primacy of seduction in newly sexually liberalised societies. It is not clear whether Houellebecq was influenced by the works of Klossowski, Lyotard or Baudrillard. If he was not, then he arrived at startlingly similar conclusions. *Whatever*, which details the miserable existence of its unnamed narrator, an IT technician with a taste for pessimistic philosophising, contains the canonical passage:

> In societies like ours sex truly represents a second system of differentiation, completely independent of money; and as a system of differentiation it functions just as mercilessly. The effects of these two systems are, furthermore, strictly equivalent. Just like unrestrained economic liberalism, and for similar reasons, sexual liberalism produces phenomena of absolute pauperization. Some men make love every day; others five or six times in their life, or never. Some make love with dozens of women; others with none. It's what's known as 'the law of the market'. In an economic system where unfair dismissal is prohibited, every person more or less manages to find their place. In a sexual system where adultery is prohibited, every person more or less manages to find their bed mate. In a totally liberal economic system certain people accumulate considerable fortunes; others stagnate in unemployment and misery. In a totally liberal sexual system certain people have a varied and exciting erotic life; others are reduced to masturbation and solitude. Economic liberalism is the extension of the domain of the struggle, to all ages and all classes of society. Sexual liberalism is likewise an extension of the domain of the struggle, to all ages and all classes of society.[22]

The sexual revolution, in Houellebecq's account, was not a liberating event along the lines that socialists had predicted. Rather it was the triumph of a certain kind of social libertarianism that in the Sixties and Seventies had been masked by the rhetoric and costume of the hippie movement and other cultural phenomena. By the Eighties and Nineties, flower power and bell bottoms were long gone, but the permissiveness of the sexual revolution had persisted. These were the same decades that saw neoliberalism triumph on both sides of the Atlantic.

For Houellebecq, this was no coincidence, as both valorised selfish individualism. His key insight, however, is that sexuality 'represents a second system of differentiation'. This is the vital distinction. Houellebecq is not arguing that all capitalist societies will be sexually liberal, or *vice versa*. There are several examples – most notably in Scandinavia – of social democracies where sexual freedoms are the norm. Houellebecq's observation is that it has proven easier to manage capitalism than it has sexual liberalism. A socially democratic society is readily conceivable but what he terms a 'sexual social democracy' is not. This is because, although sexuality mimics economics in its fundamental dynamics, it assigns value differently – it is a second system of differentiation. In a society tolerant of unrestrained sexual liberalism, the sexual 'economy' recognises seduction as its only unit of exchange. Market forces, once unleashed, might be reined in with regulation; sexual liberalism, once unleashed, is much harder – perhaps impossible – to bring under control. In this sense, it is easier to imagine the end of capitalism than the end of seduction.

With typical bathos, Houellebecq inserts this insight into a ludicrous conversation between Bruno (one of the antiheroes of *Atomized*) and an old hippie at a New Age summer camp Bruno is attending in the hope of finding a sexual partner. 'You must have a lot of stories about this place when it first opened,' Bruno asks, '– the Seventies, sexual liberation . . .' 'Liberation my arse,' the hippie replies, before going on to disabuse Bruno of the notion that free love meant on-demand sexual pleasure for all. The encounter leaves Bruno with much to consider:

> 'So, what you're saying,' said Bruno thoughtfully, 'is that there never was real sexual liberation – just another form of seduction.'
>
> 'Oh yeah . . .' agreed the hippie, 'there's always been a lot of seduction.'
>
> This didn't exactly sound promising.[23]

For almost three centuries the seduction narrative described sexual relations in societies where sexuality was still shrouded in custom and taboo. In particular, female chastity was prized highly and scrutinised closely. Seduction narratives drew their drama and their moral power from these high stakes. Indeed, the stakes were so high that seduction narratives tended to focus on the susceptibility of women to confusing passions, momentary impulses, and devastating lapses in judgement. There were also counter-narratives, those that argued for the primacy of reason in sexual relations. Hitherto the history of seduction was played out in the rivalry between these two narratives, that of passion and that of reason.

Post-sexual revolution, reason won. Sexuality was essentially rationalised. Long held in suspicion, seduction now triumphed. The seducer was no longer a villain or a transgressive figure but someone at ease in the new sexual order. Houellebecq is profoundly sceptical of this development. His *oeuvre* and his public utterances are filled with suspicion of seduction, something he sees as impure and inauthentic, something that precludes the possibility of love. His sympathy is with those men and women who cannot navigate the new sexual marketplace. His books are, in a sense, anti-seduction narratives, tales of sexual failure. Sometimes this sympathy is expressed with feeling, at others with bitter humour. However it is depicted, Houellebecq understands the experience

CLEMENT KNOX

of sexual inadequacy as among the most potent of the post-sexual revolution era.

In a shocking episode at the end of *Whatever*, when the narrator encourages his hapless colleague Rafael to kill a young couple whom they have followed to an assignation on a beach, sexual inadequacy is portrayed as the source of a murderous rage. The scene looks forward to the subculture of Incels ('Involuntary Celibates') formed online in the early years of the new millennium. Specifically, it forecasts the rage of Elliot Rodger, the twenty-two-year-old man who in 2014 published a 140-page manifesto entitled 'My Twisted World', in which he bemoaned his lack of sexual success shortly before going on a heavily armed rampage at the University of California at Santa Barbara. Rodger's killing spree began with the murder of his male room-mates. Shortly before heading to his principal target on campus, the Delta Delta Delta sorority house, he uploaded a video under the tagline 'Retribution', in which he explained that he was targeting the house because he considered the sorority sisters (none of whom he actually knew) as symbols of a world of sexual freedom from which he was excluded. In the event, nobody answered when he knocked on the door; denied access to the object of his loathing, he began shooting random passers-by. The Isla Vista attack killed seven and wounded fourteen.

In the wake of the killings Rodger became a hero in those pestilential corners of the internet where Incels congregate. Lauded as the 'supreme gentleman' (a term he had used to refer to himself in his video 'Retribution') and as the 'Saint' of the Incel community, his actions inspired a slew of copycat killings. In the years since, dozens of people have been killed in acts of Incel-related terrorism. Alek Minassian, the twenty-five-year-old who drove a van into pedestrians in Toronto in April 2018, praised the 'Supreme Gentleman Elliot Rodger' on Facebook shortly before his attack, and claimed in the same post that his actions were the first strike in an 'Incel Rebellion'. A mass uprising of sexually frustrated men has yet to occur, although the threat posed by these men is being taken seriously. In June 2019, slides were leaked from a briefing for airmen at Andrews Air Force Base in Maryland, outlining Incel ideology and the risks posed by its adherents.[24]

Houellebecq offers no solutions to the problem of Incel rage. From his vantage point, these are merely the inexorable conse-quences of sexual inequality. This does not go far in explaining the particular pathologies of the Incel subculture. Even if one accepts that the phenomenon of sexual loneliness – and indeed, loneliness and isolation of all kinds – has grown in the last fifty years, it cannot be said that this is an experience limited to men. Indeed, feminists were among the first to complain of the coars-ening of gender relations as a consequence of sexual liberation in the 1960s and 1970s. Yet only men are doing the killing. It is probably unnecessary to over-intellectualise the Incel community. It clearly arises out of the intersection of mental illness, social maladjustment and intense misogyny.[25]

There were, however, some men who recognised early on that the male loneliness, frustration and periodic rage produced as a byproduct of sexual liberation was the occasion for entrepreneur-ialism. Among them was a man named Style, who in 2003 took a couple of men to a bar in Belgrade and advised them on how to approach women. One of the group, Sasha ('who was twenty-two, said he had been with one woman, though we suspected he was exaggerating by one'), followed his recommendations and approached a girl, spoke to her, and then got her email address. Sasha was so excited that after they left the bar he skipped down the street. Watching him go, Style waxed sociological: 'A significant percentage of violent crime, from kidnappings to shooting sprees, is the result of frustrated sexual impulses and desires of males. By socialising guys like Sasha, Mystery and I were making the world a safer place.' Style was the *nom de guerre* of writer and journalist

Neil Strauss, and in 2005 he would write a best-seller titled *The Game*.

***

One of the more durable concepts developed by the French critical theorists was that of 'capital'. In 1986, Pierre Bourdieu wrote a landmark paper suggesting that the concept of economic capital could be extended to other, less tangible, forms of wealth. Bourdieu had in mind 'social capital' and 'cultural capital', both of which he identified as 'convertible' into material wealth, power and status. In 2010, sociologist Catherine Hakim extended Bourdieu's idea yet further, suggesting that in addition to these pre-existing categories of capital, individuals also possessed a stock of 'erotic capital'. 'In the sexualized culture of affluent modern societies,' Hakim wrote, 'erotic capital is not only a major asset in mating and marriage markets, but can also be important in labour markets, the media, politics, advertising, sports, the arts, and in everyday social interaction.' In the post-sexual revolution world, seduction was a competence that every individual was incentivised to develop. Unsurprisingly, ever since the early days of the sexual revolution men had been seeking to do just that.[26]

In 1965, a graduate of New York University named Eric Weber found himself working in Manhattan, toiling in a lowly job in the advertising industry and struggling to meet women. 'The Beatles had just hit, the times were changing, sex was in the air,' Weber recalled. 'I'd ride the bus home to Englewood and see the kinds of girls I always thought I should marry. But I was shy.' In the late 1960s Weber decided to take matters into his own hands. He began systematically seeking out how to improve his chances of meeting women. Part of this involved a series of frank interviews with twenty-five unattached young women, from which he tried to derive a set of rules for negotiating the new, unregulated singles scene. What Weber realised in the course of his research was that in his own lifetime the rules for sex, romance and relationships had radically altered. Sex had been decoupled from marriage. Moreover, sex had been decoupled from morality.[27] 'Twenty years ago you would have been right in assuming it was almost impossible to strike up a relationship with a strange girl,' he wrote. 'But . . . that was before the Pill and miniskirts and see-through blouses and the whole sexual revolution type thing.'

In 1970, Weber wrote up his findings in a book entitled *How to Pick Up Girls!*, which he self-published and promoted independently through magazine commercials. Within a decade he had sold 650,000 copies, grossing $5 million.[28]

Weber was the first to realise that, post-sexual revolution, men were desperate to learn how to navigate the currents of sexual liberation. He succeeded in monetising seduction. He did not, however, succeed in creating what in the fullness of time would be known as the 'seduction community'. That dubious honour belonged to Ross Jeffries, a Californian who in 1992 authored the spectacularly obnoxious and singularly successful seduction manual *How to Get the Women You Desire into Bed*. Operating in the very early days of the internet, Jeffries built an online community of several thousand men who followed his advice and shared their own experiences of putting his teachings into practice.

Jeffries very much presented himself as a guru. Whereas Eric Weber had been something of an enthusiastic dilettante, Jeffries offered his work as a coherent system. He brought into his seduction theories other strands of thought, in particular the pseudo-science of Neuro-Linguistic Programming (NLP), thus connecting his twentieth-century body of seduction theory with the old Victorian anxieties of the seducer as hypnotist, as the bridge between the rational and the irrational worlds of the mind.[29]

The conflict between reason and passion, between the rational and the irrational – the debate which has been at the heart of the history of seduction since the Enlightenment – was central to the work of the most influential seduction theorist of the post-sexual revolution era. Well into his twenties, Erik von Markovik was a luckless, lanky young man failing to find love in Toronto. Markovik did possess a passion and ability for magic, and he determined to make a career for himself as an illusionist. Plying his trade in the late 1990s, operating under the pseudonym 'Mystery', he began to develop alongside his stage routine a system of seduction that he came to believe was practically infallible. He called it the Mystery Method. A synthesis of evolutionary psychology, sales and marketing techniques, stagecraft and self-help, the Mystery Method was the most sustained attempt yet to teach men seduction. Although infamous for popularising the technique of 'negging', and widely mocked for its dependence on magic tricks and New Age-inspired personality 'tests', from a historical perspective it was also a milestone in the rationalisation of sexual relations.

For Markovik, seduction is a science. He refers variously to the 'science of courtship' and the 'algorithm for getting women'. There is an algebraic quality to his formulations (A1A2A3 – >C1C2C3 – >S1S2S3) and his scheme is meant to be obeyed, not played around with. 'The game is linear', he intones. Markovik propagated his theories in a self-published book and also in costly private seminars.[30]

In 2002, one of the men who handed over $500 to learn the secrets of seduction was Neil Strauss. Taken under Markovik's wing as a promising young student, Strauss later became a master 'pick-up artist' (PUA) in his own right. By the middle of the first decade of the twenty-first century, the seduction community had swelled to tens of thousands of men communing on online forums and in real life at 'boot camps' run by a multiplying number of seduction coaches. It was this subculture, and his participation in it, that Strauss chronicled in his 2005 book *The Game: Penetrating the Secret Society of Pickup Artists*. The book went on to sell over

2.5 million copies worldwide, propelling Strauss to media celebrity as the face of contemporary seduction. For a brief window between 2005 and 2010, the seduction community enjoyed something of a moment in the sun. There were talk-show appearances, spin-off TV shows, friendly interviews and fascinated profiles. This period of grudging acceptance was not to last.

***

If the seduction community was one product of the sexual revolution, then so too was a feminism that was sceptical of the new permissiveness. Doubts about sexual liberation had been around since the early 1960s. In 1962, in an otherwise upbeat article on the new sexual freedoms enjoyed by young women, Gloria Steinem included the proviso that 'the main trouble with sexually liberating women is that there aren't enough sexually liberated men to go around'.[31] By the time Shere Hite came to publish her epochal feminist survey of female sexuality *The Hite Report* (1976), the mood among radical women had soured. Hite's respondents described the bleak topography of sexual freedom. 'The sexual revolution liberated a vast amount of masculine bestiality and hostility and exploitativeness,' one woman wrote; others described it as 'male-oriented and anti-woman', 'the biggest farce of the century for females', and as 'late sixties bullshit. It was about *male* liberation.'[32] Everyday women recounted what feminist commentators saw abroad in Western culture at large. One feminist study of contemporary film (revealingly entitled *From Reverence to Rape*) listed the various roles women were allowed on screen: 'Whores, quasi-whores, jilted mistresses, emotional cripples, drunks. Daffy ingenues, Lolitas, kooks, sex-starved spinsters, psychotics. Icebergs, zombies, and ballbreakers.'[33]

Throughout the Seventies, the feminist vanguard identified and objected to a coarsening of attitudes towards women advanced under the standard of sexual liberation. The result was a new attitude of suspicion. At the very moment that much of the old apparatus of sexual discipline was being dismantled, radical women were beginning to agitate for the improved regulation of heterosexual relations. Andrea Dworkin and Catharine MacKinnon famously campaigned in favour of anti-pornography ordinances and helped steer feminism back towards an interest in jurisprudence, in particular with respect to the workplace. Both evinced doubts about the very possibility of sexual freedom for women. Dworkin extended this doubt to seduction itself, half-joking that 'seduction is often difficult to distinguish from rape. In seduction, the rapist often bothers to buy a bottle of wine.' One consequence of this new trend in feminist thought was a notable attempt to revive the old seduction laws (see Chapter 5), or some version of them. Jane E. Larson was a professor of law at the University of Wisconsin Law School who spent a good part of her career studying the history of sexual legislation, including the development and repeal of state seduction laws. To her mind, the repeal of the seduction statutes from the 1930s onwards was a consequence of a misplaced faith in sexual liberation. Gains in female educational achievement, economic independence and reproductive control did not obviate the need for protections in other spheres. Permissiveness, she suggested, did not simplify sexual power dynamics: 'Having gained the right to say yes, women found they had lost some of their previous power to say no. The new sexual liberalism was an attack on sexual repression . . . but it was more specifically an attack on women's control over men's sexuality.'[34]

Larson married this insight with her deep knowledge of the law and proposed a feminist defence of the now-defunct seduction statutes. In civil law, the tort of Seduction was part of a larger body of contract law that regulated how individuals dealt with one another. In business it was illegal to engage in 'intentional misrepresentation', that is to wittingly deceive one's counter-party. It was perverse, Larson argued, to allow this principle to apply to some of the blandest interactions between corporate entities but not extend it to the most intimate relations between individuals. She proposed a modern tort of Sexual Fraud that would grant similar protection to women who consented to sex under false pretences. The proposed law would provide a way out of a binary view of the sexual landscape that offered women the choice between 'Orwellian oppression and the Hobbesian jungle'.[35]

In the early 1990s Larson launched a brief and ill-fated campaign to introduce these laws. She soon discovered that there was little public appetite for a bold legislative attempt to regulate sex and courtship. In retrospect the Nineties constituted a period of ideological and institutional retrenchment, a hiatus between two great waves of feminist activism. Circa 2010, feminism and feminists burst back into public discourse. Rallying around an emergent discourse that identified the existence of 'rape culture' on college campuses and in society at large, a new generation of activists began to challenge sexual norms. The activities of the Seduction Community did not escape their attention. Self-identified pick-up artists were soon enveloped by the new critique and confronted online and in person. This was a conflict waged largely outside the public eye, until in 2014 it was thrust into the news cycle.

In November 2014, Julien Blanc was travelling in Australia for business when a hashtag, #TakeDownJulienBlanc, started circulating, first in American activist circles, then across the world. In Melbourne, an event held by his company attracted nine hundred protesters – some of them violent – and had to be cancelled. Under pressure from campaigners, businesses started to refuse to serve him or his associates, websites took down all reference to his events and venues cancelled his reservations. On 5 November, barely a week after he had entered the country, an online petition was set up called 'Cancel Julien Blanc's Visa'. It was addressed to Scott Morrison, an MP and Minister of Immigration and Border Protection, and sought the immediate withdrawal of Blanc's right to be in the country.

The next day the petition's aim was fulfilled. The Australian authorities revoked Blanc's visa and by 7 November he had been flown out of the country. Nor was this the end of Blanc's woes. The tale of his unceremonious eviction from Australia was now a global news story. Activists all over the world sought to prevent him from entering other countries. Similar petitions began to circulate in Japan, Canada, Argentina, Iceland, Ireland, Germany, Denmark, Sweden and New Zealand. Some of these met with success: Blanc was denied entry to Singapore and the United Kingdom and was told by the Brazilian and South Korean authorities that they would deny him a visa were he to apply for one. In a matter of weeks he had become an international pariah. *Time* magazine asked: 'Is Julien Blanc the most hated man in the world?'

Blanc was a seduction 'coach' associated with a company named Real Social Dynamics (RSD), referenced in *The Game*, one of a new ecosystem of seduction schools that had come into being over the previous decade. RSD was known for its hyperactive tactics and brash methodology, which bordered on harassment and assault. The immediate cause of the campaign against Blanc was the circulation of a video of him in Tokyo, where he was shown grabbing and pushing women and in one instance violently handling a woman's head. In the same period, Blanc had been bragging on social media about the effectiveness of his aggressive and manipulative techniques.

The global media storm surrounding his Tokyo misdemeanours and subsequent expulsion from Australia was the occasion for a collision between a revitalised feminism and a complacent seduction community. Feminism won. The episode marked the end of the era of the pick-up artists' social acceptability. The attitude towards them shifted from tolerance to disgust. Many seduction 'professionals' closed their businesses or rebranded as conventional self-help authors, life coaches and charisma experts. The community's final demise was signalled by Neil Strauss's disavowal of the theory and practice of seduction in a series of interviews given in 2015 to mark the tenth anniversary of the publication of *The Game*. In *The Atlantic*, Strauss characterised the PUAs' methods, the same ones he had, a decade before, practised and popularised, as 'objectifying and horrifying'.[36] In *The Guardian* he further distanced himself from the movement:

'[*The Game*] was really a book about scared men who were afraid of women. But then it became a part of the culture. And it became a reason for women to be afraid of guys.' He's sad about that. 'It was never meant to be an advocacy of a lifestyle, even though it's come to symbolise one.'[37]

Ironically, at the very same time as the seduction community was being exiled from polite society, another dehumanising, more Houellebecqian trend in seduction was rising to dominance.

***

In *Whatever*, Houellebecq had imagined a world where 'every human relationship is *reduced* to an exchange of information'.[38] A world where humans were reduced to data, managed and studied by computers. In the two decades since his novel's publication, this prediction has been vindicated in the growth and social acceptance of online and app-enabled dating. In 1995, only 2 per cent of couples met online. By 2017, 39 per cent of couples were first connected through the internet and as many as 20 per cent of newlyweds had first interacted in cyberspace.[39] Tellingly, the gains made by online dating websites and apps have been made at the expense of more traditional, communitarian ways of finding love. As late as 2000, about a quarter of couples met through family, neighbours, or in church. A decade later this number had plunged to 10 per cent, while online dating had soared in popularity.[40]

Dating apps and websites have created a genuine libidinal economy. They are marketplaces for desire where attractiveness is the dominant value, expressed in a currency of likes, swipes and messages. Houellebecq had surmised in *Whatever* that unregulated sexual markets would create huge disparities in sexual outcomes. This is a view that has been utterly vindicated online. On dating apps and websites, inequality is ubiquitous. Data for 2017 from the dating app Hinge showed that the top 1 per cent of men using the app received 16.4 per cent of all messages; the top 1 per cent of women received 11.2 per cent of all messages. To put these figures in context, consider how they would translate into economic measures of income inequality, typically measured by a Gini coefficient whereby 0 is perfect equality and 1 is perfect inequality. On this basis, the 'economy' of Hinge for women has a Gini coefficient of 0.376, and for men a Gini coefficient of 0.542. In the real world the Gini coefficient for OECD-EU nations on average is approximately 0.3. In other words, at a time of yawning economic inequality, hundreds of thousands of people are looking for love on online platforms whose dynamics are even more unequal than those they are subject to in their everyday lives.[41]

On the surface it looks as if men have a harder time online than women. The data points towards a more complex set of circumstances. Men and women seem to interact differently online. On Tinder, one study found that men typically 'like' more women but engage less when they match. In contrast, women on Tinder 'like' fewer men but are more likely to engage when they match.[42] Moreover, attractiveness is judged differently by men and women. Data from OkCupid found that women are far harsher on men than *vice versa*. On a 1 to 5 scale of attractiveness, the average man judges the average woman to be a 3.0; the average woman judges the average man to be a 2.0.[43] The obverse of this phenomenon is that female judgements of male attractiveness have less variance, whereas male judgements of female attractiveness run the gamut from 0 (perfectly ugly) to 5 (perfectly attractive). This matters, because across all dating apps and websites there is evidence that both men and women are aspirational in their pursuit of an attractive partner. On OkCupid it was estimated that the average man sought a partner 17 per cent more attractive than himself, while the average woman sought a partner only 10 per cent more attractive than herself. Another cross-platform study found that these figures were even higher: 26 per cent for men and 23 per cent for women.[44] This leads to the perverse outcome whereby at the extremes the most attractive men are getting more messages than the most attractive women, while on average women are more forgiving in terms of looks, and message men they deem to be of below-average attractiveness at far higher levels than they do men who they deem to be of above-average attractiveness. Men act differently, increasing their message flow in proportion to their judgement of the attractiveness of the woman in question.[45]

Furthermore, these inequalities are exacerbated by the relative weight given on individual profiles to visual information. When OkCupid experimented with changing the format of dating profiles such that images of each individual came to dominate the screen – at the expense of non-visual written information – then the most attractive people saw their message inflow increase by up to 75 per cent, while the least attractive people saw their already meagre message count decrease by 5–10 per cent. 'All those extra pixels allowed the pretty faces to outshine the others all the more,' OkCupid founder Christian Rudder wrote of this phenomenon, 'the rich got richer.'[46]

However the data is interpreted, it is clear that online dating rewards the beautiful and excludes the less desirable. The result is the creation of a Houellebecqian residuum of undesired and uncontacted people, a struggling middle class of middling-looking individuals just getting along, and a minority of ultra-desirable men and women under virtual siege from suitors. In 2014, *New York Magazine* profiled some of these ultra-desirable individuals by reaching out to the four most contacted OkCupid profiles in New York City. The article detailed lives of unimaginable sexual opportunity. The most contacted woman was receiving 245 messages a week. The most contacted man revealed that he was using two different dating apps and that the week before he had matched with 890 women on Tinder.[47] This theme of superabundance for an attractive minority is replicated across platforms and across studies. A 2018 study of online dating in four major North American cities identified one woman in New York who was receiving messages in such quantity that it amounted to a single message received every half hour, day and night, for an entire month.[48]

Attractiveness is not the only driver of sexual inequality on online platforms. Age is a major determinant of message traffic and acts differently for men and women – with women typically experiencing a drastic reduction of interest from men as they age, while interest in men tends to rise into their forties. Race is another factor: numerous studies show that online dating has created a racial hierarchy of attractiveness.[49] What is most wretched about the creation of these new, uncomfortable dynamics is that they seem to be a product of the particular experience of being online. Based on the data available, Christian Rudder found that on OkCupid people seemed to be operating from certain assumptions and preferences that did not reflect how they behaved in the real world. 'In short,' he wrote, 'people appear to be heavily preselecting online for something that, once they sit down in person, doesn't seem important to them.' If sexual inequality does not describe our past, then given the growing pervasiveness of online dating, it likely describes our future.[50]

Yet even this is not the whole story. Increasingly, the unequal dynamics of online dating do not simply resemble the unequal dynamics of advanced economies – they actively feed into one another. This is because the majority of the most popular dating apps are either subscription services, 'freemium' services, or some mixture of the two. Raw desirability – what Hakim called erotic capital – is no longer enough. Actual capital – money – is needed to have a hope of finding love online. The pay-to-play aspects of online dating arise out of the simple need for the companies hosting the platform to turn a profit. This is not in itself bad. But the mechanics of *how* they monetise online romance are often overlooked. This is a shame because it reveals a great deal about the workings of modern love. To start with, like much of the tech sector, the online dating world is highly concentrated. One company, Match Group, owns forty-five different platforms, grossing close to two billion dollars in revenues each year. Almost half of those revenues come from a single product: Tinder.[51]

When Tinder shot to popularity in 2014, much of its appeal derived from its democratic architecture: the app was free to download and all the users were simply thrown together and left to choose among themselves who they engaged with. Over the years, Tinder has become noticeably less open. The rise of paid subscription services like Tinder Premium and Tinder Gold, as well as the introduction and heavy promotion of in-app purchases to improve the chances of matching, have reduced the viability of simply using the app for free. The enhanced user experience given to those who pay for Tinder has come at the expense of those who do not. In the process, it has been revealed that the algorithms that run Tinder are not intended to be democratic at all. By way of example: one of the most popular products on Tinder is 'Boost', a feature that promotes the profile of the person who purchases it. Tinder claims that people who buy Boost will get tenfold exposure for half an hour when there is peak traffic on the app. Boost works because Tinder is essentially a long line of profiles queuing up to meet each other. Customers who use Boost essentially cut in front of other profiles. In 2019, Tinder introduced 'Super Boost', a product that would function the same way, allowing users, in the words of the company, to 'cut to the front and be seen by up to 100x more potential matches'. Tinder boasts that 'Super Boost' is 'the ultimate Tinder hack', essentially acknowledging that the Tinder 'economy' is rigged in favour of those willing to pay to get ahead. The real-world equivalent would be a nightclub filling up with wealthy individuals who have bribed the doormen for entry while a long, static queue builds up outside.[52]

The phenomenon is not limited to Tinder. Almost all online dating companies offer products whose workings basically admit to the inequitable premise of the services they provide. The prices of these services vary. Depending on how long a user commits to, a subscription could cost between $10 and $30 per month. Likewise, onetime app purchases can cost between $5 and $30. These are not huge amounts, but the target market tends to be younger and hence lower-income individuals. Furthermore, prices can be variable. Age and location (and, it is rumoured, attractiveness) can impact the cost of both subscriptions and app purchases. Paradoxically, the increasing popularity of these products is testament not to the merit of any one dating platform but to their failings. However, because they enjoy oligopolistic status, the companies behind the apps can afford to keep pushing paid products while systematically undermining the user experience of those who refuse to buy in.

This might matter less if the product being sold by these companies was not love. The financial statements of Match Group are filled with cynicism. Under 'Risk Factors' in the annual report, the accountants wring their hands about the possibility of 'a

meaningful migration of our user base from our higher monetizing dating products to our lower monetizing dating products
[which would] adversely affect our business, financial condition
and results of operations'. Meanwhile, in the quarterly investor
presentation, the marketing team trumpets the new Hinge brand
campaign 'resonating with users and the press'. Its slogan:
'Designed to be Deleted'.[53]

Online dating is the logical end result of a sexual revolution
more informed by liberalism than liberation. Technology has
merely better enabled an impulse unleashed many decades ago.
Writing in *Seduction*, Baudrillard suggested that:

> The sexual jurisdiction is but a fantastic extension of the common-
> place ideal of private-property, where everyone is assigned a certain
> amount of capital to manage: a psychic capital, a libidinal, sexual
> or unconscious capital, for which each person will have to answer
> individually, under the sign of his or her own liberation.[54]

This seems to capture the reality of contemporary online dating.
It is a commonplace to state that dating is now a kind of work, a
form of labour. In her 2016 book *Labor of Love: The Invention of
Dating*, Moira Weigel suggested that the work of online dating
resembled that of the unpaid internship. This, it seems now, does
not capture the extent to which online dating requires investment
– of time, money, emotion and erotic capital. The user of a dating
app or website is engaged in the work of investment rather than
the work of labour and this work is performed 'under the sign of
his or her own liberation'. In this sense, the hundreds of thousands
of online daters engaged in daily speculation on themselves are a
kind of fractal reflection of the entrepreneurial Silicon Valley business culture that gave rise to the dating apps and websites that
host them. The sexual revolution has turned its grandchildren into
startups. And most startups fail.

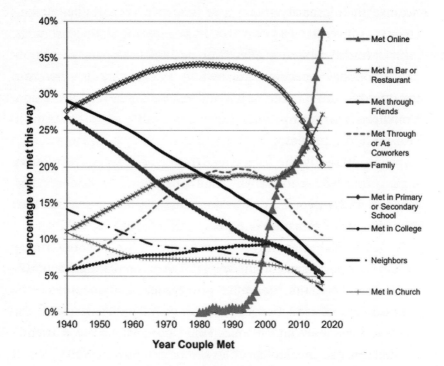

The triumph of online dating.

The general acceptance of online dating stands in stark contrast to the widespread revulsion at the seduction community. An oddity, for both are part of the same post-sexual revolution phenomenon of the rationalisation of sexual relations. Erik von Markovik dreamt of creating an 'algorithm for getting women'; the immensely profitable corporations that own and operate the online dating platforms have in their own way realised that dream, only at the level of populations rather than individuals. If the true legacy of the sexual revolution is sexual liberation with capitalist characteristics, then OkCupid, Tinder and all the other dating companies are its real beneficiaries. In the tug-of-war between reason and passion that has been the overriding feature of the history of seduction, reason, for now, seems to have won. Modern Westerners, as Houellebecq recognised earlier than most, live lonely, diminished lives in part because their capacity to forge and sustain human connections enjoys an inverse relationship to their capacity to internalise the logic of liberal capitalism. The decrepitude of the average individual's emotional vocabulary and sentimental universe is a poignant testament to this. 'Tenderness is a deeper instinct than seduction,' Houellebecq writes in *Atomized*, 'which is why it is so difficult to give up hope.' Increasingly, this small hope has been surrendered to profit-minded tech companies. The desocialisation of Western nations proceeds apace, while at the same time hundreds of thousands of lonely people flock to online dating services which treat their dreams of romantic happiness with spectacular venality.

At least, such were my own thoughts upon encountering a would-be pick-up artist in the wild. It was in London, one Saturday in January 2016, not long after Neil Strauss had renounced the methodology of seduction that he had once been a master of. The day had been grey and dismal. I had been invited to a friend's birthday drinks in Clapham that evening. Shortly before I left, it began raining torrentially. The rain stopped not long before I arrived. Water covered every surface, including the awnings and the tables in the forecourt of the pub where we were meeting, as well as the short, steep stone steps that led up to its front door. Inside, it was quiet on account of the rain. There were a few couples having dinner and a few small groups of friends. The group I joined was by far the largest and most boisterous in the place. I went to get a drink. Waiting for my order I noticed a boy – he could not have been much more than twenty-two – standing alone at the bar a few metres down from me.

Something about his pose caught my eye. He looked hunted. He held his pint glass close to his chin in between sips, the arm holding it kept tight against his chest, the other thrust into his jean pockets. His eyes moved nervously around. Occasionally he would turn to survey the room in a single, sweeping, anxious movement before turning back to the bar. On the other side, two barmen were drying glasses and chatting casually, their relaxed informality a counterpoint to his clearly agitated state. He was of average height and slight build, his upper half bulked out by a beige fatigue jacket and beneath that a blue jumper. He had dark brown hair in a slightly mussed side parting. He had soft eyes, gentle features. He looked like the kind of boy whose mother worries about him; indeed, it seemed that if his mother no longer dressed him, then the ghost of her past purchases still haunted his wardrobe. He was quite good looking, or would have been if he was not in a state of such obvious discomfort. My drink arrived; I returned to the group.

Some time later the party decamped to the beer garden out front so the smokers could smoke. Outside it was dark, cold and wet. The streetlights made moons on the pools of rainwater that now sat atop all the tables and benches. We huddled at a row of tables sheltered by an awning and warmed by a single patio heater that deactivated every couple of minutes. After a period, I went back inside to get another drink, mindful as I went of the perfectly slick steps at the entrance. I was at the bar again. The boy was no longer there. I assumed he had left, as he had arrived, alone.

I got my drink, and turned and began to walk the ten metres or so from the bar to the front door. It was then that I saw him. Just to the right of the door was a low, oblong table with two velveteen pouffes on either side and two candles in the middle. The light was particularly dim in this portion of the room and the candlelight moved atmospherically across his face, and across that of the pretty brunette now sitting opposite him. I can see the tableau in my mind: she leans forward, her right hand resting on her face, her lips apart in anticipation; there are four cards on the table and his hand is poised over one of them, but his eyes are looking up at her through his lashes with something like happiness.

I experienced a shock of recognition. This was Mystery Method in action before me.

My interests being what they are, I was now in a heartbreaking position. I was too committed to turn back to the bar and could hardly stop and stare from the middle of the room. Instead, I decelerated in order to soak in as much of the scene as possible before I was obliged to exit. Over at the table his little magic trick was arriving at its conclusion. He turned over the final card and said something in a low voice. Both hands flew to her face. She squealed and rocked back with glee. He smiled and made some modest motion with his hands, but I could see that he was basking in the glow of his success.

I was now only three metres or so from the door. One of the maxims of Mystery Method is that 'seldom will you see women of beauty alone' in a bar, or anywhere else. It occurred to me at this point that the same was likely true of this girl. Not many people go to bars alone on a Saturday night, with the exception of the guy she was now talking to. Then I noticed at a table against the wall just in front of the door a group of three, one blonde girl and two well-built men. One of them had his back to the wall and was staring with undisguised disdain at the aftermath of a card trick. His friend was hunched over the table. 'It's this thing from a book,' he said to the girl, 'so you can trick a girl into bed.' She looked utterly distraught at the news, one hand covering her mouth in horror. She half stood up in her seat, her eyes searching for her friend's attention.

I stepped outside and went back to my seat beneath the awning. Across the empty beer garden, I had a view of the front door. Barely a minute later he emerged. Defeat was stamped all over his face. He looked above at the night sky and turned his jacket collar up to the cold. He took a step down. The rain and the smooth stone collaborated in his humiliation. He slipped and collapsed down the steps onto the asphalt. Instinct saved his face from harm, but he landed hard on his forearms. He was still for a moment on the floor. Then he stood up and checked to see if anyone had seen him fall. Nobody on my table seemed to have noticed. He dusted himself down, put his hands in his jacket pockets and walked away into the night.

AFTERWORD

This book was commissioned in August 2017. In October of the same year the *New Yorker* and the *New York Times* published a series of articles detailing a long list of sexual assault allegations against film producer Harvey Weinstein. In the wake of the revelations, survivors of sexual assault began to share their stories on social media under the hashtag #MeToo. This explosion of storytelling about sexual assault – which in most (but not all) cases involved a female accuser and a male culprit – sparked a vigorous transatlantic debate about sexual mores that continues to elicit comment and generate controversy. Although this book was conceived of, planned and begun before the advent of the #MeToo era, it was largely written and researched within it and will doubtless be read by some against the background of the impassioned debates of the past few years.

It is too soon to tell whether the #MeToo era is at its beginning, middle or end. Nor can we know what its ultimate historical significance will be. Writing this book against the backdrop of blossoming scandal has been a challenge, though still an enjoyable challenge, but it has had the advantage of proving beyond doubt the basic contention of this book, namely that seduction narratives are very powerful things.

We began with Francis Charteris; we end with Harvey Weinstein. In between we have witnessed Casanova's morally questionable sexual escapades, we have heard denunciations of male rapacity from Laetitia Pilkington, Mary Wollstonecraft and Claire Clairmont, we have followed the decades-long struggle to secure legal protections for women, we have seen how sexual liberation was challenged by feminists wary of the consequences of unilaterally removing controls on male sexuality. All this resonates in the #MeToo era. The phrase that has surfaced again and again in my mind as the disclosures and dismissals have come one after the other was uttered by Pamela Andrews, the heroine of Samuel Richardson's classic novel of seduction: 'And pray, said I, walking on, how came I to be his Property? What Right has he in me, but such as a thief may plead to stolen Goods?' Pamela's protest has been the protest of the past few years, a protest not only at the abuse and assault survivors have endured but at the presumption and the entitlement of their abusers and assaulters. It is a summons for social and legal intervention as well as a demand for a change in norms and a reformation of male sexual manners.

All of which raises an obvious objection: what does any of this have to do with seduction? What do allegations of abuse, assault and rape have to do with matters of love, courtship and consensual sex? The trajectory of the #MeToo era answers its own question. Four months after the allegations against Harvey Weinstein became public, media attention alighted on a very different episode of alleged sexual misconduct. In January 2018, Babe.net published the account of a date that had taken place the previous September in Manhattan between a twenty-three-year-old woman and celebrity comedian Aziz Ansari. The woman, identified under the pseudonym 'Grace' (an incidental echo of the allegorical names favoured for the heroines of eighteenth-century seduction narratives), painted a lurid account of an innocent evening turned into an ordeal of unwanted advances that ended in her weeping in her Uber home. Once public, the episode became a flashpoint in the unrolling #MeToo moment. But whereas the response to the Weinstein allegations was unanimous revulsion and condemnation, reactions to the allegation against Ansari were divided. For Grace's partisans, it was readily apparent that her story belonged in the #MeToo pantheon alongside the criminal allegations made against Weinstein and others. Yet a number of prominent dissenting feminist voices argued that not only was her experience not comparable to serious charges of sexual assault, but that furthermore nothing had happened that night with Ansari that could credibly be understood as sexual impropriety. In the febrile atmosphere of the time, the two sets of positions were quickly (and crudely) characterised as a conflict between those who were looking to bravely push the nascent #MeToo movement into new territory and those who were arguing that #MeToo had gone too far. What was overlooked was that these two positions actually conformed to the centuries-old narrative structures discussed in this book. For some, it was obvious that a continuum existed between allegations of sexual assault (Weinstein) and a bad date (Ansari). For others, it was equally obvious that the episodes were incomparable. For one group, the distance between Weinstein's accusers and Grace was only the distance between *Pamela* and *Clarissa*. For the other group, Grace and Ansari were both knowing participants in a liberalised sexual marketplace.

This polarity in feminist responses to the #MeToo movement is often described as generational. An older group of feminists associated with the activism, ambitions and experiences of the Sixties, Seventies and Eighties is held in uniform and imaginary opposition to a new cohort of millennial feminists shaped by a separate set of circumstances and sharpened by new intellectual influences. This mothers-and-daughters narrative holds an obvious appeal. By declaring that things were that way then and they will be this way now, we can take comfort in the idea that progress is being made.

The history of seduction suggests otherwise. The contemporary divide closely mirrors the divide between the flappers and the women of the WCTU. It is the same fissure that we observed within Mary Wollstonecraft's thought. It recalls the literary differences between Samuel Richardson and Henry Fielding in Georgian London. It is a divide larger than #MeToo, and it predates modern feminism. It is a question grounded in classic Enlightenment debates over the nature of the mind – whether we are moved more by reason or by the passions, whether we are rational agents or creatures vulnerable to error, deceit and suasion – that have found expression in seduction narratives since the birth of modernity. Zooming out from individual episodes, we can see that the broad outlines of contemporary debates map on to older discussions described in the earlier chapters of this book. This is because the heart of the matter is an irresolvable conflict over first principles. We can allow that progress may occur on a material basis – women are clearly better off in 2020 than they were in 1700 – while accepting that progress in manners and mores is altogether harder to observe, or even to agree upon.

Even the briefest survey of recent history confirms this. It is important to remember that the decade that preceded the #MeToo movement was one that saw Neil Strauss, author of *The Game*, welcomed on late-night talk shows and feted at the Oxford Union, his mentor Mystery given his own reality TV show, *The Pickup Artist*, on VH1, *Fifty Shades of Grey* become the standout publishing phenomenon of the twenty-first century, and films like *Hitch*, *Wedding Crashers* and *Crazy Stupid Love* become pop-cultural touchstones. The point is that sexual culture can change very quickly. And there is no reason why it might not change again.

In the meantime, we have to contend with the present. And the present is scathing of the permissive sexual culture of their parents' and grandparents' generation. One area where this is apparent is in the renewed interest in using legal and bureaucratic devices to shape sexual behaviour. In the Sixties and Seventies sexual discipline was fought against by student radicals and activist judges.

On campuses on both sides of the Atlantic, female students fought successfully to dismantle systems of sexual control that they regarded as patronising and coercive. In America, the once formidable body of seduction law (discussed in Chapter 5) was torn down as courts ruled that it no longer reflected prevailing cultural norms. As the judges presiding over *Breece v. Jett*, a seduction suit heard in a Missouri courtroom in 1977, concluded:

> The woman of today is not the woman of yesteryear. She has a new-found freedom. The modern adult woman is sophisticated and mature. The former notion that women belong to the weaker sex has long been abandoned. The modern woman is not easily 'beguiled' and does not easily fall to the 'wiles' of man. Women desire and should be held to a reasonable responsibility.[1]

This position meets with suspicion in the #MeToo era, in part because some of the more egregious accused have sought to defend themselves by reference to the carefree mores of a bygone era. 'I came of age in the 60s and 70s,' Harvey Weinstein pleaded in a statement made in response to the allegations against him, 'when all the rules about behavior and workplaces were different. That was the culture then.' Of course, Weinstein is not the representative figure of the ethos of sexual liberation. But that he believed he could retreat into a *Mad Men*-esque popular conception of the era as an explanation for his behaviour is indicative of the ambiguous legacy of the sexual revolution. What was once regarded as a period of carefree sexual adventuring is now subjected to revisionist scrutiny. One area where this is apparent is in the discussion surrounding the existence or otherwise of the so-called 'sex recession'. When in 2019 *The Economist* posited that the decline in sexual activity could be attributed to 'economics, technology, and female empowerment', Congresswoman Alexandria Ocasio-Cortez shot back that 'if you think your "celibacy" is due to "female under pressure from activists some nations have used immigration laws to prevent the entry or expedite the departure of those deemed guilty of sexual misconduct. Another, more popular legal arena has been consent law. In Chapter 5 we saw how American seduction laws had their origins in foundational campaigns, spearheaded by Frances Willard, to raise the age of sexual consent. Under the Obama administration, activists operating with the rhetorical support of the White House and the bureaucratic support of the Department of Education sought to change the definition of consent, with an end of combating the widely discussed epidemic of sexual assault on college campuses. Rather than increase the age of consent, recent campaigns have sought to change the standard of consent from 'No Means No' to 'Yes Means Yes'. This shift has been portrayed as one broadly in line with the spirit of sexual liberation – hence the emphasis on 'enthusiastic consent' between willing and presumably joyful partners – but the tenor of the campaign has sometimes recalled the fearful language of the WCTU. Writing in support of California's recently passed 'Yes Means Yes' law in 2014, left-wing pundit Ezra Klein argued that the American left should support the new law not because it was a good law but because it was a bad one. 'If the Yes Means Yes law is taken even remotely seriously,' Klein wrote, 'it will settle like a cold winter on college campuses, throwing everyday sexual practice into doubt and creating a haze of fear and confusion over what counts as consent. This is the case against it, and also the case for it.'[3]

In 2014 Klein welcomed the attempt 'to change, through brute legislative force, the most private and intimate of adult acts'. After 2017, many people expected courts to prosecute sexual assault cases energetically. The legal realities suggest that the justice many seek will not come from the courts. The California law praised by Klein only covered the post-secondary schools that were the recipient of state money for student financial aid.[4] Jeannie Suk Gersen, a law professor at Harvard University, has cautioned that many of the legal cases sprouting as a result of #MeToo allegations 'will not end in legal vindication' because 'The alleged behavior doesn't match legal definitions, or because of statutes of limitations, or insufficient evidence, or questionable witnesses, or police misconduct, or prosecutorial overreach, or doubtful juries – in short, for all the reasons that cases can fall apart when subjected to scrutiny in court.'[5]

Extensive legal innovation is unlikely. We are not going to see contemporary equivalents of the old state seduction laws or the federal Mann Act emerge as a response to #MeToo. However, this does not mean that action will not be taken in response to the outrage of recent years – simply that it will take a different form. Elsewhere, Jeannie Suk Gersen has chronicled the rise of what she and her co-author Jacob Gersen describe as 'the Sex Bureaucracy', a cohort of administrators in American universities whose job it is to regulate sexual conduct on campus and promulgate guidelines for sexual interactions between students. The origins of the Sex Bureaucracy lie in the 1970s. In 1972 the United States Congress passed Title IX, a federal civil rights law intended to combat gender discrimination in higher education. Title IX has had a number of consequences, among them the creation of a caste of university employees tasked with ensuring that their institutions do not violate Title IX requirements in their handling (or mishandling) of sexual assault allegations on campus. In the hands of university administrators, who are themselves under pressure to ensure compliance with the most expansive readings of the law, Title IX has morphed into a wide-ranging attempt to police sexual activity on American campuses.

There are several historical ironies in play here. The first is that the pressure to create stronger codes of sexual conduct is coming from below, from the student body, rather than from above. As Laura Kipnis has observed: 'A previous generation of student activists fought against the *in loco parentis* policies of universities;

today's students are fighting to extend them.' The second is that students at American universities now abide by codes of conduct closer in spirit to the seduction legislation that governed the private lives of their great-grandparents and great-great-grandparents than to the permissive sexual culture of their grandparents and parents. Noting that universities now 'regulate conduct traditionally in the domain of morals regulation', Gersen and Suk Gersen go on to write that university consent guidelines 'are how-to's for sexual arousal, proposition, and seduction – not just consent or agreement to have sex'. The final irony is that these sexual regulations, although originating in federal law, are far more severe than any legal statute on the books at a state or federal level. Consequently, for four years while at college, typically between the ages of eighteen and twenty-two, American undergraduates will be held to a codified standard of behaviour far more stringent than any they will face once they leave campus upon graduation.[6]

Although that may be changing. #MeToo arose out of allegations about sexual impropriety in the workplace. Inevitably, there has been pressure on corporations – especially those caught up in the #MeToo allegations – to introduce new policies designed to tackle sexual harassment and misconduct in their offices. Just as in the university system, these new policies have been created, codified and promulgated by a sex bureaucracy operating extra-legally but with considerable power over the lives of the employees they oversee. The content of these new policies varies. At the extreme, employers have introduced rules that forbid employees to hug, make eye contact for five seconds or longer, or ask for one another's phone numbers. What is striking about these new guidelines is that they are grounded in the assumption that their subjects (adult employees with advanced degrees) are *either* intensely psychologically vulnerable *or* lustful predators, and then proceed to assume that all the potential human interactions that arise within the workplace environment can be rationally managed by bureaucratic fiat. This is not to deny that systematic and widespread predation has not been uncovered, much less that it should not be taken extremely seriously. It is simply to observe that there is a paradox present in the overarching narrative – a paradox that recalls the centuries-old Enlightenment debate as to whether we are rational or passionate beings.[7]

Support for a more vigorous response to #MeToo allegations and the environments that gave rise to them cuts across political divides. There are those on the left, the right, and in the centre, who will find merit in the existence and the activities of the sex bureaucracy. There will also be those who look for the introduction of new legal measures to combat sexual assault in their societies. Ultimately, individuals will have to decide for themselves what legal and bureaucratic innovations – if any – are called for in response to #MeToo. But those who do seek the empowerment of courts and bureaucracies will have to reckon with the long history of racialised policy-making in the realm of sexual conduct. And there are already signs of a renewal of the kind of racial-sexual fears described in Chapters 5 and 6 of this book.

In Europe, nationalist populist political parties have used sexual assault allegations against members of immigrant communities to advance their electoral agendas. In Sweden, a country at the forefront of progressive legislation on matters like consent, assault and harassment, this has led to peculiar dynamics. In 2013, activists successfully sought changes to how the authorities recorded and handled sexual crimes. This led, as had been expected, to a rise in the number of reported sexual crimes. The Swedish Democrats (a nationalist populist party) then claimed that this rise in sexual criminality was due to the influx of immigrants and asylum seekers in the same period of time. Their share of the vote rose from 5 per cent in 2010 to 17.5 per cent in 2018. The Swedish establishment is understandably eager to play down the issue, but is caught between campaigning pressure from the activist left for more robust sexual offence laws and the willingness of the populist right to take advantage of the statistical trends that result from the introduction of those laws. Moreover, because the authorities do not collect racial data in connection with reported sexual offences, there is no way of establishing the truth.[8]

The same risks are present in America. It is an axiom of anti-racist thought and scholarship that systemic racism finds expression in bad law.[9] As discussed in Chapter 5, this was true in the nineteenth and twentieth centuries, where loosely worded seduction statutes were used as vehicles for racial persecution. It is not hard to see how the sex bureaucracy might well replicate the wrongs of the past. This is not a matter of intentions but of consequences. One need not believe that individual university administrators are racist to recognise that the system they preside over might facilitate racist outcomes. The reality is that it already does. Gersen and Suk Gersen write that the sex bureaucracy's real-world functioning 'creates a significant risk of precriminalizing minority men'. Their concerns have been echoed by civil rights activists.[10] In America, as in Sweden, advocacy is complicated by the nature of the systems in place. The quasi-legal processes set up to rule on cases of sexual assault on American college campuses are notoriously opaque. Ezra Klein may have welcomed the 'haze of fear and confusion' generated by 'terrible law' but that haze has settled, perhaps predictably, on vulnerable students of minority background. Similarly, although there is plenty of anecdotal evidence of racial bias at work in the Title IX-mandated sexual regime on American campuses, because they do not report racial data there is no way of knowing the facts. When racial data has been released, it has confirmed the worst fears of those sceptical of the workings of the sex bureaucracy. In 2014 Colgate University, a private liberal arts college in upstate New York, made public the relevant data for the academic year 2013–14. It revealed that although black male students formed 4.2 per cent of the student body, they were accused of 50 per cent of the sexual offences reported to the university.[11]

There are no easy solutions. There are limits, also, to the usefulness of history as a guide to how to navigate the present. Much about the present has no clear antecedent. Likewise, much about the past no longer applies. When the seduction narrative was born in the eighteenth century, certain things were taken for granted. First, there was a thriving sentimental culture that valorised rich emotional experiences. To be passionate and sensible (in the eighteenth-century meaning of the word) were signs of sophistication and refinement – even of fashion. There were plenty of satires of the culture of sensibility, and there was plenty of poor behaviour despite its existence. Still, when we read the writings of Mary Wollstonecraft or Mary Shelley, highly intelligent women who were capable of writing unselfconsciously, lyrically and at length about their emotional lives, we are getting a glimpse of a portion of the emotional spectrum that is no longer visible to us. This matters, because it was self-evident to many Georgians that morality arose out of humans' emotional experiences, not from their reasoning faculties. It was Adam Smith – no swooning *ingénu* he – who declared it 'altogether absurd and unintelligible to suppose that the first perceptions of right and wrong can be derived from Reason'. Instead it was 'immediate sense and feeling', refined into sentiments, that provided the foundations for morality. #MeToo is many things, but it is surely evidence of a major breakdown in the capacity to empathise, to relate, to feel. We should not, however, hold out too much hope for the renewal of sentimental culture in an age where the median number of characters in a Tinder message sent from a man to a woman is twelve.[12]

Another aspect of eighteenth-century living we have lost is the culture of sociability, civility and conviviality. Mostly for want of alternative, our ancestors spent a great deal of time together in clubs, balls, coffee shops, taverns, churches, recitals, public gardens, readings, ridottos, carnivals, religious processions, gambling houses, the theatre, the opera, the public square. Time spent women in the West overtook men on a number of vital measures, including law school, medical school and undergraduate admissions. The trend lines still point towards economic equality. Rather than seeing these facts in opposition to one another, or worse in denial of one another, we might see that they are divergent expressions of the same phenomenon. We are living in a liberal-capitalist monoculture which has brought economic progress on paper while coarsening our social existence. It is understandable why some would react to the logic of the commodification of desire with the logic of brute legislative and bureaucratic force.

While tempting, this would not solve the underlying crisis. What we need is a return to equilibrium. Mary Wollstonecraft, like many eighteenth-century thinkers, recognised that we need a balance between logic and sentiment. 'The impulse of the senses, passions, if you will,' she wrote, 'and the conclusions of reason, draw men together.' She felt the injustice wrought in her own time by 'the fragility, the instability, of reason, and the wild luxuriancy of noxious passions', while also recognising that to permit an infantilising sentimental culture to attempt a bureaucratic takeover of our desires would be a disaster, too. We would do well to remember her dictum that 'freedom, *even* uncertain freedom – is dear'. Likewise, those who would tame the chaos of human desire with bureaucratic logic would do well to remember the words of that other great Georgian, Alexander Pope, in his *Essay on Man*:

> *Alas what wonder! Man's superior part*
> *Uncheck'd may rise, and climb from art to art;*
> *But when his own great work is but begun,*
> *What Reason weaves, by Passion is undone.*

ENDNOTES

Introduction

1   *Black Southerners and the Law, 1865–1900*, ed. Donald G. Nieman (London: Routledge, 1994), p29.

2   Ovid, *Metamorphoses*, trans. David Raeburn (London: Penguin, 2004), pp35–7, 67, 89–90, 389; Christine de Pizan, *The Book of the City of Ladies* (London: Picador, 1984), p188.

3   Stephen Greenblatt, *The Rise and Fall of Adam and Eve* (London: Bodley Head, 2017), pp90, 106–10, 122–3; St Jerome, 'On Marriage and Virginity', from Letter XXII to Eustochium and from the treatise *Against Jovinian*.

4   *Sir Gawain and the Green Knight*, trans. Bernard O'Donoghue (London: Penguin, 2013), p75.

5   Lawrence Stone, *The Family, Sex and Marriage in England 1500–1800* (London: Weidenfeld & Nicolson, 1977), p502.

6   Jonathan Rée, *Witcraft: The Invention of Philosophy in English* (London: Allen Lane, 2019), 185. This conflict also has a geographic dimension. It has become something of a trope to contrast the eighteenth-century tradition of skepticism in British philosophy with the cult of reason that reigned in France. George Orwell was nodding at this national stereotype when he remarked (in "The Lion and the Unicorn") that "the English will never develop into a nation of philosophers. They will always prefer instinct to logic and character to intelligence."

    For a contemporary iteration of the reason vs. passion debate see the opposition in Daniel Kahneman's book *Thinking, Fast and Slow* between System 1 thinking and System 2 thinking.

7   Pamela Haag, *Consent: Sexual Rights and the Transformation of American Liberalism* (Ithaca, NY: Cornell University Press, 1999), 33.

8   *The White Slave Traffic* (London: Published at the Offices of "M.A.P.", 17 and 18, Henrietta Street, 1910), 11.

9   Germaine Greer, *The Female Eunuch* (London: MacGibbon & Kee, 1970), p45.

1 Rake Culture

1 *Some Authentick Memoirs of the Life of Colonel Ch——s, Rape-Master-General of Great Britain. By an Impartial Hand* (London, 1730). See also pp1–2 for the account of the public reaction to Charteris's conviction: 'When the News was first spread about the Town, Mankind was amaz'd; People stood aghast, looking at one another like Statues . . . The Demolition of *Ch——s*, and the *Opening* of his Maid's *Port* and *Harbour*, and in what Manner he had raz'd the fortifications of her Vertue, was the Subject on which all Conversation turn'd.'

2 *Some Authentick Memoirs of the Life of Colonel Ch——s.*

3 Charteris allegedly claimed her escape as one of the greatest losses of his career, lamenting that 'A Woman that had such a large Share of Courage when on her Heels, must have had a vast deal more when between a Pair of Sheets.' *Some Authentick Memoirs of the Life of Colonel Ch——s*, p25.

4 Anon., *A Ramble Through London: Containing Observations on Men and Things* (London, 1738).

5 *The Country Gentleman's Vade Mecum* (London, 1699), p15.

6 'Philogamus', *The Present State of Matrimony or the Real Cause of Conjugal Infidelity* (London, 1739), p25.

7 Apart, on occasion, from some cosmic justice. It is recorded that Charteris's henchman Gourley once identified a particularly attractive and very devout milliner in Westminster. Charteris went to visit her store, where he engaged her in a religious discourse and then 'inveighed bitterly against the Wickedness of the Age, the licentious Manner in which all Ranks and Conditions of Christians lived; and that the unguarded Actions of the Clergy had been a great Inlet to that Sea of Atheism and Immorality that had poured in upon the Nation'. 'After this religious Courtship had been carried on some time,' we are told, he lured her to an apartment in Golden Square where 'the Colonel made a Declaration of his real Principles, professing himself a staunch Whoremaster, and that she must even, *sans Ceremony,* tumble a pillow with him that night'. After some fainting fits and other theatrics the woman agreed to do so for money. In the morning she vanished, leaving him with a vicious case of the pox and the dawning realisation that she had been a prostitute all along. Charteris was obliged to retreat from London for a period to take the painful treatment for such diseases – a hot mercury solution injected into the urethra.

8 Through extensive bribery he had secured a royal pardon for his Scottish rape charge on New Year's Day 1722.

9 Georgian slang for £100,000.

10 His testament also provided for his pistols to go to the Duke of Argyll and his stable of horses to the Prime Minister, Sir Robert Walpole.

11 *A Foreign View of England in the reigns of George I and George II: The letters of Monsieur Cesar de Saussure to his family,* trans. and ed. Madame Van Muyden (1902 edn; original letters composed 1725–30).

12 There were also other benefits to lingering in these quarters: due to ancient

privileges, those resident in houses adjacent to the canal could not be arrested for debt – the nearby Fleet Prison awaited if they strayed – and allowed for marriages to take place 'without any licence or publication of banns. Sailors and people of the common sort make great use of this latter privilege, their marriage being blessed in some tavern or pot-house, the priest being paid with half a crown and a bottle of wine.' De Saussure, *A Foreign View of England*.

13   Five printers were registered as operating in the area in 1750, growing to 32 in 1790. One of those close to Richardson was the shop of John and Paul Knapton, son of printer James Knapton, the brother of George Knapton who painted the members of the Medmenham Abbey 'Order' of St Francis – the rakes Wilkes, Dashwood et al. James Knapton moved his business to Richardson's neighbourhood in the mid-1730s, so it is plausible that the two men would have been familiar with each other.

14   Cheyne's *The English Malady* (1732), *An Essay on Regimen* (1740) and *The Natural Method of Cureing* (1742) were all published by Richardson.

15   Richardson writes in 1748 that 'by first wife I had 5 sons and one daughter; some of them living to be delightful prattlers, with all the appearances of sound health, lovely in their features and promising as to their minds, and the death of one of them, I doubt accelerating from grief, that of the otherwise laudable afflicted mother . . . I cherish the memory of my lost wife to this hour' (SR to Lady Bradshaigh, 15 Dec 1748).

16   Critics have noted the similarity between Mr B— and Colonel Charteris. See Alan Dugald McKillop, *Samuel Richardson: Printer and Novelist* (Chapel Hill, NC: University of North Carolina Press, 1936), p32: 'The worst parts of Richardson's plot, Mr B—'s clumsy and brutal attacks on the heroine, can be paralleled in the exploits of the infamous Colonel Charteris, who lures his victims to his house in town or country, comes upon them through trap-doors or disguised in women's clothes, and is aided in his schemes by one Moll Clapham, a Mrs Jewkes in real life.' Ian Watt, among others, makes much the same point in *The Rise of the Novel* (1957; new edn Berkeley, CA: University of California Press, 2001).

17   Such sham marriages actually existed. Until the 1753 Marriage Act, a variety of loopholes and folk traditions made for the possibility of genuinely misleading someone into believing they had been legitimately married. An example survives in the prison memoir of career criminal James Dalton, hanged at Tyburn in May, 1730, in which he recounts his use of this method to attain sex from women other than prostitutes: 'With this Money I purchased me a Suit of Clothes, and got acquainted with a Person that procured Husbands for unfortunate young Women. He told me that he had one at that Time, that was a Gentleman's Daughter who lived in very good Repute, and that being big with Child her Friends would not admit her into their Presence without the Sight of a Certificate; and that if I would only take the Trouble to go to Church and marry her, he would give me two Guineas for

my Trouble and upon my agreeing with his Desire, he sent for the Gentlewoman, and we went to St. Clement's Church in the Strand and were there married, my Acquaintance the Procuror performing the Part of the Father: After this we adjourned to the Tavern, where I was very handsomely entertained; and the Wine getting Influence over my Brains, I insisted on lying all Night with my Wife: A great many Arguments were made use of to persuade me to the contrary, but to no purpose upon which a Quarrel ensued, and the Landlord coming to know the Reason of the Disturbance, I related the whole Affair to him he immediately quitted the Room, and sent to the Church to know the Truth, which he was soon inform'd of; wherefore he took my part; and one of his Servants called a Coach, and my Wife and I went to the *Bell-Inn* in *West-Smithfield* where we lay together all Night. One Thing made me somewhat uneasy when I awoke the next Morning sober, and that was, I had the Foul Disease, which I knew must in all Likelihood be communicated to her, therefore I arose and left her to pay for our Night's Lodging.' Quoted in Philip Rawlings, *Drunks, Whores and Idle Apprentices: Criminal Biographies of the Eighteenth Century* (London: Routledge, 1992), pp88–9.

18 Erasmus Jones, *The Man of Manners: Or, Plebeian Polish'd* (1735).

19 *An Essay on Modern Gallantry: address'd to men of honour, men of pleasure, and men of sense: with a seasonable admonition to the young ladies of Great Britain* (London, Printed for M. Cooper, c. 1750).

20 Quoted in Faramerz Dabhoiwala, *The Origins of Sex: A History of the First Sexual Revolution* (London: Penguin, 2013), pp176–7. The sentiment is echoed in Kitty's verdict on her sister Lydia in Jane Austen's *Pride and Prejudice* (1813): 'Unhappy as the event must be for Lydia, we may draw from it this useful lesson; that loss of virtue in a female is irretrievable – that one false step involves her in endless ruin – that her reputation is no less brittle than it is beautiful, – and that she cannot be too much guarded in her behaviour towards the undeserving of the other sex.'

21 See Richardson's letter to George Cheyne of 31 August 1741: 'In my scheme, I have generally taken Human Nature as it is; for it is no purpose to suppose it angelic, or to endeavour to make it so. There is a time of life in which the passions will predominate; and ladies, any more than men, will not be kept in ignorance; and if we properly mingle instruction with entertainment, so as to make the latter seemingly the view, while the former is really the end, I imagine it will be doing a good deal.' Also his letter to Aaron Hill of 1 February 1741: 'I thought the story, if written in an easy and natural manner, suitable to the simplicity of it, might possibly introduce a new species of writing, that might possibly turn young people into a course of reading different from the pomp and parade of romance-writing, and dismissing the improbable and marvellous, cause of religion and virtue. I therefore gave way to enlargement: and so Pamela became as you see her.'

22 By 1742 a pamphlet entitled 'Lettre Sur *Pamela*' was circulating in London. A

French response to the book, it attacked its style and noted derisively of its content that if this was a fair representation of English morals then that nation was more debauched than had originally been suspected. It is improbable that Richardson read it, as he did not know French; he may well have not known it existed. He was, however, caught up in a minor contretemps over the translation of *Pamela* into French after allegations were traded over the conversion of his demotic English into highly mannered literary French. This episode gave rise to an unabashedly Little Englander tirade in a letter from Aaron Hill to Richardson in November 1741: 'Manly Decency, and modest Reserves, are the Dress, and Decorums, of Life. – But they who substitute brisk Insignificance, in the Place of a solid Vivacity, let *Them* still be called French-men – And let *us* be content to be English *John Bulls:* the only Pity is, that our Horns are no *sharper.*' In 1755 *Pamela* was published in America, where Richardson found his work in the hands of a Philadelphia printer by the name of Benjamin Franklin.

23 These were begun but, tragically, never finished and the drafts for them were later lost. In the early 1740s the painter Joseph Highmore did, however, produce a major series of twelve paintings inspired by episodes from the novel. These survive and are split between Tate Britain, the Fitzwilliam Museum and the National Gallery of Victoria.

24 AR to SR, 29 Jul 1741, in Samuel Richardson, *Correspondence with Aaron Hill and the Hill Family*, ed. Christine Gerrard (Cambridge: CUP, 2013), p105.

25 Anonymous, *Pamela Censur'd* (London, 1741). The author also agreed with Fielding, Haywood et al. that Pamela seemed far too worldly for an alleged innocent: 'Pamela instead of being artless and innocent sets out at first with as much Knowledge of the Arts of the Town, as if she had been born and bred in Covent Garden.'

26 Though not enough for Victorian publishers, who heavily redacted *Pamela*.

27 While Matthew succeeded in placing Swift's work in various publications, his attempts to ingratiate himself with the literary taste-makers of the capital were less fruitful. Swift engineered a meeting for him with Alexander Pope in his Twickenham retreat. Pope was extremely unimpressed with Matthew, writing to Swift in Ireland that the man he had talked up to him in order to secure the audience was 'a most forward, shallow, conceited fellow' who had bored and disgusted him for three whole days. This damning verdict on his protégé sent Swift into a rage.

28 Romantic marriages were increasingly the norm in England by the second quarter of the eighteenth century. Clarissa's insistence on following this practice is linked to her knowledge of the various rights and freedoms she will lose upon wedlock. 'Surely, Sir,' she writes to her uncle, 'a young creature ought not to be obliged to make all these sacrifices but for such a man as she can love.' For more on romantic marriage see Watt, *Rise of the Novel*; Stone, *Family, Sex and Marriage in England*.

Lovelace is well aware that he owes his early success with Clarissa to her family's pig-headedness: 'I knew that the whole stupid family were in a combination to do my business for me.' He crows to Belford, 'I told thee that they were all working for me, like so many ground moles; and still more blind than the moles are said to be, unknowing that they did so. I myself, the director of their principal motions; which falling in with the malice of their little hearts, they took to be all their own.' Samuel Richardson, *Clarissa* (1748; London: Penguin, 1985), p387.

29 This 'commonly received notion', as Richardson had it, was not without critics in its own day. No less an authority than Lady Mary Wortley Montagu mocked the prevailing expectations of the time as 'barbarous manners . . . well calculated for the establishment of vice and wretchedness'. *The Letters of the Right Honourable Lady Mary Wortley Montagu* (London, 1763).

30 R.F. Brissenden, *Virtue in Distress: Studies in the Novel of Sentiment from Richardson to Sade* (London: Macmillan, 1994), p22.

31 *The Polite Philosopher* (1734): 'Books may furnish us with the right ideas, experience may improve our judgement, but it is the acquaintance of the ladies only, which can bestow that easiness of address, whereby the fine gentleman is distinguished from the scholar and the man of business.' Quoted in Dabhoiwala, *Origins of Sex*.

32 See, *inter alia*, Hume on urbanisation as the essential element in the advancement of civilisation and the refinement of social discourse: 'Clubs and societies are everywhere formed. Both sexes meet in an easy and social manner; and the tempers of men, as well as in their behaviour, refine apace. So that beside the improvement which they receive from knowledge and the liberal arts, it is impossible but they must feel an increase of humanity from the very habit of conversing together.' Keith Thomas, *In Pursuit of Civility* (New Haven and London: Yale UP, 2018), p176. See also Samuel Johnson: 'man's chief merit consisted in resisting the impulses of nature', quoted in Watt, *Rise of the Novel*, p157; Dabhoiwala, *Origins of Sex*, pp180–3.

33 Locke continued with a metaphor that captured the emergent cliché of woman as the 'fairer sex' while slyly recognising the attractions of seduction: 'Eloquence, like the fair sex, has too prevailing beauties in it to suffer itself ever to be spoken against. And it is in vain to find fault with those arts of deceiving, wherein men find pleasure to be deceived.'

34 We know Richardson was familiar with Locke's writings, for he includes an extensive reflection on Lockean pedagogy in the latter portion of *Pamela*. Locke was, in any case, one of the most widely read philosophers of the period, his work running through nine editions between publication and 1760 (see Roy Porter, *Enlightenment: Britain and the Creation of the Modern World* (London: Penguin, 2001), pp67, 70). Whether or not Richardson had read or knew of Hume's writing is unknown but probably unlikely.

35 Richardson, *Clarissa*, pp262–3.

36 Lady Mary Wortley Montagu: 'This Richardson is a strange fellow. I heartily despise him, and eagerly read him, nay, sob over his works in a most scandalous manner. The first two tomes of Clarissa touched me, as being very resembling to my maiden days; and I find in pictures of Sir Thomas Grandison and his lady, what I have heard of my mother, and seen in my father.' McKillop, *Samuel Richardson*, p134.

37 HF to SR, 15 Oct 1748. Fielding was reporting his thoughts on reading *Clarissa*, apart from the last two volumes, so presumably he had read five of the seven volumes at the time of writing. He specifically praised the character of Lovelace: 'the Character of Lovelass [sic] is heightened with great Judgement. His former Admirers must lose all Regard for him on his Perseverance, and as this Regard ceases, Compassion for Clarissa rises in the same Proportion. Hence we are admirably prepared for what is to follow—' He describes in detail his reaction to the climactic rape and praises Richardson for artistry and power of sentiment: 'Let the Overflowings of a Heart which you have filled brimfull speak for me.'

He also jokes that the world believes that 'We are Rivals for that coy Mrs. Fame' before going on to declare: 'I heartily wish you Success. That I sincerely think you in the highest manner deserve it.' *The Correspondence of Henry and Sarah Fielding*, ed. Martin C. Battestin and Clive T. Probyn (Oxford: Clarendon Press, 1993), pp70–4. Sarah also recorded her impressions in a letter to Richardson of 8 Jan 1749: 'When I read of her, I am all sensation; my heart glows; I am overwhelmed; my only vent is tears; and unless tears could mark my thoughts as legibly as ink I cannot speak half I feel. . . . In short, Sir, no pen but yours can do justice to Clarissa. Often have I reflected on my own vanity in daring but to touch the hem of her garment.'

38 T.C. Duncan Eaves and Ben D. Kimpel, *Samuel Richardson: A Biography* (Oxford: Clarendon Press, 1971), p183.

39 LP to SR, 29 Jun 1745, in *The Cambridge Correspondence of Samuel Richardson* (Cambridge: CUP), Vol 3, pp373–4. She continues with a hilarious description of Cibber's hyperbole – 'I am not quite sure, whether Mr. Cibber is not so strongly enamoured with her perfections, and touched with her distresses, that, were they exhibited on the stage, he would not, like Don Quixote, rise up in wrath and rescue the lady from the hands of her violater [sic]' – before concluding with an imprecation of her own: 'Spare her virgin purity, dear Sir, spare it!'

40 SR to Lady Bradshaigh, Feb 1751, *Cambridge Correspondence*, Vols 5–7, pxv.

41 He further alleged that having conferred with 'two very delicate Minds of the Sex', he was certain that Clarissa's actions were true to life. *Cambridge Correspondence*, Vol 1, SR to AH, 29 Oct 1746; AH to SR, 23 Jan 1747.

42 She finished with a threat: 'If you disappoint me, attend to my curse: May the hatred of all the young, beautiful, and virtuous, for ever be your portion! and may your eyes never behold any thing but age and deformity! may you meet with applause only from envious old maids, surly bachelors, and tyrannical

parents! may you be doomed to the company of such! and, after death, may their ugly souls haunt you! Now make Lovelace and Clarissa unhappy if you dare.' Lady Dorothy Bradshaigh to SR, 10 Oct 1748, *Cambridge Correspondence*, Vol 5, pp3–5.

43 *Cambridge Correspondence*, Vol 5, pxxxvii. Barbauld on the first meeting of Bradshaigh and Richardson at Birdcage Walk: 'No lover ever expected his mistress with greater ardour than the grave Richardson seems to have felt for his *incognita*, when he paced so fruitlessly up and down the Mall, gazing with expectation at every lady he met.'

44 SR to DB, 26 Oct 1748, pp7–11.

45 DB to SR, 17 Nov 1748, pp20–1.

46 DB to SR, Nov 1749, and his response shortly afterwards, in *Cambridge Correspondence*, Vol 5, pp73–7. Bradshaigh's letter contained a catty remark about Richardson's propensity for pious old women. 'You know so many good old maids, Sir,' she wrote, 'that, perhaps, you may accidentally hear of some one, who would not be having the *dirty impudent baggage sent to Bridewell.*' Her allusion to Bridewell seems intended to echo some of the more callous language of Richardson's great villains, Mr B—, Sir Hargrave Pollexfen and Lovelace, though such sentiments were widespread. Lady Mary Wortley Montagu stated flatly that any girl 'that runs away with a young fellow without intending to marry him should be carry'd to Bridewell or Bedlam the next day'. Quoted in Carol Houlihan Flynn, *Samuel Richardson: A Man of Letters* (Princeton, NJ: Princeton UP, 1982), p108.

47 Richardson affirmed this connection in another letter to Bradshaigh in which, apropos of *Clarissa*, he described his heroine as 'a *second Magdalen* in her penitence, and yet not so bad as a *Magdalen* in her *faults*'.

48 DB to SR, 29 Oct 1749; SR to DB, late Nov 1749; DB to SR, Dec 1749.

49 Catherine Talbot to SR, Mar 1750: 'They much wish also, that he may have Leisure, Spirits and Inclination to comply with the repeated Requests of his Agreeable Incognita, and shew the World such a Man as would neither have been unworthy of a Clarissa, nor unagreeable to a Miss Howe.' *Cambridge Correspondence*, Vol 10, p7. See also Christian Bernhard Kaiser [translator in Hannover] to SR, 10 Jul 1753: 'When is Your Sir Charles Grandison to appear? Every body here wishes, soon to see him' (*Cambridge Correspondence*, Vol 10, p97); and Richardson's letters on the new work to Jean-Baptiste de Fréval, Jan 1750 and to Alexis Claude Clairaut, Jul 1753.

50 Eaves and Kimpel, *Samuel Richardson*, p302.

51 Allen Michie, *Richardson and Fielding: The Dynamics of a Critical Rivalry* (Cranbury, NJ: Bucknell UP, 1999), pp39–41.

52 Donald Thomas, *Henry Fielding* (London: Weidenfeld & Nicolson, 1990), p393.

53 Richardson adhered rigorously to his own moral-literary precepts. Hence the critical argument, advanced by Roger Moore, that he was the exemplary female writer of his time, and possibly of all English literature until Austen,

who was explicit in her debt to him. 'Richardson may be called, in all seriousness, one of our great women.' Robert Etheridge Moore, 'Dr. Johnson on Fielding and Richardson', *PMLA* 66.2 (Mar 1951).

54 SR to SC, 6 Dec 1750, 11 Jan 1751. *Selected Letters of Samuel Richardson*, ed. John Carroll (Oxford: Clarendon Press, 1964), pp172–3.

55 Richardson's pusillanimity need hardly be commented on; what is too easily forgotten is how his attitude towards women and literature was to predominate for the next century and a half. English society produced (against its own wishes, in many cases) many great female writers, but they were for the most part writers of the private world. There were very few Laetitia Pilkingtons in the Victorian era. As Virginia Woolf noted in the late 1920s, the belief that women ought 'to confine themselves to making puddings and knitting stockings, to playing on the piano and embroidering bags' meant they suffered 'from too rigid a restraint, too absolute a stagnation, precisely as men would suffer' in the same conditions. The miracle of women's writing was that it had achieved so much while constrained so tightly: 'She knew, no one better, how enormously her genius would have profited if it had not spent itself in solitary visions over distant fields; if experience and intercourse and travel had been granted her. But they were not granted; they were withheld; and we must accept the fact that all those good novels, *Villette, Emma, Wuthering Heights, Middlemarch*, were written by women without more experience of life than could enter the house of a respectable clergyman; written too in the common sitting-room of that respectable house and by women so poor that they could not afford to buy more than a few quires of paper at a time upon which to write *Wuthering Heights* or *Jane Eyre*.' Virginia Woolf, 'A Room of One's Own' (1929).

56 And also: 'Love, eternal Love, is the subject, the burthen of all your writings; it is the poignant sauce, which so richly seasons Pamela, Clarissa and Grandison, and makes their flimzy nonsense pass so glibly down.' *Critical Remarks on Sir Charles Grandison, Clarissa, and Pamela*, Pamphlet (1754), intro. by Alan Dugald McKillop (Los Angeles: William Andrews Clark Memorial Library, University of California), 1950.

57 This was not a new complaint, nor one limited to men. See Lady Mary Wortley Montagu:
'I am very sorry for the forlorn state of Matrimony, which is as much ridicul'd by our Young Ladys as it us'd to be by young fellows; in short, both Sexes have found the Inconveniencys of it, and the Apellation of Rake is as genteel in a Woman as a Man of Quality.' Letter of October 1723, quoted in Flynn, *Samuel Richardson*, pp56–7.

58 *Critical Remarks on Sir Charles Grandison, Clarissa, and Pamela*.

59 James Boswell, *The Life of Samuel Johnson*, p77.

60 Mark Hildesley to SR, 20 Dec 1753, *Cambridge Correspondence*, Vol 10, p168.

61 Flynn, *Samuel Richardson*, p3.

62 One such cynic was Richardson's client Daniel Defoe, who opposed an early campaign to establish the Foundling Hospital for exactly this reason. Such an institution, he believed, would 'set up a nursery for lewdness, and encourage fornication . . . Who would be afraid of sinning, if they can so easily get rid of their bastards? We shall soon be over-run with foundlings when there is such an encouragement given to whoredom.' Dabhoiwala, *Origins of Sex*, p243.

63 *The Rambler* no. 107, 26 Mar 1751: 'Properantia's hopes of a year of confusion. The misery of prostitutes.' The piece offers a fascinating insight into the world of the gadding literary men-about-town and their conflicted consciences: 'How frequently have the gay and thoughtless, in their evening frolicks, seen a band of those miserable females, covered with rags, shivering with cold, and pining with hunger; and, without either pitying their calamities, or reflecting upon the cruelty of those who, perhaps, first seduced them by caresses of fondness, or magnificence of promises, go on to reduce others to the same wretchedness by the same means!'

64 *The Gentleman's Magazine*, March 1751. The belief that seduced women and prostitutes were equivalent would linger about discussion of the institution for some time. An 1810 account discusses the important function served by what became known as the Magdalen House for 'young women who have been seduced from their friends under promise of marriage and have been deserted by their seducers. They have never been in public prostitution, but fly to the Magdalen to avoid it.' John Feltham, *The Picture of London for 1810*, pp225–8. See also Reverend William Dodd, *An Account of the Rise, Progress, and Present State of the Magdalen Hospital* (1761), pp3–4: 'Poor, young, thoughtless Females, plunged into ruin by those temptations, to which their very youth and personal advantages expose them, no less than those passions implanted in our nature for wise and good ends . . . Surrounded by snares, the most artfully and industriously laid; snares, laid by those endowed with superior faculties, and all the advantages of education and fortune; what virtue can be proof against such formidable seducers? . . . And when once seduced, how soon their golden dreams vanish! Abandoned by the seducer, deserted by their friends, contemned by the world, they are left to struggle with want, despair, and scorn. . . . It is well known, that this is the case with most of the Prostitutes in their several degrees.'

65 For example, Astrea and Minerva Hill to SR, 13 Dec 1748: 'How fast, if England has such Sanctuary Retreats as Protestant Nunneries, wou'd a Clarissa's Fate contribute to the filling of 'em!' SR to Lady Bradshaigh, 5 Jun 1759: 'Your Ladyship makes me a great Compliment, in supposing the Institution owes its beginnings to Hints in Sir Charles Grandison.'

66 His reasoning was predicated on the assumptions of the cults of sentiment and sensibility: 'I have another scheme, my lord, proceeded Sir Charles. An hospital for female penitents; for such unhappy women, as having been once drawn in, and betrayed by the perfidy of men, find themselves, by the cruelty

of the world, and principally by that of their own sex, unable to recover the path of virtue, when perhaps (convinced of the wickedness of the men in whose honour they confided) they would willingly make their first departure from it the last.

'These, continued he, are the poor creatures who are eminently intitled to our pity, though they seldom meet with it. Good-nature, and credulity the child of good-nature, are generally, as I have the charity to believe, rather than viciousness, the foundation of their crime. Those men who pretend they would not be the first destroyers of a woman's innocence, look upon these as fair prize.'

Elsewhere he makes the connection to the models of Catholic convents: 'We want to see established in every county, protestant nunneries'; 'though a Protestant, I am not an enemy to such foundations in general. I could wish, under proper regulations, that we had nunneries among us. I would not, indeed, have the obligation upon nuns be perpetual: let them have liberty, at the end of every two or three years, to renew their vows, or otherwise, by the consent of friends.' This is fairly close to what happened in the Magdalen House once it was established.

67 Dubbed 'the Macaroni Parson', Dodd's was one of the great Georgian lives. A socially ambitious and sensually profligate young clergyman who had married a domestic servant, he served as evening preacher at the Magdalen chapel 1759–77 and became an integral part of the services' appeal. He wrote an early history of the Magdalen and also a novel, *The Sisters*, on the subject of prostitution. (Ostensibly a sentimental narrative, *The Sisters* descended at times into proto-Sadean pornography: 'At their commands she was obliged to strip naked as she was born, and thus submit to the hellish purposes of either; and after having been thus abused, each presented a red hot poker, near to every part as possible, made her dance, as they called it, for all their amusements.')

Generously compensated by the charity, he developed ruinously expensive tastes, including a town house, a country house in Ealing, a carriage, and spendthrift jaunts to the West End that he could ill afford. He teetered on the edge of disgrace until 1777 when, in financial crisis, he tried to cash a fraudulent cheque under the name of his sometime pupil, the Earl of Chesterfield. Caught in the act, he was hauled before the Old Bailey, found guilty and sentenced to hang. His case attracted the intense interest of Samuel Johnson, who is said to have written Dodd's final appeal to the Recorder at the Old Bailey and maintained a close correspondence with him as he approached the day of his hanging.

Johnson also wrote on his behalf to the king, the queen, Lord Mansfield and Lord Chancellor Bathurst. He is even alleged to have written Dodd's sermon, delivered to his fellow convicts at Newgate Prison. (Johnson would later deny to Boswell that he wrote the sermon, memorably quipping, 'Depend upon it, Sir, when a man knows he is to be hanged in a fortnight, it concentrates his mind wonderfully.') The day before his execution he wrote a consoling letter to Dodd, telling him: 'Be comforted: your crime, morally or religiously considered, has no very deep dye of turpitude. It corrupted no man's principles; it attacked no man's life. It involves only a temporary and reparable injury.' Despite the best efforts of his friends to try and bribe the judge, the gaolers and the hangman, Dodd was hanged the next day, 27 June 1777. Their strenuous efforts led to persistent rumours that Dodd had escaped his fate at Tyburn and was living pleasantly in Provence. His wife died in seclusion in England in 1784. See S.B.P. Pearce, *An Ideal in the Working: The Magdalen Hospital 1758–1958* (1958); Gerald Howson, *The Macaroni Parson: The Life of the Unfortunate Doctor Dodd* (London: Hutchinson, 1973); Boswell, *Life of Samuel Johnson*.

68   DB to SR, 22 May 1759. See also SR to DB, 5 Jun 1759, where he praises her going and agrees that 'I could not have stood it'.

69   Furthermore, one of the roles of the Magdalen House was to re-induct women into the cult of sensibility. So much of the Magdalen's work, in the minds of its managers, was to make the women ready for a life of domesticity after a period of perilous misadventure in the streets. The ultimate aim was that the penitents should find a new husband, or at least a new and Christian home where they could devote themselves to suitably feminine work. Prayer, simple living and honest work would repair their damaged delicacy and pave the way for marriage. Marriage was considered a self-fulfilling prophecy, for child-rearing and home keeping would ensure a woman's loyalty to the code of domesticity; as Richardson put it in the *Familiar Letters*, 'Childbed *matronizes* the giddiest Spirits.' The governors of the Magdalen claimed a 10–15 per cent success rate in finding penitents husbands, and further claimed that two-thirds of all women who passed through their doors left satisfactorily reformed. Dabhoiwala, *Origins of Sex*, pp249–50; Feltham, *The Picture of London for 1810*, pp225–8.

70   Horace Walpole, *Letters*, Volume III, to George Montagu, Esq., 28 Jan 1760.

71   Early in his courtship Lovelace scandalises the Harlowes by turning up in their church in order to catch a glimpse of Clarissa. She has been safely stowed at home but she guesses why he came: 'Did he come for my sake; and, by behaving in such a manner to those present of my family, imagine he was doing me either service or pleasure?' Richardson, *Clarissa*, Letter XXX.

72   Dodd was known for his suggestive preaching style. For example, an extract from a sermon he included in his *An Account of the Rise* (1761), p92: 'You, who have known the fatal pleasings of passion, can more easily pity them, whom those pleadings have seduced and destroyed. And you, who are possessed of all the sweetness and delicacies of the tender mind, and happier state, can more easily guess the extreme misery which must arise to a female heart, from the foulness and horror of promiscuous prostitution.'

73   Dabhoiwala, *Origins of Sex*, pp261–4.

74   *The Gentleman's Magazine*, LXXVI (1816), Vol 1, pp577–8.

2 The Transit of Venus

1 *Boswell on the Grand Tour: Italy, Corsica, and France, 1765–1766*, ed. Frank Brady and Frederick A. Pottle (London: Heinemann, 1955). The notion that climate informed behaviour was widespread. Montesquieu's *The Spirit of Laws* (1748) was the foundational text for the claim that climate and geography shaped morality, but the idea was commonly held in the decades before its publication. See, for example, Daniel Defoe's 'True-Born Englishman' (1701): 'Lust chose the torrid zone of Italy / Where blood ferments in rapes and sodomy. / Where swelling veins o'erflow with livid streams, / With heat impregnate from Vesuvian flames: / Whose flowing sulphur forms infernal lakes, / And human body of the soil partakes. / There nature ever burns with hot desires.' Maurice Andrieux, *Daily Life in Venice at the Time of Casanova* (London: George Allen and Unwin, 1972), p126.

2 Alexander Pope, *The Dunciad*, Book IV, 310 (London, 1728).

3 John Murray was no relation to the line of John Murrays that ran the London publishing house famous for handling Byron's literary output. However, through marriage Casanova's Murray did have a connection to the Byron story: his wife Bridget Milbanke, whom he married in 1748, was the only daughter of Sir Ralph Milbanke, 4th Baronet of Halnaby Hall in North Yorkshire. Murray may have lived at Halnaby Hall for a time before going to Venice, in which case he inhabited the rooms that housed Byron during his disastrous honeymoon with Anna Milbanke (1792–1860), the only daughter of Sir Ralph Milbanke, 6th Baronet, nephew of John Murray's wife Bridget. See Christine Laidlaw, *The British in the Levant* (London: I.B. Tauris, 2010), p53.

4 Laidlaw, *British in the Levant*, p58.

5 Giacomo Casanova, *History of My Life*, trans. Willard R. Trask (12 vols; Baltimore, MD: Johns Hopkins University Press, 1966–71), Vol 4, pp136–8.

6 Andrieux, *Daily Life in Venice*, p164.

7 Carlo Goldoni, *Memoirs* (London: Alfred A. Knopf, 1926), p154.

8 Casanova, *History of My Life*, Vol 1, p92.

9 Roughly translated, the Englishman's question is: 'Teach us, grammarians, why the vagina is a masculine noun and why penis is feminine?' Casanova answers: 'It is because the slave takes his name from his master.' Casanova, *History of My Life*, Vol 1, p62.

10 Her father was Joseph Imer, the impresario behind a touring acting troupe of which Zanetta Farussi was a member. Imer and Farussi had a longstanding and furious relationship that is said to have inspired a number of Goldoni's plays.

11 In a poignant passage in Volume 6 of his memoirs he alludes, metareferentially, to the conditions of their composition: 'I have been writing memoirs for the last seven years, and though I repent of having begun, I have sworn to go on to the end. However, I write in the hope that my Memoirs may never see the light of day; in the first place the censure would not allow them to be printed, and in the second I hope I shall be strong-minded

enough, when my last illness comes, to have all my papers burnt before my eyes. If that be not the case I count on the indulgence of my readers, who should remember that I have only written my story to prevent my going mad in the midst of all the petty insults and disagreeables which I have to bear day by day from the envious rascals who live with me in this castle of Count Waldstein, or Wallenstein, at Dux. I write ten or twelve hours a day, and so keep black melancholy at bay. My readers shall hear more of my sufferings later on, if I do not die before I write them down.'

12   Casanova, *History of My Life*, Vol 2, p106.

13   Casanova, *History of My Life*, Vol 2, p101.

14   Sharpe also provides an enchanting account of seeing the ladies of Venice rowed up and down beside the *giardini* of the Giudecca by their respective *cicisbei* at dusk 'as in former days, our gentry in England frequented the Ring in Hyde-Park'.

15   Iris Origo, *The Last Attachment* (London: Pushkin Press, 2017), p52.

16   The Count did at one point try to expel Byron and rein in his wayward wife, but was met with a scorn that speaks volumes as to the entrenched status of *cicisbeismo* in this period. 'It is hard,' Teresa informed her husband, 'that I should be the only woman in Romagna who is not to have her *Amico*.' Society censured jealous husbands more than it did wandering wives; Byron stayed in their lives. Origo, *Last Attachment*, p205.

17   GGB to JH, 23 Aug 1819.

18   Tobias Smollett, *Travels Through France and Italy* (London, 1766), Letter XXVII, Nice, 28 Jan 1765.

19   Goldoni, *Memoirs*, p246.

20   See Origo, *Last Attachment*, p82: 'the essence of *Serventismo*, as he was to realize later, was that the lady should *stay* with her husband'.

21   Origo, *Last Attachment*, p151.

22   Casanova, *History of My Life*, Vol 2, p183.

23   See Jan Morris, *Venice* (1960), p47. At the end of the sixteenth century there were said to be 2,889 patrician ladies, 2,508 nuns and 1,936 middle-class wives – but 11,654 prostitutes.

24   Peter Ackroyd, *Venice* (London: Vintage, 2009), p96.

25   Andrieux, *Daily Life in Venice*, pp136–7.

26   William Alexander, *The History of Women* (1796), p137.

27   Roberto Bizzocchi, *A Lady's Man: The Cicisbei, Private Morals and National Identity in Italy* (London: Palgrave Macmillan, 2014), pp14–21. Cf. David Hume in 'The Rise of Arts and Sciences' (1742): 'Gallantry is not less compatible with wisdom and prudence, than with nature and generosity; and when under proper regulations, contributes more than any other invention, to the entertainment and improvement of the youth of both sexes. Among every species of animals, nature has founded on the love between the sexes their sweetest and best enjoyment. But the satisfaction of the bodily appetite is not alone sufficient to

gratify the mind; and even among brute-creatures, we find, that their play and dalliance, and other expressions of fondness, form the greatest part of the entertainment. In rational beings, we must certainly admit the mind for a considerable share. Were we to rob the feast of all its garniture of reason, discourse, sympathy, friendship, and gaiety, what remains would scarcely be worth acceptance, in the judgment of the truly elegant and luxurious.'

28 See Bizzocchi, *A Lady's Man*, pp191–2, Beccaria on adultery in *Dei delitti e delle pene*: 'When the interest or pride of families, or paternal authority, not the inclination of the parties, unite the sexes, gallantry soon breaks the slender ties, in spite of common moralists, who exclaim against the effect, whilst they pardon the cause.'

29 Johann von Goethe, *Letters From Switzerland, and Travels in Italy*, trans. A.J.W. Morrison (London: George Bell and Sons, 1881).

30 Charles Burney, *The Present State of Music in France and Italy* (1771), pp150–2.

31 Casanova, *History of My Life*, Vol 2, p202.

32 This made a problem for Carlo Goldoni when he had to adapt Samuel Richardson's *Pamela* for the Italian stage: nobody would believe that an Italian nobleman would ever marry his maid, however virtuous. 'For some time the novel of "Pamela" had been the delight of the Italians, and my friends urged me strongly to turn it into a comedy. I was acquainted with the work, and felt no difficulty in seizing the spirit of it, and approximating the objects; but the moral aim of the English author was irreconcilable with the manners and laws of my country. A nobleman in London does not derogate from his nobility in marrying a peasant; but at Venice, a patrician who should marry a plebeian would deprive his children of the patrician nobility, and they would lose their right to the sovereignty. Comedy, which is, or ought to be, a school for propriety, should only expose human weaknesses for the sake of correcting them; and it would be unjustifiable to hazard the sacrifice of an unfortunate posterity under the pretext of recompensing virtue. . . . I did not, however, begin the work till I had invented a denouement which, instead of being dangerous, might serve as a model to virtuous lovers, and render the catastrophe both more agreeable and more interesting.' Goldoni, *Memoirs*, pp255–6.

33 'The infamous supper' described in Casanova, *History of My Life*, Vol 3, p260.

34 Ackroyd, *Venice*, pp343–5.

35 *Selections from the Letters of De Brosses*, trans. Lord Ronald Sutherland Gower (London: Kegan Paul, Trench, Trubner & Co., 1897), pp30, 53.

36 *The history of the government of Venice wherein the policies, councils, magistrates, and laws of that state are fully related, and the use of the balloting box exactly described: written in the year 1675.*

37 'The nuns take nothing but ready money,' Carlo Goldoni (*Memoirs*, p455) grumbled apropos of the costs entailed in properly educating his niece.

38 Giuseppe Marco Antonio Baretti, *An Account of the Manners and Customs of Italy* (1768), Vol 2, p17.

39 Casanova, *History of My Life*, Vol 3, p281.

40 Either the San Giacomo di Galizzia or the Santa Maria Degli Angeli.

41 Casanova, *History of My Life*, Vol 4, pp9–10. She writes that he has become 'the puzzle of the entire convent' after five or six such attendances. 'The old nuns said that I must have some sorrow from which my only hope of being relieved was the protection of their Holy Virgin, in whom it was clear that I must have perfect trust; and the young ones said that I must be suffering from melancholia, a misanthrope who shunned the great world.'

42 Casanova, *History of My Life*, Vol 4, p17.

43 Casanova makes a memorable aside on the contents of her library: 'They included all that the wisest philosophers have written against religion and all that the most voluptuous pens have written on the subject which is the sole aim of love. Seductive books, whose incendiary style drives the reader to seek the reality, which alone can quench the fire he feels running through his veins. Besides the books there were folios containing only lascivious engravings.' Casanova, *History of My Life*, Vol 3, p75.

44 This resulted in the First Treaty of Versailles in 1756 and, indirectly, to the outbreak of the Seven Years War (1756–63).

45 It was in early 1755 that Casanova began to spend time with John Murray, the English resident in Venice, so for much of 1754 and the first half of 1755 he was indeed consorting with high-ranking foreign diplomats. In the same period he also moved out of the Palazzo Bràgadin into private apartments, possibly to protect his sponsors from lethal allegations of fraternising with diplomats.

46 J. Rives Childs, *Casanova: A New Perspective* (London: Constable, 1989), pp71–2.

47 Rives Childs, *Casanova*, pp71–2.

48 See Peter Ackroyd on the significance of Casanova's imprisonment in the *Piombi*: 'It is perhaps no wonder that the story of his imprisonment in the dungeons of the ducal palace, and of his subsequent escape, is a central text in Venetian social history; he was in the prison of his unreflecting self. It is in any case rare to find, in Venetian literature, any attempt at analysis or self-criticism. There is just no interest in the subject, the fruit of a culture in which individualism of any kind was discouraged.' Ackroyd, *Venice*, p272.

49 Casanova's description of the book is excellent: 'I read everything that the extravagance of the heated imagination of an extremely devout Spanish virgin, given to melancholy, shut up in a convent, and guided by ignorant and flattering confessors, could bring forth. All these chimerical and monstrous visions were adorned with the name of revelations . . .' *History of My Life*, Vol 3, p211.

50 The Lisbon earthquake of 1775 inspired Voltaire's famous attack on Catholic doctrine. How was it, Voltaire asked, that pious Lisbon was destroyed whilst more sinful cities were untouched?

Was then more vice in fallen Lisbon found,
Than Paris, where voluptuous joys abound?
Was less debauchery to London known,
Where opulence luxurious holds her throne?
Earth Lisbon swallows; the light sons of France
Protract the feast, or lead the sprightly dance.
Voltaire, 'Poème sur le désastre de Lisbonne' (1756)

51 Casanova gives its length both as two feet and as twenty inches. In any case, it was a sizeable device for digging through plaster and breaking through rotten wooden panelling.

52 'Nature commanded me to escape, and religion could not forbid me to do it.' Casanova, *History of My Life*, Vol 4, p293.

53 'Seingalt' is a perfect anagram of 'genitals', not likely a coincidence given Casanova's cabala-inspired fascination with hidden meaning, word games, and substitution. The Chevalier's implicit libidinism was signalled by the richness of his dress. Here is Casanova in 1763: 'I wore a suit of grey velvet, trimmed with gold and silver lace; my point lace shirt was worth at least fifty louis; and my diamonds, my watches, my chains, my sword of the finest English steel, my snuff-box set with brilliants, my cross set with diamonds, my buckles set with the same stones, were altogether worth more than fifty thousand crowns.'

54 'But Rousseau, great man though he was, was totally deficient in humour.' There is no mystery to the lack of connection between the two men – Rousseau's sexual politics were famously austere and his attitude towards female emancipation conservative in the extreme. For reference see Joel Schwartz, *The Sexual Politics of Jean-Jacques Rousseau* (Chicago: University of Chicago Press, 1984).

55 Casanova did not speak and did not seriously try to learn English. His movements around London were facilitated by a black manservant named Jarbe whom he hired upon arrival and 'who spoke English, French, and Italian with equal facility'. Despite this barrier, there were plenty of Italians in the Covent Garden area he could speak to and he also found that many well-born Englishmen and women spoke passable French. The relative ease with which he moved through London without the native language is testament to the cosmopolitan nature of the city in this period but also to the insignificance of English as a transnational language: a veteran traveller like Casanova needed only French to make his way around the world.

56 John Hawkesworth, *An account of the voyages undertaken by the order of His present Majesty: for making discoveries in the Southern Hemisphere* (London, 1773), pp480–2.

57 *The Pacific Journal of Louis-Antoine de Bougainville 1767–68*, ed. and trans. John Dunmore (London: The Hakluyt Society, 2002), p63.

58 Patricia Fara, *Sex, Botany, and Empire* (London: Icon, 2003), p114.

59 Such associations would persist for some time. Fascinated by what he heard of

Tahiti, James Boswell asked Captain Cook at dinner whether he might join the next expedition to the island. This did not happen, but he later defended Tahitian mores to a sceptical Samuel Johnson. Erasmus Darwin, in his *The Loves of the Plants* (1789), describes Tahiti as the home of the Adonis plant, with a hundred male stamens and a hundred female pistils within a single flower – a botanical metaphor for Pacific polygamy and free love. Claire Clairmont, the unhappy sometime lover of Lord Byron, described the Shelley–Byron circle as a 'tribe of the Otaheite philosophers', a joke that played on the widespread assumption that the group were practitioners of free love. Byron's grandfather, the sailor John Byron, had conducted expeditions in the South Pacific in the 1760s and had command of the *Dolphin* before it was handed over to his deputy, Samuel Wallis.

60   Denis Diderot, *Political Writings* (Cambridge: CUP, 1992), pp68, 69, 73.

61   Casanova, *History of My Life*, Vol 5, p101.

62   GGB to DK, 26 Oct 1819.

63   Compare Byron telling Teresa Guiccioli in a letter of 1819, 'I am a citizen of the world – all countries are alike to me' (Origo, *Last Attachment*, p170) with Casanova's oft-proclaimed cosmopolitan status, for example in Albert Haller's account of him: 'He tells me he is a free man, a citizen of the world' (Kelly, *Casanova*, p237).

64   Dear Madame, here's a little list
          Of the beauties my master has won.
          I've made some notes, just for fun.
          Come over here, read it with me.
          In Italy, six hundred and forty.
          In Germany, two hundred and thirty-one.
          In France, a hundred. In Turkey, ninety-one.
          But in Spain, it tops a thousand and three.
          There are your country girls,
          Maidservants and ladies in pearls.
          Countesses, baronesses
          Princesses, marchionesses.
          Women of every rank,
          Of any shape, of any age.
      From *Seven Mozart Librettos*, trans. J.D. McClatchy (New York: W.W. Norton, 2011).

65   'Ah! pieta Signori miei', 2:10b, accessed on http://www.opera-arias.com/mozart/don-giovanni/ah-pieta-signori-miei:
          Ah, be not so hard upon me,
          Give me leave, good friends, to speak!
          Wrongs like yours surely had undone me.
          But, believe me, I am not he you seek.
          I will tell you how my master, did from bad to worse descend.

Donna Elvira, do you tell them,
By what arts he gains his end;
As for thee, I've not a notion what befell thee;
As this lady here can tell thee,
For I met her, with him philand'ring,
Well I knew how all would end;
And to your lordship, I will admit it,
I've acted wrongly, not as befitted . . .
I know I've trespas'd, I ask your pardon,
Lost in the darkness, I entered the garden,
Not thought t'offend. 'Twas a blunder;
Greatly I wonder, how all was known!
Masters, I would now with speed be gone.

66   See Kelly, *Casanova*, p335; Dyneley Hussey, 'Don Giovanni', *Music & Letters* 8.4 (Oct 1927), pp470–2; Thomas Forrest Kelly, *First Nights at the Opera* (New Haven and London: Yale UP, 2004), pp78–87; *Memoirs of Lorenzo Da Ponte*, trans. Elisabeth Abbott (Philadelphia: J.B. Lippincott, 1929), pp237 and 439; Goldoni, *Memoirs*, p173: 'everybody knows the wretched Spanish play which the Italians call "Il Convitato di Pietre," the French "La Festin de Pierre," and the English "Don Juan." In Italy I always considered it with horror, and I could not conceive how such farce could for so long a time draw crowds together, and prove the delight of a polished people.' Nonetheless, it was a great success for Goldoni in the 1730s.

3 An Unsentimental Education

1   Michel Foucault, *Discipline and Punish: The Birth of the Prison* (London: Penguin, 1991), pp3–5.

2   Casanova, *History of My Life*, Vol 5, pp56–8.

3   On her travels through Scandinavia she comments unfavourably on local drinking habits, and *Maria, or The Wrongs of Women* contains this brilliant description of a hungover libertine: 'The squeamishness of stomach alone, produced by the last night's intemperance, which he took no pains to conceal, destroyed my appetite. I think I now see him lolling in an arm-chair, in a dirty powdering gown, soiled linen, ungartered stockings, and tangled hair, yawning and stretching himself.'

4   Mary Wollstonecraft, *Collected Letters*, ed. Janet Todd (London: Allen Lane, 2003), pp1–3.

5   See William Godwin, *Memoirs of the Author of a Vindication of the Rights of Woman* (1798), Ch 3, pp214–15: 'Mary was now arrived at the twenty-fourth year of her age. Her project, five years before, had been personal independence; it was now usefulness.'

6   Shortly before leaving for Ireland she had another formative pedagogical experience. That October she visited Eton College and recorded her appalled

impressions: 'I could not live the life they lead at Eton – nothing but dress and ridicule going forward – and I really believe their fondness for ridicule tends to make them affected . . . for witlings abound – and puns fly about like crackers . . . So much company without socibility [sic], would be to me an unsuportable fatigue . . . Vanity in one shape or other reigns triumphant – and has banished love in all its modifications – and without it what is society? A false kind of politeness throws a varnish over every character – neither the heart nor sentiments appear in their true colours. . . . I am in a melting mood.' MW to Everina Wollstonecraft, 9 Oct 1786, *Collected Letters*, p79.

7   See Arthur Young, *Autobiography: With Selections from His Correspondence*, pp79–80.

8   MW to EW, 30 Oct 1786, *Collected Letters*, pp84–6.

9   MW to EW, 30 Oct 1786, *Collected Letters*, p88.

10   For the quotes, see her history of the French Revolution in *Vindication of the Rights of Women* (Oxford World Classics), p291, which includes this quote; the second one comes from the *Vindication* itself, Chapter 3. Wollstonecraft's own unhappy peripatetic childhood in the countryside, and the later success she achieved in London and Paris, likely contributed to her scepticism about Rousseau's pastoralism. In Norway she described one particularly isolated community as being 'bastilled by nature – shut out from all that opens the understanding, or enlarges the heart', and while she shared in the general belief that cities were hotbeds of vice and corruption, she also saw them as places of progress, writing in her *Historical and Moral View* that 'it has been one of the advantages of the large cities of Europe, to light up the sparks of reason, and to extend the principles of truth' (p359).

11   MW to EW, 24 Mar 1787, *Collected Letters*, pp114–15. She reaffirms this attitude of admiration in a review of the second part of his *Confessions* for the *Analytical Review*: 'The writer of this article will venture to say, that he should never expect to see that man do a generous action, who could ridicule Rousseau's interesting account of his feelings and reveries – who could, in all the pride of wisdom, falsely so called, despise such a heart when naked before him.' Mary Wollstonecraft, *Works*, Vol 7, ed. Janet Todd and Marilyn Butler (London: William Pickering, 1989), p228.

12   MW to EW, 24 Mar 1787. See also Janet Todd, *Mary Wollstonecraft: A Revolutionary Life* (London: Orion, 2011), p105 for Wollstonecraft on Lady Kingsborough, whom she judged to be 'devoid of sensibility . . . *vanity only* inspires her immoderate love of praise – and *selfishness* her *traffick* of civility'.

13   For the Magdalen House, see Chapter 1. There is a passing but pointed allusion to the Magdalen in *A Vindication of the Rights of Woman*: 'Many innocent girls become the dupes of a sincere affectionate heart, and still more are, as it may emphatically be termed, RUINED before they know the difference between virtue and vice: and thus prepared by their education for infamy, they become infamous. Asylums and Magdalens are not the proper

remedies for these abuses. It is justice, not charity that is wanting in the world!' (p143)

14 Knowles, *Fuseli*, pp163–4. A cultivated disregard of fashion had been pioneered by Rousseau and remained in vogue throughout the pre-revolutionary period. During the revolution itself, Helen Maria Williams noted: 'The greatest simplicity in dress is observed, and is sometimes carried even to negligence. Every man seems at pains to shew that he has wasted as few moments as it was possible at his toilette, and that his mind is bent on higher cares than the embellishment of his person.' Deborah Kennedy, *Helen Maria Williams and the Age of Revolution* (Cranbury, NJ: Bucknell UP, 2002), pp85–8).

15 Her first recorded review, in June 1788, of *Edward and Harriet, or the Happy Recovery, a Sentimental Novel. By a Lady*, was typically combative: 'The Happy Recovery is an heterogeneous mass of folly, affectation, and improbability. Metaphors and vulgarisms abound. The countess, "wrapt up in the sable and all-encircling mantle of despair, is seized with a violent puking of blood." An analysis of novels will seldom be expected, nor can the *cant* of sensibility be tried by any criterion of reason; ridicule should direct its shafts against this fair game, and, if possible, deter the thoughtless from imbibing the wildest notions, the most pernicious prejudices, prejudices which influence the conduct and spread insipidity over social converse.' Wollstonecraft, *Works*, Vol 7, p19.

16 Godwin, *Memoirs*, p226.

17 Jenny Uglow, *In These Times: Living in Britain Through Napoleon's Wars 1793–1815* (London: Faber, 2014), p14.

18 Richard Price, 'A Discourse on the Love of Our Country' (1789).

19 In Isaac Cruikshank's 1790 cartoon 'The doctor indulged with his favorite scene', Dr Price is shown watching the *poissardes'* National Guard henchmen ransack Marie-Antoinette's bedroom during the night of 5–6 October through a peephole, with a little black demon for company. Price watches the scene kneeling, his hands in prayer. A speech bubble says: 'Lord now lettest thou thy Servant depart in peace for mine Eyes have Seen.' This is a line lifted from his lecture 'A Discourse on the Love of Our Country'.

20 Edmund Burke, *Reflections on the Revolution in France* (Oxford: Oxford World Classics), pp14, 72, 76, 77.

21 Kennedy, *Helen Maria Williams*, p80.

22 Godwin's diary quoted in Nicholas Roe, *Wordsworth and Coleridge: The Radical Years* (Oxford: OUP, 1997), p42.

23 *Women in Revolutionary Paris, 1789–1795*, ed. Darline Gay Levy, Harriet Branson Applewhite, Mary Durham Johnson (Urbana, IL: University of Illinois Press, 1978), pp76–7.

24 Todd, *Wollstonecraft*, p179.

25 *Women in Revolutionary Paris*, pp89–93.

26 Wollstonecraft, *Vindication*, p65.

27 Wollstonecraft, *Vindication*, p66.
28 Wollstonecraft, *Vindication*, p106. Shortly afterwards (p108) she takes an amusing potshot at Rousseau's proposed system of education for girls: 'The mother, who wishes to give true dignity of character to her daughter, must, regardless of the sneers of ignorance, proceed on a plan diametrically opposite to that which Rousseau has recommended with all the deluding charms of eloquence and philosophical sophistry.'
29 Wollstonecraft, *Vindication*, p71.
30 Wollstonecraft, *Vindication*, p93. Wollstonecraft perceived and decried the notion that a woman would under-educate herself in order to appear unthreatening to a potential partner as 'quitting a substance for a shadow' (p99).
31 Wollstonecraft, *Vindication*, p196.
32 Wollstonecraft, *Vindication*, p219: 'I have before observed, that men ought to maintain the women whom they have seduced.'
33 Wollstonecraft, *Vindication*, p113.
34 MW to JJ, Oct 1792, *Collected Letters*, p205.
35 Rachel Hewitt, *A Revolution of Feeling: The Decade that Forged the Modern Mind* (London: Granta, 2017), pp192–3.
36 For Tahiti see Chapter 2. Southey even considered travelling there, writing that 'Otaheitii independent of its women had many inducements, not only for the sailor but the philosopher.' This came to nothing, while the Pantisocratic scheme was also abandoned, but not before notions of free love were pre-emptively abandoned too. 'I am for Liberty & Long Petticoats,' Southey decided in the end. For a brilliant survey of the Pantisocracy and free love, and a critique of the self-serving male aspects of the imagined sexual utopias, see Hewitt, *A Revolution of Feeling*, Chs 7 and 8.
37 Godwin, *Political Justice* (1793), Vol 2, Ch VI. Godwin also seemed to believe that in this exulted state of liberty, individuals would cease to be the 'slave of sensuality and selfishness' and that their interest in sex would become almost purely functional: 'Reasonable men then will propagate their species, not because a certain sensible pleasure is annexed to this action, but because it is right the species should be propagated; and the manner in which they exercise this function will be regulated by the dictates of reason and duty.' It should be noted that Godwin also argued that, in a world of perfect freedom, the mind would conquer matter and then mortality: 'In a word, why may not man be one day immortal?' A crucial step on the path to immortality was the abolition of sleep: 'before death can be banished, we must banish sleep, death's image' (*Political Justice*, Ch VII).
38 Virginia Woolf, 'Four Figures', in *The Common Reader*, Vol 2 (London, 1932).
39 MW to WR, 3 Jan 1792, in *The Collected English Letters of Henry Fuseli*, ed. David H. Weinglass (Millwood, NY: Kraus International Publications, 1982), p79.
40 Knowles, *Fuseli*, p165.

41 Wollstonecraft, *Collected Letters,* pp204–5.

42 By this point Wollstonecraft had, in the eyes of the conservatives, joined the ranks of the Francophile radical vanguard. See Horace Walpole to Ms Hannah More, 21 Aug 1792:

'But it is better to thank Providence for the tranquility and happiness we enjoy in this country, in spite of the philosophising serpents we have in our bosom, the Paines, the Tookes, and the Woollstoncrofts [sic]. I am glad you have not read the tract of the last-mentioned writer. I would not look at it, though assured it contains neither metaphysics or politics; but as she entered the lists on the latter, and borrowed her title from the demon's book, which aimed at spreading the *wrongs* of men, she is excommunicated from the pale of my library.'

43 Knowles, *Fuseli,* pp167–8.

44 David Andress, *The Terror* (London: Abacus, 2006), p114.

Roland's friend and English champion, Helen Maria Williams, whose hotel had a prospect on to the storming of the Tuileries on 10 August, was aghast at the violence and was in no doubt that it had been carefully organised. In a letter to Hester Thrale Piozzi on 4 September – to which she was too terrified to even sign her name for fear of interception – she described the orgy of violence in Paris as 'a dark stain on the annals of the revolution – you will hear accounts of it as if it were the mob – but it is a well-known fact that the plan was laid the list of the proscribed marked by those to whom the people have been an instrument'. Kennedy, *Helen Maria Williams,* p91.

45 MW to WR, 12 Nov 1792. Wollstonecraft, *Collected Letters,* pp206–8.

46 MW to JJ, 26 Dec 1792. Wollstonecraft, *Collected Letters,* pp216–17.

47 'Letter on the Present Character of the French Nation', Paris, 15 Feb 1793; see also John Hardman, *The Life of Louis XVI* (New Haven and London: Yale UP, 2016), pp438–40.

48 Helen Maria Williams, Letter V, p77; see also Kennedy, *Helen Maria Williams,* p94.

49 Kennedy, *Helen Maria Williams,* p63; HMW, Letter V, p77.

50 Williams's obituary in the *Gentleman's Magazine* in 1828, where she was damned as 'among the violent female devotees of the French revolution', was also home to some choice words for Stone. Writing apropos of her later disavowal of the revolution, the *Magazine* declared that 'she thus showed that her democratic consistency equalled the republican morality she had previously exhibited by living "under the protection" (as the phrase is) of the quondam Rev. Mr Stone, – one of those singularly black sheep, which even the liberal politics of modern ecclesiastical government cannot tolerate'. Kennedy, *Helen Maria Williams,* pp240–1.

51 Todd, *Wollstonecraft,* p211.

52 Todd, *Wollstonecraft,* p236.

53 For a concise survey of the themes of *The Emigrants,* see John Seelye, 'The

Jacobin Mode in Early American Fiction: Gilbert Imlay's "The Emigrants"', *Early American Literature* 22.2 (Fall 1987), pp204–12.

54 Virginia Woolf wrote of Imlay's courtship of Wollstonecraft that 'tickling minnows he had hooked a dolphin', a view that captures the persisting view that Imlay was a romantic chancer and a human mediocrity, who ran amok in the emotional world of one of Europe's greatest female writers and thinkers with little care or concern for the disastrous consequences of his coquetry. This view is anchored in an oblivion of literary evidence. We have none of Imlay's letters and consequently only Wollstonecraft's side of the story. For an even-handed treatment of the Imlay/Wollstonecraft connection, see Richard Holmes's essay 'The Feminist and the Philosopher' (1987) in *Sidetracks: Explorations of a Romantic Biographer* (London: HarperCollins, 2000).

55 Andrew Cayton, *Love in the Time of Revolution: Transatlantic Literary Radicalism and Historical Change, 1793–1818* (Chapel Hill, NC: University of North Carolina Press, 2013), p56.

56 Godwin, *Memoirs*, pp241–2.

57 MW to GI, Aug 1793, *Collected Letters*, p228; Todd, *Wollstonecraft*, p216; Andress, *The Terror*, pp155–70.

58 MW to GI, Sep 1793, *Collected Letters*, p232; Nov 1793, *Letters*, p231.

59 MW to GI, 1 Jan 1794, *Collected Letters*, p238.

60 Cecilia Lucy Brightwell, *Memorials of the Life of Amelia Opie* (1854), pp58–9.

61 Rousseau argued that by installing women in the house they would become the true rulers of France. His model was Sparta, which he argued was nominally run by men but whose controlling influence were Spartan wives and mothers. See 'Dedication to the Republic of Geneva', the preface to the *Discourse on Inequality*: 'I must not forget that precious half of the Republic, which makes the happiness of the other; and whose sweetness and prudence preserve its tranquillity and virtue. Amiable and virtuous daughters of Geneva, it will be always the lot of your sex to govern ours. Happy are we, so long as your chaste influence, solely exercised within the limits of conjugal union, is exerted only for the glory of the State and the happiness of the public. It was thus the female sex commanded at Sparta; and thus you deserve to command at Geneva.' See also Joan B. Landes, *Women and the Public Sphere in the Age of Revolution* (Ithaca, NY: Cornell University Press, 1988), pp70–5.

62 Dorinda Outram, *The Body and the French Revolution: Sex, Class, and Political Culture* (New Haven, CT: Yale UP, 1989), p126.

63 *Women in Revolutionary Paris, 1789–1795*, p180.

64 Helen Maria Williams recorded that, even among hardened Jacobins, the masturbation slander was regarded as needlessly overblown: 'When, Hebert accusing Antoinette of having committed the most shocking crime, she turned with dignity towards the audience, and said, "I appeal to the conscience and feelings of every mother present, to declare if there be one amongst them who

does not shudder at the idea of such horrors," Robespierre, struck with this
answer as by an electrical shock, broke his plate with his fork. "That blockhead
Hebert!" cried he, "as if it were not enough that she was really a Messaline, he
must make her an Agrippina also, and furnish her with a triumph of exciting
the sympathy of the public in her last moments.'" Helen Maria Williams,
Letters Written in France in 1790, ed. Neil Fraistat and Susan S. Lanser
(Broadview Press, 2001), pp172–3.

65   *Women in Revolutionary Paris, 1789–1795*, pp213–16.
66   See Simon Schama, *Citizens: A Chronicle of the French Revolution* (London:
Penguin, 1989), pp637, 653, 686; Joan B. Landes, *Visualizing the Nation:
Gender, Representation, and Revolution in Eighteenth-Century France* (Ithaca,
NY: Cornell UP, 2001), pp112, 126.
67   Wollstonecraft would consistently refer to herself as Mrs Imlay until 1796, and
it was widely believed that she was legally married to him until she married
William Godwin.
68   MW to RB, 20 May 1794, *Collected Letters*, pp253–4.
69   MW to GI, 22 Sep 1794, *Collected Letters*, pp263–4.
70   MW to GI, 12 Jun 1795, *Collected Letters*, p297.
71   Wollstonecraft, *Letters Written in Sweden*, p130.
72   See Holmes, 'The Feminist and the Philosopher'.
73   MW to GI, 27 Sep 1795, *Collected Letters*, p322.
74   Godwin, *Memoirs*, pp258–9.
75   Knowles, *Fuseli*, p170.
76   Wollstonecraft, *Maria*, p102.
77   Wollstonecraft, *Maria*, p137.
78   For a full treatment of seduction laws in England and America, see Chapters 4
and 5.
79   Wollstonecraft, *Maria*, pp170–1.
80   Godwin, *Memoirs*, p256.
81   Holmes, 'The Feminist and the Philosopher', p210.
82   Purely by coincidence, Godwin's memoir was published at the same time as
another scandal broke whose particulars were skewed to defame the late
Mary Wollstonecraft. Shortly after she died, her former student Mary King
was at the epicentre of a salacious affair seemingly lifted from the pages of
Clarissa. In October 1797, Mary eloped with her cousin, Henry Gerard
Fitzgerald. She was retrieved and sent back from London to Castle
Mitchelstown. Her brother, Colonel Robert Edward King, fought a duel with
Fitzgerald in Hyde Park on the morning of 1 October. This was inconclusive,
so they agreed to meet again the next day, but were arrested under the
orders of the Duke of York before they could do so. Shortly before
Christmas, Fitzgerald was spotted lurking about Castle Mitchelstown in
disguise. Robert found out which inn Fitzgerald was staying in, went to his
room and shot him dead 'on the account of [him] seducing his sister'. In

between his duel in Hyde Park and the murder in County Cork, Lord Kingsborough had died, and Robert had inherited the title. Consequently, he was permitted to request a trial in the House of Lords where he was unanimously acquitted in May 1798. In the prelude to the trial, the press began to pick up on the connection between Mary King and her governess (for a very brief period) Mary Wollstonecraft. The unhappy events in the King household were subsequently held to have been part of the perverse legacy of Wollstonecraft's 'detestable system' of morality and education. See *Dictionary of National Biography, 1885–1900*, Vol 31, 'King, Robert (1754–1799)'; N.F. Lowe, 'Mary Wollstonecraft and the Kingsborough Scandal', *Eighteenth-Century Ireland* 9 (1994), pp44–56.

83   *The Anti-Jacobin review and magazine*, Vol 1 (Jul–Dec 1798), p98 and Index; William Stafford, *English Feminists and Their Opponents in the 1790s: Unsex'd and Proper Females* (Manchester: Manchester UP, 2002), pp13–16, 28.

84   William Hazlitt, *The Spirit of the Age* (1825).

4 Circling Mary Shelley

1   HS to Catherine Nugent, 20 Nov 1814, in *A Shelley Library, A Catalogue of Printed Books, Manuscripts, and Autograph Letters, Collected by Thomas James Wise* (London, 1924).

2   Shelley, for his part, believed the whole phenomenon of 'seduction' was a product of a corrupt and oppressive moral order, a view he delineated in a letter to Sir James Lawrence of 17 August 1812: 'Love seems inclined to stay in the prison, and my only reason for putting him in chains, whilst convinced of the unholiness of the act, was a knowledge that, in the present state of society, if love is not thus villainously treated, shew who is the most loved will be treated worse by a misjudging world. In short, seduction, which term could have no meaning in a rational society, has now a most tremendous one; the fictitious merit attached to chastity has made that a forerunner to the most terrible ruins which in Malabar would be a pledge of honour and homage. If there is any enormous and desolating crime of which I should shudder to be accused of it is seduction. I need not say how I admire "Love"; and, as a British public seems to appreciate its merit, in not permitting it to emerge from a first edition, it is with satisfaction I find that justice had conceded abroad what bigotry has denied at home.'

3   HS to CN, 20 Nov 1814, in *A Shelley Library*.

4   MS to Unknown, 1 Jun 1816.

5   Leslie A. Marchand, *Byron: A Portrait* (London: John Murray, 1971; Pimlico, 1993), p127.

6   This disastrous sojourn was later dubbed their 'treacle-moon' by Byron.

7   'Lord Byron took every pains to convince his wife of improper relations subsisting between himself and his sister.' Harriet Beecher Stowe, *Lady Byron Vindicated: A History of the Byron Controversy* (Boston, 1870).

8   Marguerite Gardiner, Countess of Blessington, *Conversations of Lord Byron with the Countess of Blessington* (1834), p142.

9   This was at first part of her appeal to him. In one (pre-nuptial) encomium Byron described her as 'a poetess, a mathematician, a metaphysician; yet, withal, very kind, generous, and gentle, with very little pretension'. Later he would parody these same traits in *Don Juan*: 'Her favourite science was the mathematical, . . . / Her thoughts were theorems, her words a problem, / As if she deem'd that mystery would ennoble 'em.' The notion that Lady Byron was especially 'cold and mathematical' would become something of a trope among Byron's partisans. One defender in the *Atlantic Monthly* wrote: 'finding that she could not reduce him to the mathematical proprieties and conventional rules of her own mode of life, [she] suddenly, and without warning, abandoned him in the most cruel and inexplicable manner.'

10 Marchand, *Byron*, pp211–12.

11 In her 1830 testimony, Lady Byron described her flight from her husband in January 1816: 'The facts are, I left London for Kirkby Mallory, the residence of my father and mother, on the 15th of January, 1816. Lord Byron had signified to me in writing, Jan. 6, his absolute desire that I should leave London on the earliest day that I could conveniently fix. It was not safe for me to encounter the fatigues of a journey sooner than the 15th. Previously to my departure, it had been strongly impressed on my mind that Lord Byron was under the influence of insanity.

    'This opinion was in a great measure derived from the communications made to me by his nearest relatives and personal attendant.' Stowe, *Lady Byron Vindicated*, p108.

12 Fewer than 350 such divorces had been approved by this method in all English history.

13 Medora Leigh herself believed she was Byron's daughter and said as much in her memoir. There is no genetic evidence available to confirm or deny the allegation.

14 GGB to Scrope Davies, 7 Dec 1818, in *Byron's Letters and Journals: A New Selection*, ed. Richard Lansdown (Oxford: OUP, 2015), p306.

15 'From the time Mrs L – came to Bennet St. in the year 1813 – Lord B – had given her various intimations of a criminal intercourse between them.' Marchand, *Byron*, pp229–30.

16 Marchand, *Byron*, p236.

17 'The English women are the only good-looking women in Brussels; though, with true English Bullism, they vest *here* a complete Anglomanian costume, preserving their French fashions for the English winds to waft.' Polidori, *Diary* (London, 1911), p58.

    Thomas Moore, in *The Life of Lord Byron* (London: John Murray, 1835) Vol III, records a hilarious conversation between Polidori and his employer that took place as they travelled from France to Switzerland: 'A dialogue which Lord Byron himself used to mention as having taken place between them during their journey on the Rhine, is amusingly characteristic of both the persons concerned. "After all," said the physician, "what is there you can do that I cannot?" "Why, since you force me to say," answered the other, "I think there are three things I can do which you cannot." Polidori deigned him to name them. "I can," said Lord Byron, "swim across that river and I can snuff out that candle with a pistol-shot at the distance of twenty paces and I have written a poem of which 14,000 copies were sold in one day".

18 Polidori, *Diary*, p97.

19 Polidori, *Diary*, p98. On the way to Dover they had visited the grave of Charles Churchill (1732–64), a poet, satirist and legendary rake. This layover produced a poem, 'Churchill's Grave': 'I stood beside the grave of him who blazed / The Comet of a season . . .'

20 Marchand, *Byron*, p288. Robert Southey had observed the group in Geneva and spread rumours back in England about them, leading Byron to rage in an 1820 letter to Hobhouse: 'The son of a bitch on his return from Switzerland, two years ago, said that Shelley and I "had formed a League of Incest, and practised our precepts with, &c." He lied like a rascal, for they *were not sisters* . . . he lied in another sense, for there was no promiscuous intercourse, my commerce being limited to the carnal knowledge of Miss C.' He later took his revenge on Southey, a radical turned conservative, in the bitter dedication to *Don Juan*:

> Bob Southey! You're a poet – Poet-laureate,
> And representative of all the race;
> Although 'tis true that you turn'd out a Tory at
> Last – yours has lately been a common case;
> [. . .]
> Europe has slaves – allies – kings – armies still,
> And Southey lives to sing them very ill.

21 Moore, *Life of Lord Byron*, p279.

22 The very first reference Polidori makes to Mary and Claire is revealing. Shelley, he records, 'keeps the two daughters of Godwin who practise his theories [free love]'. Leaving aside his clear ignorance of the stepsisters' actual relationship (he was not alone in either his confusion or his indifference to clearing it up), it suggests a certain presumption on his part: perhaps Mary might practise Godwin's theories on him?

23 Giovanni Aldini, *An Account of the Late Improvements in Galvanism* (1803), p216.

24 Byron, *Don Juan* (1819), Canto I, CXXX, 35. The full quotation makes the allusion to Aldini's Newgate experiments even more explicit:

> And galvanism has set some corpses grinning,
> But has not answer'd like the apparatus
> Of the Humane Society's beginning
> By which men are unsuffocated gratis

The Humane Society had collaborated with Aldini in his 1803 experiments.

Richard Holmes in *Shelley: The Pursuit* (London: HarperCollins, 1994), p44, notes that Shelley had been passionately interested in electricity since his Oxford days, when he had kept an 'electrical apparatus' in his room and spoke 'with vehemence of the marvellous powers of electricity, of thunder and lightning' while he tinkered with it.

25   The same point is made in Sandra Gilbert and Susan Gubar, *The Madwoman in the Attic: The Woman Writer and the Nineteenth-Century Literary Imagination* (New Haven and London: Yale UP, 1979): 'At the same time, just as surely as Eve's moral deformity is symbolized by the monster's physical malformation, the monster's physical ugliness represents his social illegitimacy, his bastardy, his namelessness. . . . Mary Shelley's monster has also been "got" in a "dark and vicious place." Indeed, in his vile illegitimacy he seems to incarnate that bestial "unnameable" place.' And significantly, he is himself as nameless as a woman is in patriarchal society, as nameless as unmarried, illegitimately pregnant Mary Wollstonecraft Godwin may have felt herself to be at the time she wrote *Frankenstein*.

'"This nameless mode of naming the unnameable is rather good," Mary commented when she learned that it was the custom at early dramatizations of *Frankenstein* to place a blank line next to the name of the actor who played the part of the monster. But her pleased surprise was disingenuous, for the problem of names and their connection with social legitimacy had been forced into her consciousness all her life.'

26   She also wrote to her estranged husband: 'My dear Bysshe let me conjure you by the remembrance of our days of happiness to grant my last wish – do not take your innocent child from Eliza who has been more than I have, who has watched over her with such unceasing care. – Do not refuse my last request – I never could refuse you & if you had never left me I might have lived but as it is, I freely forgive you & may you enjoy that happiness which you have deprived me of.' (Accessed at http://shelleysghost.bodleian.ox.ac.uk/harriet-shelleys-suicide-letter#Transcript)

27   The Shelleys also tried, more gently, to dissuade him. In a letter from Pisa, dated 21 October 1821, Percy offered to take Allegra into his own household: 'The Countess tells me that you think of leaving Allegra for the present at the convent. Do as you think best; but I can pledge myself to find a situation for her here such as you would approve in case you change your mind.' *A Shelley Library*, p66.

28   MS to CC, 11 May 1821. *My Best Mary: The Selected Letters of Mary Wollstonecraft Shelley*, ed. Muriel Spark (London: Allan Wingate, 1953).

29   This is now known to history as 'A Fragment of a Novel'. It is only a few pages long and contains no reference to vampires or vampirism.

30   *The Vampyre* was quickly translated into French and German and was wildly popular in both countries. In France it also became the basis for the popular

plays *Lord Ruthann ou les Vampires* by Cyprien Bérard (1820), *The Bride of the Isles, a Tale*, by J.R. Planché (1820), *Le Vampire* by Charles Nodier (1820) and *La Guzla* by Prosper Mérimée. Many imitations of *The Vampyre* claimed to have been written by Byron himself, and for many in Europe it was the first piece of Byron they ever read. Goethe famously, and hilariously, described it as 'the English poet's finest work'. See Christopher Frayling, *Vampyres* (London: Faber, 1992), Ch. 2.

31 Confusingly, 'Oneirodynia' is now the technical term for nightmares, but in the early nineteenth century the word was used to refer to sleepwalking, or somnambulism.

32 The connection of sleep with the disabling of man's reasoning faculties was widespread. Describing her sister in a delirious fever, Mary Wollstonecraft had compared her condition to 'something like strange dreams when judgement sleeps and fancy sports at a fine rate' (Todd, *Wollstonecraft*, p45).

33 Anthelme Richerand and John Howell, *Elements of Physiology* (Bristol Royal Infirmary, 1815).

34 Joseph Deleuze, *A Critical History of Animal Magnetism* (London, 1816).

35 Tim Fulford, 'Conducting the Vital Fluid: The Politics and Poetics of Mesmerism in the 1790s', *Studies in Romanticism* 43.1 (Spring 2004).

36 Deleuze, *A Critical History of Animal Magnetism*.

37 Dr John Bell, *The General and Particular Principles of Animal Electricity and Magnetism* (1792), pp65–70; see also *The Sceptic* (1800) (accessed at British Library http://explore.bl.uk/primo_library/libweb/action/search.do?vid=BLVU1)

38 Richard Holmes, *The Age of Wonder: How the Romantic Generation Discovered the Beauty and Terror of Science* (London: HarperCollins, 2008), p273; *The Sceptic*.

39 James Gillray, 'The apples and the horse-turds; – or – Buonaparte among the golden pippins' (1800).

40 *Anti-Jacobin Review* (1806), review of *Du Fluide-Universel, de son Activité et de l'Utilité de ses Modifications, &c.*

41 Louis Odier (1748–1817), a Swiss doctor whose research was, typically of his era, diverse, encompassing paediatrics, vaccinations, laughing gas and Animal Magnetism. Intriguingly, in the aforementioned *Anti-Jacobin Review* article on Universal Fluid the author notes that somnambulism is associated with the doctors of Lyons and Geneva but not Paris, who hold it 'in just contempt'.

42 Polidori, *Diary*, pp119–22.

43 *New Monthly Magazine*, Vol 31, pp180–5.

44 Byron may well have approved of the comparison with Caroline, for he was a huge fan of her grandfather's work both on the stage and in Parliament, and had of course sat on the board of the Sheridan family's Drury Lane Theatre for a period. The great man died in July 1816, and Byron composed his elegy 'On the Death of Richard Brinsley Sheridan' while staying in the Villa Diodati.

45 Thornton Butterworth, *The Journal of Henry Edward Fox* (London, 1923), p292.

46   There is scholarly debate as to whether the story was Mary's or Claire
     Clairmont's. See Bradford A. Booth, 'The Pole: A Story by Clare Clairmont?',
     ELH 5.1 (Mar 1938), pp67–70.

47   *The Diary of Benjamin Robert Haydon*, Vol 4, ed. Willard Bissell Pope
     (Cambridge, MA: Harvard UP, 1960–3), pp110–11.

48   During the same period Haydon records a conversation he had with Edward
     Ellice, an acquaintance of Byron and a minister in Lord Grey's cabinet, on the
     subject of Byron's wife that is revealing of contemporary male sexual attitudes:
     'I said, "She was a prig – she married him to reform him." "Yes," said Mr.
     Ellice, "not only to *reform* him but to *refuse* him."'

       Haydon confides in his diary that if Lady Byron should have actually
     'checked his [Byron's] natural appetites' then he should have 'prostrated her by
     force! – at any rate a man can't be hung for a rape on his wife.' *Diary of
     Benjamin Robert Haydon*, pp99–100.

49   Following his participation in the Greek War of Independence, Trelawney had
     proposed marriage to both Claire Clairmont and Mary Shelley. The latter rejected
     him in brutal fashion, with a wonderfully backhanded compliment thrown in for
     good measure: 'My name will never be Trelawney. I am not so young as I was
     when you first knew me, but I am as proud. I must have the entire affection,
     devotion, &, above all, the solicitous protection of any one who would win me.
     You belong to womankind in general, & Mary Shelley will never be yours.'
       Muriel Spark, *Mary Shelley* (London: Constable, 1993), p122.

50   MS to MG, 13 Oct 1835, in *Letters of Mary W. Shelley*, ed. Frederick L. Jones
     (Norman, OK: University of Oklahoma Press, 1944), p106.

51   Under Breach of Promise to Marry, plaintiffs could seek damages on the
     grounds of seduction – that is, if the promise of marriage led to sex – but even
     in the absence of that were secure in claiming compensation for the psychic,
     emotional and reputational damage sustained by the unexpected and undesired
     end to their nuptial plans. The results could be ridiculous but also fortuitous at
     a time when social mobility was limited and women's life prospects were
     particularly tightly constrained. In 1828, 58-year-old Sally Simpson was
     overjoyed to discover that an obviously humorous offer of marriage made
     nineteen years earlier by a local landlord resulted in a court-ordered payout of
     £350. Nonetheless, leading English jurists took the suit seriously. Referring to
     the survival of 'contract marriage' in Scotland, Lord Brougham observed in
     1849: 'the promise [of marriage] is made secretly, in the course of a seduction,
     and is parcel of the act of seducing the female. Then the difficulty is for the
     female to prove it.' See Denise Bates, *Breach of Promise to Marry: A History of
     How Jilted Brides Settled Scores* (Barnsley: Pen & Sword, 2014); Lawrence Stone,
     Road to Divorce: England 1530–1987 (Oxford: OUP, 1990), pp80–1.

52   Fluke had been castrated by shrapnel at the Battle of Waterloo and was
     thereafter taken into the household service of the Nortons, one of whom was
     his commanding officer in the Lowlands.

53 Much like the lawyers and jurists in nineteenth-century Crim. Con. cases, contemporary historians have probed the historical record for conclusive evidence as to whether Melbourne and Norton were, in fact, intimate. The closest to a smoking gun is a letter Melbourne's brother sent to their sister five days after the trial: 'Quel triomphe ! J'ai ta letter du 23 . . . Don't let Wm think himself invulnerable for having got off again this time; no man's luck can go further.' The 'again' refers to Lord Brandon's Crim. Con. suit, which Melbourne had rid himself of earlier in the decade. The affair was common knowledge at the time. Lord Malmesbury, hearing of Melbourne's acquittal, joked that to accept the court's ruling one would have to believe that 'Melbourne had had more opportunities than any man ever had before, and made no use of them.' Quoted in *The Letters of Caroline Norton to Lord Melbourne*, ed. James O. Hoge and Clarke Olney (Chapel Hill, NC: Ohio State UP, 1974); see also Stone, *Road to Divorce*, p280.

54 For an account of the trial, see Diane Atkinson, *The Criminal Conversation of Mrs Norton* (London: Preface, 2012), pp8–22.

55 CN to MS, 25 Jun 1836, quoted in Jane Gray Perkins, *Life of Mrs. Norton* (London: John Murray, 1910), p95.

56 CN to JM, 1838, quoted in Perkins, *Life of Mrs. Norton*, p151.

57 Brothels, &c. Suppression Bill, HL Debates, 14 Jun 1844, Vol 75 cc877–91.

58 See Hansard, HC Debates, 23 Jun 1847, Vol 93 cc811–14.

59 The *Spectator*, for example, praised the bill: 'Such a law would entail responsibility on another; it would operate as a check on seducers, and a powerful one – for all deceivers of women are mean men. The prospect of having to pay heavily for their "successes" would convert many a Don Juan into Scipios.' (Scipio was the Roman general known for his temperance and moral rectitude.) In *Littell's Living Age*, Vol 14 (Jul–Sep 1847).

60 *Married Women and the Law*, ed. Tim Stretton and Krista J. Kesselring (Montreal: McGill-Queen's University Press, 2013), p7.

61 'The Hon. G.C. Norton and the Hon. Mrs Norton', *Morning Post*, 19 Aug 1853.

62 Caroline Norton, 'English Laws for Women in the Nineteenth Century' (1854).

63 Allen Horstman, *Victorian Divorce* (London: Croom Helm, 1985), p77.

64 These clauses were: 21 – 'Protects earnings of a wife deserted by her husband'; 24 – 'Court could direct payment of separate maintenance to a wife or to her trustee'; 25 – 'A wife can inherit and bequeath property like a single woman'; 26 – 'A Separated wife was given power of contract and suing, and being sued, in any civil proceeding'.

65 Sybil Wolfram, 'Divorce in England 1700–1857', *Oxford Journal of Legal Studies* 5.2 (Summer 1985), pp155–86.

66 Daisy Hay, *Young Romantics: The Shelleys, Byron and Other Tangled Lives* (London: Bloomsbury, 2010), pp307–8.

5 Of Mann and Men

1   Jack Johnson, *My Life: In the Ring and Out* (New York: Dover, 2018), p48.

2   Ida B. Wells, *The Red Record: Tabulated Statistics and Alleged Causes of Lynching in the United States* (1895), Ch 3.

3   Wells, *The Red Record*, Ch 3.

4   As opposed to the English tradition, which required that fathers or guardians bring suits on behalf of their daughters, using the fiction of a putative 'loss of services' from the seduced women. See Chapter 4 for an overview of the English actions.

5   The states were Alabama, Alaska, California, Georgia, Idaho, Indiana, Iowa, Kentucky, Michigan, Mississippi, Montana, Nevada, Oregon, South Dakota, Tennessee, Utah, Virginia and West Virginia. Washington, D.C. also enacted the reform. All but Alabama eliminated the lost services clause; five states (Georgia, Kentucky, Michigan, Virginia, West Virginia) did not extend the right to sue to woman on her own behalf. The rest enacted both reforms simultaneously.

6   M.B. Sinclair, 'Seduction and the Myth of the Ideal Woman', *Law & Ineq.* 5.1 (1987), pp57, 64. Note how closely the language of the law ('priceless jewel') mimics that of sentimental literature, such as Richardson's *Pamela*: 'that jewel, your virtue, which no riches, nor favour, nor any thing in this life, can make up to you'.

7   Larry Whiteaker, *Seduction, Prostitution, and Moral Reform in New York, 1830–1860* (London: Routledge, 2016), p143.

8   H.W. Humble, 'Seduction as a Crime', *Columbia Law Review* 21.2 (Feb 1921).

9   Absurd and condescending as these ideas now seem, they do not devalue the NYFMRS's attempt to introduce seduction legislation. The attempt to introduce these laws cannot be understood without a proper understanding of the legal and political landscape within which these women were operating. Nineteenth-century American women had very few sexual rights. The age of consent was ten in the majority of states, and as low as seven in some. Rape convictions were very hard to come by, as the law assumed that any failure to actively resist at any point in an assault was evidence of consent. The threat or use of violence by men to extract sexual compliance was not automatically considered rape, while the demonstrative injustices posed by the rape laws filtered into other aspects of sexual existence. Identifying genuine sexual consent in such a deeply unequal, deeply patriarchal society was very hard. Furthermore, women were punished in the marriage market for any extra-marital sexual encounters, consensual or otherwise, they might have had, damaging their prospects for long-term financial and physical security. Finally, women could not vote and were not expected to involve themselves in politics in any way. They were locked out of the only institutions that could have improved their position. In such an environment, the fact that the NYFMRS proved themselves capable of mobilising women activists to generate popular support for improved sexual protection and extract such protections from an all-male legislature was no small feat.

10   Mary Frances Berry, 'Judging Morality: Sexual Behavior and Legal
     Consequences in the Late Nineteenth-Century South', in *Black Southerners and
     the Law: 1865–1900*, ed. Donald G. Nieman (London: Routledge, 1994). See
     also, for instance, the case of Emmett Till and his accuser Carolyn Bryant,
     who later admitted that her allegation was completely fictitious; Timothy B.
     Tyson, *The Blood of Emmett Till* (New York: Simon & Schuster, 2017).
     Lynching was a wedge issue within the feminist cause, with black women
     reformers constantly at odds with their white allies over the issue. Black
     women recognised that the uncompromising rhetoric of the WCTU and
     similar organisations on matters of sexual discipline actually endangered black
     lives. When white reformer Mrs Ormison Chant voted against an anti-
     lynching resolution at the National Conference of Unitarian Churches in 1894,
     black reformer Florida Ruffin Ridley wrote an open letter declaring: 'We here
     solemnly deny that the black men are the foul fiends they are pictured; we
     demand that until at least one crime is proved upon them, judgement be
     suspended.'
         Frances Willard was famously silent on the subject of lynching – she
     wished not to antagonise her Southern allies – leading to a public spat with
     Ida B. Wells, who dedicated a whole chapter of *The Red Record* to criticising
     Willard and the WCTU for their policy towards lynching. The upshot of these
     internal tensions was that black women stayed out of the age of consent
     campaign. See Mary E. Odem, *Delinquent Daughters: Protecting and Policing
     Adolescent Female Sexuality in the United States, 1885–1920* (Chapel Hill, NC:
     University of North Carolina Press, 1995), pp29–33. (It is important to note
     that policing sexuality was not the only motivating factor for lynch mobs. The
     desire to appropriate the property of a new class of black landowners was
     often a material factor in designating the victim. See https://features.
     propublica.org/black-land-loss/heirs-property-rights-why-black-families-lose-
     land-south/: 'Ray Winbush, the director of the Institute for Urban Research, at
     Morgan State University, told me, "There is this idea that most blacks were
     lynched because they did something untoward to a young woman. That's not
     true. Most black men were lynched between 1890 and 1920 because whites
     wanted their land."')
11   Johnson, *In the Ring and Out*, pp33–5.
12   Johnson, *In the Ring and Out*, p38.
13   Johnson, *In the Ring and Out*, pp37–9.
14   Ada 'Bricktop' Smith would later write of Johnson's smile: 'There were reasons
     why his smile was so famous. It reflected the real champion, the warm
     generous, impulsive, wonderful, loveable man. That smile gave him the
     handsomeness his looks didn't really deserve.' Ada 'Bricktop' Smith with James
     Haskins, *Bricktop* (New York: Atheneum, 1983), p43.
15   Indeed, Johnson experienced the global sporting scene as his travels, celebrity
     and legal misadventures took him across the world. 'I had opportunities to

observe denizens of the underworld in nearly every country of the world,' he wrote in his memoirs, 'I have witnessed scenes among them that have no parallel even in the most imaginative fiction of melodramatic writers.' Johnson, *Inside the Ring and Out*, p112. Bricktop would later describe him as 'this champion of the world, driver of fast cars, escorter of beautiful women, symbol of the wild, irresponsible sporting man'. Smith, *Bricktop*, p46.

16   Johnson, *Inside the Ring and Out*, pp63–5; Geoffrey C. Ward, *Unforgivable Blackness: The Rise and Fall of Jack Johnson* (London: Yellow Jersey Press, 2015), p77.

17   Johnson, *Inside the Ring and Out*, p65.

18   Smith, *Bricktop*, p185.

19   Ward, *Unforgivable Blackness*, p44.

20   Johnson, *In the Ring and Out*, p52.

21   Johnson, *In the Ring and Out*, p66.

22   'He made Chicago his home. I can understand why – it was big and sprawling, full of vitality and excitement, just like Jack.' Smith, *Bricktop*, p43.

23   The Ketchel fight was one of Johnson's more gruesome encounters. Ketchel, a former bouncer, was a brutal puncher but was 49lb (22kg) lighter than the champion. Johnson quite literally carried Ketchel around the ring for eleven rounds. In the twelfth, Ketchel launched a blistering attack that sent Johnson to the ground and sent the almost entirely white crowd to their feet. An enraged Johnson got up and threw a brawling right hand with such conviction that it carried him over Ketchel and onto his knees on the other side of the ring. Ketchel was out for a minute and a half, a starfish in centre ring. Even in the grainy black and white film, Johnson can be clearly seen picking out three of Ketchel's teeth from his glove and letting them sprinkle down onto the canvas. Then he leans back with one arm across the rope to admire his work.

24   Johnson had no illusions about Jeffries' motivations. In his memoirs he describes him as 'a one-time champion . . . coaxed back to contend for the title in order to satisfy jealousy, hatred, and prejudice'. He also recalled with some bitterness how Jeffries had diminished his victory over Tommy Burns by attacking 'Burns for fighting me, saying that he was money-mad and that he had sold his pride and the pride of the caucasian race by fighting me'. Johnson, *In the Ring and Out*, p134.

25   Ward, *Unforgivable Blackness*, p197. The 'bull fiddle' was in fact a bass viol that Johnson had learnt to play with some skill during his nomadic youth. Essentially the largest type of viola, the bass viol is smaller than a cello but is played in the same way. It is not clear when Johnson learned to play or why he chose this particular type of instrument, though possibly it was simply the type best suited to his size. Full string sections were common in the better sort of clubs and bars that Johnson frequented at this time, and one of his party tricks was to join in these bands when the fancy took him. As a voracious reader, it might have pleased Johnson to know that the bass viol had a

Shakespearean pedigree. The instrument was popular among sixteenth- and seventeenth-century players and is referenced on occasion in Shakespeare's plays. One allusion, from *The Comedy of Errors*, is especially fistic: in Act 4, Scene 3, Dromio describes Adam, the sergeant of the guard, as 'he that goes in the calf's skin . . . he that went, like a bass-viol, in a case of leather'.

26   Ward, *Unforgivable Blackness*, p198.

27   All examples from Al-Tony Gilmore, *Bad Nigger* (Port Washington, NY: Kennikat Press, 1975), pp60–6.

28   Louis Armstrong, *Satchmo: My Life in New Orleans* (New York: Da Capo Press, 1954), p36.

29   In a striking example of how anti-Johnson feeling ran concurrent with progressive sentiment, Thetus Sims of Tennessee was a passionate supporter of women's suffrage. In the official history of the suffrage movement he is named alongside the eponymous champion of the Mann Act as one of those who went above and beyond to ensure the passage of a suffrage bill in the house in 1918: 'Republican Leader Mann of Illinois at much personal risk came from a hospital in Baltimore. He had not been present in Congress for months and his arrival shortly before five o'clock caused great excitement in the chamber. Representative Sims of Tennessee, who had broken his shoulder two days before, refused to have it set until after the suffrage vote and against the advice of his physician was on the floor for the discussion and the vote. Representative Barnhart of Indiana was taken from his bed in a hospital in Washington and stayed at the Capitol just long enough to cast his vote. One of the New York Representatives came immediately after the death of his wife, who had been an ardent suffragist, and returned on the next train.' *The History of Woman Suffrage*, Vol V, ed. Ida Husted Harper et al. (1922).

30   Gilmore, *Bad Nigger*, p90.

31   'Women Denounce Vice', *New York Tribune*, 1901. As early as 1885 – amid the campaign for age of consent laws – Willard had called for the 'punishing with extreme penalties such men as inflict upon women atrocities compared with which death would be infinitely welcome'. The same logic was at work in her subsequent campaign against the White Slave Trade. See Odem, *Delinquent Daughters*, p19.

32   *Fighting the Traffic in Young Girls, or War on the White Slave Trade*, ed. Ernest A. Bell (1910), Ch 30.

33   In his memoirs, Johnson mentions in passing that the Café de Champion's art collection included 'a few real Rembrandts which I had obtained in Europe'. This is a casual and quite transparent lie, but it reflected his interest in being taken seriously as a man of the world with refined tastes. Through his travels, notably his recent trip to Paris and London, Johnson 'had gained a comprehensive idea of decorative effects; I had viewed some of the most notable amusements centers of the world, both as to their exterior and interior arrangements. I also had collected many fine works of art, curios, and

novelties.' He wanted his club to be a showcase for his cultivation/discernment. Johnson, *In the Ring and Out*, p59.

34   Johnson, *In the Ring and Out*, p68.

35   Suicide seems to have dominated the *Times'* columns that September. Excluding the coverage of Etta Duryea's death, the newspaper ran no fewer than twenty-two stories on, or closely related to, suicide, including the incredible 'SHOOTS HIMSELF; WINS GIRL. Rejected for Another, Young Georgian Sways Her by Trying Suicide'.

36   Ward, *Unforgivable Blackness*, p301.

37   Ward, *Unforgivable Blackness*, pp302–3.

38   Ward, *Unforgivable Blackness*, pp302–12.

39   Al-Tony Gilmore, 'Jack Johnson and White Women: The National Impact', *The Journal of Negro History* 58.1 (Jan 1973).

40   Gilmore, *Bad Nigger*, p97.

41   *Chicago Defender*, 26 Oct 1912.

42   Lucille 'begged me to marry her', Johnson wrote in his memoirs, 'declaring that not only had she been ruined in the eyes of the world, but that furthermore her mother was making her the object of abuse and nagging which she could not bear.' Johnson, *In the Ring and Out*, p70.

43   Gilmore, *Bad Nigger*, p107.

44   *New York Times*, Dec 1912. For context, it should be noted that these declarations were widely condemned by politicians and by commentators in the press. The *Times* joked that Blease 'Out-Tillmans Tillman in South Carolina and elsewhere'. (Benjamin Tillman was a notorious racial demagogue, rabid Redeemer and South Carolina senator.) In 1928 Blease would have the dubious distinction of being the last American legislator to agitate for a constitutional amendment that would have outlawed interracial marriage.

45   Gilmore, *Bad Nigger*, p108.

46   In the same December 1912 conference, Blease cited in defence of lynching a 'higher law' than the Constitution. This was an exact duplication of abolitionist William Seward's famous statement that there was a 'higher law' than the Constitution which justified resistance to slavery. Abolitionists, like lynchers, were disdainful of the Constitution, which they called a 'covenant with death' on account of its codifying of slavery.

47   Gilmore, *Bad Nigger*, p122.

48   Gilmore, *Bad Nigger*, p125.

49   Johnson, *In the Ring and Out*, p72.

50   http://montrealgazette.com/news/local-news/second-draft-champion-boxer-jack-johnson-got-under-white-peoples-skins; see also Ward, *Unforgivable Blackness*, pp344–9.

51   Jessica R. Pliley, *Policing Sexuality: The Mann Act and the Making of the FBI* (Cambridge, MA: Harvard UP, 2014), p101.

52   For more on how women with interracial lovers and/or clients were treated in

court, see the example of Ray Vernon discussed in Sharon R. Ullman, *Sex Seen: The Emergence of Modern Sexuality in America* (Berkeley: University of California Press, 1998), pp131–5.

53 David J. Langum, *Crossing Over the Line: Legislating Morality and the Mann Act* (Chicago: University of Chicago Press, 2006).
54 Pliley, *Policing Sexuality*, pp107–13.
55 Pliley, *Policing Sexuality*, pp112–13.
56 All quotes from *Caminetti v. US* (1917) No. 139, http://caselaw.findlaw.com/us-supreme-court/242/470.html
57 Additional biographical material is available in *100 Americans Making Constitutional History: A Biographical History*, ed. Melvin I. Urofsky (Washington, D.C.: CQ Press, 2004). Three justices dissented from the judgment. Justice McKenna wrote the minority opinion, in which he attacked the 'immoral purposes' clause as imprecise, but also argued that in the context of the law's specific mission to erase the threat of white slavery, 'immoral purposes' could only reasonably be applied to 'commercialized vice, immoralities having a mercenary purpose'. He then went further and challenged the assumptions underlying both the law itself and the majority opinion of the court: 'There is much in the present case to tempt to a violation of the rule. Any measure that protects the purity of women from assault or enticement to degradation finds an instant advocate in our best emotions; but the judicial function cannot yield to emotion – it must, with poise of mind, consider and decide. It should not shut its eyes to the facts of the world and assume not to know what everybody else knows. And everybody knows that there is a difference between the occasional immoralities of men and women and that systematized and mercenary immorality epitomized in the statute's graphic phrase "white slave traffic." And it was such immorality that was in the legislative mind, and not the other.'

McKenna also concurred with the *Times* that the law's naive view of prevailing social and sexual morality opened the door to abuses, blackmail in particular: 'There is danger in extending a statute beyond its purpose, even if justified by a strict adherence to its words. . . . The present case warns against ascribing such improvidence to the statute under review. Blackmailers of both sexes have arisen, using the terrors of the construction now sanctioned by this court as a help – indeed, the means – for their brigandage. The result is grave and should give us pause. It certainly will not be denied that legal authority justifies the rejection of a construction which leads to mischievous consequences, if the statute be susceptible of another construction.'

Both Diggs and Caminetti were out within a year, and there was a happy ending to this story for Maury Diggs at least. Maury and Marsha married in San Francisco in 1915 and remained so until his death in 1953 in St Helena, California. After his release from prison Diggs resumed his career as an architect and became a specialist in the design and construction of horse racetracks. He was responsible for designing some of the largest in the state, including the Golden Gate Fields in Albany, San Francisco.

58 Johnson, *In the Ring and Out*, pp76–80.

59 Ward, *Unforgivable Blackness*, pp379–81.

60 Johnson, *In the Ring and Out*, p115.

61 There is a long and revealing passage in his memoirs where he describes an indigenous tribe his party encountered during their travels in Mexico: 'We discovered that it was not uninhabited, but that it was the camping place of a tribe of Indians, the name of which I never learned. Perhaps they had never acquired any designation for they were without doubt the lowest in the human scale that I had ever seen. They had human forms but other than that they were animals. They were even worse than animals so unclean and lazy as they were. They were naked and their skins were filthy with slime. They lay about in camps like vermin, men, women and babies piled up together with dogs who had the same privileges as the others – privileges which permitted them to nurse at the breasts of the human mothers who lolled listlessly about, a suckling babe on one side, a dog on the other.' Even Johnson, who knew all there was to know about racial prejudice, was not free of the racist assumptions of his time. Johnson, *In the Ring and Out*, p95.

62 Johnson, *In the Ring and Out*, p98.

63 Zelda made it clear to her friends, at least, that her acceptance of his proposal was contingent on his acceptance by a publisher. A friend of both F. Scott and Zelda recalled the latter's attitude as: 'If Scott sells the book, I'll marry the man, because he is sweet.' But sweetness was no substitute for financial security. In the event, Zelda became Mrs F. Scott Fitzgerald a mere eight days after the publication of *This Side of Paradise*. This was a book that contained the observation (from Rosalind, a Zelda avatar) that 'given a decent start any girl can beat a man nowadays'. David S. Brown, *Paradise Lost: A Life of F. Scott Fitzgerald* (Cambridge, MA: Belknap Press, 2017), pp75, 90.

64 Paula S. Fass, *The Damned and The Beautiful: American Youth in the 1920s* (Oxford: OUP, 1977), pp22–3.

65 Ward, *Unforgivable Blackness*, p425.

66 All Fitzgerald quotes are taken from F. Scott Fitzgerald, *The Best Early Stories* (New York: Modern Library, 2005).

67 *Recent Social Trends in the United States; Report of the President's Research Committee on Social Trends* (1933), pp417–19.

68 M.B.W. Sinclair, 'Seduction and the Myth of the Ideal Woman'.

69 Pippa Holloway, *Sexuality, Politics, and Social Control in Virginia, 1920–1945* (Chapel Hill, NC: University of North Carolina Press, 2006), pp40–6.

70 Pliley, *Policing Sexuality*, p132.

71 Angus McLaren, *Sexual Blackmail: A Modern History* (Cambridge, MA: Harvard UP, 2002), pp87–8, 93, 95–7.

72 Anita Loos, *Gentlemen Prefer Blondes & But Gentlemen Marry Brunettes* (London: Penguin, 1998); McLaren, *Sexual Blackmail*, p172

73 The senator's interpretation continued to baffle her long into her life: 'The thing that was so amazing and truly surprising to me was that it was widely interpreted as giving free rein to predatory males to take advantage of chaste maidens which, of course, was diametrically opposed to what my conception was. I thought – and I still think – that it was an early blow for women's liberation.'

74 The seven states that passed anti-heart balm legislation in 1935 were Indiana, Illinois, Alabama, New Jersey, New York, Michigan and Pennsylvania. California, Colorado and Massachusetts followed over the next five years, while Florida abolished the actions in 1945. Arizona, Connecticut, Idaho, Maryland, Minnesota, Missouri, Nebraska, North Carolina, Oklahoma, Oregon, Rhode Island, Texas, Washington, Wisconsin and Ohio would try and fail to pass similar legislation in 1935.

Among the states that abolished was Illinois. A state which had searched the law books for any pretext to hold Jack Johnson for the crime of seducing a very willing white woman now described the heart balms as 'action conducive to extortion and blackmail' and abolished them.

75 Sinclair, 'Seduction and the Myth of the Ideal Woman'. For all details relating to Roberta West Nicholson, see the Roberta West Nicholson Oral History Transcript at the Indiana State Library Digital Collections: http://cdm16066. contentdm.oclc.org/cdm/ref/collection/p16066coll40/id/77.

76 Sinclair, 'Seduction and the Myth of the Ideal Woman'.

6 Blood Out

1 Daniel Pick, *Svengali's Web: The Alien Enchanter in Modern Culture* (New Haven and London: Yale UP, 2000), p66.

2 Irving knew exactly what he was doing to the impressionable Stoker. 'The effects of his recitation upon Stoker was all that Irving had hoped,' Irving's son, Laurence, would later write, '– as welcome as the effects of the "Murder of Gonzago" on his uncle were to Hamlet.'

Laurence Irving, *Henry Irving: The Actor and His World* (London: Faber & Faber, 1951), p279.

3 Du Maurier would later state that Florence Stoker was among the three most beautiful women he had ever met. 'Filial Reproof', *Punch*, 11 Sep 1886; E.V. Lucas, 'The Creator of Trilby', *The Times*, 6 Mar 1934 (on the one-hundredth anniversary of Du Maurier's birth).

4 Oscar Wilde, in contrast, praised Irving effusively for resisting the lure of public favour and staying true to his artistic vision: 'With his marvellous and vivid personality, with a style that has really a true colour-element in it, with his extraordinary power, not over mere mimicry but over imaginative and intellectual creation, Mr Irving, had his sole object been to give the public

what it wanted, could have produced the commonest plays in the commonest manner, and made as much success and money as a man could possibly desire. But his object was not that. His object was to realize his own perfection as an artist, under certain conditions, and in certain forms of Art.' Oscar Wilde, *In Praise of Disobedience: The Soul of Man Under Socialism and Other Writings* (London: Verso, 2018), p28.

5   Irving, *Henry Irving*, pp310–11.
6   The Lyceum became one of the few places where the two men could be found together. By the 1880s Gladstone was going blind and had to be given a special seat in the prompt corner so he could follow the action. A very old and very frail Disraeli remained mischievous, however. When he came to see *The Corsican Brothers* in 1880, his companion Corry asked Stoker as they left the performance whether 'we could have supper somewhere and ask some of the Coryphées to join us, as we used to do in Paris in the fifties?

   'Stoker hastened to explain that the ballet dancers at the Lyceum would be deeply shocked at such a suggestion and that Loveday had been driven frantic in trying to persuade them to overcome their suburban primness in the abandon of the bal masqué. . . . The Conservatives would be slow to change their view of the theatre as an Arcadia populated with captivating and warm-hearted nymphs who could be lured into "cabinets particuliers" where their slippers, brimming with champagne, could be raised to Love, Life and Laughter.'
   Irving, *Henry Irving*, pp363–4.
7   Horace Wyndham, *The Nineteen Hundreds* (London, 1922), p118.
8   The 1881 select committee recorded the causes of mass juvenile prostitution: 'A vicious demand for young girls; overcrowding in dwellings, and immorality arising therefrom; want of parental control, and in many cases parental example, profligacy, and immoral treatment; residence, in some cases, in brothels; the example and encouragement of other girls slightly older, and the sight of dress and money which their immoral habits have enabled them to obtain; the state of the streets in which little girls are allowed to run about, and become accustomed to the sight of open profligacy; and sometimes the contamination with vicious girls in schools.'
9   Josephine Butler was later one of the vice-presidents (the president was the Duke of Westminster) of the National Vigilance Association (NVA), an organisation created to ensure the enforcement of the 1885 Criminal Law Amendment Act and the pre-eminent combatant of the white slave trade in the United Kingdom. The offices of the NVA were on 267 Strand, a short walk from the Lyceum.
10   Susan Kingsley Kent, *Sex and Suffrage in Britain, 1860–1914* (Princeton, NJ: Princeton UP, 1987), pp10, 120.
11   W.T. Stead, 'If Christ came to Chicago!', *Review of Reviews* (London, 1894),

p262; John D'Emilio and Estelle B. Freedman, *Intimate Matters: A History of Sexuality in America* (Chicago: University of Chicago Press, 1997), pp152–3.

12 See also Oscar Wilde's criticism of sentimental philanthropy in 'The Soul of Man Under Socialism': 'Charity they feel to be a ridiculously inadequate mode of partial restitution, or a sentimental dole, usually accompanied by some impertinent attempt on the part of the sentimentalist to tyrannise over their private lives.' The bill was certainly regarded as a seduction statute by its most vigorous supporters. In response to an 1899 survey of European and North American seduction laws conducted by the International Congress on the White Slave Trade, the British delegation declared that the 1885 Criminal Law Amendment Act was the governing British law on such matters and 'has been used to punish married men who have seduced girls under promise of marriage'. Indeed, the successful campaign by Butler and Stead to introduce and enforce the 1885 law was the inspiration for Frances Willard and the WCTU in their campaign to increase the age of consent in American states discussed in Chapter 5. See *The White Slave Trade: Transactions of the International Congress on the White Slave Trade* (London: Office of the National Vigilance Association, 1899), pp19, 60.

13 One of the prominent victims of the law in its early years was Captain Verney, MP, whom *The Times* on 7 May 1891 described as 'conspicuous for his zeal in the "purity movement" and for the unction of his language in discussing questions of morality, while he was leading a double life and methodically employing a procuress in the service of his profligacy. . . . His evil practices were deliberate, systematic, and apparently long continued. His punishment is heavy, and the 12 months imprisonment is, perhaps, the lightest part of it. As Sir Charles Russell said: – "His position is lost, his rank in the Navy is gone, his honoured name has departed from him."'

14 Ironically, Stead was charged with abduction of a minor and tried under the new legal procedures stipulated in the Criminal Law Amendment Act of 1885 (See *The Times*, 11 Nov 1885). There were a number of high-profile campaigns to have Stead released from prison, including a direct appeal by Josephine Butler to the Home Secretary (*The Times*, 13 Nov 1885). In the end Stead served his full three-month sentence, the majority of it in Holloway Prison where he continued to edit the *Pall Mall Gazette*. He took some pride in his imprisonment, and each year would pose for photos in his old prison uniform to commemorate the day of his conviction.

15 Letter from Dighton Macnaughten Probyn to Henry Irving, 4 Jul 1885. Irving's own antipathy towards evangelical Christianity was shaped by his mother, an unbending Methodist, who disowned her son for his decision to work in the theatre.

16 For Stead, as places of entertainment theatres were scenes of seduction; as places of business they were scenes of debauch. For example, in the 'Maiden

Tribute' series: 'It is said that at a certain notorious theatre no girl ever kept her virtue more than three months.'

17 Through Watts, Terry met all the major figures in this circle: Millais, Rossetti (who was John Polidori's nephew; see Chapter 4), Hunt and Leighton. She married Watts not long after the most famous Pre-Raphaelite muse, Elizabeth Siddal – most famous for being the model of Ophelia in Millais's famous painting – died of a laudanum overdose. Despite her own immense success, Terry lived in the shadow of Siddal's legend and her own breakout performance was of Ophelia in Irving's *Hamlet*, the first play run at the Lyceum in 1878. Terry and Siddal's portraits (posing as Lady Macbeth and Ophelia respectively) can now be found on the same wall at Tate Britain.

18 Nina Auerbach, *Ellen Terry: Player in Her Time* (London: Phoenix House, 1987), pp116–17.

19 'Strange Case Of Dr. Jekyll And Mr. Hyde', *The Times*, 25 Jan 1886.

20 From the outset Lankester made it clear that he saw this law at work in human society:

'Any new set of conditions occurring to an animal which render its food and safety very easily attained, seem to lead as a rule to Degeneration; just as an active healthy man sometimes degenerates when he becomes suddenly possessed of a fortune; or as Rome degenerated when possessed of the riches of the ancient world. The habit of parasitism clearly acts upon animal organisation in this way. Let the parasitic life once be secured, and away go legs, jaws, eyes, and ears; the active, highly-gifted crab, insect, or annelid may become a mere sac, absorbing nourishment and laying eggs.' Edwin Lankester, *Degeneration: A Chapter in Darwinism* (London, 1880).

21 Cesare Lombroso, *Criminal Man, Briefly Summarised By His Daughter Gina Lombroso Ferrero* (New York: G.P. Putnam, 1911), p xiv.

22 *Pall Mall Gazette*, 25 Oct 1881.

23 *Pall Mall Gazette*, 10 Oct 1887.

24 Letter in the British Museum, https://www.bl.uk/collection-items/anonymous-letter-to-city-of-london-police-about-jack-the-ripper. The letter also says: "'I thought it Strange this Play Should have Commenced before the Murders for it is Really Something after the Same Stile. The Murders take place on Saturday nights Mr M never has A Performance on Saturday. The Murders Once Took PLace on Friday & once Mr M Was to ill to Perform at the Saturday Morning Performance . . .'"

25 *Daily Telegraph*, 12 Oct 1888.

26 Stoker also knew another man suspected of being the murderer: his great friend Hall Caine's acquaintance Francis Tumblety.

27 *Spectator*, 6 Oct 1888.

28 Irving, *Henry Irving*, pp333–4.

29 *Pall Mall Gazette*, 8 Sep 1888.

30 Neil R. Davison, '"The Jew" as Homme/Femme-Fatale: Jewish (Art)ifice,

"Trilby", and Dreyfus', *Jewish Social Studies*, New Series 8.2/3 (Winter–Spring 2002), pp73–111: '"The Jew" remained subversive, powerful yet morally inferior, and degeneratively feminized throughout the decade and beyond.'

31 Lombroso, *Criminal Man*, p140. See also the Austrian delegation's comment on the white slave trade, made in 1899: 'The agents [of the trade] themselves are invariably Jews. The victims are not sent directly to Constantinople. . . . But they at length arrive in that city. From thence some are forwarded to Cairo, some to Trebizond: none of them ever come back to their native country.' *The White Slave Trade*, p83.

32 'Is It Not Time?', *Pall Mall Gazette*, 16 Oct 1883. See also William Henry Wilkins, *The Alien Invasion* (London, 1892), Ch 3.

33 Colin Holmes, *Anti-Semitism in British Society: 1876–1939* (London: Arnold, 1979). For specific association with the Ripper case, see *Jewish Chronicle*, 12 Oct 1888 (accessible on http://www.casebook.org/press_reports/jewish_chronicle/jc881012.html).

34 See Anthony S. Wohl, '"Dizzi-Ben-Dizzi": Disraeli as Alien', *Journal of British Studies* 34.3 (Jul 1995), pp375–411; Pick, *Svengali's Web*, pp130–1: Carlyle on Disraeli: 'a superlative Hebrew conjurer, spellbinding all the great Lords, great parties, great interests of England'.

35 Christopher J. Probst, *Demonizing the Jews: Luther and the Protestant Church in Nazi Germany* (Bloomington, IN: Indiana UP, 2012), pp48–9. Luther called the Jews 'a whoring and murderous people', 'bloodthirsty bloodhounds and murderers of all Christendom', witches and magicians capable of 'conjuring signs, figures, and the tetragrammaton of the name, that is, with idolatry, envy and conceit'.

36 The epicentre of late Victorian discourse on hypnosis was the Parisian hospital of Salpêtrière, where Jean-Martin Charcot conducted his famous experiments on 'hysterical' women. In 1885 Sigmund Freud was one of his students. The fissure within the field of hypnosis was between the 'Parisian school' led by Charcot and the 'Nancy school' led by Hippolyte Bernheim. The latter argued that all women were susceptible to the power of suggestion and hypnosis, not just hysterics. The debate was followed in England and was the subject of discussion at the Second International Congress of Psychology in London in 1892. Pick, *Svengali's Web*, pp66–7.

Charcot is directly alluded to in *Dracula* during a conversation between Seward and Van Helsing: '"Yes," I said. "Charcot has proved that pretty well." He smiled as he went on: "Then you are satisfied as to it. Yes? And of course then you understand how it acts, and can follow the mind of the great Charcot – alas that he is no more! – into the very soul of the patient that he influence. No? Then, friend John, am I to take it that you simply accept fact, and are satisfied to let from premise to conclusion be a blank? No? Then tell me – for I am a student of the brain – how you accept the hypnotism and reject the thought reading. Let me tell you, my friend, that there are things done to-day in electrical science which would have been deemed unholy by the very men who discovered electricity – who would themselves not so long before have been burned as wizards. There are always mysteries in life."'

See also Ralph M. Leck, *Vita Sexualis* (Urbana, IL: Illinois UP, 2016). Charcot's 1882 *Inversion du sens genital et autres Perversions sexuelles* was one of the first books to link degeneration with sexual deviance, which became a trope of French medical and scientific discourse in the last decade of the nineteenth century.

37 The geographic reach and temporal endurance of this canard is remarkable. When Olga Ivinskaya was questioned in Moscow's Lubyanka prison in 1949 on account of her romantic association with the poet Boris Pasternak, her interrogator expressed disbelief that a Russian woman could be attracted to a Jewish man: 'I can't believe that a Russian woman like you could really be in love with this old Jew – there must be some ulterior motive here! I've seen him myself. You can't love him. He's just mesmerised you, or something.' Anne Pasternak, *Lara* (London: William Collins, 2016), p98.

Hypnotism was also posited as an explanation for the Ripper killings, either as a tool for the murderer to use on his victims or as a device used to compel the murderer to kill. See e.g. 'Has the Miscreant Been Hypnotised?', *Evening News*, 16 Oct 1888; *Daily Chronicle*, 'Hypnotism and Crime'. For the connection made between hypnotism and crime see Ruth Harris, 'Murder Under Hypnosis', in *The Anatomy of Madness*, Vol 2, ed. W.F. Bynum, R. Porter and M. Shepherd (London: Tavistock, 1985); for a contemporary account of the connection between seduction and hypnosis, see Ernest Mesnet, *Outrages Against Modesty* (1890).

38 'Svengali's vanity, treacherousness, selfishness, personal uncleanliness and so forth', George Orwell observed, 'are constantly connected with the fact that he is a Jew.'

George Orwell, 'As I Please', *Tribune*, 6 Dec 1946.

39 Jonathan Freedman, *The Temple of Culture: Assimilation and Anti-Semitism in Literary Anglo-America* (Oxford: OUP, 2000), pp91–2.

40 *Trilbyana: The Rise and Progress of a Popular Novel* (New York, 1895), p8.

41 'No such magnificent or seductive apparition has ever been seen before or since on any stage or platform – not even Miss Ellen Terry as the priestess of Artemis in the late Laureate's play, "The Cup."' Du Maurier, *Trilby*, p209. Nina Auerbach argues that Terry was in fact the inspiration for Trilby. When she was newly wed to artist George Watts in the 1860s, Du Maurier had been a visitor to her husband's home at Little Holland House and had been scathing of the pretentious old artists who gathered there and the women who fawned over them. Whether this image of the teenage Terry – then Nelly Watts – as the beautiful plaything of older, bohemian men survived the thirty-year interval between his visits and the publication of *Trilby* is hard to know, but alluring nonetheless. See Auerbach, *Ellen Terry*, p109.

42 Rossetti had himself indulged in some pretty ghoulish antics in his time. In 1860 he had married Elizabeth Siddal, the Pre-Raphaelite muse and model. When Siddal died in 1862, Rossetti had buried her with a notebook of his unpublished poetry, much of which concerned his love for her, nestled amid her golden hair. In 1869 he decided he wanted the notebook back and had her corpse exhumed by the light of an enormous fire lit by her grave in Highgate Cemetery. According to Hall Caine, her body had not decomposed and they found her as beautiful as ever, the volume of poetry still in her hair. The book was retrieved, the body returned to the ground and the verses returned to Rossetti. It is not clear whether Stoker knew about this story, though given Caine's role in recording the event for posterity, and that Rossetti was long dead by the time *Dracula* was written, it is plausible that he told Stoker at some point during the writing process or before. He could also have heard it from Ellen Terry, who was a part of the Pre-Raphaelite circle as a young woman. William Michael Rossetti, *Dante Gabriel Rossetti: His Family-letters, with a Memoir* (1895), pp274–5.

43 'With his left hand he held both Mrs. Harker's hands, keeping them away with her arms at full tension; his right hand gripped her by the back of the neck, forcing her face down on his bosom. Her white nightdress was smeared with blood, and a thin stream trickled down the man's bare breast which was shown by his torn-open dress. The attitude of the two had a terrible resemblance to a child forcing a kitten's nose into a saucer of milk to compel it to drink.' For a critical discussion of this scene and others, see Dejan Kuzmanovic, 'Vampiric Seduction and Vicissitudes of Masculine Identity in Bram Stoker's "Dracula"', *Victorian Literature and Culture* 37.2 (2009), pp411–25.

44 Stoker had a personal connection with the region through his brother, George, who had served as a doctor there during the Russo-Turkish war and published a book recounting the experience. David J. Skal, *Something in the Blood: The Untold Story of Bram Stoker* (New York: Liveright, 2016), p109.

45 *Spectator*, 10 Nov 1888, 'Transylvania' book review. Interest in the region was piqued in this period by the 'Eastern Question', a slow-moving geopolitical crisis generated by the decline of the Ottoman Empire. The English public's concern with the Eastern Question helped stoke mainstream anti-Semitism, partially because Disraeli was largely indifferent to the matter, which his more scurrilous critics, Gladstone included, alleged was a reflection of his Jewish indifference to the suffering of Christians in the Ottoman domains. See Anthony Julius, *Trials of the Diaspora: A History of Anti-Semitism in England* (Oxford: OUP, 2010), pp264–5.

46 Dracula is described as 'a tall thin man, with a beaky nose and black moustache and pointed beard'; Svengali as 'bold, brilliant, black eyes, with long heavy lids, a thin, sallow face, and a beard of burnt-up black, which grew almost from under his eyelids; and over it his moustache, a shade lighter, fell

in two long spiral twists'. See Bram Dijkstra, *Idols of Perversity* (Oxford: OUP, 1986), p343.

47 Stoker had used anti-Semitic tropes in his other novels. 'The Watter's Mou' (1895) features the wicked German-Jewish money lender Solomon Mendoza, an 'elderly man with a bald head, keen eyes, a ragged grey beard, a hooked nose, and an evil smile'.

48 Historian Anthony Julius (*Trials of the Diaspora*, p271) notes that anti-Semitic discourse in 1890s England attached itself to the Boer War, which was allegedly orchestrated by and for Jewish 'gold bugs' intent on securing the mineral wealth of the Transvaal.

49 There is an interesting if somewhat opaque allusion to Dracula's Jewishness in his ability to transform into a wolf. Jews had long been associated with magical powers, including the ability to assume animal form. 'The Discoverie of Witchcraft', a 1584 treatise on witches, includes a description of 'one Bajanus a Jew, being the sonne of Simeon, which could, when list, turne himselfe into a wolf'. It is of course highly improbable that Stoker would have been familiar with this obscure text, but he did know *The Merchant of Venice* and may have absorbed, by osmosis if nothing else, Gratiano's attack on Shylock in Act IV, Scene I:

> O, be thou damn'd, inexecrable dog!
> And for thy life let justice be accused.
> Thou almost makest me waver in my faith
> To hold opinion with Pythagoras,
> That souls of animals infuse themselves
> Into the trunks of men: thy currish spirit
> Govern'd a wolf, who, hang'd for human slaughter,
> Even from the gallows did his fell soul fleet,
> And, whilst thou lay'st in thy unhallow'd dam,
> Infused itself in thee; for thy desires
> Are wolvish, bloody, starved and ravenous.

50 Max Nordau was a German-Jewish author whose best-known work, *Degeneration*, was published in England in 1895. Stoker would not necessarily have had to read Nordau in order to be familiar with the broad contours of his theory of cultural and metaphysical decay. It includes a sustained attack on Ibsen along lines illustrative of what many contemporaries found objectionable in the playwright's work. Nordau saw in Ibsen's plays 'such unqualified approval of all feminine depravities, was bound to secure the applause of those women who in the viragoes of Ibsen's drama – hysterical, nymphomaniacal, perverted in maternal instinct – recognise either their own portrait or the ideal of development of their degenerate imagination'. He also considered the proliferation of ghost stories that include themes of 'hypnotism, telepathy, somnambulism' a hallmark of the collapse of high culture – ironic, given the positive allusion to him in *Dracula*.

George Bernard Shaw's *The Quintessence of Ibsenism* (1891) made the robust case for the connection between Ibsen and 'the woman question'. For a more balanced, modern take on the relationship between Ibsen and late-nineteenth-century feminism, see Joan Templeton, 'The Doll House Backlash: Criticism, Feminism, and Ibsen', *PMLA* 104.1 (Jan 1989), pp28–40.

51 'In some faculties of mind he has been, and is, only a child'; 'The criminal always works at one crime – that is the true criminal who seems predestinate to crime, and who will of none other. This criminal has not full man-brain. He is clever and cunning and resourceful; but he be not of man-stature as to brain. He be of child-brain in much. Now this criminal of ours is predestinate to crime also; he, too, have child-brain, and it is of the child to do what he have done. The little bird, the little fish, the little animal learn not by principle, but empirically; and when he learn to do, then there is to him the ground to start from to do more.'

52 Pick, *Svengali's Web*, pp63–6; Harris, 'Murder Under Hypnosis', pp207, 217–18. The latter contains an account of the 1878 rape trial of a French-Jewish doctor, Paul Lévy, who allegedly used hypnosis to molest a young gentile girl. He received ten years' imprisonment. The case was referred to in the more famous Bompard trial of 1890 in which the defendant, Gabrielle Bompard, alleged she had been hypnotised by her lover, Michel Eyraud, and made an accessory to the murder of Toussaint-Augustin Gouffé while his powerless tool.

53 As defined by Thomas Hardy, the New Woman was 'The woman who was coming into notice in her thousands every year – the woman of the feminist movement – the slight, pale "bachelor" girl – the intellectualized, emancipated bundle of nerves that modern conditions were producing, mainly in cities as yet; who does not recognize the necessity for most of her sex to follow marriage as a profession, and boast themselves as superior people because they are licensed to be loved on the premises.' Thomas Hardy, Postscript to *Jude the Obscure*, 1st edn (1895).

54 Inevitable comparisons were made with the French Revolution. See the *Quarterly Review* on the 'New Woman' in 1894: 'she advances, with drums beating and colours flying, to the sound also of the Phrygian flute, a disordered array, but nowise daunted, resolute in her determination to end what she is pleased to define as the slavery of one-half the human race.' *Quarterly Review* 179, 1894, quoted in Elaine Showalter, *Sexual Anarchy* (London: Bloomsbury, 1991), p39.

55 *The New Woman, and Other Emancipated Woman Plays* (Oxford: OUP, 1998).

56 'Drama at Royal Academy', *The Era*, 18 May 1895.

57 Edy helped radicalise her mother, who by 1914 was boasting to Australian journalists, 'Of course you know I'm a suffragette. Of course I am and so is my daughter Edith Craig.' From 1909 Edy was involved with the Actresses' Franchise League; she directed *A Pageant of Great Women*, which opened on 12 November 1909 featuring Ellen Terry as eighteenth-century Drury Lane

actress Nance Oldfield. See Michael Holroyd, *A Strange and Eventful History: The Dramatic Lives of Ellen Terry, Henry Irving and their Remarkable Families* (London: Chatto & Windus, 2008), pp426, 432.

58 'Woman, however, if physically and mentally normal, and properly educated, has but little sensual desire. If it were otherwise, marriage and family life would be empty words. As yet the man who avoids women, and the woman who seeks men are sheer anomalies.' Dr. R. v. Krafft-Ebing, *Psychopathia sexualis*; only authorised English adaptation of the twelfth German edition by F.J. Rebman (1893).

59 In *Man and Superman* John Tanner, the Don Juan stand-in, accuses Ann Whitefield of being a vampire in the play's final line.

60 In Chapter VIII: 'We had a capital "severe tea" at Robin Hood's Bay in a sweet little old-fashioned inn, with a bow-window right over the seaweed-covered rocks of the strand. I believe we should have shocked the "New Woman" with our appetites. Men are more tolerant, bless them! Then we walked home with some, or rather many, stoppages to rest, and with our hearts full of a constant dread of wild bulls. Lucy was really tired, and we intended to creep off to bed as soon as we could. The young curate came in, however, and Mrs. Westenra asked him to stay for supper. Lucy and I had both a fight for it with the dusty miller; I know it was a hard fight on my part, and I am quite heroic. I think that some day the bishops must get together and see about breeding up a new class of curates, who don't take supper, no matter how they may be pressed to, and who will know when girls are tired. Lucy is asleep and breathing softly. She has more colour in her cheeks than usual, and looks, oh, so sweet. If Mr. Holmwood fell in love with her seeing her only in the drawing-room, I wonder what he would say if he saw her now. Some of the "New Women" writers will some day start an idea that men and women should be allowed to see each other asleep before proposing or accepting. But I suppose the New Woman won't condescend in future to accept; she will do the proposing herself.'

61 After Marie Stopes published *Married Love*, a celebration of female sexuality, in 1918 she received an angry letter from an anonymous aristocrat enraged at her proselytisation of the joys of sex. 'Once you give women a taste for these things,' he wrote, 'they become vampires, and you have let loose vampires into decent men's homes.' Quoted in Carol Dyhouse, *Heartthrobs* (Oxford: OUP, 2017).

William J. Robinson of Bronx hospital in *Married Life and Happiness* (1922) describes wives who want sex every two weeks/ten days as normal, but 'there is the opposite type of woman, who is a great danger to the health and even the very life of her husband. I refer to the hypersensual woman, to the wife with an excessive sexuality. It is to her that the name vampire can be applied in its literal sense. Just as the vampire sucks the blood of its victims in their sleep while they are alive, so does the woman vampire suck the life blood and exhaust the vitality of her male partner – or victim. And some of them – the pronounced type – are utterly without pity or consideration.' Dijkstra, *Idols of Perversity*, p344.

62 One prominent male ally of the women's movement was W.T. Stead, who voiced his support in an article entitled 'The Novel of the Modern Woman' (*Review of Reviews* 10, 1894). The New Woman was only claiming 'rights, privileges, and responsibilities of a human being', he wrote, '[she] is not going back to her old position. Through whatever stormy seas and across no matter what burning desert marked by the skeletons and haunted by the ghosts of those who have fallen by the way, she will press on, fleeing from monogamic prostitution of loveless marriage and the hideous outrage of enforced maternity.'
    A.L. Ardis, *New Women, New Novels* (New Brunswick, NJ: Rutgers UP, 1990), pp21–2.

63 Ruth Brandon, *The New Woman and the Old Men: Love, Sex and The Woman Question* (London: Secker & Warburg, 1990), p197.

64 Sheila Rowbotham, *Dreamers of a New Day* (London: Verso, 2010), p61.

65 Charlotte Despard, *Woman in the New Era* (London: The Suffrage Shop, 1910), pp32–3.

66 Winnifred Harper Cooley, *The New Womanhood* (New York, 1904).

67 Rowbotham, *Dreamers*, p65.

68 Christabel Pankhurst, *The Great Scourge and How to End It* (London, 1913).

69 See Sir T.S. Clouston: 'The ideals which would exalt culture above motherhood are suicidal and should be abandoned. It will not do to say that women should have a choice either to take up culture and intellectual work, whether it has a lessened capacity for motherhood or not, or to select domestic life. Mothers of high brain power are as much needed for an advancing race as fathers – rather more so, in fact.' Quoted in Carol Dyhouse, *Girls Growing Up in Late Victorian and Edwardian England* (London: Routledge, 2016), p154.

70 David J. Skal, *Hollywood Gothic* (New York: W.W. Norton, 1990), pp43–4, 54–5; of course, at least one copy survived the purge and the film remains in circulation.

71 Ewers would later become an in-house novelist for the Nazi elite, writing, in one instance, a hagiographic portrayal of Nazi martyr Horst Wessel at Hitler's request. See Eric Kurlander, *Hitler's Monsters: A Supernatural History of the Third Reich* (New Haven and London: Yale UP, 2016), p79.

72 Siegfried Kracauer, *From Caligari to Hitler* (London: Dennis Dobson, 1947), pp77–9.

73 See Kurlander, *Hitler's Monsters*, Chs 1 and 2.

74 Adolf Leschnitzer, *The Magic Background of Modern Anti-Semitism* (New York: International Universities Press, 1956), p144. Leschnitzer notes that this magical conception of Jews allowed for the suspension of certain logical precepts – clear causation, consistency of argument, generalisation of

behaviour to large, inchoate groups – which permitted aggression towards an out-group without recourse to reality.

75 Kurlander, *Hitler's Monsters*, p42.

76 One of Hitler's favourite rhetorical turns was to describe Jews as '*Schadlinge am Volkskorper*', 'parasites on the body politic'. The German *Volkskorper* better captures the anthropomorphic imagery. Combined with the near-constant equation of Jewish men with sexual predation, the listener's thoughts are practically led to the image of the vampire feasting on a sleeping woman's arteries. Robert Gellately, *The Gestapo and German Society* (Oxford: OUP, 1990), p92.

77 The assumption that Jews ran the white slave trade in central Europe was, by the 1920s, several decades old. 'The majority of unfortunate girls who form the prostitutes of the larger towns have fallen through Jewish depravity,' Theodor Fritsch wrote in *Antisemiten-Katechismus* (1893), 'the notorious "girl commerce" will soon be carried on exclusively by the Jews.'

78 Dennis E. Showalter, *Little Man, What Now?: Dür Stormer in the Weimar Republic* (Hamden, CT: Archon Books, 1982), p100.

79 Theodor Fritsch, *The Riddle of the Jew's Success* (1927), p191.

80 Fritsch, *The Riddle of the Jew's Success*, p260.

81 This had been a recurring theme of *Der Stürmer*'s depiction of Jews as constantly seeking to entrap German women into sex through ostentatious displays of wealth. Such encounters always resulted in the ruin of the gentile woman. See for instance 'The Talmudist', in which a brutish Jewish lothario dresses himself while an Aryan swoons in post-coital shame in a soiled hotel bed. Alcohol lies around the room. The caption says: 'The Goy's Temple is Our Toilet' (Showalter, *Little Man, What Now?*, p89). Another cartoon shows 'The Beginning' (a Weimar flapper with a bob, professional clothes and a clutch, hopping into a sleek car driven by a Jew) and 'The End' (the same woman shivering on the street, now a prostitute with her Jewish pimp leering over her shoulder). http://research.calvin.edu/german-propaganda-archive/images/ sturmer/sturm06.jpg

82 James Q. Whitman, *Hitler's American Model* (Princeton, NJ: Princeton UP, 2017). Coincidentally, in the same year the Prussian Memorandum was published, an anti-Semitic forgery now known as the 'Franklin Prophecy' appeared in a pro-Nazi paper in the United States. It purported to be an extract from a 'lost' speech given by Benjamin Franklin in 1787 and contained the following description of Jews: 'They are vampires and vampires cannot live on other vampires – they cannot live among themselves. They must live among Christians and others who do not belong to their race.'

83 One of the priorities of the exclusionary campaign was to exclude Jews from the practice of medicine. This had a clear sexual subtext, as anti-Semitic propagandists believed that the Jewish monopoly on medical practice was a ruse to access Aryan bodies for sexual purposes. 'Now we know why the Jew uses every artifice of seduction in order to ravish German girls at as early an age as

possible,' Julius Streicher had written in *Der Stürmer*'s New Year issue of 1935, 'while the Jewish doctor rapes his patient while they are under anaesthetic. He wants the German girl and the German woman to absorb the alien sperm of a Jew.' Louis W. Bondy, *Racketeers of Hatred* (London: Newman Wolsey, 1946), p48.

Nazis also believed that Jewish doctors were responsible for undermining the Aryan race through the provision of abortions. 'The racial hatred Jews had for their Aryan host people extended to the growing life in a mother's womb. Jewish scoundrels made this part of the programs of political parties. How many millions of unborn children and how many hundreds of thousands of mothers fell prey to the greed and racial hatred of Jewish doctors?' Hanns Oberlindober, *Ein Vaterland, das allen gehört! Briefe an Zeitgenossen aus zwölf Kampfjahren* (Munich: Zentralverlag der NSDAP, 1940), pp152–67; 'The "Decent" Jew: A Letter to an Englishman' (1937).

84 See Daniel Goldhagen on anti-Jewish legislation and social death in *Hitler's Willing Executioners*, 1996.

85 Kurlander, *Hitler's Monsters*, pp81–3.

7 Seduction Remains

1 See *The Communist Manifesto*: 'Our bourgeois, not content with having the wives and daughters of their proletarians at their disposal, not to speak of common prostitutes, take the greatest pleasure in seducing each other's wives.'

2 Quoted in Kristen Ghodsee, *Why Women Have Better Sex Under Socialism* (London: Vintage, 2018), p116.

3 Bellamy saw a eugenic benefit in allowing women to be the arbiters of the sexual marketplace under socialism: 'You were speaking, a day or two ago, of the physical superiority of our people to your contemporaries. Perhaps more important than any of the causes I mentioned then as tending to race purification has been the effect of untrammeled sexual selection upon the quality of two or three successive generations. I believe that when you have made a fuller study of our people you will find in them not only a physical, but a mental and moral improvement. It would be strange if it were not so, for not only is one of the great laws of nature now freely working out the salvation of the race, but a profound moral sentiment has come to its support. Individualism, which in your day was the animating idea of society, not only was fatal to any vital sentiment of brotherhood and common interest among living men, but equally to any realization of the responsibility of the living for the generation to follow. To-day this sense of responsibility, practically unrecognized in all previous ages, has become one of the great ethical ideas of the race, reinforcing, with an intense conviction of duty, the natural impulse to seek in marriage the best and noblest of the other sex. The result is, that not all the encouragements and incentives of every sort which we have provided to develop industry, talent, genius, excellence of whatever kind, are comparable in their effect on our young men with the fact that our

women sit aloft as judges of the race and reserve themselves to reward the winners. . . . Our women have risen to the full height of their responsibility as the wardens of the world to come, to whose keeping the keys of the future are confided. Their feeling of duty in this respect amounts to a sense of religious consecration. It is a cult in which they educate their daughters from childhood.'

4   Ghodsee, *Why Women*, pp118–19. It was this 'communist morality' that Yevgeny Zamyatin was satirising in his great dystopian novel *We* (1921), in which the citizens ('ciphers') of the One State have free sexual access to one another through the state distribution of pink tickets: 'Having subjugated Hunger . . . , the One State began an offensive against the other master of the world – against Love. Finally, even this natural force was also conquered, i.e., organised and mathematicised, and around three hundred years ago, our historical *Lex Sexualis* was proclaimed: "Each cipher has the right to any other cipher as a sexual product."' Yevgeny Zamyatin, *We* (1921; London: Vintage, 2007), p21.

5   Herbert Marcuse, *Eros and Civilization: A Philosophical Inquiry into Freud* (Boston: Beacon Press, 1955), p202.

6   Marcuse, *Eros and Civilization*, p198.

7   Marcuse always deftly denied that he was in any way the intellectual leader of the New Left, though he did coyly admit on at least one occasion that 'it would have been better to call me not the father, but the grandfather of the New Left'. His influence on the student movement has likely been overstated, even if his theories were taken seriously by the intellectual elite of the new left-wing and radical movements of the Sixties and Seventies. He was in any case an odd choice of hero for the *Easy Rider* generation, this man who once described the motorcycle as 'a fascist invention which equates speed and power with virility and besides it makes such a dreadful noise and pollutes terribly'. See Tom Bourne, 'Herbert Marcuse: Grandfather of the New Left', *Change* 11.6 (Sep 1979); Herbert Marcuse, *Philosophy, Psychoanalysis and Emancipation*, Collected Papers of Herbert Marcuse Vol 5, ed. Douglas Kellner and Clayton Prince (London: Routledge, 2011), pp201–5.

8   See Michel Houellebecq, *Whatever* (London: Serpent's Tail, 1998), p40: 'This progressive effacement of human relationships is not without certain problems for the novel. How, in point of fact, would one handle the narration of those unbridled passions, stretching over many years, and at times making their effect felt on several generations? We're a long way from *Wuthering Heights*, to say the least. The novel form is not conceived for depicting indifference or nothingness; a flatter, more terse and dreary discourse would need to be invented.'

9   Francis Fukuyama, *The Great Disruption: Human Nature and the Reconstitution of Social Order* (New York: The Free Press, 1999), pp5–6: 'The changing nature of work tended to substitute mental for physical labor, thereby propelling millions of women into the workplace and undermining the traditional

understandings on which the family had been based . . . [B]roadly speaking, the technological change that brings about what economist Joseph Schumpeter called "creative destruction" in the marketplace caused similar disruption in the world of social relationships.'

Shere Hite argued for the primacy of economic factors to the success or failure of the sexual revolution. 'It is important to remember that *you cannot decree women to be "sexually free" when they are not economically free*; to do so is to put them into a more vulnerable position than ever.' See Shere Hite, *The Hite Report: A Nationwide Study on Female Sexuality* (London: Talmy Franklin, 1977), p305. This was echoed by Kate Millett in 1970: 'The goal of revolution would be a permissive single standard of sexual freedom, and one uncorrupted by the crass exploitative economic bases of traditional sexual alliances.' Quoted in David Allyn, *Make Love Not War: The Sexual Revolution: An Unfettered History* (London: Little, Brown, 2000), p104.

A similar point is made at the end of Alix Shulman's best-selling 1972 novel *Memoirs of an Ex-Prom Queen* (London: Serpent's Tail, 2019), when Sasha, the female protagonist, complains (p249): 'To find myself at thirty locked under a dryer eagerly studying ads in magazines while I worry about the sitter and my husband is away on a business trip; now, after my schemes and triumphs, my visions and dares, to be, without income or skill, dependent on a man and a fading skin – it can only be the fulfilment of a curse!'

10   See *Je T'Aime: The Legendary Love Story of Jane Birkin and Serge Gainsbourg* (London: Icon, 2019). For a contemporaneous perspective on the cultural influences of the sexual revolution, see the brilliant scene in John Updike's *Couples* (London: Penguin, 1969), pp63–4, where the adulterous Piet surveys his lover's husband's bookshelf: 'Curiously he would finger and skim through Thorne's bedside shelf – Henry Miller in tattered Paris editions, Sigmund Freud in Modern Library. *Our Lady of the Flowers* and *Memoirs of a Woman of Pleasure* fresh from Grove Press, inspirational psychology by the Menningers, a dove-grey handbook on hypnosis, *Psychopathia Sexualis* in textbook format, a delicately tinted and stiff-paged album smuggled from Kyoto, the poems of Sappho as published by Peter Pauper, the unexpurgated Arabian Nights in two boxed volumes, works by Theodor Reik and Wilhelm Reich, various tawdry paperbacks.'

11   See Kate Millett, *Sexual Politics* (London: Rupert Hart-Davis, 1971), p63: 'Save for [the pill], the "New Woman" of the twenties was as well off, and possibly better provided with sexual freedom, than the woman of the fifties.'

12   Perhaps not unrelated to the foregrounding of Enovid in cultural discourse of the sexual revolution was the high rates of uptake among the demographic consuming and producing such literature. By 1965 more than 80 per cent of unmarried, white, non-Catholic college graduates aged 20–24 had used oral contraceptives. See Elizabeth Siegel Watkins, *On the Pill: A Social History of Oral Contraceptives 1950–1970* (Baltimore, MD: Johns Hopkins UP, 1998), p34.

13 There is a comparable trend in divorce, which was not legalised in Italy until 1970, Spain until 1981, Ireland until 1985 and Malta until 2011. See https://ec.europa.eu/eurostat/statistics-explained/pdfscache/6790.pdf

14 Roy Baumeister and Kathleen Vohs, 'Sexual Economics: Sex as Female Resource for Social Exchange in Heterosexual Interactions', *Personality and Social Psychology Review* 8.4 (2004), pp339–63.

15 In Nora Ephron's 1983 novel *Heartburn* (London: Virago, 2018), p81, Nora Samstat's verdict on the sexual revolution makes much the same point in pithier terms: 'Their wives went out into the world, free at last, single again, and discovered the horrible truth: that they were sellers in a buyer's market, and that the major concrete achievement of the women's movement in the 1970s was the Dutch treat.'

16 Elizabeth Hardwick, 'Seduction and Betrayal', *New York Review of Books* (May and Jun 1973); Margaret Drabble, 'The Sexual Revolution', *Guardian*, 11 Oct 1967.

17 Stuart Jeffries, *Grand Hotel Abyss: The Lives of the Frankfurt School* (London: Verso, 2016), pp303 and 305 describes Marcuse speaking in the summer of 1964 at a conference on the island of Korcula in Croatia: 'Why should the overthrow of the existing order be of vital necessity for people who own, or can hope to own, good clothes, a well-stocked larder, a TV set, a car, a house and so on, all within the existing order?' and quotes him in *One-Dimensional Man* (1964): 'Here, the so-called equalization of class distinctions reveals its ideological function. If the worker and his boss enjoy the same television program and visit the same resort places, if the typist is as attractively made up as the daughter of her employer, if the Negro owns a Cadillac, if they all read the same newspaper, then this assimilation indicates not the disappearance of classes, but the extent to which the needs and satisfactions that serve the preservation of the Establishment are shared by the underlying population.'

18 The factors he lists, which are those Angela Davis had identified in 'Women and Capitalism' (1971), are these: 'alleviation of heavy physical labor, the reduction of labor time, the production of pleasant and cheap clothing, the liberalization of sexual morality, birth control, general education'.

19 In 'Marxism and Feminism' (1974), Marcuse pinned his hopes on the revolutionary potential of feminism as a political movement: 'Feminism is a revolt against decaying capitalism, against the historical obsolescence of the capitalist mode of production. This is the precarious link between Utopia and reality: the social ground for the movement as a potentially radical and revolutionary force is there; this is the hard core of the dream. But capitalism is still capable of keeping it a dream, of suppressing the transcending forces which strive for the subversion of the inhuman values of our civilization.'
    This was the same argument Shulamith Firestone made in *The Dialectic of Sex* (1970), where she decried the 'pseudo-liberation' of Western women: 'They

were told then as we still are now, "You've got civil rights, short skirts and sexual liberty. You've won your revolution. What more do you want?" But the "revolution" had been won within a system organized around the patriarchal nuclear family. And as Herbert Marcuse in *Eros and Civilization* shows, within such a repressive structure only a more sophisticated repression can result ("repressive de-sublimation").'

20 Pierre Klossowski, *Living Currency* (1970); trans. Jordan Levinson (London: Bloomsbury, 2017); Jean-François Lyotard, *The Libidinal Economy*, trans. Iain Hamilton Grant (Indiana University Press, 1993); Jean Baudrillard, *Seduction*, trans. Brian Singer (New World Perspectives, 1990).

21 Michel Houellebecq, *H.P. Lovecraft: Against the World, Against Life* (London: Weidenfeld & Nicolson, 2006), pp115–16.

22 Houellebecq, *Whatever*, p99.

23 Michel Houellebecq, *Atomized* (London: Vintage, 2001), pp161–2.

24 Zack Beauchamp, 'Incel, The Misogynist Ideology that Inspired the Deadly Toronto Attack, Explained', vox.com, 25 Apr 2018; https://edition.cnn.com/2014/05/24/us/elliot-rodger-video-transcript/index.html; Chris Perez, 'Air Force Warns About Nationwide Threat of Incels', *New York Post*, 21 Jun 2019; Zack Beauchamp, 'Our Incel Problem', vox.com, 23 Apr 2019.

25 Houellebecq, *Whatever*, p148: 'No civilization, no epoch has been capable of developing such a quantity of bitterness in its subjects. In that sense we are living through unprecedented times.' See also W. Bradford Wilcox, 'The Happiness Recession', theatlantic.com, 4 Apr 2019; Kate Julian, 'Why Are Young People Having So Little Sex?', theatlantic.com, Dec 2018.

26 Pierre Bourdieu, 'The Forms of Capital', in J. Richardson, *Handbook of Theory and Research for the Sociology of Education* (Westport, CT: Greenwood, 1986), pp241–58; Catherine Hakim, 'Erotic Capital', *European Sociological Review* 6.5 (2010).

27 Weber's own methods were unabashedly amoral and casually misogynistic. They also relied heavily on the cultural tropes of his day. For example: 'March in a peace demonstration, even if you're secretly for war. I've heard countless stories of guys who've picked up fantastic broads at peace demonstrations' (p163); 'One of the best ways to compliment a woman is to tell her you dig something about her she had no idea was particularly digable' (p60); 'What else will make you look sexy? Experiment. When you find something that works you'll know it from the way chicks start looking at you. Try on some of the new wild clothes. Bell bottoms and English boots and wide ties. Wear a body shirt or leather dungarees or a groovy vest. Be dramatic. Leave the top button on your shirt open. Wear shades or those new rimless glasses. *Think sexy*. Think, I am a virile male animal' (p43); 'Now you know damn well that the way these girls would like you to feel is not necessarily the way you're going to feel. Half the time you want to pick up a girl it's because she's got a set of breasts that makes you dizzy. Or the face of a movie star. Or the hips of

a belly dancer. Not because she has some magnetic inner quality. . . . But you can't let them know that. You've got to pretend otherwise' (p53).

28 Randall Rothenberg, 'Copywriter's Foray into Book Writing', *New York Times*, 15 May 1990; Eric Weber, *How to Pick Up Girls!* (New York: Bantam, 1977), p17; Suzanne Chazin, 'Some Women Would Tell Eric Weber to Buzz Off, but Men Are Buying His Line on Picking Up Girls', *People*, 17 Aug 1981.

29 Neil Strauss, 'He Aims! He Shoots! Yes!!', *New York Times*, 25 Jan 2004.

30 The counterpoint to this mathematical attitude is a profound distrust of emotion (what Locke and Hume would have called the passions). See Strauss, *The Game*, p22: "'All your emotions are going to try to fuck you up," Mystery continued. "They are there to try to confuse you, so know right now that they cannot be trusted at all. You will feel shy sometimes, and self-conscious, and you must deal with it like you deal with a pebble in your shoe. It's uncomfortable, but you ignore it. It's not part of the equation."' This was an attitude adopted by Mystery's successors. In its promotional material, Real Social Dynamics promised to 'Make girls beg to sleep with you after short-circuiting their emotional and logical mind.'

31 Gloria Steinem, 'The Moral Disarmament of Betty Coed', *Esquire*, Sep 1962. Interestingly Eric Weber made much the same point in his landmark seduction manual: 'Women have come a long way recently. They're learning they have the same right to sexual freedom that men have. In fact I think it's going to be harder for men to adjust to the sexual revolution than it is for women.' Weber, *How to Pick Up Girls!*, p22.

32 Hite, *The Hite Report*, pp311, 319, 320.

33 Molly Haskell, *From Reverence to Rape: The Treatment of Women in the Movies* (London: New English Library, 1975), pp327–8.

34 Linda R. Hirshman and Jane E. Larson, *Hard Bargains: The Politics of Sex* (Oxford: OUP, 1999), p165.

35 Jane E. Larson, 'Women Understand so Little, They Call My Good Nature "Deceit": A Feminist Rethinking of Seduction', *Columbia Law Review* 93.2 (Mar 1993), pp374–472.

36 Kathy Gilsinan, '*The Game* at 10', theatlantic.com, 13 Oct 2015.

37 Tom Lamont, 'Neil Strauss: "My Thinking Was: If This Woman Wants to Be Naked with Me, I Must Be OK"', *Guardian*, 10 Oct 2015.

38 Houellebecq, *Whatever*, p41.

39 These figures are for heterosexual couples; the figure for same-sex couples is 60 per cent. See 'How Couples Meet and Stay Together' survey data, managed by Michael Rosenfeld at Stanford University. For wedding data, see Lea Rose Emery, 'How Do Most Couples Meet These Days? Online is the Top Way People are Finding their Spouses Today, Survey Finds', bustle.com (10 Nov 2017), although estimates vary widely as to both how many couples and marriages originate online. The only certainty is that online dating has increased a great deal and continues to rise.

40 See the chart in Michael Rosenfeld et al., 'Disintermediating Your Friends', *Proceedings of the National Academy of Sciences* 116.36 (Jul 2019).

41 https://hingeirl.com/hinge-reports/whats-the-biggest-challenge-men-face-on-dating-apps-a-qa-with-aviv-goldgeier-junior-growth-engineer/; Dan Kopf, 'These Statistics Show Why it's So Hard to Be an Average Man on Dating Apps', quartz.com (15 Aug 2017). This is data for heterosexual men and women. The country data for Gini coefficients comes in this instance from the *CIA World Factbook*, the OECD-EU figures from 'Understanding the Socio-Economic Divide in Europe: Background Report', 26 Jan 2017, p7, https://www.oecd.org/els/soc/cope-divide-europe-2017-background-report.pdf

42 http://www.eecs.qmul.ac.uk/~tysong/files/Tinder.pdf, p4

43 See Christian Rudder, *Dataclysm: What Our Online Selves Tell Us About Our Offline Selves* (London: Fourth Estate, 2016), pp23–4: 'Translate this plot to IQ, and you have a world where the women think 58% of men are brain damaged.'

44 'A Woman's Advantage', okcupid.com, 5 Mar 2015; Elizabeth E. Bruch and M.E.J. Newman, 'Aspirational pursuit of mates in online dating markets', *Science Advances* 4.8 (8 Aug 2018).

45 Rudder, *Dataclysm*, p98.

46 Rudder, *Dataclysm*, p133. Given the lack of data one can only speculate, but it seems likely that Tinder's format, which consists of single images and very little written information, would tend to exaggerate this effect.

47 https://www.thecut.com/2014/02/okcupid-most-desired-people-in-new-york.html

48 Bruch and Newman, 'Aspirational pursuit of mates'. This is not to suggest that this is necessarily an enjoyable situation to be in. Many women on online dating platforms experience harassment, and obscene and objectifying proposals. However, one of the false intuitions about the dynamics of online dating is that the sheer quantity of messages (crude, polite or otherwise) that women receive is dampening their enthusiasm to participate equally in contacting potential partners. Heterosexual women are 3.5 times less likely to send the first message than men, but curiously this holds true whether the women are deemed attractive or not, *and* whether they are receiving a huge volume of messages or very few. https://theblog.okcupid.com/a-womans-advantage-82d5074dde2d

49 https://theblog.okcupid.com/race-and-attraction-2009-2014-107dcbb4f060; Jevan Hutson, Jessie G. Taft, Solon Barocas, and Karen Levy, 'Debiasing Desire: Addressing Bias & Discrimination on Intimate Platforms', *Proceedings of the ACM on Human-Computer Interaction* 2, CSCW (Nov 2018).

50 Rudder, *Dataclysm*, p98.

51 Kaitlyn Tiffany, 'Nearly all of the big dating apps are now owned by the same company', vox.com, 11 Feb 2019.

52 Tinder Boost, https://www.help.tinder.com/hc/en-us/articles/360029087891-Super-Boost

53 Rebecca Jennings, 'Dating apps like Tinder and Bumble are free. But people say paying for them is worth the money', vox.com, 19 Sep 2018; 'Match Group, Inc. Report on Form 10-K for the Fiscal Year ended December 31, 2018', https://ir.mtch.com/financials/sec-filings/default.aspx; 'Q1 2019 Investor Presentation – May 7 2019', https://ir.mtch.com/news-and-events/quarterly-results/default.aspx

54 Baudrillard, *Seduction*, p39.

Afterword

1   Quoted in Sinclair, 'Seduction and the Myth of the Ideal Woman'.

2   Weinstein was quoted in Caroline Frankie, 'Deciphering Harvey Weinstein's bizarre defense against sexual harassment claims', vox.com, 5 Oct 2017; Chantal Da Silva, 'Alexandria Ocasio-Cortez: If You Think U.S. Spike In Celibacy Is Due To "Female Empowerment," You're Missing the Point', *Newsweek*, 13 May 2019; Yvonne Roberts, 'The sex revolution of my youth wasn't so great. Maybe today's celibacy is a sign of progress', *Guardian*, 7 Apr 2019.

3   Ezra Klein, '"Yes Means Yes" is a terrible law, and I completely support it', vox.com, 13 Oct 2014.

4   The California State University and University of California systems backed the legislation having already adopted similar consent standards that year. See https://abc7chicago.com/news/yes-means-yes-california-sb-967-sex-assault-bill-signed/328741/

5   Jeannie Suk Gersen, 'Unpopular Speech in a Cold Climate', *New Yorker*, 14 Mar 2019.

6   Laura Kipnis, *Unwanted Advances: Sexual Paranoia Comes to Campus* (London: Verso, 2018), p76; Jacob Gersen and Jeannie Suk, *The Sex Bureaucracy*, 104 *California Law Review* 881 (2016). For a general overview of the state of Title IX, the growing backlash against its execution and a profile of Jeannie Suk Gersen, see Wesley Yang, 'The Revolt of the Feminist Law Profs', *Chronicle of Higher Education* (7 Aug 2019).

7   See 'Netflix film crews "banned from looking at each other for longer than five seconds" in #metoo crackdown', *The Independent*, 13 Jun 2018. For a comprehensive code of conduct that reflects the substance of progressive modern thought on sexual harassment in the workplace, see the Code of Conduct of the International Faculty and Staff Sexual Misconduct Conference (FASSM), available at: https://facultysexualmisconduct.com/code-of-conduct.

8   'Reality Check: Is Malmo the "rape capital" of Europe?', BBC News, 24 Feb 2017.

9   See Bryan Stevenson: 'The explicit use of race to codify different kinds of offenses and punishments was challenged as unconstitutional, and criminal statutes were modified to avoid direct racial references, but the enforcement of the law didn't change. Black people were routinely charged with a wide range

of "offenses," some of which whites were never charged with.' http://www.nybooks.com/articles/2017/07/13/presumption-of-guilt/

10   See 'The Sex Bureaucracy', and https://reason.com/2017/09/14/we-need-to-talk-about-black-students-bei/

11   Emily Yoffe, 'The Question of Race in Campus Sexual-Assault Cases', *The Atlantic*, 11 Sep 2017. The article also notes a serious disparity between the proportion of Asian students at Colgate (3 per cent) and the number of Asian students accused of sexual assault (13 per cent).

12   Adam Smith, *The Theory of Moral Sentiments* (1759), quoted in Dennis C. Rasmussen, *The Infidel and the Professor: David Hume, Adam Smith, and the Friendship that Shaped Modern Thought* (Princeton, NJ: Princeton UP, 2017), p89; Gareth Tyson, Claudiu Perta, Hamed Haddadi and Michael Seto, 'A First Look at User Activity on Tinder', 8th IEEE/ACM International Conference on Advances in Social Networks Analysis and Mining (ASONAM), San Francisco, CA (2016), accessed at http://www.eecs.qmul.ac.uk/~tysong/#selectedpublications. The same report notes that 25 per cent of messages from men to women are six characters or less in length.

LIST OF ILLUSTRATIONS

Plate section

Road to Ruin by Thomas Rowlandson (The Elisha Whittelsey Collection, The Elisha Whittelsey Fund, 1959)

Covent Garden by Pieter Angillis (Yale Center for British Art, Paul Mellon Collection)

The Harlowe Family, from Samuel Richardson's Clarissa by Joseph Highmore (Yale Center for British Art, Paul Mellon Collection)

Magdalen Chapel by Thomas Rowlandson (The Elisha Whittelsey Collection, The Elisha Whittelsey Fund, 1959)

The Meeting by Pietro Longhi (Gift of Samuel H. Kress, 1936)

The Visit by Pietro Longhi (Frederick C. Hewitt Fund, 1912)

The Parlatorio delle Monache by Giuseppe de Gobbis

The Doctor Indulged with his Favourite Scene by James Gillray (Yale Center for British Art, Paul Mellon Collection)

Mary Wollstonecraft by John Opie (bequeathed by Jane, Lady Shelley, 1899)

Mary Shelley by Samuel John Stump

Coloured lithograph of Caroline Norton (Wellcome Collection)

Illustration of 'the Love Game'

Jack Johnson at the wheel (American Photo Archive / Alamy)

Patients in Paris receiving Mesmer's animal magnetism therapy (Wellcome Collection)

A Clinical Lesson at the Salpêtrière by Pierre Aristide André Brouillet

Poster advertisement for *Trilby* by George Du Maurier (Smith Collection / Gado / Getty)

Der Stürmer cartoon (reproduced with the kind permission of Randall Bytwerk)

Integrated

Page 24 *A Harlot's Progress* by William Hogarth (Harris Brisbane Dick Fund, 1932)

Page 38 *Pamela Swooning* by Guillaume Philippe Benoist (Yale Center for British Art, Yale Art Gallery Collection, Gift of the Library Associates)

Page 74 *The Magdalen Hospital* by Eastgate (Wellcome Collection)

Page 111 *View of the Brenta, near Dolo* by Giambattista Cimaroli (Robert Lehman Collection, 1975)

Page 128 Illustration in Casanova's *Story of my Flight*

Page 130 Escape from Venice (Clement Knox)

Page 153 Contemporary Illustration of the Women's March on Versailles

Page 168 *The Nightmare* by Henry Fuseli

Page 210 Lord Byron at the Villa Diodati (Rischgitz / Getty)

Page 214 Frontispiece to *Frankenstein* by Theodore Von Holst

Page 224 A practitioner of Mesmerism using Animal Magnetism (Wellcome Collection)

Page 232 Caroline Norton (Bettmann / Getty)

Page 272 Jack Johnson with his wife Etta Duryea in Reno, Nevada (Popperfoto / Getty Images)

Page 274 Jack Johnson knocks out Jim Jeffries (Bettmann / Getty)

Page 277 Illustrations of young woman and man at party from *Fighting the Traffic in Young Girls* (Wellcome Collection)

Page 301 Jack Johnson beaten by Jess Willard in the world heavyweight boxing championship (JHU Sheridan Libraries / Gado / Getty)

Page 311 American actress Ruth Taylor reads *Gentlemen Prefer Blondes* by Anita Loos (George Hommel / John Kobal Foundation / Getty)

Page 315 Anti-heart cartoon (Reproduced with the kind permission of University of Evansville Libraries)

Page 325 Illustration of the Lyceum Theatre portico (DEA / Biblioteca Ambrosiana / Getty)

Page 340 W. T. Stead in prison uniform (Chronicle / Alamy)

Page 354 Anti-Semitic cartoon from *Trilby* (World History Archive / Alamy)

Page 371 Anti-Semitic cartoon of women by night and day (Reproduced with the kind permission of Randall Bytwerk)

Page 377 Herbert Marcuse at a lectern (ullstein bild / Getty)

Page 412 Online dating graph (Reproduced with the kind permission of Michael J. Rosenfeld)

ACKNOWLEDGEMENTS

This book was many years in the making and many people directly and indirectly supported it and contributed towards its completion. I am grateful to them all.

Dom Pakenham has been there since the beginning and read some of the earliest and least promising versions of this book. Alex Hunting gave valuable advice on the introduction. Chris Clube provided pointers on Greek vocabulary as well as insights from the classical context. Carlotta Bonafini was the first to read the entire manuscript through and was the source of immeasurable encouragement and solace besides. Josh White was tolerant of the moody writer under his roof these past years. I am grateful to all those at Waterstones, especially Richard Humphreys, who put up with me whilst I ground away at this project. I owe a great debt to the staff of the London Library where much of that grinding took place. At William Collins, Arabella Pike, my wonderful and indulgent editor, made all of this possible and Paul Erdpresser was the indispensable man. Julian Humphries produced a beautiful cover and was remarkably tolerant of my meddling. Steve Gove, Katy Archer and Jo Thompson were all invaluable in goading the manuscript into publishable form. In America, I am grateful for Alison Lewis's hard work on my behalf as well as her close reading of all that I have written. Katie

McGuire and Claiborne Hancock at Pegasus have been fantastic to work with. This book would not exist without the mercurial brilliance of my agent Sophie Scard, hers is the kingdom, the power and the glory.

INDEX

#MeToo 416, 417, 419, 428
  responses to 425
#TakeDownJulienBlanc 403–4

abortion 385, 386
Acker, Kathy 376
Ackroyd, Peter 126
Acquaviva, Cardinal 89–91
actresses, association with prostitutes 341–2
Adair, Robert 45–6
Adèle et Théodore (de Genlis) 149
Adler, Chief Rabbi Hermann 352
Adorno, Theodor 372
adultery 44–5, 242–3, 245
  consequences for women 44–5
Advocate, The (NYFMRS) 257
Affair of the Diamond Necklace 224
Alabama 258
alcohol 143
Aldini, Giovanni 211–12
Algerian Communist Party 378
Ali, Yusuf 91
Alienation of Affection law 234, 254, 315
Amar, André 179–80
Amelia (Fielding) 66
American Legion 376
American Revolution 154
Analytical Review 152
Ancilla 81
Andrews, Pamela (character in book) 33–6, 51, 417
Anglo-Saxon Clubs of America (ASCOA) 308
animal magnetism 224, 226
Ansari, Aziz 417–18
anti-heart balm legislation 314–15, 470n74
  partial success of 316

perception of 316
Anti-Jacobin Review 193, 226
Anti-Pamela; or Feign'd Innocence Detected (Haywood) 39, 40
anti-pornography campaigns 402
anti-Semitism, British 349, 352
Antoinette, Marie 179, 224
Apology (Philips) 49
app-enabled dating 405–6
Appotomax Club 285
apprentices, printing industry 28
Apprentice's Vade Mecum, The (Richardson) 32–3
Apron, Leather 351, 358
Arden, Jane 144
Armstrong, Eliza 340–1
Armstrong, Louis 273–4, 306
Ars Amatoria (Ovid) 3
Ashkenazim Jews 350–1
Asylum for Female Orphans 151
atavistic humans 344
Atkins, Emily (character in book) 9
Atomized (Houellebecq) 393, 394–5, 413
attractiveness 406–8
Augustus 3
Austin, Mary 263
Axur (Salieri) 139

Babe.net 417–18
Balbi, Marin 127, 129–30
Balcombe, Florence *see* Stoker, Florence
Baltimore Afro-American Ledger 285
Bankes, William 199
Banks, Ada 281, 284
Banks, Joseph 134

Barbaro, Marco 100
Bardot, Brigitte 383
bare-knuckle boxing 260
Barlow, Joel 173, 175
Barlow, Ruth 173, 181
bastardy *see* illegitimate children
Baudrillard, Jean 391–2, 411
Baumeister, Roy 386–7
Baxter of Dundee, William 195
Bebel, August 373–4
Bell, Dr John 224–5
Bellamy, Edward 374, 482–3n3
Benson, Edward White 337–8
'Bernice Bobs Her Hair' (Fitzgerald) 304–5
Bertati, Giovanni 140
Bill of Rights 24
Blackfriars Bridge 151
blackmail 309–10
Blake, William 151, 163, 166
Blanc, Julien 403–5, 421–2
Blavatsky, Madame 319
Blease, Governor Cole 288
Blessington, Lady 202
Blood, Fanny 144, 146–7
Bonafede, Countess 125
Bonaparte, Napoleon 225, 226
Bond, Anne 13, 22
Bondini, Pasquale 140
Boswell, James 20, 71, 79, 133, 447–8n59
Bougainville, Louis-Antoine de 134
Bourdieu, Pierre 398
bourgeois sexuality 387
boxing 260
  bare-knuckle 260
  brutality of 260
  illegality of 260
  racial element 266
  white rescue 268
Bradshaigh, Lady Dorothy 'Belfour' 59–62, 63,
  77, 437–8n42
  letter to Samuel Richardson 62, 438n46
  visit to Magdalen House 75
Bradshaigh, Sir Roger 60
Bragadin, Senator Matteo Giovanni 99–100,
  110, 111–12
Bramwell, Lord 339
Branden, Lord 235
Breach of Promise to Marriage law 234, 254,
  315, 461n51
Breece v. Jett (1977) 420, 421
Brenta Canal 106, 111, 113
Brissot, Jacques-Pierre 173, 175, 177

Britain, declaration of war on France 173
The British Club 173
British Embassy (Venice) 80
Brougham, Lord 246
Bryant, William 264
Bureau of Investigation 279, 286
Burgh, James 146
Burgh, Mrs 146, 147
Burke, Edmund 154–5
  Reflections on the Revolution in France 155
Burne-Jones, Edward 362
Burney, Charles 107
Burns, Tommy 266–7, 268
Butler, Josephine 333, 336–7, 471n9
  double standards of sexual morality 337
  view of women as innocent 337
Byron, Clara Allegra 'Alba' 215–18
  death 218
Byron, Lady *see* Milbanke, Anna Isabella
  'Annabella'
Byron, Lord 8, 84, 136
  affair with Lady Caroline Lamb 200, 200–1
  Cicisbean experience 96–7, 98
  death 227
  false use of name 218–19
  friendship with Percy Shelley 208
  ill health 216
  marriage to Anna Milbanke 201–2
    courtship 199–200, 201
    cruelty towards 202
    fights divorce suit 203–4
      agrees legal separation 205
      sodomy allegation against 205
    unhappiness 201–2
  meeting of young Romantics 208–15
    ghost stories 212
  Napoleonic carriage 205–6
  nightmares 201
  rages 202
  relationship with Claire Clairmont
    daughter Alba 215–18
      sends to convent 217–18
    letters from 204–5
  scandal with Augusta Leigh 204
  travel with John William Polidori 205–7
  writings
    Childe Harold's Pilgrimage (1812) 199
    Don Juan (1819–24) 212
    Mazeppa (1819) 220

Cabinet of Dr. Caligari, The 366
Café de Champion 280–1, 284, 286, 466–7n33

Café de Luxe (later Cotton Club) 305–6
Cagliostro, Alessandro 224
Caine, Hall 355, 356
Callisto 3
Cameron, Archibald 71
Cameron-Falconet, Mrs F. 282–3, 288
Cameron, Lucille 281, 282–4, 287–8, 293
  arrest for disorderly conduct 283–4
  and Jack Johnson
    divorce 311
    marriage 288, 311–12
    on the run 293, 298–9
      Havana 300–1
      London 299, 301–2
    witnesses defeat to Willard 301
Camille (Casanova's acquaintance) 135–6
Caminetti, Anthony 294, 295, 468n57
Caminetti, Drew 294–7
Caminetti v. United States 294–7, 468n57
Campo San Moisè 112
Canterbury Tales, The (Chaucer) 4
Capet, Citizen Louis 171
capital 398
capitalism
  commodification of interpersonal relation-
    ships 373, 387
  libidinal intensities 391
  repressive sexual order 374
  sexual origins of fascism 375
  and sexuality 373, 392
  surplus-repression 375
Capretta, Caterina 113–14, 114–15, 116–17
  ménage à trois 124
  pregnancy and miscarriage 117
  recovery 118
  visited by Casanova 118
Capretta, Pietro 111–13, 114–15
Captive of the Castle of Sennaar (Cumberland)
  163
Carlisle House 132
Carnot, Lazare 173
Carpentier, Georges 298, 299
Caruso, Enrico 310
Casanova, Francesco 83
Casanova, Gaetano 83
Casanova, Giacomo 8, 81
  adopted title of Chevalier de Seingalt 131,
    447n53
  arrest and imprisonment 125
    escape 126–31
  barella crash incident 111–13
  cicisbeo to Signora F. 94–5

clerical work in Rome 89–91
Constantinople, visit to 91
death 140
Don Giovanni
  attendance 137, 139
  libretto, collaboration on 139–40
Enlightenment philosophy 110
failure, feelings of 99
female companions
  Camille 135–6
  Caterina Capretta 113–14, 114–15,
    116–17, 118, 124
    illicit encounters with 'M.M.' 118–24
  Mesulla 98
  Signora F. 93–4, 98
  Teresa Imer 87, 88, 114, 132
France, living in 110, 131–2
gambling 92, 109, 110, 123
humour 86
ill-health 84
'imposter' servant incident 92–3
  assault of 93
kerdaleophron, describes himself as
  possessing 131
London, visits to 132, 447n55
Martorano, short visit to 88–9
memoirs 85, 87, 98, 100–1, 108, 110, 133,
  136, 142, 443–4n11
military service 91–3
musician at wedding 99
patronage of Senator Alvise Malipiero 86–7
performance 82
pursuit of women 109–10
rational pleasures, belief in 121
rococo sexual escapades 88
scrutiny from Venetian Inquisition 124–5
seduction technique 82
self-reflection 117, 118
and Senator Bragadin
  dropped letter incident 99
  flees Venice 109
  homecoming 111
  lives at the Palazzo Bragadin 101–2, 109,
  111
  oracle story 100–1
  saves life of 99–100
student acquaintances 85–6
studying in Padua 84–5
  law degree 86
virginity, loss of 88
wealth of 131
writings about Venice 107–8

Casopo 93
Castelli, Leonilda 91
Castiglione, Baldassare 5
Catherine the Great 132
Catholic institutions 73
Ceccaldi, Janine 377–80
  birth of son 379
  communist sympathies 378
  marriage and separation 379
  medical studies at university 378
Ceccaldi, Michel Thomas (later Houellebecq) 379
  lives with maternal grandmother 380
  lives with paternal grandmother 380
  'Lost Kingdom' 381–2
  spiritual awakening 380–1
  world of the struggle 381
  see also Houellebecq, Michel
Cercle Social 157
Chamfort, Nicolas 173
Chapman, Annie 346
Chapone, Sarah 49, 68
Charcot, Jean-Martin 474–5n36
charities 72–4
Charles II 14
Charteris, Colonel Francis 13–17, 21–2, 22–3, 432n1, 432n3, 432n7
Charteris, Janet 15, 22
chastity 36, 48, 134
Chestnut Street Opera House 331
Cheyne, Dr George 31, 53
Chicago 278
Chicago Daily News 283
Chicago Daily Tribune 278
Chicago Defender 288
Chicago Tribune 272
Childe Harold's Pilgrimage (Byron) 199
Chivers, Emma 1–2, 9–10
Choynski, Joe 261–2
Christianity 4
Christie, Rebecca 173
Christie, Thomas 173
Church of England Purity Society 338
Cibber, Colley 46, 47, 58, 64
cicisbeismo, culture of 94–8
cicisbeo, life of 95–6, 97
City of London 26
civil law, and seduction 234–5
Civilisation and Its Discontents (Freud) 374
Clairmont, Claire (formerly Mary Jane) 8, 448, 448n59
  birth of Clara Allegra 'Alba' 215–16

agrees custody with Lord Byron 216
  reclaims from Lord Byron 217
free love 198
helps the Shelleys to elope 197
illegitimacy 214–15
letters to Lord Byron 204–5, 207
meeting of young Romantics 208–15
memoir 247–8
relationship with Percy Shelley 198
Clarissa: or, the History of a Young Lady (Richardson) 50, 51–2, 54–62
  criticisms of 57, 58
    Lady Dorothy Bradshaigh 59–60
    Richardson's defence of 58–9
  gestation and long birth 57
  praise of 57–8
  rape 51
  reason and passion 54–5
  reformation 52–3
  seduction 52
Clarke, Charlotte 49
Cleveland Daily News 292
Coleridge, Samuel 163–4
Collier, Jane 49
Colonda, Maria 111–13, 115
Commerce Clause 278–9
Communist Manifesto, The (Marx and Engels) 373, 392
communist morality 374
Compagnoni, Giuseppe 105
Condulmer, Antonio 124
consent law 422
Contagious Diseases Act (1867) 336
contraception 385–6, 389
convents 115–16
  fees from upper-class parents 116
  permissiveness of 115–16
Cook, Captain 134
Coram, Thomas 72
Corbett, Gentleman Jim 260, 272
Corday, Charlotte 178, 179
Cordeliers Club 158
Corinthian (liner) 293
Cornelys, Teresa 132
Council of Ten 108
Council of Three 108
Court Magazine and Belle Assemblee, The 230
Court of Common Pleas 235
courtesans 178
Courteville, Ralph 39
Covent Garden 17–18, 326
  Piazza 19

Covent Garden Gout 18
coverture 243, 245
  principle of 242
Craig, Edy 361–2, 478–9n57
Cranston, Isabella 21
Cravan, Arthur 302–3
Crim. Con. Gazette, The 235
Criminal Conversation law 234–5, 236–7, 254, 315
Criminal Law Amendment Act (1885) 355
  passing of 340
  proposal 333, 335, 336, 338–9
  seduction, confusion over 338–40, 472n12
criminals 344, 345
  criminal genus 345
Critical Remarks on Sir Charles Grandison, Clarissa, and Pamela (anon) 69–70
Crosby, Mrs 148
Cult of Sensibility 53–4
cultural capital 398
Cumberland, George 163
Curley, Jack 299
Custody of Infants Act (1839) 237, 239–40, 240

Da Ponte, Lorenzo 138, 139
Daily Journal 31
Damiens 141–2
Dandolo, Marco 100
Daniel, Mary 65
Darwin, Charles 318, 343, 346
Darwin, Erasmus 211, 213, 448n59
dating apps 406
Davis, Angela 376, 390
Davy, Humphry 225
de Bernardis, Bernardo 88–9
de Bernis, François-Joachim 124, 131
De Brosses 115
de Genlis, Madame 149, 173, 179
de Gouges, Olympe 159, 178, 180
de la Houssaye, Abraham Nicolas Amelot 116
de la Rochefoucauld, Prince 92–3
de Pizan, Christine 3
Declaration of Independence 8
Declaration of the Rights of Woman (de Gouges) 159
Defoe, Daniel 31, 440n62
degeneration 343, 477n50
Degeneration: A Chapter in Darwinism (Lankester) 343
Delaney, Dr Patrick 42, 47
Deleuze, Joseph 223
Dempsey, Jack 310, 312

Dennigan, Senator William P. 315
Der Stürmer (Streicher) 367–8, 481n81
Descent of Man, The (Darwin) 343, 346
Deutsche Arbeiterpartei (DAP) 367
Devonshire, Duchess of 199
Diana 3
Diderot, Denis 77, 135
Diggs, Maury 294–7, 468–9n57
Disraeli, Benjamin 329, 352, 471n6
divorce 45, 157, 159, 170, 174, 190, 203, 205, 240, 245
  simplification of 246
Dodd, Reverend William 75, 441–2n67, 442n72
Dohrn, Anton 343
Dolphin (ship) 133–4
domesticity 67–8
Don Giovanni (Mozart) 137, 138, 139–40
Don Juan (Byron) 212
d'Orléans, Duc 172
Doyle, Arthur Conan 326, 355
Dr. Jekyll and Mr. Hyde (Stevenson) 342–3, 345–6, 347
Dr. Mabuse the Gambler 366
Drabble, Margaret 385, 389
Dracula (Stoker) 356–60, 362–3, 364–5
  unlicensed adaption 366–7
'The Dream of Eugene Aram' (Hood) 322
Drury Lane 17–18, 19
Drury-Lane Ague 18
Drury Lane Theatre 132
Du Maurier, George 324, 353, 355, 470n3
  Trilby 353–5
Dublin Evening Mail 321
Ducal Palace 109, 125
  dungeons 125–30
d'Urfé, Madame 131, 132
Duryea, Clarence 270
Duryea, Etta 270, 280, 317
  suicide 281–2
Dworkin, Andrea 402, 421
Dyer, Alfred 332–3

Eddowes, Catherine 346–7
education
  higher 360
  self-education 144, 149–50
  and women 160–1, 161–2
Edward I 349
Edwards, Thomas 67
El Burlador de Sevilla y Convidado de Piedra (Molina) 137

Elements of Physiology (Richerand) 223
Elise (nanny of Alba Byron) 217
Eller v. Lord (1915) 256
Ellington, Duke 306
embryology 343–4
Emigrants, The (Imlay) 174–5
Émile (Rousseau) 150
'End of History' thesis 382
Engels, Friedrich 373, 392
English Laws for Women in the Nineteenth Century (Norton) 244
Enlightenment 6, 104
  culture of sociability 104–5
  feminine influence 105
  playful attitudes towards sex and courtship 105, 444–5n27
  reason vs. passion debate 6, 8, 9, 399–400
  reasoned pursuit of happiness 120–1
Equal Pay Act (1970) 384
The Era 361
Eros and Civilization (Marcuse) 389, 390
erotic capital 398, 409
An Essay Concerning Human Understanding (Locke) 53, 54
Eton College 449–50n6
Europa, princess 3
Europe
  cultural tropes 318–19
  sex trade 318
  sexual permissiveness 318
European Slave Trade in English Girls, The (Dyer) 332–3
Eve 4
Everleigh Club 269–70
evolution, theory of 318, 343
extra-marital sex 308

Farussi, Zanetta 83, 84, 88–9
fashion, Venetian women 102, 103
Fear of Flying (Jong) 383, 385
Federal Bureau of Investigation (FBI) 309
Female Eunuch, The (Greer) 10
Female Quixote, The (Lennox) 49
Female Spectator, The (Haywood) 49
feminism 239, 365
  Marcuse on 485–6n19
  rape culture 403
  sceptical view of permissiveness 401–2
  and sexual liberation 363–4
Fenton, Lavinia 20
Ferdinand, Archduke Franz 298
Fielding, Henry 8, 37, 39, 40, 71

  character of 65
  feuding with Samuel Richardson 65, 67
  illness 66
  letter to Samuel Richardson 57–8, 437n37
Fielding, Sarah 49, 67, 68
Fielding, Sir John 132, 151
Fighting the Traffic in Young Girls, or War on the White Slave Trade 276
Firestone, Shulamith 376
Firpo, Luis 312
Fisher, Kitty 20–1, 132
Fitzgerald, F. Scott 304, 306–7
  'Bernice Bobs Her Hair' 304–5
  flapper profile 304–6
  'The Ice Palace' 304
  'The Offshore Pirate' 304, 305
flapper profile 304–6
Fleet Street 29, 30
Fluke, John 237, 461n52
Fort Venus 134
fortune telling 249–50
Foster's Giants 293
Foundling Hospital 72–3, 440n62
Fox, Henry Edward 230
France 152–3
  see also French revolution
Frankenstein (Shelley) 212–15
Franklin, Benjamin 132
Frederick the Great 132
free love 243
  Claire Clairmont 198, 248
  Mary Shelley 228
  notions of 163, 164, 165
  William Godwin 197
free will 56
Freisler, Roland 368
French Revolution 142–3, 153
  Amazon Allies 156
  arrest of royal family 169
  Burke's opposition to 155
  Committee of Public Safety 176
  executions 172
  Jacobins/Girondins infighting 175–6
  Jacobins purge of prisoners 169
  new constitution 157
    women's political aspirations ignored 158–9, 178
  poissardes 153, 155, 156
  septembriseurs 171
  September Massacres 169–70
  sexual politics 143
  Surveillance Committees 176

Terror 177–8, 180–1
women
    demands of 157–8
    forced to flee France 179
    political aspirations 158
    political clubs 157–8
    political exclusion 179–80
    prosecution of 179
    protection of rights 158
Women's March on Versailles 153–4
Freud, Sigmund 374
Friedrich, Caspar David 166
Fritsch, Theodor 368
From Reverence to Rape (film study) 401
Fukuyama, Francis 382–3, 483–4n9
    'End of History' thesis 382
    The Great Disruption 382–3
Fuseli, Henry 165–9, 188, 192
Fuseli, Sophia 167

gallantry 105, 110, 444–5n27
Galvani, Luigi 211
Galveston 251, 259
    fighting dockworkers 259–60
galvinism 211–12
gambling 15
Ganymede 3
Gardiner, Marguerite (Countess Blessington) 218
Garrick, David 132
Garrick Theatre, New York 354
Gawain 4–5
General and Particular Principles of Animal Electricity and Magnetism, The (Bell) 224–5
Gentleman's Magazine, The 73, 440n64
Gentlemen Prefer Blondes (Loos) 310–11
George II 22, 71, 83
George III 132
George Street 151
Germany 366–7
    vampire metaphor for Jewish threat 367–8
    see also Hitler, Adolf; Nazi Germany
Gersen, Jacob 423, 424, 426
Gersen, Jeannie Suk 422–3, 424, 426
Gilbert, W.S. 330
Gillray, James 225
Gimbel, Frederick 310
Girondins 173
    fratricidal infighting with the Jacobins 175–6, 177

reconfiguration of sexual politics 177–8
Gisborne, Maria 227, 232
Gladstone, William 329, 471n6
Glorious Revolution 24, 25, 153, 154
Gobbis, Giuseppe de 116
Godwin, Mary *see* Shelley, Mary
Godwin, William 157, 167, 185, 191, 225, 452n37
    appearance 186–7
    character and personality 186, 187
    free love 197
    loan from Percy Shelley 197
    marriage to Mary Wollstonecraft
        biography of Mary 192
        commonalities with 187
        coping with Mary dying 191–2
        courtship 187
        marriage 187–8
        unconventional relationship 188
    Memoirs 193
    Political Justice 164, 197
    stepfather to Fanny Imlay 188
Goethe, Johann von 106
gold-diggers 310
Gold-Diggers bill (1935) 315
    see also anti-heart balm legislation
Goldin, Claudia 428–9
Goldoni, Carlo 83, 97, 139–40, 445n32
Goodchild, Francis (Hogarth character) 29
Gordon Riots 151
Gourley, John 16, 21, 23, 432n7
Gover v. Dill (1856) 255
Gozzi, Doctor 85
Graham, David 66
Grand Tour 79
Grandison, Sir Charles (character in book) *see* *History of Sir Charles Grandison, The* (Richardson)
Grau, Fritz 369, 370
Great Disruption, The (Fukuyama) 382–3, 483–4n9
Great Reform Act (1832) 236, 240
Great Reform Bill 230
Great White Fleet 267
Greer, Germaine 10
Grimani, Alvisi 84
Grimani, Michele 83
Grub Street 13, 23, 30
Guardi, Francesco 115–16
Guiccioli, Count 96, 444n16
Guiccioli, Teresa 84, 96, 97–8

Haeckel, Ernst 343–4
Hakim, Catherine 398
Halford, Sir Henry 205
Hall, Violet 293–4
Hamlet 186, 329–30
Hammond, William 45
Hardwick, Elizabeth 388–9
Hardy, Thomas 478n53
Harlot's Progress, The (Hogarth) 23, 24
Hart, Marvin 266
Havana 300–1
Haydon, Benjamin 230–1, 461n48
Haygood, Bishop 252
Haymarket Theatre 355
Hays, Mary 187
Haywood, Eliza 39, 40, 49
Hazlitt, William 193
heart balm acts 254–5, 314
Hell-Fire Club (Dublin) 45
Hell-Fire Club (London) 18
Her Majesty's Theatre 355
Hewlett, Reverend John 146, 147
Highmore, Joseph 60, 77
Hill, Aaron 31, 40, 58
Hinge (dating app) 406, 411
Historical Society 320
Histories of Some of the Penitents in the
     Magdalen House, The (Richardson) 74
History of Sir Charles Grandison, The
     (Richardson) 63–4, 73
   ideal man, notion of 64, 65
Hite Report, The (Hite) 401
Hite, Shere 401, 484n9
Hitler, Adolf 367
   vampire metaphor 367
Hobhouse, John 96, 200–1, 221
Hogarth, William 23, 24, 29, 39, 71
Hood, Thomas 322
Hoppner, Richard 217
Horkheimer, Max 372
Hornby Lodge 15–16
Horrors of the White Slave Trade: The Mighty
     Crusade to Protect the Purity of Our
     Homes (Roe) 278
Hôtel d'Angleterre 198, 207, 208
Hôtel de Ville 153
Houellebecq, Michel
   contentions about post-1968 world 382
   sexual revolution 394
   sexual social democracy 394
   sexuality and capitalism 392
   suspicion of seduction 395–6

work as computer engineer 392
writings
     Atomized (1998) 393, 394–5, 413
     Whatever (1994) 393, 396, 405, 406
How to Get the Women You Desire into Bed
     (Jeffries) 399
How to Pick Up Girls! (Weber) 399
Hoxton 144–5
Humane Society 186
Hume, David 54, 436n32
Hundreds of Drury Lane 19
Hunt, Leigh 216, 227
hypnosis/hypnotism 9, 223, 474–5n36
   in Dracula 359
   and seduction 353

Idle, Thomas (Hogarth character) 29
Ilive, Jacob 20
illegitimate children 213, 214–15
Imer, Giuseppe 132
Imer, Sophie 132
Imer, Teresa 87, 88, 114, 132
   see also Cornelys, Teresa
Imlay, Fanny 181, 183, 188, 215
Imlay, Gilbert 174–5, 176–7, 180–3, 185, 192,
     454n54
   false marriage to Mary Wollstonecraft 180–1
   mistresses 183, 186
immigration, fear of swamping 365
immoral purposes 294, 297, 468n57
Incel community 396–7
Indiana, Gold-Diggers bill (1935) 315
Indiana Republican Party 313
Indianapolis Freeman 285
industrial capitalism 318
Industry and Idleness (Hogarth) 29
infidelity 45
Information Age 383, 384
Institute for Social Research 372
intellectual labour 383
interracial gatherings, banning of 308–9
interracial marriage 289, 292
   criminalisation of 308
interracial sexual relations 258–9
Io (nymph) 3
Irving, Henry 321–2
   dinner with Bram Stoker 322–3
   encounters with Jews abroad 349–50
   knighthood 355
   Lyceum Theatre
      ethos of selected plays 328
      Hamlet 329–30

profitability 330
renovation costs 328
success 329–30
Shylock 350
see also Lyceum Theatre
Italy 63–4
cicisbeismo, culture of 94–8
cicisbeo's life 95–6, 97
culture and learning 79
marriage market for women 105–6
new sociability of the Enlightenment 105–6
see also Venice
Ivinskaya, Olga 475n37

Jack the Ripper murders 346–8, 349
characteristics of Jack, perceived 349
hypnotism 475n37
Jewish culpability, belief in 351
profile of victims 351
Jacobins 169
fratricidal infighting with the Girondins
175–6, 177
ideas on women's role in society 178, 180
James II 24
Jarbe (manservant) 132
jazz 305–7
Jefferies, Jack 266
Jeffries, Jim 266, 270–1
vs. Jack Johnson 271–3
Jeffries, Ross 399
Jenkins, Nettie 293
Jew and Woman: The Theory and Practice of
Jewish Vampirism (Schwartz-Bostunitsch)
370
Jewish Chronicle 352
Jewish Ladies' Association for Preventative
and Rescue Work 352
Jewish Question 370
Jews 350
Ashkenazim 350–1
and crime 351–2
and hypnotism 353
Jewishness 349, 350
and prostitution 351
living in England 349, 350
magical abilities, perceived 352–3
persecution in Russia 350
see also Germany; Nazi Germany
Jim Crow caste system 251
Johnson, Henry 251
Johnson, Jack 468–9n57
Ada Banks, relationship with 281, 284

appearance 262–3, 268–9
Belle Schreiber, relationship with 269–70,
270, 271, 280, 286–7
arrest for violation of the Mann Act
287–8, 290
Booker T. Washington, criticism from 284–5
boxing career
arrest and detention 261–2
vs. Arthur Cravan 302
diminishing 312
exhibitions during the war 317
facing the Color Line 266
heavyweight champion 268
vs. Jess Willard 299–301
vs. Jim Jefferies 271–3
race riots following 273–5
vs. Joe Choynski 261–2
vs. John 'Must Have It' Lee 260
learns from Choynski 262
lessons 260
mocking Tommy Burns 267
need for greater challenges 266
personal accounts of 261, 464–5n15
vs. Stanley Ketchel 270, 465n23
style 263
vs. Tommy Burns 268
Café de Champion 280–1, 466–7n33
Café de Luxe venture 305
childhood 251
Clara Kerr, relationship with 264–5
death 317
defends freedom and rights 285
effigy 285
Etta Duryea, relationship with 270, 271, 280
burial next to 317
marriage 280, 317
suicide 281–2
Hattie McClay, relationship with 269, 270,
271, 280
Irene Marie Pineau, marriage to 312
and Joe Louis 316–17
life on Galveston docks 259–60
love affairs 250
Lucille Cameron, relationship with 281, 282–4
arrest for abduction 284
divorce 311
marriage 288, 311–12
on the run 293, 298–9
Barcelona 302–3
Havana 300–1
London 299, 301–2
returns to America 304

Johnson, Jack *cont'd*
  Mary Austin, marriage to 263
  memoirs 290, 300
    indigenous tribe in Mexico 303
  Napoleon, admiration for 300
  Nellie O'Brien, bogus marriage to 269
  personality 263
  physique 263
  poverty 265
  United States v. John Arthur Johnson (1913) 289–92
    conviction 291–2
    defence 291
    escape 292–3, 298
    prison sentence 292
  visits fortune teller 249
  and white women 265
  Zeppelin bombers story 302
Johnson, Joseph 147, 150, 151, 152, 155, 167, 192
Johnson, Samuel 18, 50, 71, 73, 132, 146, 441–2n67
Johnson, Sol C. 291
Johnson, Tiny 251, 270, 303
Jong, Erica 383
Josie's Beer Garden 260
Journey of a Voyage to Lisbon (Fielding) 67
Joyce, James 310
Juan, Don 137–8

Keane, Reverand 254
Kelly, Mary 347
Kerr, Clara 264–5
Ketchel, Stanley 270, 465n23
King, Margaret 149, 455n82
King, Robert, Viscount Kingsborough *see* Kingsborough, Lord
Kingsborough, Lady 148, 149, 150
Kingsborough, Lord 148
Kinnaird, Lord 136
Kipnis, Laura 423
Klein, Ezra 422, 426
Klossowski, Pierre 390–1
Knapton family 433n13
knowledge economy 390
Kollontai, Alexandra 374
Ku Klux Klan 313

La Monnaie vivante (*Living Currency*) (Klossowski) 390–1
la Tour d'Auvergne, Count de 135–6
La Valeur 92–3

Labor of Love: The Invention of Dating (Weigel) 411
labour market, gender equality 383
Lac Léman 207, 208
Lacombe, Claire 179
Ladies National Association (LNA) 333, 336
Lamarioux, Agent 293–4
Lamb, Lady Caroline 200, 200–1, 205, 219, 235
Lamb, William, 2nd Viscount Melbourne, *see* Melbourne, Lord
Langford, Sam 298
Lankester, Ray 343, 473n20
Larson, Jane E. 402–3
laughing gas 225, 226
Laura (intermediary of Casanova/Caterina) 117, 123
law 9–10
  medieval legal system (UK) 238
  questions of morality 238
  see also civil law
Lawrence, Dr William 211, 213, 216
Le Fanu, Joseph Sheridan 321, 356
Leake, John 29
Lee, John 'Must Have It' 260
Lee, Lorelei (character in book) 310–11
Leigh, Augusta 200, 204
Leigh, Medora 204
Lennox, Charlotte 49
Léon, Pauline 179
A Letter to the Queen on Lord Chancellor Cranworth's Marriage & Divorce Bill (Norton) 244
Letters Written in France (Williams) 156
Letters Written in Sweden, Norway, and Denmark (Wollstonecraft) 184–5
Levee 278
liberalism 6
libertinism 25
libidinal economy 406
Libidinal Economy, The (Lyotard) 391
Ligonier, General 48
Lipski, Israel 351
Lisbon earthquake 126, 446n50
Locke, John 53, 54, 436n34
Lombroso, Cesare 344–5, 351–2
London
  buying and selling of virgins, claim 333–4
  East End Jews 350–1
  furore caused by *Pall Mall Gazette* 331–2
  life in 17–18
  murders of alleged prostitutes 346–7

prostitution 334–5
 rich and wealthy clients 335
sexual activity 18–19
 of women 21
sexual vocabulary 18
underworld 334–5
Victorian 326
 crime 327
 fog 327
London Committee for Suppressing the
 Traffic in British Girls 333
London, Jack 268
London Revolution Society 154
Longhi, Pietro 115
Looking Backward (Bellamy) 374
Loos, Anita 310
Louis, Joe 316–17
Louis XIV 104
Louis XV 141
Louis XVI 142, 171, 172
Loveday, Harry 329
Lovelace, Robert (character in book) 51–2, 55,
 56, 58–60, 61
L'uomo Delinquente (Criminal Man)
 (Lombroso) 345
Lyceum Theatre 325–6, 328–30
 Beefsteak Room 341
 Dr. Jekyll and Mr. Hyde 342–3, 345–6, 347,
 348
 ethos of selected plays 470–1n4
 leasing out 342
 Macbeth 348
 negative publicity 348
 Prince Karl 348
 touring 330–1, 342
lynchings 251, 254, 259
Lyndhurst, Lord 246
Lyotard, Jean-François 391

Macaulay Graham, Catherine 156
MacKinnon, Catharine 402
Magdalen 62, 63
Magdalen House/Hospital 73–4, 151, 440n64
 chapel 74–5, 76
 safari of seduction 76
 sensibility, re-induction of women into
 442n69
magnum opus, Eros and Civilization (Marcuse)
 376
Maison Chapuis 208
male liberation 401
Malipiero, Senator Alvise 86–7, 88

Malleus Maleficarum 5
Man and Superman (Shaw) 362
Man of Feeling, The (Mackenzie) 9
Man, The (Stoker) 361
Mann Act (2010) 275, 275–6, 279, 287–8, 296
 blackmail 309–10
 convictions for violations of 309
 double standards 310
 Drew Caminetti and Maury Diggs 294–7
 exploitation by devious women 296
 immoral purposes 294, 297, 468n57
 imprisonment of women 293
 Nettie Jenkins 293
 see also United States v. John Arthur Johnson
 (1913)
Mann, James Robert 279
Mansfield, Richard 342, 346, 347–8, 354
Manuzzi, Giovanni Battista 124–5
Manzoni, Signora 114
Marat, Jean-Paul 176, 178–9, 225
Marcuse, Herbert 372
 adaptability of capitalism 390
 'angel of the apocalypse' 376
 capitalism and sexuality. relationship
 between 373
 economic and sexual spheres 376
 Freud and Marxist theory 374–5
 joins the Institute for Social Research 372
 joins the Office of Strategic Services (OSS)
 373
 Marxist influence 373
 opposition to Nazi regime 372
 socialist and sexually liberated civilisation
 375–6
 socialist revolution, doubts of imminent
 arrival 389
 supporters 376–7
 surplus-repression 375
 writings
 Eros and Civilization (1955) 390
 magnum opus, Eros and Civilization
 (1955) 376
 'Marxism and Feminism' (1974)
 485–6n19
 One-Dimensional Man (1964) 390
Maria: or, The Wrongs of Woman
 (Wollstonecraft) 188–91
Markovik, Erik von 'Mystery' 400, 412, 419
 Mystery Method 400
marriage 242
 accommodating female independence 364
 adultery, consequences of 242–3

marriage 242 cont'd
  contradictions of 244–5
  Godwin's attack on 164
  immovability of 242
  interracial 289
  issues 6
  legal reform 244–6
  male immorality 245
  market for 105–6
  private choice 6
  reform of 364
  romantic 433–4n17, 435–6n28
  and sexual inequality 242
  sham 433–4n17
Married Love (Stopes) 479n61
Marshalsea prison 47
Martín, Vicente 139
Martorano, bishopric of 88–9
Marx, Karl
  The Communist Manifesto 373, 392
Marxism
  commodification of interpersonal relation-
    ships 373, 387
  and feminism 485–6n19
  sexual liberation for women 373–4
  social and economic independence for
    women 373–4
Mary, A Fiction (Wollstonecraft) 150, 152
Mary of Talfourd 239
Match Group 409, 410–11
Matrimonial Causes Act (1857) 246, 247
Maunsell, Dr Henry 321
Maxwell-Stirling, Sir William 247
Mazeppa (Byron) 220
McClay, Hattie 269, 270, 271, 280
McIntosh, Hugh D. 267–8
McKenna, Justice 468n57
McMillan, Margaret 364
McNabe, Senator 314
McNeil Island 297
Mein Kampf (Hitler) 367
Melbourne, Lady 199
Melbourne, Lord 233–4
  cuckolded by Byron 235
  friendship with Caroline Norton 236
  relationship with George Norton 235–6
  seduction charges brought against 235
    Trial of the Century 236
Memmo, Lucia 125
Memoirs of Laetitia Pilkington, The
  (Pilkington) 48
Memoirs of the Author of A Vindication of the

  Rights of Woman (Godwin) 192–3
men
  characterisations of 53
  ideal man, notion of 64, 65
  reformation of 63
mesmerism 222, 223, 224, 225
Mesulla 98
Metamorphoses 3
Milbanke, Anna Isabella 'Annabella' 199
  birth of Ada 202
  intelligence 202
  marriage to Lord Byron 201–2
    courtship 199–200, 201
    divorce suit 203–4, 205
      legal separation agreed 205
      threatens sodomy allegation 205
    psychological diagnosis of 202–3
      madness 203–4
      madness, unproven by doctors 203–4
  meeting with Caroline Lamb 205
Millais, John Everett 330
Millar, Andrew 30
Minassian, Alek 396–7
miscegenation 258–9
misogyny 4–5
mistresses 178
M.M. (Casanova's lover) 118–24
  ménage à quatre 124
  ménage à trois 124
Modern Jew, The (White) 352
Mohocks 18
Molina, Tirso di 137
Monmouth, Duke of 25
Mont Blanc 207
Montagu, Lady Mary Wortley 57, 437n36,
  439n57
  aversion to John Murray 80
Montesquieu 105
moons of Jupiter 3
moral economy 255–6
Moral Essays (Pope) 21, 23
moral hypocrisy 98
moralists 39
morality, legal questions 238
Moran, Frank 298
Morisson, Fynes 102
Morley, John 332
Morris, William 374, 387–8
Morrison, Jim 383
Morrison, Scott 404
Mount Tambora 208
Mozart, Wolfgang Amadeus 137, 138, 139, 140

Murano convent 115, 116–17
Murnau, F.W. 366
Murray, Fanny 20
Murray, John 80, 206, 239, 446n45
  popularity 80–1
Mystery Method 413–15
'Mystery' pseudonym *see* Markovik, Erik von

narrative *see* seduction narrative
Narrative of the Life of Charlotte Charke, The
  (Clarke) 49
National Assembly 157, 158, 170
  trial of Louis XVI 171
National Governors Conference 288
National Sozialistische Deutsche
  Arbeiterpartei (NSDAP) 367
National Vigilance Association (NVA) 471n9
natural rights 238, 245
natural selection 343
Nazi Germany
  anti-Semitic legislation 368–9
    intensification 370
  Commission on Criminal Law Reform 369
  dismantling of Jewish economic power 370
  exclusion of Jews from practice of medicine
    481–2n83
  Final Solution 370
  Jewish Question 370
  Nuremberg Laws 369
  Prussian Memorandum 368
  race treason 368–9
    modelled on United States 368–9
  racial utopia 369
  sexual threat of Jews 369–70
  'Superstition in Film' memo 370–1
    Nosferatu 366, 371
  Wannsee Conference (1942) 370
Needham, Mother 21, 23
neoliberalism 394
Neuro-Linguistic Programming (NLP) 399
New Left 483n7
New Man 364
New Monthly Magazine 229
New Woman 318, 360, 360–1, 478n53
  characteristics of 360, 362
  patronising image of 364
  sexual aggression 363
  theatre 360–1
New Woman, The (Grundy) 360
New York Female Moral Reform Society
  (NYFMRS) 257, 463n9
New York Magazine 408

New York Sun 254
New York Times 282, 296
New York World 282
News from Nowhere (Morris) 374, 387–8
Nichols, Mary Anne 346
Nicholson, Roberta West 313–14
  anti-heart balm legislation 314–16
Nootbaar, Captain Max 283–4
Nordau, Max 477n50
Norman, Stephen 361
Norris, Lola 294–5
Norton, Caroline 228–9
  breakdown of marriage 236
    damage to reputation 236–7
    lawsuit 243–4
    legal deed of separation 240
    letters in *The Times* 244
    redirects debts to husband 243
    reunification with sons 240
    separation from sons 237
  comparison with Lord Byron 230
  death 247
  and feminism 239
  friendship with Lord Melbourne 236–7,
    462n53
  friendship with Mary Shelley 231–2, 232–3
    letters to and from 240
    offers legal assistance 233–4
  inheritance from mother's death 243
  legal reform 237–9
    Custody of Infants Act (1839) 237, 239–40
    of marriage 244–6
    and married women 244–5
    Matrimonial Causes Act (1857) 246, 247
    natural rights 238, 245
    requests Mary Shelley's help 237–8
    sovereignty of property rights 238–9
    writings 237, 244–5
  marriage 229
  marriage to Sir William Maxwell-Stirling 247
  mischief-making personality 230
  paid work 229
  sons 230
  as a source of fascination in society 230–1
  writings 229, 244
    legal reform 237, 244–5
    *English Laws for Women in the
      Nineteenth Century* (1854) 244
    *A Letter to the Queen on Lord
      Chancellor Cranworth's Marriage &
      Divorce Bill* (1855) 244
    Sorrows of Rosalie, The (1829) 229

Norton, George 229, 235
  breakdown of marriage 236
    lawsuit 243–4
    legal deed of separation 240
    letters in *The Times* 244
    refuses financial maintenance 243
  death 247
  friendship with Lord Melbourne 235–6
    seduction charges against 236
  Norton v. Viscount Melbourne 236
Norton, William 240
Nosferatu (Murnau) 366, 371
Nostitz Theatre 137–9
Notorious Mrs. Ebbsmith, The 361
novels 41
  see also *Pamela; or, Virtue Rewarded*
    (Richardson)
Nugent, Catherine 196
Nuremberg Laws 369

O'Brien, Nellie *see* McClay, Hattie
Ocasio-Cortez, Alexandria 420–1
Odier, Dr Louis 226, 460n41
Odysseus 131
Office of Strategic Services (OSS) 373
'The Offshore Pirate' (Fitzgerald) 304, 305
OkCupid 406–7, 408
One-Dimensional Man (Marcuse) 389
one drop rule 308
online dating 405–6
  acceptance of 412
  and age 408
  attractiveness, importance of 406–8
  as a kind of work 411
  logical end result of sexual revolution 411
  men/women interaction differences 406–7
  paid subscriptions 410
  and race 408
  sexual inequality 406–9
  subscription services 409
  visual information 407
  see also Tinder
oral contraceptives 'the pill' 385
Origin of the Species, The (Darwin) 343
Original Stories from Real Life (Wollstonecraft)
  163
Osborn, John 30
Osborne, Walter 361
Ovid 3
Oxford, Lady 200

Padua 84–5

Paine, Thomas 157, 173, 225
Palazzo Bragadin 101–2
Palazzo di Spagna 90
Palazzo Soranzo 99
Pall Mall Gazette 331–2, 345
  buying and selling of virgins, story 335–6
  influence of 332
  Jack the Ripper murders 347–8, 351
Palmerston, Lord 246
Pamela Censur'd (anon) 40–1
Pamela; or, Virtue Rewarded (Richardson)
  33–42, 50
  adulation for Richardson 38–9
  anonymous publication of 38
  critics of 39
  French translation 434–5n22
  modification of text 41
  satirical attacks on 39–40
  success of 38–9
Pankhurst, Christabel 364, 421
Pantisocracy 164
Parsons, Mrs 22
Pascal, Blaise 381
passions 54
Pasternak, Boris 475n37
Pensées (Pascal) 381
permissiveness 103, 116, 318, 394, 401–2
  Venice convents 115–16
Philadelphia Port News 284
philanthropy 72–4
Phillips, Teresia Constantia 49, 68
Philosophical Society 320
Philpotts, Henry, Bishop of Exeter 241
physical labour 383
Pilkington, Betty 47
Pilkington, Laetitia 42–3, 44–7, 68
  financial support from Samuel Richardson
    47
  The Memoirs of Laetitia Pilkington 48
Pilkington, Matthew 42–5, 45–6, 435n27
pill, the *see* contraception
Pillars of Acre 129–30
Pineau, Irene Marie 312
Pinero, Arthur Wing 361
Pitt the Younger, William 152–3
Place de Grève 141
Place de la Révolution 172
Planned Parenthood 313
Plecker, Walter 308–9
poissardes 153, 155, 156
Polidori, John William 205–7
  De Oneirodynia 222

death 227
ghost stories 212
injury 209–10
Lord Byron, declining relationship with 220–1
Mary Shelley, infatuation with 209–10, 458n22
Percy Shelley, jealousy of 209
studying somnambulism 226–7
The Vampyre 218–22, 227
Political Justice (Godwin) 164, 197
Polwhele, Reverend Richard 192–3
Poor Law (1834) 240
Pope, Alexander 21, 23, 429, 435n27
Potter, Paul 354–5
Powell, John 309
Prana-Film 366
Preserve Racial Integrity Act (1924) 308
Price, Dr Richard 146, 154–5
Priestley, Joseph 225–6
Printing Act, demise of 24
printing industry 28
  growth 30
prizefighting *see* boxing
procuration 338, 339
Prohibition 303, 309
property rights, sovereignty of 238–9
prostitutes/prostitution 19–20, 62, 63, 73
  alien faiths 352
  Angel of the House 336
  and the Contagious Diseases Act (1867) 336
  juvenile 333, 338
  in London
    life of 334–5
    rich and wealthy clients 335
  policing of 241
  traditional morality, demise of 352
  vulnerability of women 333, 471n8
provident nature 70
Prussian Memorandum 368
Public Assemblages Act (Virginia, 1926) 308–9
Punch 327, 347, 349
Pushkin, Alexander 78
Putnam, Robert 428
Puységur, Marquis de (Amand-Marie-Jacques de Chastenet) 223–4

Queensberry, Duchess of 15
Queensbury, Duke of 15
quiet revolution 386

race riots 273–5
racial segregation 308–9
racial violence 252–4
racism 426
Rambler, The (Johnson) 73, 440n63
rape 7, 13, 51
rape culture 403
Rapport sur l'instruction publique (Talleyrand) 160
rational passions 8
Real Social Dynamics (RSD) 404
reason 54
  vs. passion debate 6, 8, 9, 54–5, 56, 399–400
  power of 8
recapitulation, theory of 343–4
Recent Social Trends in the United States 307
Reconstruction 250, 251, 289
Redemption 250
Rée, Jonathan 431n6
Reflections on the Revolution in France (Burke) 155
Refuge Fund for the Poor of the East-end of London 348
Reich, Wilhelm 376
Religious Courtship (Defoe) 31
repression 374
Republic of Letters 104
Richard III (Shakespearian character) 5
Richardson, Samuel 24
  appearance 31
  appointed Master of Stationers' Company 70
  book of letters 33–4
  as a collector of women 47–8
  countryside home 33
  criticises female writers 68, 439n55
  criticises Fielding's *Tom Jones* 65–6
  criticisms of 39, 57, 58, 59–60, 69
  death 77
  domestic values of women 67–8
  early life in London 25–7
  fame 71
  health issues 31
  Henry Fielding, feuding with 65–7
  influence on literature 77–8
  Lady Dorothy Bradshaigh, friendship with 59–63
  letters
    to Aaron Hill 434n21
    to George Cheyne 434n21
    to Sarah Fielding 67
  literature and letter writing 26–7
  Martha, marriage to 29, 31, 433n15

Richardson, Samuel 24 cont'd
  moral system 68–9
  philanthropy 72–4
  printing apprenticeship 28, 29
  printing business
    contracts 30–1
    premises in Salisbury Court 29–30, 31, 70
    success of 70–1
  prosperity of 42, 47
  satirical attacks on 39–40
  self-satisfaction 71–2
  writings
    The Apprentice's Vade Mecum (1733) 32–3
    Clarissa: or, the History of a Young Lady (1748) 50, 51–2, 52–3, 54–62
    The Histories of Some of the Penitents in the Magdalen House (1759) 74
    The History of Sir Charles Grandison (1753-4) 63–4, 73
    New World circulation 78
    Pamela; or, Virtue Rewarded (1740) 33–42, 50
    translations into foreign languages 78
Richardson, Samuel Sn. 25
Richardson, Thomas Verren 32
Richerand, Anthelme 223
Richmond Planet 292
Rickard, Tex 271
Riddle of the Jew's Success, The (Fritsch) 368
Ridotto 103, 123
Rights of Man, The (Paine) 157
Rivington, C. 30
Rivington, C. and Osborn, J. 33
Robespierre, Maximilien 176, 177, 225
Roddenberry, Seaborn 275, 288–9
Rodger, Elliot 396
Roe, Clifford G. 278, 279
Roebuck, John Arthur 241–2
Roland, Madame 169–70, 173, 179, 180
romantic marriages 435–6n28
Romantics 185
Roosevelt, President Theodore 267
Roscoe, William 166–7, 170
Ross, David 20
Rossetti, Dante Gabriel 356, 476n42
Rousseau, Jean-Jacques 77, 131, 150, 447n54
  Émile 150
  ideas on women's role in society 178, 454n61

Royal Academy 361
Rudder, Christian 407, 408

Sacramento Bee 295
Salieri, Antonio 139
Salisbury Court 29–30, 31
San Francisco Examiner 273
satirists 39
Saturday Evening Post, The 304
Sayre, Zelda 304, 469n61
Scala dei Giganti 129
Scala d'Oro 129
Sceptic, The (anon) 225
Schlabrendorf, Gustav von 174
Schmeling, Max 316
Schreiber, Belle 269–70, 270, 271, 280, 286–7, 294
  testifies against Jack Johnson 287
Schwartz-Bostunitsch, Gregor 370
Scott, Benjamin 332–3, 333–4
Sebottendorf, Rudolf von 366–7
seduction
  charges against Lord Melbourne 235–6
  civil laws 234–5
  Criminal Law Amendment Act (1885) 338–40, 472n12
  defining 256
  distinction from rape 7
  in the eighteenth century 34–6
  extinction under Marxist revolution 373, 374
  Great Social Evil 241
  illegitimate children 213
  investigations of 2
  legislation 314
    campaign to repeal 314–15, 470n73
    Gold-Diggers bill (1935) 315
  Percy Shelley's view on 456n2
  policing of 241
  regulation of (US) 255–9
  repeal of legislation 402–3
  risks to women 160–1, 228
  as a science 400
  sexual danger 55
  and the sexual revolution 388–9
  technique 82
  as a unit of exchange 394
  and the white slave trade 336
'Seduction and Betrayal' (Hardwick) 388–9
Seduction and Prostitution Suppression Bill, proposal for 241–2
Seduction (Baudrillard) 391, 411
seduction community 399, 400–1, 403

exile of 404–5
revulsion at 412
Seduction law 234, 254, 256
seduction narrative 2–6
  assumptions 427
  Christian values 36
  classic form 6–7
  counter-narratives 395
  custom and taboo of sexuality 395
  dilemma 56
  Enlightenment period 6
  powerlessness of victims 7–8
  reason vs. passion debate 6, 8, 9, 54–5, 56,
    399–400
  seducer as hero 8–9, 10
  seducer as villain 7–8, 10
  see also Dracula (Stoker)
seduction professionals 403–5
seductresses 21
segregation, racial 308–9
Seingalt, Chevalier de (Casanova's adopted
    title) 131, 447n53
sensibility 53–4, 72
Sephardic Jews 349
September Massacres 170
Seven Years War 132
Seward, Thomas 49
sex
  conducted along entrepreneurial lines 391
  mediation between individuals 391
      seduction as mediation 391–2
  privatisation of 390–1
Sex Bureaucracy 423, 426
Sex Discrimination Act (1975) 384
sex recession 420–1
sex trade, in Europe 318
sex workers see prostitutes/prostitution
sexual assault 338, 422
sexual behaviour
  legal and bureaucratic devices 419–20, 422–3
  monitoring of 309
  new language to describe 255
sexual conduct
  codes of conduct 423–4
      initiated by students 423–4
  university campuses, regulation of 423–4
  in the workplace 424–5
sexual criminality and immigration 425–6
sexual culture 419
sexual economics 386–7, 388
sexual economy 394
sexual exploitation 10

of women through somnambulism 224
Sexual Fraud 403
sexual freedoms 2, 8
  consequences of 242–3
  and contraception 385
sexual ideology 69
sexual immorality 72
sexual liberation 164–5, 363, 394
  doubts about 401
sexual loneliness 397
sexual markets, unregulated 406
sexual morality 135
  double standards 337
  single standard 421
  in the Twenties (US) 307
sexual permissiveness 318
sexual rationalism 10
sexual regulation
  in universities 423–4
  in the workplace 424–5
sexual relations
  commodification of 373
  exploitation of 373
  rationalisation of 400
sexual revolution 304–8
  abortion 385, 386
  authoritarian legislation 308
  capitalist characteristics 390, 391
  changing behaviour 308
  contraception 385–6, 389
  cultural influences
      1920s 384
      1960s and 1970s 383–4
          legislation 384–5
  economic factors, primacy of 484n9
  gender equality in labour market 383
  and intellectual labour 383
  low-price sexual-economic market 388
  multiplication of potential sexual encounters
    392
  rationalisation of sexuality 395
  social libertarianism 394
  suffrage 385
  trends 382–3
  twentieth century 388
Sexual Revolution, The (Reich) 376
sexual social democracy 394
sexuality
  and capitalism 373, 392
  poetry of desire 392
  rationalisation of 395
  'second system of differentiation' 394

Shakespeare, William 5
sham marriages 433–4n17
Shamela (Fielding) 39, 40
Sharpe, Samuel 95
Shaw, George Bernard 321, 323, 328, 355, 362, 470–1n4
Shelley, Clara 197, 215, 217
Shelley, Harriet (née Westbrook) 196, 197
  suicide 215
Shelley, Mary 8, 191, 427
  appearance 195
  Caroline Norton, friendship with 228–9, 231–2, 232–3
    commonalities 230
    letters to and from 240
    profile of 229
    seeks legal assistance from 233–4
  death 247
  free love 228
  haunted by Harriet Westbrook 197
  illegitimate children, writing about 214–15
  intelligence 195
  meeting of young Romantics 208–15
    ghost stories 212
    Frankenstein 212–15
  Percy Shelley, relationship with 196–7
    birth of Clara 197, 215
    birth of William (Wilmouse) 198
    death of Clara 217
    declares love for 196
    elopement to Europe 197
    grief at death of 227
    marriage 215
  Switzerland, visit to 198–9
  visits mother's graveyard 196
Shelley, Percy Bysshe 8, 196
  death 227
  Harriet Westbrook, marriage to 196
  ill health 216
  Lord Byron, friendship with 208
  Mary Shelley, relationship with 196–7
    assignations in St Pancras Churchyard 196
    elopement to Europe 197
    marriage 215
  meeting of young Romantics 208–15
    ghost stories 212
  seduction, views on 456n2
Shelley, William (Wilmouse) 198, 215
  death 227
Sheridan, Richard Brinsley 228
Shylock 350

Sidney, Philip 5
Sign of the Four, The (Doyle) 326
Signora F. 93–4, 98
Sims Act (1912) 275, 466n29
Sims, Attorney Edwin W. 278, 279
Sin Against the Blood, The (Dinter) 366
Single Moral Standard 246
Sir Gawain and the Green Knight (anon) 4–5
slave trade
  English girls 332–3
  white 275–9, 289–90
sleepwalking 222
Smith, Ada 'Bricktop' 281–2, 464n14
Smith, Adam 427
Smith, Henry 252–4, 273
Smollett, Tobias 97
social capital 398
social mobility 20
socialism
  economic equality for women 387
  price of sex 388
  sexual liberation for women 373–4
  social and economic independence for women 373–4
Société fraternelle 157
Societies for the Reformation of Manners 26–7, 72
Society for the Suppression of Vice 72
Society of Revolutionary Republican Women 158
sodomy 205
Somers Town 186, 188
somnambulism 222–4, 226–7
  see also artificial somnambulism
Soradaci 127
Sorrows of Rosalie, The (Norton) 229
Southey, George 163–4, 452n36
Southey, Robert 192
Spectator 349, 357, 476n45
Spooner, Richard 241
sport 263–4
St Augustine 4
St James's Palace 204
St Jerome 4
St Mark's 103, 112, 122, 126
St Pancras Churchyard 196
St Peter Damian 4
Stanley, Edward Lyulph 339
Stationers' Company 29, 70
'The Statues: or, The Trial of Constancy. A Tale for the Ladies' (Pilkington) 46–7
Stead, William Thomas 331–2, 333–4, 352

associated actresses with prostitutes 341–2
jail for abducting a minor 340–1
journey into London's underworld 334
opposition to Criminal Law Amendment
Act 340
shares Josephine Butler's view of women 337
story in the *Pall Mall Gazette* 335–6
women's rights 363
Steinem, Gloria 401
Stevenson, Robert Louis 342–3, 345–6
Stewes Bank 19
Stoker, Abraham Sn. 319, 320
Stoker, Bram (Abraham) 319
appearance 319, 324
death 366
Dracula 356–60, 362–3
anti-Semitic tropes 358
hypnosis 359
male anxiety 364–5
motivation for writing 356
and race 357–8
seductive narrative 356–9
themes 356
family life in London 325, 326–7
family portrait 324
Florence Balcombe, marriage to 323–4
Henry Irving, dinner with 322–3
investment in publishing scheme 355
legal training 355
Lyceum Theatre 325–6
acting manager 329
behind the scenes 329
crossroads of career 355
front of house 330
outside role 329
public function 329
reputation for omnipotence and ubiquity
330–1
touring arrangements 330–1
The Man 361
theatre critic for *Dublin Evening Mail* 321
Trinity College Dublin 320
auditor of Historical Society 320
Dublin civil service 321
high achiever 320
performing on stage 320
president of Philosophical Society 320
Stoker, Charlotte 319–20
Stoker, Florence (née Balcombe) 323–4, 325,
361, 366–7
Stoker, Irving Noel Thornley 324
Stoker, Thomas 319

Stone, John Hurford 174
Stopes, Marie 479n61
storytelling 2
Strand (London Street) 326
Strauss, Neil 'Style' 397–8, 400, 405, 413, 419
The Game: Penetrating the Secret Society of
Pickup Artists 400–1, 405
Streicher, Julius 367–8
Stride, Elizabeth 346–7
Stuart, Mary 24
Style (Neil Strauss) *see* Strauss, Neil 'Style'
Sublime Porte 91
suffrage, women's 360, 362
Sullivan, Arthur 330
Sullivan, John L. 260, 266, 272
Summer of Love 377
surplus-repression 375
Sweden 425–6
Swift, Jonathan 23, 43, 435n27
Swinburne, Algernon Charles 329

Tahiti 133–5, 163
mores 133–4, 447–8n59
sexual morality 135
Talbot, Catherine 438n49
Talbot, John 230
Talfourd, Sir Thomas 239
Talleyrand, Charles Maurice de 158, 160, 225
Teatro San Samuele 83, 99
Tellez, Gabriel 137
Templer Bar 29–30
Tennyson, Alfred 330
Teresa, Empress Maria 110
Terriss, William 331
Terror 177–8, 180–1
Terry, Ellen 341–2, 354, 473n17, 475n41
Tertullian 4
The Game: Penetrating the Secret Society of
Pickup Artists (Strauss) 400–1, 405
Theatre Royal 321
theatres, association with seduction 341–2,
472–3n16
Thelwall, John 226
This Side of Paradise (Fitzgerald) 304
Thomas, George 299
Thomas, René 379, 380
Thomas, Sheriff Henry 262
Thoughts on Education (Burgh) 146
Thoughts on the Education of Daughters
(Wollstonecraft) 147, 148
Thule Society 367
Tillman, Ben 295

Tinder 406, 408, 409–10
    paid subscription services 409–10
titillation 37
Title IX 423, 426
Toleration Act (1649) 24
Tom Jones (Fielding) 65–6
Torbillon, Robert A. 310
Tosello, Father 86
Tower Hamlets 26
Tower of London 25, 26
Transit of Venus 134
Transylvania 357–8
Treatise of Human Nature, A (Hume) 54
Tree, Herbert Beerbohm 355
Trelawney, Edward 'Corsair Trelawney' 227,
    231, 232, 461n49
Trial of the Century 236
Trilby (Du Maurier) 353–5
    stage adaption
        Garrick Theatre, New York 354
        Haymarket Theatre, London 355
Trinity College Dublin 320
Tuileries Palace 169
Tunney, Gene 310
Twenge, Jean 428
Tyburn 17, 29

unfaithful wives 178
United States of America (USA)
    Alabama law 258
    Commerce Clause 278–9
    Eller v. Lord (1915) 256
    Gover v. Dill (1856) 255
    heart balm acts 254–5, 314
    Henry Smith 252–4
    inheritance of English civil law 254–5
    Jazz Age 305–7
    lynchings 252–4, 259
    Prohibition 303, 309
    race riots 273–5
    racist South 252–4
    regulation of seduction 255, 256
        judgement of women's character 258
        miscegenation 258–9
        protection of young women 257–8
        punishments 256–7
        race and social standing 258
    in the Twenties 305–7
United States v. John Arthur Johnson (1913)
    289–92
'The Unsex'd Females' (Polwhele) 192–3
unsexed 336–7

Updike, John 383
urbanisation 436n32

Vallati, Anna Maria d'Antoni 90–1
Valmy, Battle of 170
vampire metaphor 367–8
Vampire, The (Burne-Jones) 362
Vampire, The (Ewer) 366
Vampyre, The (Polidori) 218–22, 227,
    459–60n30
Vance, Myrtle 251–2
Vanderbilt, Cornelius 310
Vane, Lady Frances 68
Vaulting School 18
Vauxhall Leisure Gardens 19
venereal disease 98
Venice 80
    Brenta Canal 106
    British Embassy 80
    convents 115–16
        fees from upper-class parents 116
        permissiveness of 115–16
    Council of Ten 108
    Council of Three 108
    culture 106–7
    Doge 112, 129
        Bucentaur 112
    Ducal Palace 109
    exuberance of street life 106–7
    fame 80
    Feast of the Ascension 111, 112
    Golden Book 108, 445n32
    gondolas, travelling by 106
    Inquisition 108, 124
    life during the eighteenth century 106
    patrician class 108–9
    police state 108
    printing industry 104
    sexual licence 102
    surveillance and spying 108–9
    Venetian state, unchanging 103–4
    Venus of the Adriatic 102
    women
        captivity of 102
        expansive freedom 103
        fashion 102, 103
        private apartments 103
        sexual revolution 103
        ubiquitous in public 103
Venus 134
Victoria (liner) 324
Victoria, Queen 237

Victorian society
  New Woman, spectre of 318, 360
  'the Sex,' women portrayed as 337
  women as sex objects 337
Vienna 110
Villa Aldobrandini 90
Villa Diodati 208, 221
Villa Foscarini 84
Villa Pisani 84
villainous seduction narrative 7–8, 10
A Vindication of the Rights of Men
  (Wollstonecraft) 155–6
A Vindication of the Rights of Woman
  (Wollstonecraft) 159–61, 163
Virgin in Eden, The 40
Virginia 308
  Public Assemblages Act (1926) 308
  racial segregation 308–9
  state sterilisation act 308
virgins, buying and selling of 333–4
virtue 36–7, 70
Visions of the Daughters of Albion (Blake)
  163
Vitalism 226
vocabulary, sexual 18
Vohs, Kathleen 386–7
Volstead Act (1920) 303
Voltaire 8, 132, 133

Wade, Senator 314
Wales, Prince of 329, 330
Wallis, Captain Samuel 133–4
Walpole, Horace 37, 453n42
  visit to Magdalen House 75–6
Wannsee Conference (1942) 370
Ward, Genevieve 321
Warrington, Marsha 294–5, 468–9n57
Washington, Booker T. 284–5
Watts, George 342, 473n17
Waugh, Arthur 355
Webb, Beatrice 363
Weber, Eric 398–9, 486–7n27
Webster, Sir Richard 339
Weekly Miscellany 31
Weigel, Moira 411
Weinstein, Harvey 416, 418, 420
Wells, Bombardier 299
Wells, Ida 252
Wemyss, 7th Earl of 23
Westbrook, Harriet *see* Shelley, Harriet (née
  Westbrook)
Whaley, Florette 282

Whatever (Houellebecq) 393, 396, 405, 406
Whistler, James 330
White, Arnold 352
White Cross League 338
white slave trade 275–9, 289–90
  and Jewry 367
  and seduction 336
White-Slave Traffic Act *see* Mann Act
white supremacy 250
Whitechapel Mystery 346–8, 349
  see also Jack the Ripper murders
whiteness, definition of 308
White's 46, 48
Whitman, Walt 321
whore-mongers 18
whores 20
Wilberforce, William 72
Wilde, John 28, 29
Wilde, Oscar 323, 327, 330, 355, 472n12
Willard, Frances 276, 422
Willard, Jess 299–301
William of Orange 24
Williams, Helen Maria 156, 173, 174, 179
Wilson, Woodrow 294, 295
Winckelmann, Augustus 132
witch tales 319
witches 5
Wollstonecraft, Edward 143–4
Wollstonecraft, Eliza 145
Wollstonecraft, Elizabeth 143, 145
Wollstonecraft, Everina 145, 149
Wollstonecraft, Mary 8, 192–4, 427
  appearance 151–2
  childhood 143
  death 191–2
  dislike of alcohol 143, 449n3
  Edmund Burke, anger at 155
  education and women 160–1, 161–2
  employment
    as companion 145
    governess 148–51
  establishment of school in Newington Green
    145–6
  Eton College, impressions of 449–50n6
  Fanny Blood, friendship with 144, 145, 146
    travels to Lisbon 146–7
  France, living in 171–82
    avoiding the Terror 180–1
    connections to French revolutionaries
    173–4
    disillusionment with revolutionary
    politics 177

Wollstonecraft, Mary 8, 192–4, 427 *cont'd*
  French Revolution, living through
    171–81
      moving to France 171–2
  free love, experiments with 165–9, 182
  Gothenberg trip 183–4
  ideas on women's role in society 180
  imagination 184–5
  letters
    to Gilbert Imlay 183
    to Joseph Johnson 162, 171–2
    to William Roscoe 170
  lifestyle 151–2
  logic and sentiment, balance 429
  and love 162, 163
    theory of 183
  loves and lovers
    Gilbert Imlay 174–5, 176–7, 180–3, 185,
    186, 192
      false marriage 180–1
      pregnancy and birth of Fanny 177,
      181
      Gustav von Schlabrendorf 174
      Henry Fuseli, passion for 165–9
  nature, calming impact of 184–5
  reason and rational thought 147–8
  reason vs. passion 162
  Rousseau, contempt and admiration for
    150
  self-education 144, 149–50
  self-sufficiency 152
  sexual freedom, individual 164–5
  suicide attempts 183, 186
  William Godwin, marriage to 187–8
    birth of Mary 191
    commonalities with 187
    courtship 187
    unconventional relationship 188
  writings
    Letters Written in Sweden, Norway, and
    Denmark (1796) 184–5
    literary reviews 152
    Maria: or, The Wrongs of Woman (1798)
    188–91
    Mary, A Fiction (1788) 150, 152
    Original Stories from Real Life (1788)
    163
    Thoughts on the Education of Daughters
    (1787) 147, 148

    A Vindication of the Rights of Men
    (1790) 155–6
    A Vindication of the Rights of Woman
    (1792) 159–61, 163
Wollstonecraft, Mary (daughter) 191–3
Woman's Christian Temperance Movement
  (WCTU) 276
women
  access to higher education 360
  domestic values, Richardson's view 67–8
  and education 160–1, 161–2
  equality in labour market 383
  exploitation by men 62
  injustices against 48
  and Marxism
    sexual liberation 374
    social and economic independence
    373–4
  moral superiority 49
  rights of 158–60, 363
    growing 240–1
    sexual 331–2
  and sensibility 53–4, 72
    Magdalen House 442n69
  'the Sex,' Victorian portrayal as 337
  sexual exploitation through somnambulism
    224
  sexualising of politics, need for 337
  special protections 62–3
  writings by 49–50
  see also feminism; French Revolution; New
    Women; Venice: women
Women and Socialism (Bebel) 373–4
Women's March on Versailles 153–4
Women's Organization for National
  Prohibition Repeal 313
women's suffrage 360
Wood, Myron 1–2
Woolf, Virginia 165, 439n55
Worsdale, James 44, 45
Wyndham, Horace 330

Yorke, Henry Galgacus Redhead 241
Young, Arthur 148
Young, Edward 58

Zelmi 91
Zeppelin bombers 302
Zeus 3